D1707595

CONFLICTING WORLDS

New Dimensions of the American Civil War

T. Michael Parrish, Editor

LEGACY OF

THE ENDURING SIGNIFICANCE

OF THE AMERICAN CIVIL WAR

DISUNION

Edited by

Susan-Mary Grant and Peter J. Parish

Louisiana State University Press
Baton Rouge

Copyright © 2003 by Louisiana State University Press
All rights reserved
Manufactured in the United States of America
First printing
12 11 10 09 08 07 06 05 04 03
5 4 3 2 1

Designer: Amanda McDonald Scallan
Typeface: AGaramond
Typesetter: Coghill Composition Co. Inc.
Printer and binder: Thomson-Shore, Inc.

Library of Congress Cataloging-in-Publication Data:

Legacy of disunion : the enduring significance of the American Civil War / edited by Susan-Mary
Grant and Peter J. Parish.
     p.   cm.—(Conflicting worlds)
Includes bibliographical references and index.
   ISBN 0-8071-2847-3 (alk. paper)
   1. United States—History—Civil War, 1861–1865—Influence.   I. Grant, Susan-Mary.   II. Parish,
Peter J. III. Series.
   E468.9 .L44   2003
   973.9—dc21   2002013638

The paper in this book meets the guidelines for permanence and durability of the Committee on
Production Guidelines for Book Longevity of the Council on Library Resources. ∞

CONTENTS

ACKNOWLEDGMENTS

Composing the acknowledgments of any publication is normally a pleasurable task. For this particular volume, however, it is a task tinged with more than a degree of sadness since my coeditor, Peter J. Parish, did not live to see the book published. Peter had been ill for some time, although that had not hampered his intellectual enthusiasm nor his good humor. The end, when it came on May 16, 2002, was far more sudden than anyone had anticipated. Those of us who knew and worked with him—and that includes all the contributors to this volume—miss him greatly. We have lost a remarkable friend and colleague, and the academic world has lost one of foremost historians of the American Civil War.

It is fitting that Peter has contributed two chapters to this volume. His chapter "Abraham Lincoln and American Nationhood" is a substantially revised version of the Harry Allen Memorial Lecture delivered at the Institute of United States Studies (where Peter served as director for many years), University of London, on May 22, 2000, and subsequently published by the institute as a pamphlet under the same title. I am grateful to Prof. Gary McDowell, director of IUSS, for his generous permission to publish this revised version. Indeed, the volume itself grew out of a conference that McDowell organized in 1997, "The Enduring Significance of the Civil War." His support—both intellectual and financial—for British Americanists in general, and Peter and myself in particular, has been unstinting over the years and is very much appreciated. Thanks are also due to the Office of Public Affairs, Embassy of the United States of America in London, and especially to the cultural attaché, Dennis Wolf, for financial assistance in completing this book.

Two of the chapters in this collection have previously appeared as articles. Richard N. Current's chapter, "From Civil War to World Power: Perceptions and Realities, 1865–1914," first appeared in Stig Förster and Jörg Nagler, eds., *On the Road to Total War: The American Civil War and the German Wars of Unification, 1861–1871* (Cambridge University Press, 1997), 621–39. I am grateful to the German Historical Institute, Washington, D.C., for permission to reprint this article here. Susan-Mary Grant's chapter, "'The Charter of Its Birthright': The Civil War and American Nationalism," is a revised version of an article that previously appeared in *Na-*

tions and Nationalism 4 (1998): 163–85, and I am grateful to Cambridge University Press for permission to reprint it. Finally, James M. McPherson's chapter, "'For a Vast Future Also': Lincoln and the Millennium," was first presented as the annual Jefferson Lecture (2000), sponsored by the National Endowment of the Humanities, and previously appeared as a limited-edition pamphlet.

Last, but not least, thanks are due to the contributors to this volume, all of whom have responded to my (frequently last-minute) requests for additional information promptly and cheerfully. The overall editor of this series, Michael Parrish, and the staff at Louisiana State University Press, have been extremely efficient and supportive, especially since Peter's illness was diagnosed. I particularly want to thank Sylvia Frank Rodrigue, Gerry Anders, Margaret Hart and, for outstanding editorial work, independent editor Kevin Brock. The completion of this book would have been so much harder without their much appreciated help.

Susan-Mary Grant
August 2002

LEGACY OF DISUNION

INTRODUCTION

Susan-Mary Grant and Peter J. Parish

The war has made us a nation of great power and intelligence. We have but little to do to preserve peace, happiness, and prosperity at home, and the respect of other nations. Our experience ought to teach us the necessity of the first; our power secures the latter.

—Ulysses S. Grant, *Memoirs*

> Turn your eyes to the immoderate past,
> Turn to the inscrutable infantry rising
> Demons out of the earth—they will not last.
>
> —Allen Tate, "Ode to the Confederate Dead"

The ideal outcome will be the reconciliation, at long last, of North and South based on factual, imaginative, and spiritual recognition by each citizen that his or her personal identity and destiny are grounded in the historical event that most crucially shaped our national character.

—David Madden, on the Civil War's forthcoming sesquicentennial.

Historians often have more difficulty with the consequences than the causes of great events. The origins of the Civil War have inspired endless and often fierce debate, but at least all the participants in the controversy are clear about the conclusion of their argument: the bombardment of Fort Sumter and the ensuing four years of bloody conflict. Discussion of the consequences, or the legacy, of the war has a clear starting point at Appomattox Court House, but it can then spread out over the whole of subsequent American history. The subject becomes increasingly diffuse, for it becomes more and more difficult to avoid the *post hoc, ergo propter hoc* fallacy and to establish which developments were or were not shaped by the war, how great an effect the war had and how far its influence spread.

Those who had lived through the conflict, and especially those who had played prominent parts in it, were in little doubt that it had left a huge legacy to the United

States, even if they had not yet seen the details of the will. As he prepared to meet death, Ulysses S. Grant reflected on his life and on the Civil War, which had proved so central to him and to his nation. He believed that his country was "on the eve of a new era, when there is to be great harmony between the Federal and Confederate" and that America had emerged from the Civil War a stronger and wiser nation. "We must conclude," he wrote, "that wars are not always evils unmixed with some good." Since Grant, a great many individuals both in America and beyond have reflected on the influence of the Civil War upon the United States and on its legacy for the nation. Many like Grant have seen the war's bequest to America as one combining increased self-knowledge and power with global recognition. The outcome of the Civil War eradicated slavery, united North and South, and proved to a frequently skeptical world that, in Lincoln's words, "a nation so conceived" could in fact "endure."[1]

The claims made for the long-term consequences of the American Civil War have been substantial, and some have a solid foundation. In this, as in many other historical situations, the thoughts and feelings of men and women about what happened are at least as important as the facts of what actually happened. If generations of Americans (and not only Americans) have treated the war as a major historical event with consequences that spread far and wide, that in itself forms part of its enduring legacy. If there has been a widely shared belief that the war was the great watershed of American history, that consensus of opinion has acquired something of the power of a self-fulfilling prophecy. For many Americans it has been convenient and, at least superficially, plausible to identify the war as a fault line between two Americas. On one side lies the world of Thomas Jefferson and James Madison, Andrew Jackson and John Calhoun, on the other the world of Theodore and Franklin Roosevelt, Woodrow Wilson, and Herbert Hoover. On one side lies the mythical "Old" South invoked by Margaret Mitchell, and on the other the more complex South explored by William Faulkner. Prior to the Civil War was the era of the family farm, the small workshop, and the village store; afterward came the age of Standard Oil, United States Steel, and J. P. Morgan and Company. Even if such clear-cut differentiation between antebellum and postbellum America is too simplistic, there is no denying the substantial and significant influence of the war on many different aspects of American life. Furthermore, this spread far beyond the United States. The war has often been regarded as a watershed in global terms too. In the words of one historian, the war's outcome "forever changed the course of American history, and thereby of world history." Another has argued that the Civil War, "like the French and Russian Revolutions, was so critical a moment in the formation of the world in which we live that it compels us to contemplate the most basic features and values of modern society."[2]

The Civil War claimed more American lives than all of the nation's other wars up to Vietnam combined. Its physical and emotional effects on nineteenth-century America must not be underestimated. What, though, of its legacy? Did the Civil War, as Grant believed, bequeath power, intelligence, and sectional harmony to the United States, or did it, as many have argued since, leave a legacy of racial and sectional bitterness that has blighted the nation since 1865? What exactly was the legacy of the American Civil War? This present volume, which considers that question from a variety of angles, originated at a conference in London in 1997 devoted to exploring—from a transatlantic perspective—just some of the short- and long-term implications of the war of 1861–65 for the United States. From the papers delivered on that occasion, and from the ongoing debates held at various subsequent conferences and seminars, it is clear that the Civil War's legacy is less straightforward than it has sometimes seemed. The conviction that the war left a massive legacy has generally been much clearer than the definition of what that legacy has actually been.

As the essays in this volume show, in certain areas the war's influence was far less than has been supposed; in others it was far greater. In broad terms, however, the debate over the war's legacy has tended to rotate around a tripartite axis, comprising the South, race relations, and above all, the role played by Abraham Lincoln. In recognition of this fact, but also with a view to incorporating new elements, this volume is divided into three rather different parts that, while they each take account of the South, race, and Lincoln, juxtapose chapters on these subjects with chapters exploring alternative areas of debate. The first part certainly has a strong southern focus and explores the increasingly significant debate over the Civil War's place in American memory. Opening with one southerner's very personal account of the war's legacy, this section's main emphasis is on the means by which the myth of the war came to have the resonance it did in the South, exploring the roles of history, myth, and the media—in the form of the movie business—in creating and sustaining the memory of the war. These chapters also bring together the black and white Civil War, reminding us that one of the main legacies of the conflict was to bequeath a lasting sense of "unfinished business" to the United States, not just between North and South but also between African Americans and the nation as a whole.

The second part shifts the focus away from the South. It opens with a chapter that explores the fast-growing subject of the North's Civil War before moving on to look in depth at Lincoln and his individual legacy to the nation he helped hold together. The third part explores some of the war's consequences in less well-developed fields. It covers the effect of the conflict on civil-military relations, explores the war's role in the construction of American national identity, and finally assesses its influence on the development of the United States on the international stage. Together, these sections, through their juxtaposing of American and non-American explorations of the subject, highlight the continuing worldwide fascination with the central event of America's history. They show too that the European perspective can, in places, shed a different light on aspects of the war's legacy that, from an American perspective, are sometimes too close for comfort.

The Civil War retains its fascination both inside and far beyond the United States, and each generation continues to discover and explore it afresh. Despite the many thousands of volumes published on the war, it seems unlikely that the final word on this most significant of conflicts is in sight. If anything, recent years have witnessed a resurgence in America's Civil War industry. This is reflected in the popularity of recent novels such as Charles Frazier's *Cold Mountain* and the republication of older works such as Harold Sinclair's *Horse Soldiers.* Another novel, Michael Shaara's *Killer Angels,* was the inspiration behind the epic film *Gettysburg*—though one can still wonder why it took American moviemakers so long to get around to the subject. Shaara's son, Jeff, has since published *The Last Full Measure,* a sequel to his father's work, that focuses on Grant and Lee. Whether this too will appear in a film version remains to be seen. A very different recent film, Ang Lee's *Ride with the Devil*—based again on a novel, in this case Daniel Woodrell's *Woe to Live On*—portrayed the vicious guerrilla warfare along the western border. These films are more successful in portraying the horrors of the war rather than conveying any message about its long-term significance. The popularity of nonfiction works such as Tony Horwitz's *Confederates in the Attic*—revealingly subtitled *Dispatches from the Unfinished Civil War*—offers further testimony to the enduring fascination the war retains. This attraction is also expressed, and encouraged, by the rapid proliferation of Civil War sites on the World Wide Web, including Edward Ayers's mammoth ongoing Civil War project *The Valley of the Shadow.* Through the Web one can find a range of information—and sometimes not wholly factual—about the war, learn how to trace ancestors who fought, and peruse a wide selection of contemporary images and photographs of individuals and battlefields. Nor have Americans ceased to commemorate the Civil War in very public ways. The year 1998 saw the eventual unveiling of a statue in Washington, D.C. dedicated to the many African American troops who fought in the war. The publicity that attended the dedication of *The Spirit of Freedom* memorial, unveiled on the anniversary of the assault on Fort Wagner, South Carolina, referred to the lack of black troops at the Grand Review in Washington in 1865 as the "final insult" and "symptomatic of the national attitude toward the valuable service of African American soldiers," an attitude that, to some degree at least, *The Spirit of Freedom*'s creation attempts to correct.[3]

Indeed, interest in the many monuments and memorials to the Civil War has been slowly growing. A number of recent studies that examine the background to and influence of Civil War monuments and statuary go far beyond the sporadic interest that has been shown in Augustus St. Gaudens's memorial to the Fifty-fourth Massachusetts Infantry, which stands on Boston Common. Books such as Kenneth Foote's *Shadowed Ground: America's Landscapes of Violence and Tragedy,* Kirk Savage's *Standing Soldiers, Kneeling Slaves: Race, War, and Monument in Nineteenth-Century America,* and Kathryn Allamong Jacob's *Testament to Union: Civil War Monuments in Washington, D.C.* cross the line between the academic and the public world with studies that address the interests of a broad section of the American population. A further contribution to this process comes from studies of the popular image of the two opposing sides in the Civil War, notably Mark E. Neely, Harold Holzer, and Gabor Boritt's *Confederate Image: Prints of the Lost Cause* and Neely and Holzer's *Union Image: Popular Prints of the Civil War North.*[4]

Civil War scholarship shows no sign of going into decline and, partly by extending its range of subject matter, continues to hold its own in the world of twenty-first-century academia. A limited but growing proportion of this scholarship also focuses on the legacy of the Civil War as academics such as Gaines Foster, Stuart McConnell, Cecilia O' Leary, and David Blight probe the multiplicity of meanings inherent in the war's legacy. The continued fascination that the Civil War exercises over both the public and the academic worlds suggests that interest in the conflict goes beyond the mere romance of a time in America's history that is "gone with the wind." Rather, in their preoccupation with the Civil War and its outcome, Americans, but not only Americans, are expressing the conviction that its lessons continue to have meaning today. The great issues of the Civil War era—nationalism, democracy, liberty, equality, race, majority rule and minority rights, central authority and local self-government, the use and abuse of power, and the horrors of all-out war—are as alive in the early twenty-first century as they were in the mid–nineteenth century.[5]

The modernity of the issues at stake ensures the Civil War's lasting appeal to Americans and non-Americans alike. For Americans specifically, however, the appeal is surely tinged with the recognition that the war's legacy was a divided one, which left many issues unresolved. Allen Tate's belief that the demons invoked by the conflict would not last was at best premature. The United States shows no signs yet of exorcising those particular demons. For example, although the public reaction to Ken Burns's epic series on the Civil War, which first appeared over a decade ago, was overwhelmingly positive, the academy proved more cautious in its praise and indeed was frequently critical. Opinion was, and remains, divided. Some historians felt that Burns had gone a long way toward demythologizing the conflict, stressing instead the dark heart of the war and juxtaposing both antiwar and abolitionist elements in his series. Others argued that he had effectively downplayed the problematic and divisive legacy of the war, particularly as it related to the betrayal of African

American hopes and dreams during the Reconstruction era and beyond. In *Race and Reunion,* David Blight presents a sobering and detailed account of how exactly such dreams came to be betrayed. As North and South struggled toward reconciliation, the emancipationist vision of the war's memory was relegated to the sidelines and, in time, overshadowed altogether by the rhetoric of reunion. "The Civil War had become the nation's inheritance of glory," Blight argues, "Reconstruction the legacy of folly, and the race problem a matter of efficient schemes of segregation."[6]

The crux of the issue, for today's historians as well as for individuals during the war itself, was freedom or liberty and the many possible interpretations of that concept. In the third year of the war, before the start of the last great Union offensive against the Confederacy, Abraham Lincoln summed up the problem facing the still divided nation: "The world has never had a good definition of the word liberty," he observed, "and the American people, just now, are much in want of one. We all declare for liberty; but in using the same *word* we do not all mean the same *thing*." As W. E. B. Du Bois saw it many years later, the problem was not resolved by the war's outcome: "to the Negro, 'Freedom' was God; to the poor white 'Freedom' was nothing—he had more than he had use for; to the planter 'Freedom' for the poor was laziness and for the rich control of the poor worker; for the Northern business-man 'Freedom' was the opportunity to get rich."[7]

Neither black and white nor North and South could reach any agreement on the implications, or transcend the limitations, of America's "new birth of freedom" in the aftermath of the war. Grant's optimistic assessment of relations between Federals and Confederates notwithstanding, the debate over what had been won and lost continued, and continues in some quarters to this day. The "Lost Cause" elevated Southern defeat into the stuff of legend. It created heroes out of the horrors of the battlefield, inculcated resentment rather than reconciliation, and provided an ideal platform on which to construct, for our own times, a brand of Southern nationalism no more closely attuned to the reality of the South than was its nineteenth-century predecessor. Southern nationalism, of course, was and is not the same thing as Confederate nationalism, although the two are frequently seen as synonymous. Gary Gallagher has recently explored the depth and the persistence of Confederate national sentiment, but for the South as a whole, a nationalism predicated on race distinctions was never likely to prove a winner. The shadow of the Confederacy continues to cloud not just the South but also the nation. To this day reconciliation, for some, remains an ideal to be striven for rather than one already achieved. Recently David Madden, the director of the U.S. Civil War Center at Louisiana State University, the flagship institution for the sesquicentennial commemoration of the war in 2011, expressed his hope that the "Sesquicentennial will celebrate our Civil War heritage. . . . The ideal outcome will be the reconciliation, at long last, of North and South, based on factual, imaginative, and spiritual recognition by each citizen that his or her personal identity and destiny are grounded in the historical event that most crucially shaped our national character."[8]

These various themes—reconciliation, destiny, imagination, nationalism, sectionalism, and patriotism—form the focus of this collection of essays, each of which in its individual way explores the evolving legacy of the Civil War. In recognition of the fact that it is often the losers who have the longer historical memories, the opening chapter, by leading Southern historian Charles Joyner, examines the Confederate myth, the importance of defeat and memory to southerners, from a personal and consequently very probing perspective. In many ways, the opening chapter sets the tone for the entire volume, its transatlantic perspective, and its general thrust. History "studied only by insiders, or any history studied only by outsiders, is only half-studied," Joyner argues, and certainly both perspectives are present in this collection. Joyner too draws out the parallels between America's Civil War era and our own. "Our postmodern world," he points out, "seems to be moving toward a proliferation of smaller and weaker nations, each lacking in political or economic stability, each unified mainly by the bitter hostility of its citizens toward their neighbors." The world now, as then, could do worse than explore the implications of the American nineteenth-century experience. Joyner also considers various attendant themes, many of which have been the subject of new research, such as the role of religion in the South and the important role that the memory of the Civil War plays in that region today.

In the view of Allen Tate, the South, more than the North, is "conscious of the past in the present." The memory and the legacy of slavery, in particular, continue to work against racial and sectional harmony throughout America today. If slavery is, as Joyner suggests, the curse that the South needs to work out, then the Civil War and its outcome left a legacy that the nation as a whole is still working through. The chapters that follow explore many aspects of that challenging and often burdensome inheritance. Joyner's very personal, southern perspective on the war is followed by an alternative view of the "Myth of the South" and a close examination of the reality that this myth produced. Bruce Collins also focuses on the important role that the past plays in the present. He traces the legitimization of the Confederate legacy after 1880, examining the effect of such events as the establishment of the United Daughters of the Confederacy in 1894, the reopening of the Citadel in 1882, and the gradual "nationalizing" of the central figure of the Confederacy, Robert E. Lee. "The emotional bonds forged by the war lived on (if not with their wartime intensity)," he concludes, "and became a central part of the national heritage and a vital contribution to the national spirit."

The obvious flaw in the newly mended national fabric was, of course, the swift relegation of African Americans to the sidelines. Although historians have done much in the last few decades to correct the view of the Civil War as a "white man's war," the African American Civil War experience is still not fully incorporated into Civil War scholarship. It is still portrayed, both in the historiography and more generally, as a war apart from that experienced by the American nation, North and South, as a whole. Although Americans today are much more aware of the "role taken by African Americans in fighting for their freedom during the Civil War," it remains the case that the black soldier is still regarded as distinct and separate from his white comrades. Robert Cook's aptly titled chapter, "Unfinished Business," examines the African American challenge to this aspect of the Civil War's legacy. African Americans, Cook argues, rather quickly lost the battle over the meaning of the war. But, he concludes, the battle is far from over in this particular arena. By means of a penetrating study focusing on the centennial celebrations of 1961–65, Cook shows how African Americans contested, and continue to contest, the white version of the war, particularly the white southern version. With the approaching sesquicentennial comes the opportunity to rectify the African American Civil War, on which much remains to be said.[9]

Although the multiplicity of books and monuments testifies to America's fascination with the Civil War, this has not been expressed to any comparable degree in film. Melvyn Stokes examines some of the reasons for this in his study, "The Civil War in the Movies." Looking at familiar films such as *The Birth of a Nation* (1915), *Gone with the Wind* (1939), and *The Red Badge of Courage* (1951), Stokes shows how a combination of "emotional resistance," in C. Vann Woodward's phrase, and practical considerations relating to the intended audiences inhibited filmmakers' attempts to bring the Civil War to the big screen. Those films that did appear, Stokes concludes, did little to foster sectional reconciliation, and much more to perpetuate the "Myth of the Old South." For a great many people, their understanding of the South, and indeed of the Civil War generally, has never moved beyond *Gone with the Wind*.

The second section of this volume turns the spotlight on to Abraham Lincoln. Four chapters examine "The Leader and the Legacy," with a specific exploration of party politics in the North and the role that Lincoln played—particularly after his death—in the development of U.S. national identity. Even in today's climate of renewed interest in nationalism as a worldwide phenomenon, as so many small nations struggle to define a separate identity, American nationalism has continued to be a rather neglected subject. In many societies, as Joyner notes, the search for definition involves the construction of a negative reference point, a people against whom to define one's own nationality. The parallels with America's sectional divisions in the antebellum period are instructive here. Similarly, the positioning of the Civil

War as the defining act of U.S. national construction is comparable with the ways in which many European nations have gone about the process of creating a national identity.

Although the Civil War is widely regarded as a watershed in U.S. history, Adam Smith and Peter Parish remind us that, in the context of American political development, it has too often been treated as a "sideshow." Political historians have too readily sidestepped the war, arguing that the American political nation was not much altered by the conflict. Smith and Parish contest this view. There are, they argue, "serious questions to be asked about the dominant historiographical interpretation of nineteenth century politics, which stresses continuity and does not identify the war as a time of transition." They show that here as elsewhere, the war's legacy was one of division, of opportunity, and of change. "Viewed from outside," they conclude, "the structure of the house of American politics may have retained much the same appearance, but during the 1860s and 1870s, there was a good deal of renovation within and much rearrangement of the furniture."

If the Civil War is the central event of American history and national development, then Abraham Lincoln is assuredly the central figure of the Civil War, and three chapters are devoted to the president and his legacy. First, political scientist Jeffrey Leigh Sedgwick examines the effect of Lincoln's statesmanship during the crisis itself and in the context of American nationality. Lincoln, Sedgwick argues, "clarified the options and asked Americans to choose, finally, between two competing interpretations of the nation's civic identity." Sedgwick examines Lincoln's understanding of the Declaration of Independence, his opposition to the Dred Scott decision of 1857, and the intricacies of the Lincoln-Douglas debates the following year. Lincoln's statesmanship, he suggests, was "an attempt through rhetoric to move a wandering nation back to a firm belief in those true principles upon which it was founded." Again, the parallels with the present day are instructive. Lincoln's position, Sedgwick concludes, offered a form of "third alternative, civic friendship, well worth consideration for its depth of understanding of the problem of modern politics."

Two historians of the Civil War present different perspectives on Lincoln's contribution to the legacy of the conflict. Intriguingly, it is the British scholar Peter Parish who focuses on Lincoln's role in the construction of American nationhood, while the American James McPherson places the president's contribution in a broader international context. Parish emphasizes that Lincoln's determination to save the Union even as the war escalated and the casualties soared to new levels of horror was the prerequisite of all his other contributions to the shaping of American nationhood. But not content to be simply the savior of the Union, he also placed his own unmistakable stamp upon the character of the United States. His conception of

American nationhood was inclusive, as demonstrated by his scornful rejection of nativist restrictiveness. More gradually and uncertainly, he moved toward a recognition of black Americans as fellow citizens—a process dramatically accelerated by wartime emancipation and given constitutional confirmation in the Thirteenth and Fourteenth Amendments. In Parish's view Lincoln saw the nation as process, and that process implied constant striving for political, economic, social, and moral improvement. Parish describes this as ameliorative or aspirational nationalism.

McPherson is greatly impressed by Lincoln's sense of history and also his sense of the universality and timelessness of the issues at stake during the Civil War. The president's belief that the fate of liberty was the core issue in the conflict was shared, says McPherson, by many of the Union soldiers who fought and died in the war as well as those on the political left and right in Europe who either welcomed or feared the triumph of American freedom and equality. Lincoln saw the war as a crucial test of the viability of popular government, not merely for the United States but also for the world, and he was equally aware of the universal implications of emancipation. Reflecting on the meaning of the Gettysburg Address, McPherson places alongside each other three sets of three images: past, present, and future; continent, nation, and battlefield; and birth, death, and rebirth. He then seeks to show how Lincoln wove them all together in one brief address. McPherson concludes with a discussion of the transition from negative to positive concepts of liberty, stimulated by Lincoln and consolidated in the Thirteenth, Fourteenth, and Fifteenth Amendments.

It is noteworthy that Sedgwick, Parish, and McPherson all take as their starting point Lincoln's reverence for the ideals of the Declaration of Independence. But they differ in the direction taken by their respective interpretations and in the emphasis they give to particular issues. Sedgwick sees Lincoln attempting to guide the nation back to its founding principles. In Parish's eyes Lincoln saw the ideals of the Declaration as a guide to future progress and continuing improvement of the American nation. For McPherson, Lincoln gave substance and meaning to the abstract ideas of the Declaration of Independence, and he understood the war as a critical moment on which depended the fate of those ideas throughout the world.

The final section of this volume ranges still more widely over the disputed territory of the war's legacy and draws together many of the points touched on throughout the preceding chapters. It highlights several areas where the war's influence was rather less than has commonly been supposed, where its legacy has been one of continuity rather than dramatic change, or where the war may have hindered rather than aided America's development. Surprisingly perhaps, civil-military relations is one such area. Brian Holden Reid considers the effect of the conflict on U.S. military institutions and points out that in this area "a fundamental paradox . . . needs to be confronted at the outset, namely that the Civil War represents a massive upheaval yet seems to have bequeathed little in the way of structural change or innovation." In this particular case, Holden Reid concludes, Americans had to work through the war and its consequences. American military development was hampered by the dominance of the very strong personalities that emerged from the war. Until they left the scene, little substantial in the way of organizational or structural change in the U.S. military could take place.

There are other areas where changes wrought by the Civil War may have been less clear cut and predictable than they seemed at first sight. One obvious example lies in the field of U.S. constitutional and legal history. Pat Lucie examines the long-term consequences of the Civil War constitutional amendments. "The journey from slavery to freedom transformed the Constitution," she reminds us, and debates over the Thirteenth, Fourteenth, and Fifteenth Amendments remain "central to contemporary constitutional law." These three amendments have, she points out, effectively "become the framework within which every other contest about individual rights has been shaped for all Americans. The most modern dilemmas of gender identity and equality, access to contraceptives, and control over the technology of death come to courts throughout the land as cases demanding interpretation of the Civil War's legacy." Although there are, she concludes, "enduring core values in the Civil War amendments," these "have always had to fight for space with some other enduring aspects of American constitutionalism," most notably the traditional interpretation of the Constitution as "a charter of negative liberties." Nevertheless, the Civil War amendments lie at the heart of America's "ongoing dialogue about freedom and citizenship."

Returning to the theme of U.S. nationalism and the Civil War's part in the development of American identity, Susan-Mary Grant looks at the ways in which the war was transformed from a brutal internecine conflict into the "salvation drama" of American nationhood that has much in common with the construction of nationality in many European nations. Although the war left a divided legacy, it is one to which both sides have had access. It simultaneously draws North and South together even as it remains the source of so much disagreement. In the volume's concluding chapter, Richard Current questions whether the rise of the United States to global dominance and its eventual position as a "world power" can really be credited to the Civil War. In line with Holden Reid's argument concerning America's military development, Current argues that Americans had to "live down the Civil War before the country could become a great power and they could accept and applaud its new status." He identifies a variety of "requirements" before the United States could achieve a position of global dominance, including a unifying party system that was not divided along sectional lines, "a sense of psychological as well as political reunion," a strong presidency, an expansive foreign policy backed by military and naval capacity, and an industrialized and productive economy. By the eve of the First World War, the nation had many of these elements in place, but, Current suggests, this had little to do with the Civil War. The war, indeed, intensified sectionalism, and it was not until the Spanish-American War of 1898 that northerners began "to look back on the Civil War in more or less the same way that southerners did." Not until the "intellectual southernization of the North" was achieved was the nation in any position to venture with any degree of confidence onto the world stage. Certainly, the Union victory was essential to America's eventual rise to global prominence, but in the short term the Civil War did more to hinder than to help the nation toward its new world role.

For America, therefore, the legacy of the Civil War is a divided one, and some of those divisions continue to have an effect today. This is perhaps unsurprising. For both the United States and the world, the enduring significance of the Civil War lay not only in what it achieved but also in what it prevented, not only in what it changed but also in what it preserved. Rather than transforming America beyond recognition, the effects of the war were more complex, subtle, and varied—sometimes surprising, often contested. This was a conflict in which continuity was as important as change, and the juxtaposition of these—frequently contradictory—elements influenced the legacy that the war left to the nation. If the preservation of the Union, the North's first and main "war aim," represents continuity, then the emancipation of the slaves represented not just change but also an opportunity to reconstruct the nation according to the ideals set forth in its founding document, the Declaration of Independence. If the postwar reality fell far short of that ambition, one significant part of the war's legacy is that the ideal could not again be dismissed. In one sense, certainly, continuing racial and sectional conflict represents a substantial aspect of the Civil War's legacy; in another, however, it ensures that the ideal for which so many had died could never again be ignored.

The Civil War touched virtually all late-nineteenth-century Americans, and new immigrants coming to the nation had to take account of its legacy in the same way as those whose families had fought. All, therefore, had a stake not just in America's future but, more significantly, in the nation's past as well. Lincoln had invoked the Declaration of Independence in just this way. Even those not born in the United States, he asserted, had a right to American nationality via the Declaration of Independence. It was this document, he averred, that constituted the "electric cord" holding the nation together. For the Civil War generation and those who came after them, the war fulfilled a similar function. It became the new basis for U.S. national identity, though by no means a wholly solid nor an entirely secure one. America's post–Civil War nationality was constructed on contested ground. But as the continuing fascination with the Civil War proves, the ground retains its appeal and draws each generation of combatants to the same battlefields in the search for a resolution, in the working out of the war's legacy. It is worth recalling in this context one of the observations made by Alexis de Tocqueville during his visit to the United States during the 1830s, namely that for Americans the future was of more significance than the past. "Democratic nations," Tocqueville asserts, "care but little for what has been, but they are haunted by visions of what will be." It is "in this direction," he suggests, that "their unbounded imagination grows and dilates beyond all measure." This was no longer the case for America after the Civil War. The war, as several historians and writers have argued, gave the United States a truly usable past; it became the central event of its history. In Robert Penn Warren's words, the Civil War could "be said to *be* American history." The ultimate legacy of the war, perhaps, is the continued debate over it. In their continued fascination with the Civil War, with all that it achieved and all that it failed to achieve, Americans reveal themselves to be, now as then, truly aspirational nationalists.[10]

I

THE MYTH AND
THE MEMORY

The Civil War in American Memory

1

"FORGET, HELL!"

The Civil War in Southern Memory

CHARLES JOYNER

The wind goeth toward the south,
and turneth about unto the north;
it whirleth about continually,
and the wind returneth again
according to his circuits.

—Ecclesiastes: Prologue

When I see all these,
My own people, thirsting for battle,
My limbs fail me and my throat is parched,
My body trembles and my hair stands on end. . . .
Should not we, whose eyes are open,
Who consider it to be wrong
To annihilate our house,
Turn away from so great a crime?

—The Bhagavad-Gita

The passion of the sword rages high,
The accursed fury of war, and wrath over all:
Even as when flaming sticks are heaped roaring loud
Under the sides of a seething cauldron,
And the boiling tides leap up;
The river of water within smokes furiously
And swells high in overflowing foam,
And now the wave contains itself no longer;
The dark steam flies aloft.

*—*Virgil, *The Aeneid,* Book 7

The poor fools did not know
That they had reached the end
And were now bound fast in the bonds
Of utter destruction.
　　　　　　—Homer, *The Odyssey,* Book 22

The American Civil War had been over for seventy years when I was born, but as the ranks of living Confederate veterans became thinner and slower, as the rebel yells from their ancient throats became softer and weaker, the cause they had lost grew stronger and shriller. Defeat and memory strengthened the bonds that united those who survived. The Confederacy continued to live in the distant memories of aging men and aging women and in stories passed down from generation to generation. As a boy I was touched with the tacit understanding that the disastrous Confederate experience continued to define the people of the South—my people.

The effort to examine the Civil War in southern memory is hedged about with more than the usual set of problems. History exists in time, as the anthropologist-turned-historian Greg Dening points out, and time passes, resisting our efforts to set its reality in stone or to freeze it in memory.[1] The Civil War is blurred now into mythology, into signs and symbols. Historians have learned from painful experience how hard it is to convey the awesome and awful quality of that war, how difficult to recapture its grief and sorrow or even its pride, how perplexing to try to make sense of its senseless slaughter.

A few years ago when I was a visiting professor at the University of Sydney, I was asked "What are the difficulties of being a southerner and writing Southern history?" I responded that I thought of it less as a difficulty than as an opportunity.[2] But of course that was an overstatement. All history is difficult. Marc Bloch said that history is impossible. And there are particular hazards in writing the history of "Ourselves," whether we define "Ourselves" in national, regional, ethnic, racial, or gender terms. If we confuse history with autobiography, if we write history to glorify "Our" ancestors, we are likely to write some pretty bad history. But there are equal hazards for those who specialize in writing the history of the "Other," the history of those who are postulated to be "different." I think any history studied only by insiders, or any history studied only by outsiders, is only half-studied.

For good or ill, I am a southerner who writes of his native region. I am of the South, and I confess an emotional attachment to it. But as a historian I am also part of the modern world, and I am bound to hold the South and the modern world up against each other in mutual comprehension and in mutual criticism. Not only do comparisons with other parts of the world illumine southern history, but comparisons with the southern past also illuminate the present of many parts of the modern world. I learned one example in Australia. How strange Anzac Day seems to most of the world! What a bizarre triumph to have discovered a national identity in the slaughter at Gallipoli![3] Yet as a southerner visiting in the *real* Deep South, I found something familiar in the intense pride Australians feel in a disastrous but gallant defeat.

And when I participated in a 1989 anthropological congress in what was then Yugoslavia, it was obvious to anyone that the country was coming apart.[4] I asked Croat friends if they were not afraid they might destroy the union. "Well, we certainly hope so!" they exclaimed. I ventured that perhaps we should discuss this since I am from South Carolina and we have had some experience with such matters. I come from a region of secessionists, I told them, and I have studied its causes and consequences for most of my adult life. I told them I did not see much to recommend it and warned them that they might be in for a bit of trouble.

Perhaps nowhere is the enduring significance of the Civil War more clearly revealed than in its influence on this phenomenon of nationalism.[5] As a child growing up in war-torn Virginia and South Carolina, Woodrow Wilson had seen with his own eyes the failure of the War for Southern Independence, had seen a people's aspirations for national self-determination crushed under the weight of superior firepower. He had seen a generation of southern men and women pour out their blood and their treasure until Appomattox determined that there would be no "Southern Nation." During the First World War, Wilson first articulated his doctrine of the "self-determination of peoples" in Point Ten of his famous Fourteen Points. All "peoples," according to Wilson's doctrine, have an inalienable right to what he called "autonomous development" under a government of their own choosing.[6] It proved easier for Wilson and his colleagues at Versailles to legitimate nationalism with the rhetoric of self-determination (in the charters of the League of Nations and later in the United Nations) than to embody the actuality of self-determination on the map. Nonetheless, it is easy to see how the "primordial affinities and attachments" of twentieth-century nationalism grow directly out of the Confederate experience.[7]

The future of nationalism promises to be no more peaceful than its past. In the gory and well-publicized dismembering of Yugoslavia, conflicts both ancient and recent have been fought out not only in the press and in various legislative forums but also on the killing fields. And such bloody transformations are hardly limited to the former Yugoslavia. But nationalist ideologies would appear to have taken a decisive step. Movements of "unification nationalism" based on broad visions of national union (such as those of Abraham Lincoln) have been elbowed aside by movements of "separatist nationalism" based on narrower definitions of national identity (such as those of Jefferson Davis). Our postmodern world seems to be moving toward a proliferation of smaller and weaker nations, each lacking in political or economic stability, each unified mainly by the bitter hostility of its citizens toward their neighbors.[8]

This is only the postmodern counterpart of the Civil War's long, sad legacy of sectional bitterness, of Dixie denigration on one hand and "Yankeephobia" on the other. The War for Southern Independence taught many lessons, but for the defeated rebels none was more humiliating than learning that you can strive and sacrifice and do your best and still lose. In the months after Appomattox, hatred crackled and seared among former Confederates. They had lost control of their destiny; and the experience left them frustrated and outraged. For at least fifteen years after Appomattox, a kind of post-traumatic stress disorder settled upon the late Confederacy.

Perhaps the mood of the vanquished rebels was best captured by Father Abram Joseph Ryan, a former Confederate chaplain, in his poem "The Conquered Banner." "Furl that banner," he wrote,

> For there's not a man to wave it,
> And there's not a sword to save it. . . .
> Oh! 'tis hard for us to fold it;
> Hard to think there's none to hold it. . . .
> Touch it not—unfold it never.
> Let it droop there, furled forever,
> For its peoples' hopes are dead.[9]

Although North-South animosity has abated somewhat in recent decades, it still persists in mutually slanderous stereotypes and *blaison populaire.* Even so reconstructed a southerner as I must confess to an occasional unseemly satisfaction at evidence of Yankee hypocrisy on racial matters.

The American Civil War continues to cast what filmmaker Ross Spears has called "long shadows." Perhaps the longest is that cast upon historical writing. One of the consolations of the bloodiest war in American history is that it has inspired some of our greatest historical literature. The history of war has been a thriving enterprise ever since the origins of our discipline in the studies of Herodotus and Thucydides; and the splendid opportunities inherent in the "Late Unpleasantness" have certainly not been neglected. Unfortunately, too much of the military history of the Civil War has been of the bugles-and-sabers variety, deriving ultimately from the Roman tradition of Caesar's *Commentaries,* with its oversimplified motivation, its armies of automatons, and especially its glorification of the commander. But fortunately there is another tradition that has produced distinguished military histories of the Civil War and its battles. The Greek tradition fathered by Herodotus and Thucydides in the fifth century B.C. is, as John Keegan describes it, "a great deal richer, more subtle, more psychological, above all more frank in its treatment of how men behave in battle" and why, above all, they choose to fight.[10]

As a boy I had been taught that we southerners were a righteous people, a chosen people, that God was on our side. I then had great difficulty comprehending Appomattox, comprehending the Confederate defeat. As a youth the historian C. Vann Woodward confronted the same historical problem: "If Marse Robert was all that noble and intrepid, if Stonewall was all that indomitable and fast on his feet, if Jeb Stuart was all that gallant and dashing, and if God was on our side, then why the hell did we *lose* that war?" Southern literature may be more helpful than the platoon of historians who have addressed the problem. Miss Rosa Coldfield in William Faulkner's *Absalom, Absalom!* explains that southerners entrusted "our . . . future hopes and past pride" to "men with valor and strength but without pity or honor. Is it any wonder that Heaven saw fit to let us lose?"[11]

When Faulkner was asked why the South had created a vital literature out of the Civil War and the North had not, he replied that "the Northerner had nothing to write about regarding it. He won it." In Robert Penn Warren's memorable phrases, the war gave the South "the Great Alibi" and gave the North "the Treasury of Virtue." The Treasury of Virtue was a plenary indulgence awarded by the hand of history for saving the Union and freeing the slaves. It redeemed all sins past, present, and future. It did not need writing about. But the Great Alibi was, by its very nature, for public consumption. By the Great Alibi the South explained, condoned, and transmuted defeat into victory, defects into virtues, and ignorance into divine revelation. The Great Alibi required mythmakers.[12]

Growing up among the survivors of the Civil War bred among the writers of Faulkner's generation a certain mentality that Allen Tate characterized as "the peculiarly historical consciousness of the Southern writer." They created a literature treating the past as something that still shapes our present, something that still affects us today—a literature, in Tate's words, "conscious of the past in the present."[13] For such writers, born a generation too late to know the Civil War at first hand, a generation too late to have seen for themselves "the bright eyes of the beardless boys go up to death," the survivors became living symbols, tangible connections with the living past. For such writers, listening to the survivors made the Civil War a central experience of their own lives and of the lives of the characters they created. And so they wrote not only of the war, they wrote also of listening to the survivors tell stories of the war. In so doing they also created a literature conscious of evil in the past—the evil of slavery, the evil of racial injustice, the evil of the inhumanity of war.[14]

If historians have concentrated on military and political history, novelists have turned instead to the tragic realities of the war's effects on those at home—hardship, defeat, evil, and what Faulkner called "the problems of the human heart in conflict with itself." In the fiction of such writers as Faulkner, Tate, Caroline Gordon, Andrew Lytle, Margaret Mitchell, and Stark Young, the war is significant as a defeat that heightens southern devotion to a past imagined to be sacred and inviolable. Their heroes and heroines eke out a bare living and brood over the past. As Yankee capitalism invades the region (transforming its society and economy even more than Sherman's urban renewal program), they baptize themselves in the blood of Confederate martyrs and make the Lost Cause into a civil religion. And as the planter class proves itself incapable of handling the modern world, a new class arises—a rapacious breed that Faulkner calls Snopeses. Commerce supplants agrarianism as the keystone of the "New Departure." These novelists at their best bring to realization for the first time the powerful literary potential of southern social history. In their hands, the South's yearning for a sacred past is offset by a nagging sense of the evil and fraudulence of that same past. Their moral tone is ironic, grounded in their judging the inadequacies of the present by the standards of a past that never was.[15]

And the sheer tragedy of the Civil War continues to haunt us. The word "tragedy" is often used loosely. I mean more than that the Civil War was sad. I mean more than the shivery sensation we get squinting down an alley of melancholy, moss-draped live oaks that lead to somber ruins—or to an archaeological site. I intend the word at its deepest Aristotelian significance: the purgation by pity and terror of the most profound questions of human fate.[16] The tragedy began not with the war itself, but with our embrace of human slavery. The existence of human bondage—in a new nation that consecrated itself to liberty in its Declaration of Independence—divided the heart of the nation against itself and put its two parts in conflict with one another.

Slavery was called "the Peculiar Institution" in the Old South, but there is nothing very peculiar about the institution of slavery—at least not in the most common definitions of peculiar as "odd," "eccentric," or "unusual." Slavery existed before the dawn of human history, in the most primitive societies that anthropologists have ever studied and in the most advanced societies of western civilization. There is no region on earth where slavery has been unknown. So widespread was slavery in human history that it is highly improbable that any of us are not descended from both slaves and slaveholders.[17]

Tragedy is the result of choices. Without choice—however sharply and painfully restricted—there can be no tragedy. Slavery was the deliberate choice of men who sought to reap what they did not themselves sow, men who sought greater returns than they could earn by the sweat of their own brows. Slavery—placing a property or monetary value on our fellow human beings—was the tragic flaw of the South.

Those who chose to adopt and to preserve slavery could no more escape responsibility for their choice than they could escape its consequences. That it might have been otherwise, that other choices might have been made, makes the Civil War not just an exercise in predestination but also a subject of tragic stature.

Alone among the slaveholders of the New World, southern planters thought slavery was worth fighting for. They thought it was worth the blood of their sons. And like no other Americans before or since, they made a major effort to overthrow the government of the United States by force and violence. They courted catastrophe by doing conscious violence to the nation their parents had created—and to their own deepest values. We need not question their sincerity nor doubt their courage to point out the obvious fact that results have proved their judgment terribly inept. At least three generations of southern men and women paid a horrible price for the erratic behavior of their ancestors.

There was scarcely a family, North or South, that did not mourn dead soldiers or harbor disabled veterans. Until well into the twentieth century, Civil War veterans missing an arm or leg remained common sights in the South. The crutch and the empty sleeve made boys who had unflinchingly faced death into men without resources to face the future.[18] Modern combat videography has not improved on the haunting old photographs of cocky young soldiers posturing before the battles and of tangled bodies in the Bloody Lane afterward. Even now it is a moving experience to be reminded that real blood gushing from real men soaked the ground at Bloody Angle and darkened the waters at Bloody Pond.[19]

When I taught at the University of Mississippi a few years ago, Willie Morris pointed out a statue on the campus commemorating the University Grays, a Confederate unit comprised of Ole Miss students. Willie said that 103 of the University Grays, average age nineteen, charged up Cemetery Ridge at Gettysburg. One of the first to fall was Jeremiah Gage. On the battlefield he was able to scribble a last letter to his mother:

My dear Mother
This is the last you may ever hear from me. I have time to tell you that I died like a man. Bear my loss as best you can. Remember that I am true to my country and my greatest regret at dying is that she is not free and that you and my sisters are robbed of my worth whatever that may be. I hope this will reach you and you must not regret that my body can not be obtained. It is a mere matter of form anyhow. This is for my sisters too as I can not write more. Send my dying release to Miss Mary . . . you know who.

The University Grays made it to the Union trenches, where they engaged in fierce hand-to-hand combat with saber and bayonet. Some now call that spot at

Gettysburg "the High Water Mark of the Confederacy." The South's doomed effort to realize itself as a separate national entity never again came so close to success. Not one of the University Grays survived to boast of their achievement.[20]

According to Charles Kuralt, in the secret room of his fraternity at the University of North Carolina there is a handwritten record of everyone who has ever been a member, noting in a few lines what they did in life and when they died. Seven of the fraternity were members of the class of 1863. Two years later six of them were dead. Those six young men, like their counterparts in Mississippi's University Grays, were going to be the leaders of their state. They were the college generation, but that generation was decimated in the Civil War. Of course decimated, as Kuralt points out, is not quite the right word. Decimated just means the death of one in ten.[21] A generation of potential leaders was annihilated, leaders we could ill afford to lose. The long decades of race baiting and political demagoguery that followed set an unsavory precedent for similar politics in our own day.

Thus, the enduring significance of the Civil War—the issue of human slavery and its consequences—offers us the most distinguished theme in our history, for its contradictions and spiritual stresses haunt us still. Faulkner suggested that there is a curse on the South. "The curse," he said, "is Slavery, which is an intolerable condition . . . and the South has got to work that curse out."[22]

Perhaps the most visible symbol of the enduring significance of the Civil War has been the so-called "Confederate battle flag." It flew over the capitol in my native state of South Carolina from 1962, when the state's segregationist government had to confront the civil rights movement, until 2000. To some of my fellow South Carolinians the flag was a sacred symbol of their heritage, and they sought to keep it there. To others, it was a shameful symbol of slavery and racism, and they sought to have it removed. Sacralization of the flag helped one group forget the immensity and horror of the war. But it was a constant reminder to the other of the immensity and horror of slavery.

What any object "symbolizes" is slippery at best. And in South Carolina the symbolism is especially enigmatic since the banner atop the state house was neither the flag commissioned by the Confederate government to serve as its official symbol nor banner under which most Confederate troops made war against the United States. It neither adorned the Confederate capitols in Montgomery or Richmond nor fluttered atop any state capitol within the Confederacy. Debate continues over whether its rectangular shape ever flew over any Confederate military unit until late in the war. Its use in South Carolina was a blatant example of what Eric Hobsbawm has called an "invented tradition."[23]

Many southerners insisted nonetheless upon the flag's sanctified nature. But when it was seen everywhere adorning license plates, bumper stickers, beach towels, and beer cans (often accompanied by the slogan "Forget, Hell!"), where were its defenders to protest the gaudy commercialization and tacky desecration of their sacred symbol? And if it was not an emblem of racism, where were its defenders to protest its blasphemous appropriation by the Ku Klux Klan and the American Nazi Party? Not least among my revulsion at such displays is that they amounted to a form of trivialization of this bloodiest of American wars and callousness toward a conflict that claimed the lives of more than half a million soldiers and countless civilians, that claimed the lives of one out of every four white southern males between the ages of twenty and forty; a form of callousness toward a death toll more than five times greater than that for World War II, toward military casualties greater than those of all our other wars put together through the first five years of Vietnam, toward the war's incalculable devastation and destruction, toward the billions of dollars of property destroyed, toward the crops and cities burned, and toward the countless widows and orphans created. And I should add that I take such callousness quite personally. One of those orphans was my grandfather.

The flag controversy in South Carolina was resolved in 2000 with a legislative compromise that supplanted the "rebel flag" atop the state house with the "Stars and Bars" elsewhere on the capitol grounds. If one is going to display "the Confederate flag," I suppose there is something to be said for displaying an official one. But the compromise may be only temporary. Those southerners who find the "rebel flag" a daily reminder of the slavery and segregation that have shamed too much of our past are unlikely to be bought off by replacing it with the official emblem of a nation created for the specific purpose of perpetuating slavery.

Of course the nub of the controversy lay not in the flag itself but in conflicting interpretations of the meaning of the Civil War. In ceremonies marking Confederate Memorial Day in 1994, the senior U.S. senator from South Carolina, Strom Thurmond, spoke for many of his white constituents when he declared that he was "irked" by people who say the Civil War was fought over slavery. Given that affronts to southern honor require an appropriately savage reaction (and indeed the senator's own record of virility and martial prowess is legendary), his being merely "irked" was occasion for some of us to breathe a sigh of relief. The war, he maintained, was fought over the rights of the states to control their own destinies. "Slavery," he added, "was incidental."[24]

There is a difference, to be sure, between the senator's history and ours, even if we speak (in some sense) of the same historical events. How could it be otherwise? We are historians, scavengers of evidence. He is a griot, a singer of tales. In another rhythm his history might well have been a chanted epic or a mythic genealogy, helping his people make sacramental sense of a great calamity. Thurmond served the same function two years later when he called for removal of the Confederate flag

from the South Carolina State House. If we wish to comprehend the war in southern memory, if we wish to comprehend these myths and signs and symbols, we
must—as Greg Dening notes—observe them at work in culture in all their creativ-
ity, their transformations, and their attachments to the present moment (or, more
accurately, to the fleeting series of present moments that make up all our lives). We
must construct not only a history of their pasts but also an ethnography of their
presents.[25]

Thurmond's 1994 interpretation was the same one advanced by Jefferson Davis
and Alexander H. Stephens. As Stephens expressed it, the war was caused by "opposing ideas as to the nature of what is known as the General Government. The contest
was between those who held it to be strictly Federal in character and those who
maintained it to be thoroughly national." Slavery was not the cause but merely the
"question" upon which the two "antagonistic principles" came into "actual and active collision with each other on the field of battle." The arguments of Davis and
Stephens were weakened, however, by the fact that as president and vice president
of the late Confederacy, they had important axes to grind. Furthermore, their arguments were advanced after the war had been lost and the Lost Cause was in need of
justification. But in 1861, as top leaders of a Confederacy that they confidently expected to endure, each had candidly acknowledged that the cause of the war was
slavery. In an address to the Confederate Congress in April 1861, Davis had declared
that "a persistent and organized system of hostile measures against the rights of the
owners of slaves in the Southern States" had culminated in a political party dedicated to "annihilating in effect property worth thousands of millions of dollars."
Since "the labor of African slaves was and is indispensable" to the "productions in
the South of cotton, rice, sugar, and tobacco," Davis had said, "the people of the
Southern States were driven by the conduct of the North to the adoption of some
course of action to avert the danger with which they were openly menaced." In a
speech in Savannah, Stephens had made it even clearer that the establishment of the
Confederacy had "put to rest forever all the agitating questions relating to our peculiar institutions—African slavery as it exists among us—the proper status of the
negro in our form of civilization. This was the immediate cause of the late rupture
and present revolution," he wrote, adding that the Confederacy was "founded upon"
what he called "the great truth that the negro is not equal to the white man; that
slavery, subordination to the superior race, is his natural and normal condition."[26]

Moreover when South Carolina delegates walked out of the 1860 Democratic
National Convention in Charleston as a prelude to secession, their spokesman de-
clared that "slavery is our King; slavery is our Truth; slavery is our Divine Right."
And a few months later when the South Carolina secession convention issued its
Declaration of the Causes of Secession, they advanced as their grounds for breaking

up the Union that the free states have "assumed the right of deciding upon the propriety of our domestic institutions." They complained further that the free states have "denied the rights of property established in fifteen of the States." The "domestic institution" to which they referred was slavery. The "rights of property" to which they referred were rights to *human* property. A few sentences later the secessionists finally abandoned such embarrassed euphemisms and called slavery by its name, objecting that the free states have "denounced as sinful the institution of Slavery." The secessionists alleged that the free states had "encouraged and assisted thousands of our slaves to leave their homes; and those who remain have been incited by emissaries, books, and pictures, to hostile insurrection."[27]

The efforts of a group of people to control their own destinies, to "separate themselves from the political sovereignty under which they live and set up a new political community" that they expect to promote their safety and happiness, "must always command a certain respect," Lord Charnwood writes in his biography of Lincoln (published during Woodrow Wilson's presidency). But to him it was another question entirely whether such a separation was "entitled further to the full sympathy and to the support or at least acquiescence of others." The idea that it was of "no concern of their neighbours" was surely ridiculous. The "slave interests," he notes, with their filibustering expeditions to the Caribbean as well as their expansionist activities in the western territories, had already made plain their imperialistic appetite. Had the loyal states acquiesced in secession, they would have faced "an aggressive and disturbing power upon the continent of America." The Confederacy, Charnwood writes, was "a nation dedicated to the inequality of men." He does not find it "really possible" to think of the "new and peculiar political society" initiated by the seceding states as "a thing to be respected and preserved." His words are reminiscent of Mary Boykin Chesnut's plaintive lament, "How can I honor what is so dishonorable or respect what is so little respectable, so disreputable?"[28]

Running for governor of South Carolina in the critical election of 1860, Francis W. Pickens left little doubt of his support for disunion and even war to perpetuate slavery. His sentiments were echoed by his old friend Edward Bryan, who declared during the campaign, "Give us slavery or give us death!" In proclaiming his support for slavery today, slavery tomorrow, slavery forever, Pickens committed his state— and mine—to a ruinous course. "I would be willing to appeal to the god of battles," he defiantly declared, "if need be, cover the state with ruin, conflagration and blood rather than submit."[29] Pickens won the governorship in 1860, and the state was indeed covered with ruin, conflagration, and blood. In the end she submitted anyway. These are not interpretations by so-called "revisionist historians," they are statements made *at the time* by Confederate leaders explaining what they were doing and why.

* * *

I am a southerner, and I love the South. But I reject the notion that the test of one's loyalty to the region is reverence for the Confederacy. Some identify that temporary entity with the South itself, but the secessionists represented only a part of the South and served the interests of only a part of the region. They precipitated the bloodiest war in American history to preserve the right of some southerners to hold other southerners in perpetual bondage. In retrospect, it is difficult to see how anyone who truly loves the South can ponder the disastrous Confederate experiment without more regret than pride. When the folly of our forefathers in breaking up the Union brings down pain and poverty upon three generations of southerners, we do not serve the region well by praising them for it.

I do not claim that everyone who put on a Confederate uniform between 1860 and 1865 did so primarily to defend slavery. After Fort Sumter, young South Carolinians volunteered for Confederate service by the thousands. Robert Conway Wilson, my grandfather's grandfather, was one of them. I do not know how he felt about slavery, but I do know that he owned no slaves. I do know that he said, "I have no quarrel with the Yankees." I do know that that he lived and farmed in Horry County, South Carolina, a unionist stronghold of small farmers who considered secession foolish. The Confederate army—"Lee's Miserables"—was filled with young men like Robert Conway Wilson. They came from all over the South, enduring four years of arduous service and fighting with almost unbelievable bravery.[30]

Many of those who sought to keep the "rebel flag" flying today are descendants of such men, and they are entitled to be proud of the courage of their ancestors. But it is less clear why they should wish to celebrate the Confederacy, which wasted the lives of such young men in the service of a dubious cause contrary to their own interests. Robert Conway Wilson lost his life in the Tennessee campaign of 1864. A Confederate victory would have ensured that he—and other southerners neither slave nor slaveholder—would have continued to struggle in uneven economic competition with rich planters and slave labor.

But Appomattox determined that there would be no southern nation. Seldom has a war been lost more thoroughly than the Confederacy lost the Civil War; seldom has a "nation" crumbled more completely than did the Confederate States of America. Robert E. Lee surrendered more than a sword at Appomattox; he offered up the whole South as a living sacrifice on the altar of slavery. And Lee knew better. He had said in 1861 that he was "one of those dull creatures that cannot see the good of secession." There was little in the next four years, or in the rest of his life, to change his mind.

Young Woodrow Wilson, growing up in war-gutted South Carolina and Georgia, saw at first hand what the Confederacy's quixotic attempt to make the world safe for slavery had cost the South. Unlike Lee, he came to believe that the reverence southerners showered upon the Confederacy was misguided, that building monuments to the men who had led the South into disaster was not the best way to demonstrate one's love for the region. He came to believe that the Confederacy's defeat benefited the South more than its success could have. He rejoiced, he is reported to have said, in the failure of the Confederacy.[31] Only the transaction at Appomattox could have freed the southern people—not merely the slaves but all southerners—to move ahead toward realizing what Lincoln called "the better angels of our nature."

How long the South will allow itself to be symbolized by retrogressive politicians, irreligious evangelists, and pseudo-Confederate battle flags I have no way of knowing. But I know we will never reach our potential until we can accept the past as it was. Jack Burden, the protagonist of Robert Penn Warren's *All the King's Men*, tells Anne Stanton how "if you could not accept the past and its burden there was no future, for without one there cannot be the other, and how if you could accept the past you might hope for the future, for only out of the past can you make the future."[32] Exactly. Forget, hell. The past is within us, part of us; we forget its lessons at our peril. But we ought to *learn* its lessons before we refuse to forget them.

Southerners, like other Americans, have tried to move into the future without facing up to the past. Defeat and social upheaval have fostered decades of self-destructive politics, economic Snopesism, and moral stagnation. But confronting the tragic past has the potential to impart a deeper and more compassionate understanding of the modern world and of the universal human condition. Ralph Ellison acknowledged being motivated by what he called "an old slave-born myth . . . not the myth of the 'good white man,' nor that of the 'great white father,' but the myth, secret and questioning, of the flawed white southerner who while true to his Southern roots has confronted the injustices of the past and been redeemed. Such a man, the myth holds, will do the right thing however great the cost . . . and will move with tragic vulnerability toward the broader ideals of American democracy." The figure evoked by this myth is one who will grapple with complex situations that have evolved through history, and is a man who has so identified with his task that personal considerations have become secondary.[33] That is the kind of southerner who has gone back into the South's tragic and enduring past and confronted both the myths of Confederate nationalism and the realities of racial and class injustice. That is the kind of southerner who can finally furl that banner. That is the kind of southerner the region needs now.

2

CONFEDERATE IDENTITY AND THE SOUTHERN MYTH SINCE THE CIVIL WAR

Bruce Collins

In 1958 C. Vann Woodward began an essay on southern identity on a skeptical note: "The time is coming, if indeed if has not already arrived, when the Southerner will begin to ask himself whether there is really any longer very much point in calling himself a Southerner." He therefore proceeded to point out what might constitute "southernness" in an age of economic boom and boosterism. The South, unlike the rest of the country, had experienced long periods of recent and grinding poverty, humiliation in war and military occupation after it, a sense of guilt (over slavery) totally at odds with Americans' customary "innocence" of any significant defects in their society or polity, and finally a notably powerful sense of place. Even though business values dominated the South of the 1950s, so powerful a cultural heritage and set of perceptions arising from a troubled past might, Woodward implied, prove a useful counterpoint to America's overwhelming self-confidence in facing the future. Visiting the United States at the same time that Woodward reflected on the possibly enduring value of southernness, John Keegan (later to become one of Britain's foremost analysts of warfare) came to a similar conclusion about the cultural importance of defeat. Writing decades later, he noted: "I have often tried to analyse why I should have a sense, however slight, of being at home in Dixie. Class system, yes; history, yes; but more important, I suspect, the lingering aftermath of defeat. Europe is a continent of defeated nations. . . . Victorious America has never known the tread of occupation, the return of beaten men. The South is the exception. . . . Pain is a dimension of old civilizations. The South has it. The rest of the United States does not."[1]

A sense of the limitations and failings of the human condition, of the entrapments that the past has a habit of bequeathing to later generations, and of the sobering and enduring restraints created by historic reverses flowed from the four hectic years when the Confederacy was born, struggled for life, and then suffered dismemberment and death. The legacy of the Confederacy—what and who created it, how and why it collapsed or was crushed—has formed almost as vital a theme in the definition and redefinition of the South since 1865 as the issues of race and power that spurred its formation in the first place.

At the time when Woodward and Keegan were reflecting on the South's peculiar legacy of defeat, the image of the Confederacy was about to undergo a major change. Generalizing broadly, it is possible to argue that the Confederacy had a positive image nationally from the 1880s to the 1940s, that the Confederacy's reputation then declined significantly, but that the last few decades have witnessed a Confederate revival among some writers, though scarcely among professional historians in academe.

From the 1880s, the Confederate legacy was powerfully legitimized in national politics and culture. The northern retreat from Reconstruction and the partisan political compromises of the late 1870s meant that prominent service in the Confederate government and army no longer impeded, indeed helped propel, political careers. For example, of the twenty-two senators who represented the eleven ex-Confederate states in the Forty-seventh Congress (1881–83), fourteen had served in the Confederate army, with eight becoming generals and another three reaching the rank of colonel (no rank was provided for Isham G. Harris). Three others served in the Confederate Congress and Joseph E. Brown was the wartime governor of Georgia. Three, all lawyers, did not play a public part in the Confederacy, and one, William P. Kellog from Illinois, fought on the Union side and became a leading figure in the reconstruction of Louisiana from 1865. Overall, eighteen of the seventy-six U.S. senators in 1881, nearly one-quarter, had been active Confederates. The restoration of men was accompanied by a finality over the suppression of key political measures, which is often overlooked. There was no revival of theoretical debate or political agitation concerning the constitutional issues of ultimate state sovereignty and the right of secession, which had burgeoned in the 1840s and 1850s. Although the tension between state governments' rights and the powers and the responsibilities of the federal government continued to dog and divide politicians, the ultimate claim of states' rights doctrine died with Reconstruction.[2]

What had not died by the late 1870s, of course, was the experience that hundreds of thousands of northerners and southerners possessed of having fought each other so fiercely and determinedly for so long. This experience was increasingly commemorated and indeed celebrated during the last two decades of the nineteenth century. To a large extent what Pres. Charles de Gaulle hoped to achieve between the French and the Algerian revolutionaries in 1959—a "peace of the brave"—was forged by ex-Union soldiers and ex-Confederates in those years.³ The most dramatic literary attempt to reconcile these former enemies came in the series of articles published in *The Century* magazine from 1884 to 1887 and then pulled together in the four fat volumes of *Battles and Leaders of the Civil War*. The series was credited with almost doubling *The Century*'s sales and with reaching about two million readers. By offering detailed accounts of the battles by senior officers on both sides, this exhaustive series achieved at least three things. First, it brought together former enemies in an atmosphere of professional debate, where animosity or disagreement was directed as much at colleagues within each army as against the leaders of the opposite side. Second, the series focused in immense detail on war as fighting, not as politics, and virtually ignoring the home front and the struggle for African Americans' freedom, which grew in vigor and extent as the conflict proceeded. Military events became virtually depoliticized, divorced from the moral fervor that impelled and sustained the war. They were subject to passionate arguments about tactics, strategy, and individual leaders' decisions and blunders in a way similar to those engendered by modern sporting events rather than to the venomous commitment to a cause that one would associate with modern nationalist movements. Finally, the focus on campaigning and fighting and the elucidation of competing claims within each camp opened the way to reconciliation. Gen. Ulysses S. Grant, in his essay on Shiloh, typified the approach adopted. He noted postwar assertions about superior Confederate skills displayed in the battle: "The Confederates fought with courage at Shiloh, but the particular skill claimed I could not, and still cannot, see; though there is nothing to criticize except the claims put forward for it since. But the Confederate claimants for superiority in strategy, superiority in generalship and superiority in dash and prowess are not so unjust to the Union troops engaged at Shiloh as are many Northern writers. . . . It is possible that the Southern man started in a little more dash than his Northern brother; but he was correspondingly less enduring." Having established the brotherhood of the fighting men and distanced those engaged in the fighting from those who later prattled or wrote about it, Grant added a powerful additional point: "The troops on both sides were American, and united they need not fear any foreign foe."⁴ The way was clear for the full rehabilitation of Johnny Reb and his descendants into America's armed forces. Wars against Native Americans and the Spanish-American War of 1898, partly fought in Cuba, whose acquisition by the United States had been a central demand of Southern Democrats during the 1850s, completed this process of restoration.⁵

While sectional resentment against the conquering Yankee remained intense, southerners flourished on the national scene in politics and in the armed forces. This restoration did not inhibit the continuing celebration of the Confederate military record. The United Daughters of the Confederacy, established in 1894, became extraordinarily active by the 1900s, principally in erecting monuments to the glorious dead. Some 1,120 memorials and monuments had been dedicated to the Confederate cause by 1982, with 368 of them just in Virginia and Georgia. Equally potent as a symbol of military rehabilitation was the reopening in 1882 of the Citadel, the Military College of South Carolina. Originally founded as an amalgam of training college and garrison for use in the event of a slave uprising in 1842, the institution took on a larger collegial role in Charleston on the eve of the Civil War. According to the story current in the 1930s, cadets from the Citadel fired the first and last shots of the war. The federal government occupied the site from 1865 to 1881. It then passed it back to the state of South Carolina, which chose to reopen the college as a unique state-funded institution providing higher education in a military setting. The Citadel expanded, being rehoused on a new two-hundred-acre campus in the 1920s, with barracks bordering a spacious parade ground. By the mid-1990s the college enrolled two thousand full-time students, and only after bitter controversy did it admit women undergraduates in that decade. So too the Virginia Military Institute, founded at Lexington in 1839, was resuscitated after the war. By the mid-1990s it boasted twelve hundred full-time undergraduates. Not only were the Confederate dead commemorated publicly and with honor, but also the new generation was positively encouraged, with state funding, to embrace the military legacy of the South.[6]

The process of Confederate rehabilitation was further assisted by two influential factors. One was the use of the character and generalship of Robert E. Lee. Despite the fact that the preeminent Confederate field commander absorbed a higher proportion of casualties among his own armies than the notorious "butcher" General Grant did among his, Lee developed and subsequently enjoyed a reputation for dashing, highly intelligent, determined, and indomitable leadership that set him head and shoulders above his northern opponents in the pantheon of heroic generals. The idea of the Civil War as a chivalric, honorable contest owed a great deal in subsequent commentary to Lee's personal values, deportment, and behavior, including his dignity in surrender at Appomattox.[7]

The image of Lee as the preeminent Confederate general had been fashioned after his death in 1870. This development was helped by the early date of his passing—with no public expression of views about the war by him—and by blaming the defeat at Gettysburg on Lt. Gen. James Longstreet. The image was further advanced in, for example, some thirteen biographies of Lee published from 1928 to 1941. Pres. Woodrow Wilson used the nationwide respect accorded to Lee as an important theme in a brief address in memory of the Confederate dead: "I remember one day in the *Century Cyclopedia of Names* I had occasion to turn to the name of Robert E. Lee, and I found him there in that book published in New York City simply described as a great American general. . . . Our solemn duty is to see that each one of us is in his own consciousness and in his conduct a replica of this great united people." Similarly, when Pres. Franklin D. Roosevelt was present at the unveiling of the Robert E. Lee Memorial Statue at Dallas, Texas, in June 1936, he emphasized: "All over the United States we recognize him as a great leader of men, as a great general. But, also, all over the United States I believe that we recognize him as something more important than that. We recognize Robert E. Lee as one of our greatest American Christians and one of our greatest American gentlemen."[8] This eulogy to an officer who dedicated himself thoroughly to destroying the United States, who placed loyalty to Virginia above loyalty to conscience or nation, and who engaged with energy, commitment, and tactical imaginativeness in the bloodiest campaigning Americans experienced before the 1940s assuredly testifies to the success of the Confederacy's rehabilitation.

The image of a heroic war, of a sustained passage of honorable arms somehow isolated from the conflicting political and social values for which its combatants struggled, gained further strength by the way in which the victorious North's worst excesses were associated not with the war itself but with Reconstruction. The Dunning "school" of historians reduced the postwar period to a story of unremitting corruption and political disaster. A dramatic expression of this view comes in John Gunther's *Inside U.S.A.*, published in 1947. Gunther was a serious analytical journalist who had written lengthy political-social-cultural travelogues on Asia, Latin America, and Europe before turning his attention to his native land. He introduced his section on the South as follows: "It will be almost literally impossible for an outsider, whether a man from Mars, the moon, Moscow or Jersey City to understand the South, if he does not accept as a concrete and contemporaneous fact the cataclysm of the Civil War or, as it is usually called by die-hard Southerners, the War Between the States, together with what followed. Perhaps the four years of actual warfare were not quite so important as the aftermath. . . . Nobody in the South ever forgets Reconstruction. To this day the South has not recovered from Reconstruction. This was one of the most cruelly outrageous episodes in all the wantonness of history." The arrival en masse in 1867 of northern carpetbaggers to rule the South, the African Americans' enfranchisement from 1870, and the division of the section into military districts constituted, in Gunther's account, the main instruments of this terrible tyranny. But Gunther went even further. An experienced reporter of European events during World War II, he drew a shocking comparison with those events: "Atlanta in the 1870s must have startlingly resembled Budapest or Warsaw under the Nazis in the 1940s." Given such demonization of Reconstruction, it became increasingly difficult to understand why the Civil War had been fought so hard and so long; hence the plausibility of the view that attributed the coming of the war to a "blundering generation" of politicians rather than to more profound causes.[9]

Accompanying this steady process of sanitizing the war and the Confederate experiment was an increasing nostalgia for the antebellum South. Such regard, particularly for the physical fabric and cultural symbols of the slave South, in turn legitimized the Confederate effort to defend that "civilization," as it continued to be described. One expression of this interest emerged in films building on the success of *The Birth of a Nation* (1915). Following the financial crash of 1929, Hollywood engaged in a remarkable love affair with all things "southern." Perhaps some seventy such films were made from 1929 to 1941, appealing to a national rather than simply sectional audience. The genre reached its apogee with the screen adaptation of Margaret Mitchell's *Gone with the Wind*, the movie appearing in December 1939. It is worth reminding ourselves of just how extraordinarily popular the film proved to be and how it reiterated contemporary historiographical orthodoxies on Reconstruction that were only just beginning to be challenged. Its rendition of slavery reflected historical writings that were not seriously revised until the 1950s. The Confederacy thus stood as a heroic defense of a reasonable, indeed civilized, order that was finally crushed by northern politicians and their unscrupulous agents—during Reconstruction it has to be emphasized—and not by the soldiers of the war itself.[10]

It is possible to speculate on the film's wider appeal. A disquiet with industrial capitalism was matched by a fierce loyalty to values of community resting on attachment to the land. Scarlett O'Hara's earthy pledge to Tara presumably had a powerful emotional resonance for American farming families dispossessed of, or driven by low prices from, their homesteads during the 1930s, and many other Americans were related to such families. The Confederate cause almost became part of a struggle against an industrial capitalism that had wreaked such devastation for so many Americans. In addition, the film depicted the Civil War and its grievous human losses in such a way as to achieve the effect of being an antiwar film that positively commemorated Confederates individually and, in a paradoxical way, the cause they so enthusiastically but naively espoused. *Gone with the Wind* thus tapped both admiration for the Lost Cause and the powerful antiwar spirit of the 1930s.[11]

The deification of the Confederacy went a step further when that transient nation was portrayed as an effort to defend a lost but once admirable "civilization." The "southerns" of the 1930s created a wholly inflated image of the grandeur and elegance of the antebellum plantation house as a symbol of that allegedly cultured and refined society. Such a portrayal could be interpreted as evidence of social criticism in the 1930s, of a linking of conspicuous consumption with rejected elites. In fact, the more probable effect of such depictions of the elegance of antebellum living was to stimulate romantic escapism in the viewer and to make the social caste that enjoyed such lifestyles admirable by the very sumptuousness and remoteness of their pattern of living. The distinctiveness and disciplined magnificence of the British monarchy's lifestyle, for example, was systematically and repeatedly invoked in the twentieth century to stimulate a respect tinged with awe for the royal family. Although the image of the antebellum plantation house and the elegance of existence within it were grossly exaggerated in the Hollywood sagas of the 1930s, that image increased the sympathy due to those who gallantly and honorably defended their homeland during the Civil War. So too, the war's destruction of the plantation house as exemplified by Tara strengthened a sense that the northern war effort smashed the locus classicus of the southern household and all those values of stability, family, and culture it fostered and protected.

The 1950s turned the Confederate cause, outside the South, from an emblem of understandable, even respectable, remembrance to one of potent, objectionable reaction. Writers in the 1940s typically referred to the difficulties facing the South as "the Negro problem," reflecting the need for racial control—if at "best" paternalistic—that had sustained the secessionists. By the 1960s the civil rights movement had successfully cast white racism as the southern problem. As late as William R. Taylor's *Cavalier and Yankee* (1957) and Clement Eaton's *Growth of Southern Civilization, 1790–1860,* it was possible for serious historians to describe the Confederate cause as a misguided but honorable defense of an anachronistic but civilized way of life. Of course, there were important earlier urgings that the South's defensiveness about its recent past, its racial intolerance, and its suspicion of outside influences impeded the region's future development. Yet there was also a powerful argument that no conservative ideology could be sustained in America because of the Confederacy's defeat. Russell Kirk argued in 1953 that the Civil War had discredited the principal case for states' rights, removed any future possibility of secession, and undermined any prospect of maintaining a link between familial traditionalism, rural values, a religious sense of men's essential sinfulness, and the primacy accorded to community over the individual. Kirk deplored the liberal consensus on individualism, with its optimism, commitment to improvement, and rejection of the wisdom of the past. The Confederacy's resistance to northern policies of improvement represented a last stand for assertive, spirited conservatism.[12]

Most of these principal assumptions about the nature of the Confederacy have been cast aside in the decades since the 1950s. The idea that the antebellum South spawned a particularly attractive civilization took a severe mauling from the work of historians who treated the slaves as individuals with their own emotions, aspirations, and agendas. Plantation life has been seen increasingly as an arena of violence and conflict at worst or of endemic tussling over workloads and rights at best rather than as a paradigm for cultured agrarianism. The image of the plantation house itself may be readily dented. Far from being spacious and lavishly furnished, as portrayed in the film of *Gone with the Wind*, most were small, cramped, and basic in fabric and contents. The vast majority of such houses had been thrown up in the thirty years before the Civil War. The notion that the Confederacy embodied some longstanding way of life resting on a contented plantation order and epitomized by the elegance produced in plantation houses has collapsed in recent decades.[13]

Beyond this—and more controversially—it has been argued that the Confederacy commanded relatively limited popular backing, either in its formation or in its heyday. One group of historians has described the origins of the Confederacy in terms of a counterrevolution by the slaveowning elite to ward off the consequences of Lincoln's election to the presidency both on the national political scene and within the South itself. The Confederacy represented, therefore, the political handiwork of a class intent on defending its self-interests. This view of the Confederacy as a reactionary vehicle for the maintenance of slaveowners' brutally acquired wealth and consequent privileges has gained further strength from the work of Drew Gilpin Faust on the creation of Confederate nationalism. She views the Confederates' creation of a national identity as the work of an elite bent on dominating "the masses." It involved an attempt to purge southern state governments of the influence of poorer voters and an effort by southern ministers to raise spiritual awareness and commitment. Yet according to Faust, this systematic and wide-ranging attempt to forge a sense of Confederate nationality collapsed under the weight of wartime suffering. Ideas of community values, local self-rule, and mutuality among whites fell to pieces when sparing wartime inflation provoked protests and then food riots in southern towns. By 1863 the Confederate consensus had (apparently) broken down, and southern urban newspapers denounced and deplored the allegedly socialist rhetoric and demands of the urban hungry and poor. The accompanying debate over wartime extortion and profiteering dented the moral and political claims of the Confederacy to embody even white social unity.[14]

If the Confederacy did not build upon a highly distinctive "civilization" and in some interpretations represented the political interests of the southern planter class rather than the wider white popular will, then it becomes possible to argue that its downfall marked a far less significant historic shift than was indicated by earlier accounts.

This conclusion has been reinforced by recent research by Charles Royster and Mark Grimsley. In reexamining Maj. Gen. William T. Sherman's operations in the Deep South in 1864–65, both have concluded that the depiction of his march as a form of annihilatory warfare grossly exaggerates what occurred. Although Sherman himself described the conflict in terms of annihilating his opponent, his language was more severe than his practice. In a way his description of events was more lurid than one might expect from a general because Sherman remained a conservative unionist; not wishing to unleash punitive war upon the Confederate population, he needed therefore to explain and justify measures that other commanders might have resorted to without much agonizing. Royster has stressed that Sherman's march missed most of the population of Georgia and South Carolina. Few whites saw the army. Inhabited houses were rarely destroyed, although they were often looted and their owners may have been harassed. The march demonstrated, as Sherman intended, that the Confederate army by 1864 was powerless to defend the civilian population of most of the Deep South. Grimsley goes further in pointing out that only rarely did the Federal troops burn a dwelling in Georgia, no murders of whites were recorded, and very few and very vague accounts of rape have come down to us. Only in South Carolina was a deliberate policy of wanton destruction pursued, and that was tempered by strict orders and by the northern soldiers' own sense of the moral dilemmas raised by the war. Once the Federal army moved on from the hot-house of secession in South Carolina, it ceased to inflict such widespread damage upon civilian property. Indeed, Sherman regarded the burning of Columbia, the capital of South Carolina, as a sufficiently powerful and dramatic signal to intimidate the rest of the Confederacy and therefore to require no repetition. It might also be noted that Charleston, by far the most populous and wealthiest South Carolinian town, held out against Federal forces until the end of the war and thereby denied Sherman a chance to destroy the storm center of secession. Grimsley concludes that the later southern myth about the extent of Yankee violence and destructiveness in the Deep South, deeply entrenched during the first half of the twentieth century, helped intensify the southerners' sense that they were beaten unfairly—and not through military ineptitude—and that their postwar economic ills resulted as much from the wartime destruction of the southern economy as from their own subsequent economic decisions or failures.[15]

These historiographic developments have challenged the model of Confederate identity that was so powerful until the 1950s. Yet there are three principal countervailing trends to this powerful revisionism. Without restoring the discredited stereotype of the Old South defended by the "heroics" of the Confederacy, these counterarguments demonstrate why the legacy of the Confederacy remains a significant cultural/ideological debating point.

Following the tide of federal government activism and interventionism arising from the New Deal, the Second World War, the civil rights movement, the Great Society, and the Vietnam War, conservative efforts have been made, not surprisingly, to reinvigorate notions of limited government and states' rights. Such notions have been canvassed since the early 1970s, and in the 1980s a more energetic rhetoric of states' rights erupted to accompany assaults on federal government spending on domestic programs. During the mid-1990s the Republican majority in the House of Representatives, led by its Speaker, Newt Gingrich of Georgia, sought to rollback many of the federal government's extensions of power. Some writers on jurisprudence and political science reopened the case made most elaborately in the nineteenth century by John C. Calhoun for a formal reassertion of states' rights doctrines. Calhoun had been one of the first and remained for antebellum southerners one of the most inspiring ideological theorists of secession. This has led some to recast the Confederate cause as essentially a political crusade against the constitutional encroachments aimed at and then affected by the northern Republicans of the 1860s. With the southern states out of the Union, Congress passed protective tariffs, which ran counter to modern classical liberals' theories, and then proceeded after the war to enact the Fourteenth Amendment, which was originally intended to be and in the second half of the twentieth century became a principal constitutional mechanism for the assertion of federal power. Classical liberals thus regard the Civil War as a constitutional disaster because the North brushed aside states' rights and established powerful precedents for the later expansion of federal authority. By contrast, the Confederate Constitution and practice of politics both nurtured states' rights.[16]

This dichotomy has long been described by historians. Allan Nevins, for example, stressed that the Civil War led to the development of more thoroughgoing national organization, and liberal historians have regretted that the advance of national ideals and programs did not continue beyond the early years of Reconstruction. Against this progressive interpretation of the necessary unfolding of federal power classical liberals have set the extensive writings of John C. Calhoun. Unfortunately, they have tended to overlook the fact that, although Calhoun made no mention of slavery in his disquisitions, the whole course of his political theorizing and scheming was directed to the defense of slavery. Late twentieth-century states' rights advocates ignore this context to Calhoun's political thought but claim that, under various possible scenarios, slavery within the Confederacy would have ended anyway. One could speculate that the worldwide depression in agricultural prices during the 1880s and 1890s would have made plantation slavery unprofitable. Others have suggested that the Confederacy would have been incapable of preventing slave runaways; the battle of the 1850s to enforce the Fugitive Slave Act outside the slave states would have palled into insignificance compared with the problems of trying to prevent the flights of slaves into the United States from the Confederacy. But against arguments that slavery might have been eroded by events must be set the strenuous guarantees set out in the Confederate Constitution to protect the peculiar institution. To see the seceded South as offering a path to eventual emancipation reverses the situation. The Confederate Constitution forbade the passage of any law "denying or impairing the right of property in negro slaves" and emphasized that no state or future territory of the Confederacy could free slaves held by owners in other states or territories. To amend the constitution required a decision by a convention of all the states and approval by two-thirds of the states' legislatures or specially called conventions. The creation of the Confederacy made gradual or eventual emancipation less rather than more likely to occur.[17]

The most obvious objection to the argument that slavery would have ended eventually under a Confederate government is that this counterfactually assumes that the abolition that did occur was accompanied by the sort of social, political, and economic disruption—indeed ruin—postulated by the Dunning school of early-twentieth-century historians. Instead, as Eric Foner has insisted, although emancipation marked an extraordinary gain for the former slaves, it led to an ambiguous and severely qualified improvement in African Americans' economic fortunes and social status. The potential benefit of emancipation under a Confederate government was actually achieved as a result of the war, with no major change—by the 1880s—in the structure of white political control within the southern states. But this potential for emancipation within the Confederacy is scarcely the classical liberals' main argument in favor of the southern experiment. The preeminent claim of the Confederacy to contemporary political theorists' interest was its insistence on states' rights and rejection of the federal political activism that wartime Republicans unleashed upon the nation.[18]

Just as the Confederacy has begun to reemerge in the guise of a romantic embodiment of states' rights ideology, so the image of the civilization it defended has been reburnished as one of culture and refinement. During the 1930s Hollywood treated the plantation house as an icon of a lost way of life notable for elegance and splendor. But most antebellum plantation houses by then were either dilapidated or had been transformed into hunting lodges for wealthy northerners. Few people regarded them as viable houses for middle-class life. By the 1980s a new "lifestyle" interest in the antebellum plantation house had emerged. Magazines such as *Southern Living* depicted the decoration and furnishings of the restored plantation houses as major statements of good taste and reawakened interest in refined living. Houses that were overequipped and overlavish in color schemes and furniture beyond any measure of historical authenticity won glowing endorsements as tasteful restatements of antebellum reality. This revival of older buildings as desirable dwellings was not limited to the South or to the United States. But when seen in conjunction with local campaigns to maintain the right to fly the Confederate flag as part of the region's "heritage," renewed assertions about the elegant legacy of southern plantation houses confirmed a particular perspective on the Confederacy as the defense of "culture" well worth defending.

These newly revamped images of the Confederacy have been reinforced by a third revival. The strongest contemporary image of the Confederacy remains its fighting prowess. The sheer amount of writing on the military history of the Civil War remains extraordinary. We have minute, detailed "micronarratives" of virtually every battle—one is tempted almost to say every engagement—of the war, and the grand ebb and flow of the conflict is frequently recounted as well. All this narration serves to commemorate, if not celebrate, the Confederate cause and to lend it credibility, if not legitimacy. This latest surge in Civil War historical writing had been accompanied by a drive to tell the stories of individuals or small groups of fighting men. Until the mid-1980s little scholarly work had been done on the soldiers themselves since Bell Irvin Wiley's important books of 1943 and 1952. Modern research on the war represents an expanding working out of one part of the postmodern agenda by historians who would, mostly, reject the tenets of postmodernism.

But this aspect of recent historiography, of recreating individuals' unpatterned existences and experiences, has an extremely important consequence. It treats the fighting men of both sides as equal in their shared involvement in protracted warfare. Gerald Linderman's *Embattled Courage* offers an influential example of the approach in no longer distinguishing between Confederate and Federal in understanding the national experience of fighting. Reid Mitchell concludes his study *Civil War Soldiers* by underscoring this shared legacy: "The soldiers who had fought had shared the political culture of America in the last years of the old Republic, whether they embraced its Northern or its Southern expression. Between 1861 and 1865, they had created a new American history, a potent source of myth and identity."[19] When James McPherson completed his revisionist study of Civil War soldiers' motivation, he concluded that beliefs, not simply peer pressure from fellow soldiers, deeply influenced the fighting men: "Civil War soldiers willingly made extraordinary sacrifices, even of life itself, for the principles they perceived to be at stake in the war." Tracey Power's study of Lee's soldiers again stresses the transcendent moral values which infused their experience: "Those who persevered from the Wilderness to Appomattox and called themselves 'Lee's Miserables' set a standard that is a fitting testament to the resiliency of the human spirit, that quality above all others made the Army of Northern Virginia such a cohesive community of men and such a formidable body of soldiers."[20] In this respect the study of military history both smoothes, even almost romanticizes, the image of the Confederacy and strengthens the view of the conflagration as indeed a "brother's war."

Biographies of generals—few of which follow William McFeeley into the paths of righteous indignation against the principal practitioners of war—add to this analysis of warfare as a skilled craft, an elaborate game with its own internal rules, logic, emotions, demands, rewards, and penalties. The sense that Confederate leaders fully shared the experience, risks, and suffering of war was underscored by the fact that nearly a quarter of the Confederacy's 425 general officers died during the course of the conflict. Yet it is curious that the most frequently remembered maxim of Clausewitz—that war is, in effect, the continuation of politics by alternative means—should so often be ignored when military history is written. The underlying rationale of the Confederacy—to uphold slavery and the constitutional rights to make the basic political decisions on the fate of slavery—disappears largely from view. Too often the history of battle and the history of fighting become the history of the war; for the image of the Confederacy, this is pure gain.[21]

The last two decades have thus witnessed significant developments in softening the Confederacy's image. Southerners' states' rights arguments, it has been suggested, were interesting and legitimate even if, unfortunately, they became intertwined with the root-and-branch defense of slavery. There was after all, we are told, a cultured, tasteful lifestyle that the Confederacy attempted to maintain and that was indeed swept aside by its defeat. And the fighting of the Confederate cause was done by honorable men skilled in the technical craft of warfare, exposed to the physical and emotional hardships and hardening experiences shared by all fighting men, and inspired by a high sense of their political and cultural identity.

Given this revival of the Confederacy as a historical experience worthy of respect, it is necessary to return to consider that aspect of the Confederate legacy that so impressed Vann Woodward in the 1950s and that has recently been restated by John Keegan—the notion that the experience of defeat has marked the South off from the rest of the United States since the 1860s. One consequence of that defeat has been, so runs the argument, that the South has not shared the "can-do" mentality that flows from Americans' customary optimism and orientation to the future. Insofar as the contemporary positive image of the Confederacy arises from political and cultural characteristics that are essentially backward looking, what has been stated here confirms that view. But even in stressing that the ex-Confederacy differed from the rest of the United States, Woodward and Keegan imply that the Confederate legacy is a salutary one, affording southerners a sense of perspective and caution about political/public life that might not be undesirable.[22]

The effect of defeat upon southern attitudes toward the armed services and involvement in foreign wars scarcely suggests that southerners have felt chastened by the experience of military defeat.

First, the presidents who led the United States into major wars during the twentieth century have also been those who won the support of the majority of southern whites. Woodrow Wilson—a Democrat and Virginian by origin, though not by residence in the 1910s—was the first southern-born president elected after the Civil War. His victory in 1912 appeared virtually as a victory for the South, resuscitating the region's pride. Not only did he take America into the war of 1914–18, but also he sought to entrench America's active postwar world role. In 1917, Confederate veterans marched down Pennsylvania Avenue to the cheers of 250,000 people as they waved placards proclaiming "Send us if the boys can't do the job."[23]

Franklin D. Roosevelt, as a Democrat, was also the southern whites' choice of president. Although his domestic activism drew opposition from the southern wing of his own congressional party from 1937, Roosevelt's foreign policy was endorsed by southern opinion. John Gunther noted just after 1945 that "The South was . . . [the] part of the nation that from the beginning and most vividly took the allied side in both World War I and World War II." In 1940–41, Texas, Georgia, and South Carolina had ratios of volunteer enlistments to inductions through selected service higher than the national average. When Gallup conducted surveys in 1940–41 on Americans' attitudes toward entering the European war, it found that southern respondents favored U.S. involvement to a greater extent than did respondents in any other region. In September 1938 the South led all regions, though only by a very small margin, in supporting the enlargement of the American army. A year later, just after the outbreak of the European war yet well before Pearl Harbor, southerners emphatically supported a change in the Neutrality Law to enable Britain and France to buy war materials in the United States; 77 percent of the southern sample favored this proposal compared with 55–57 percent of respondents in the three regions of New England, East Central, and West Central. By December 1940 the South was far more favorable to helping Britain win the war, even at the risk of U.S. involvement, than the East Central and the West Central regions and appreciably more favorable than New England (75 percent compared with 54 percent for the two central regions and 62 percent in New England). In January 1941 the South decisively outvoted all other regions in backing a suggestion that U.S. ships should be used to supply Britain with goods if the need arose and in supporting the Lend-Lease bill. On the latter legislation, 77 percent favored Roosevelt's initiative compared with only 54 percent in New England and the Middle Atlantic states and even lower proportions in the central regions. When respondents were asked in May 1941 whether they would support going to war with Germany and Italy or staying out of the European war, eight of the former Confederate states were among the eleven states with the highest proportions approving entry. Since the other three were Colorado, Wyoming, and Arizona, one might reasonably suggest that these responses had as much to do with militaristic attitudes as with a fine calculation of interests.[24]

When it came to American involvement in Vietnam two decades later, the two presidents most directly responsible for deepening their country's commitment, John F. Kennedy and Lyndon B. Johnson, were strongly backed by the South. In the wake of rising antiwar sentiment, southern respondents in 1970–71 wanted U.S.

involvement in Vietnam to continue more than did the population of any other section of the country. In September 1970 the South was the only region that did not give a majority in favor of the United States bringing all its troops back from Vietnam by the end of 1971. The difference was largest between the South (49 percent) and the East (62 percent). In June 1917 southern respondents gave the lowest percentage of any region in support of a proposition to withdraw all American troops from Vietnam by July 1972 and in support of a more general proposition that war was outmoded as a means of resolving international disputes. Following the shift of southern whites into the Republican party of the 1970s and 1980s, the assertive approach to military preparedness and in the conduct of foreign policy under Ronald Reagan proved popular among white southern voters.[25]

Nothing in this record suggests that the Confederate experience of defeat made for twentieth-century restraint. Nor is this surprising. The defeated separatists of the United Kingdom of the eighteenth and early nineteenth centuries, the Scots and the Irish, did not resort to pacific introversion; instead they played a very active role within the British army of the nineteenth century. The Scots battalions consistently won renown for their bravery, and Irishmen in the nineteenth century volunteered in disproportionately large numbers for the British army. The French defeat at the battle of Waterloo in 1815 did not deter France from adopting Bonapartism once again after the revolutions of 1848 and pushing a program of military adventurism in the 1850s and 1860s under Napoleon III. Nor did German defeat in 1918 discredit the army of militaristic values.

The southern commitment to the military acquired an additional edge through the redistribution of federal tax revenues in favor of defense spending in the South. This phenomenon is well illustrated by the pattern of spending by the Department of Defense in 1972, at a time when such expenditures were necessarily high owing to America's deep involvement in Vietnam. According to the federal census of 1970, some 24.73 percent of the U.S. population lived in the eleven states of the former Confederacy. Yet while those states paid only 19.8 percent of the federal tax burden in 1972, they received 27.6 percent of Department of Defense spending. This gain in share above both population and tax contribution was especially significant given the sheer size of the Defense budget. Not all eleven ex-Confederate states achieved these gains, and the success of Texas and Virginia in drawing in federal expenditure boosted the total.[26]

Such net gains had not been accidental; they rewarded consistent political effort. Under the long period of virtually uninterrupted Democratic control of the U.S. Senate from 1933 to 1981 and the longer period of very rarely broken Democratic control of the House of Representatives from 1933 to 1995, southern Democrats were able to gain powerful positions in Congress from which to influence the federal government's allocation of spending. Some examples indicate the extent of this southern influence. Carl Vinson of Georgia long served as chairman of the House Armed Services Committee; in 1972, Georgia received 2.88 percent of Defense Department spending compared with its contribution of 1.82 percent to federal tax revenues and (in 1970) its 2.27-percent share of the country's population. John C. Stennis of Mississippi served in the Senate from 1947 to 1989, becoming chairman of the Senate Armed Services Committee for many years from 1969, having sat on that panel since 1951. From his earliest years on the committee, he proved a persistent advocate of the Department of Defense's case for increased spending. His state received 1.49 percent of defense spending compared with its 0.59 percent federal tax burden and 1.10 percent share of the U.S. population. The majority of that defense spending went to the Litton Shipbuilding Complex and the city of Pascagoula in the Fifth Congressional District. That district in turn was represented from 1933 to 1973 by William M. Colmer, who held an extremely powerful committee chair in the House. He was succeeded in 1973 by Trent Lott, who later secured a seat in the Senate, where he became Republican majority leader.

In South Carolina defense spending was concentrated in the First District, which includes Charleston, the cradle of secession. L. Mendel Rivers, a congressman for thirty years until his death in late 1970, was chairman of the House Armed Services Committee from 1965. By the early 1970s some 35 percent of all payrolls in the First District were estimated to come from military bases or the defense sector; the district boasted no fewer than eleven naval installations. The joke went that if any more naval installations were built on Charleston's harbor fronts, the fronts would sink under their overwhelming weight. Defeat in war had scarcely destroyed South Carolinians' enthusiasm for the military. So too in the poor, relatively nonurbanized, and low-wage economy of eastern North Carolina was there considerable enthusiasm for the armed services. The region produced a higher percentage of volunteers for the army than any other part of the country during the early 1970s, when the draft ended. A large Marine Corps base at Camp Lejeune and a huge army base at Fort Bragg aided this process. Although poor employment prospects help explain this phenomenon, these areas also endorsed a strong "southern" political identity. In the presidential election of 1968, some 44 percent of the First District's voters opted for George Wallace, the candidate associated with the defense of racial segregation, while Wallace secured 36 percent of the vote in Fort Bragg's Seventh District. In Virginia the focus of defense activity lay at Norfolk, which boasts one of the world's largest naval bases and the headquarters of the Atlantic Fleet. Texans did extremely well from the expansion of the space program at a time when Lyndon Johnson served as Senate majority leader, vice president, and president. Southern whites have consistently welcomed federal activism and spending when it has not impinged upon their freedom to control race relations and their internal domestic agenda.[27]

Finally, it is worth reminding ourselves of the influence of the Confederate legacy on the training of America's top officers at West Point. Until the 1960s at least, Generals Lee, "Stonewall" Jackson, and "Jeb" Stuart formed part of a very small pantheon of heroes for an incoming cadet. Lee's portrait—as a former superintendent of the Point—honored the dining hall, and his description of duty as the most sublime noun in the language was disseminated among cadets. The cadets themselves in the mid–twentieth century came overwhelmingly from farm families or from towns with under twenty-five hundred people, a demographic background most strongly associated with "southern" values. More specifically, from the mid-1970s the military doctrine of active defense taken up in teaching at the academy emphasized the importance and benefits of Lee's and Jackson's maneuvering. The idea that war required bludgeoning strategies of annihilation, associated however unfairly with Grant, became unpalatable in the wake of U.S. involvement in Vietnam and in the face of growing needs for America to be able to intervene more effectively in limited campaigns.[28]

The historian of the South is faced with contradictory interpretations of the Confederate legacy. On the one hand, we are told that the legacy lost its power long ago. According to Gaines M. Foster, "The ghosts of the Confederacy . . . had become too elusive and ephemeral to define" the modern South's identity. On the other hand, there remains the tendency for intellectuals and academics to depict the South as an empirical fact that they record, comment on, and even celebrate.[29]

No celebratory revival of interest in the Confederacy has occurred in recent times to match the sentimental and often enthusiastic commemoration of the Confederate experiment that occurred in the late nineteenth and early twentieth centuries. But elements of the Confederate legacy and ideals or myths that the Confederate cause embodied and depended on for its legitimacy have been resuscitated separately and piecemeal over the last two decades. The political reaction against liberalism as a doctrinal portmanteau and the rhetoric concerning a new federalism that emerged in the 1970s gained mainstream approval under Ronald Reagan's presidency for ideas that flowed from the Confederacy's defense of states' rights. The doctrine of states' rights was by no means solely linked to the Confederate States of America. The northern Democrats of the 1850s and probusiness Republicans of the late nineteenth century and later both supported states' rights while rejecting secession. But the revival of interest in and support for such arguments has lessened the sense in which the Confederate cause could be discussed as alien and anachronistic. In a completely different arena of America's intellectual and cultural life, the antebellum South, for whose preservation the Confederacy was established, has gained from a marked revival of interest in the image of the plantation house, following decades of neglect from the mid-1940s to the 1980s, and of interest in such structures as physical legacies and contemporary representations of "good taste" in architecture and interior design—a phenomenon of relatively limited significance from the 1860s to the 1980s. Again, this aesthetic/commercial interest is directed toward a lifestyle that the Confederacy was established to maintain rather than to a phenomenon that the Confederacy created.

Quite different has been the cultural influence of the Confederacy's fighting traditions. While most southern academics and intellectuals have tended to ignore, regret, or deplore the military legacy of the Confederate armies, there has been a remarkable continuity—perhaps, more accurately, growth—of interest in the Confederates' individual commitment to heroism. Recent histories of the fighting war—as distinct from accounts of the home front—provide us with an alternative interpretation to that offered by histories emphasizing the horrors of slavery and social conflicts among white southerners in the 1860s. As a result of these historical developments since the early 1980s, the interest in the Confederacy as a Lost Cause has been rekindled and the Confederate legacy has been depicted less in terms of black and white moral opposites and, perhaps appropriately enough, in more varying hues of gray.

3

UNFINISHED BUSINESS

African Americans and the Civil War Centennial

ROBERT COOK

Historical memory in the United States, as elsewhere, is notoriously contested ground. Different constituencies at all levels of the American polity possess their own interpretations of past landmarks. When the time comes to commemorate such events, the result is seldom harmonious—witness, for example, the furor over plans by the Smithsonian Institution in Washington, D.C., to stage a major exhibition on the dropping of the atomic bombs on Japan. The exhibition, whose central attraction was to be the *Enola Gay* itself, was finally cancelled early in 1995 after veterans groups launched a successful campaign decrying the exhibition's interpretative script as revisionist and offensive to those who had fought in the Pacific War.[1] Professional scholars, represented primarily by the Organization of American Historians, fought in vain to convince both Congress and the public that the veterans were attempting to put a patriotic gloss on a complex event that was open to more than one interpretation. Different forms of "vernacular" or "particularist" memory (such as the one held by veterans of the war against Japan) coexist uneasily with each other and with official ones dominated by the powerful national state of the twentieth century.[2]

During what black activist Bayard Rustin called "the classical period" of the civil rights movement in the early 1960s, African Americans found their campaign for equal rights under the law vigorously opposed by white southern supporters of de jure segregation. Among the most potent cultural weapons in the armory of white bitter-enders were nationalist and regional memories of the American Civil War that in their own ways glorified the Confederacy's tenacious fight for independence in the mid–nineteenth century. The Civil War Centennial seemed to provide segregationists with an ideal opportunity to mobilize popular support for the crumbling status quo by linking contemporary concerns to past heroics. Although black leaders proved slow to respond to the challenge, ultimately they were able to further their cause by trumping the prevailing white orthodoxies with their own emancipationist reading of the war.[3]

As David Blight has revealed, after the Confederate defeat in the spring of 1865, African American leaders found themselves fighting a losing battle over the meaning of the Civil War. For blacks and their white allies inside and outside the Republican party, the war had been intertwined with the problem of race in antebellum American life. In their view secession was the work of treacherous southern slaveholders whose principal concern in the aftermath of Abraham Lincoln's election victory in November 1860 had been to defend their peculiar institution against external aggression. The war itself had soon become a struggle for human freedom as a consequence of the Emancipation Proclamation (1863), and blacks themselves had played a valuable role in the North's eventual triumph by abandoning the plantations and enlisting in large numbers in the Union army and navy. After Appomattox, congressional Reconstruction had witnessed positive advances for blacks both in terms of their civil rights and their ability to construct their own institutions free from interference by white overlords. The problem was that by 1872, white northerners such as that year's Liberal Republican and Democratic presidential candidate, Horace Greeley, who had once been vociferous in their support for antislavery measures, had begun to advance the cause of sectional reconciliation. As war memories began to fade rapidly during the 1870s and 1880s, blacks discovered that northern whites were losing not only their hatred of Confederates (a hatred that race leaders like Frederick Douglass had done their utmost to instill) but also any sense that the war had much to do with either slavery or blacks.[4]

With African American rights being eroded in the South and in the federal courts, the growth of a racially exclusive definition of the Civil War as an exercise in white nation-building (one in which southern whites had participated as bravely as their northern peers) was a menacing threat to many of the gains that blacks had made during the mid–nineteenth century. An aging Douglass did his best to stem the onset of national amnesia. "There was a right side and a wrong side in the late war which no sentiment ought to cause us to forget," he insisted in a Memorial Day speech in 1878. By the time of his death in 1894, however, African Americans had lost the battle to define the meaning of what northerners had once been happy to call "the War of the Rebellion." If it is possible to speak of a collective American memory at the end of the nineteenth century—and here it is worth stressing the view of one modern scholar that "forgetting is one of the most powerful forces that shape national remembering"—then it is evident that that memory did not encompass those blacks, free born and slave, who had risked, and in many cases sacrificed, their lives in defense of the Union.[5]

African Americans did not remain passive as white novelists, historians, and filmmakers devoted their efforts to the process of sectional reconciliation by rewriting the Civil War and Reconstruction. Black ex-servicemen belonging to the influential veterans organization the Grand Army of the Republic labored proudly at the local and supralocal levels to sustain memories of their wartime contribution to national unity. Inevitably, as death began to thin the ranks of the 170,000 surviving African American veterans, the twin scourges of racism and poverty meant that Civil War recollections were far from central to the lives of most ordinary blacks by the 1930s. But even though the majority of them continued to live in the South, where schools were at pains to devalue the African American experience in the war, former slaves retained vivid memories of the conflict, handing down oral narratives of emancipation and in some cases naming their children after those Union generals who had contributed to their liberation.[6] And while the black masses certainly had more pressing concerns than the fundamental meaning of the Civil War, African American historians such as George Washington Williams, W. E. B. Du Bois, and Charles H. Wesley, aided by the National Association for the Advancement of Colored People (NAACP) and the Association for the Study of Negro Life and History (ASNLH), continued with the struggle to preserve a distinctive black "countermemory" in the face of waves of racist violence and magnolia-blossom kitsch rolling in on the tide of national reunification. Regarding history as a potent weapon in the ongoing fight against segregation and discrimination, they flayed the hegemonic, racially charged interpretation of the Civil War as a tragic (white) brothers' war that had resulted in the unfortunate imposition of "Negro rule" on the proud (white) people of the South. Their efforts found favor with a small number of liberal and left-leaning scholars during the New Deal era and beyond but had only a minimal effect on the American public in the first half of the twentieth century.[7]

In many ways attempts to highlight the positive role that blacks had played in saving the Union may have been hampered by the powerful grassroots image of Abraham Lincoln as the Great Emancipator. For while the martyred president's consistent popularity among ordinary African Americans undoubtedly served to link the present with the past, it also fueled a sense that blacks had been passive actors in the 1860s. By the mid–twentieth century the Civil War had lost its grip on the national imagination. The minority of northern whites positively interested in the Civil War belonged to round-table associations and battle reenactment groups that focused primarily on the military aspects of the war rather than on its fundamental causes and consequences. The sheer trauma of defeat, the persistence of segregation, and the work of organizations like the United Daughters of the Confederacy meant that white southerners retained a much more vivid sense of what their grandfathers had fought and died for. Inevitably, this was a memory entirely at odds with its African

American counterpart, a vernacular variant that in truth exerted only a limited influence on the hard-pressed black community itself.

In September 1957 Dwight D. Eisenhower signed into law a bill to create the U.S. Civil War Centennial Commission (CWCC), a temporary federal body set up to oversee events commemorating the centenary of what the president himself preferred to call the "War between the States." The initial momentum for the creation of the commission had been generated by round tables and business interests in the Washington area, but the bill had garnered impressive bipartisan support from northerners and southerners in Congress—an early indication that the centennial was widely perceived as an opportunity not only to generate tourist revenues but also to educate the public about the central event in the nation's history. Predictably, the federal government was intent upon imposing its own agenda on the forthcoming festival. Throughout its existence, the commission would seek to depict the Civil War as a unifying experience—a sad yet heroic conflict that had finally given birth to the home of western democracy. At a time when the country was embroiled in a global conflict against Communism and less than united over the burgeoning issue of black civil rights, it made obvious sense for the government to depict the Civil War as a defining moment when northerners and southerners finally became Americans.[8]

From the outset the CWCC pursued a decentralized approach to commemorative activities. The individual states were encouraged to create their own centennial commissions to plan events. Interest was most pronounced in the South, where white legislators appear to have had the clearest understanding of the connection between identity, memory, and current affairs. Normally cash-strapped Mississippi voted $2 million for centennial observances; Virginia, $1.4 million. African Americans made little contribution to these early developments. A few individuals such as black historian John Hope Franklin became members of northern state commissions, but as a group blacks lacked the resources to compete effectively in the race to commemorate the Civil War. In the autumn of 1959 Dr Albert D. Brooks, the secretary-treasurer of the ASNLH, met with Karl Betts, a Washington-area businessman who had been appointed executive director of the Centennial Commission. Betts made it clear that the commission had no funds to distribute to participating organizations and that if the ASNLH wished to follow through with its commemorative efforts, it would have to do so without federal money. Although the association was loaned (and subsequently published) a list of blacks who had been decorated for their wartime endeavors, the paucity of financial resources forced it to shelve ambitious plans to sponsor a touring Civil War pageant with associated chorus.[9]

If African American leaders found money hard to come by, and perhaps understandably were preoccupied by the developing civil rights movement in the aftermath of the 1955–56 Montgomery bus boycott and the student sit-ins of 1960, they did not ignore the centennial completely. The foremost institutional conduit for black history, the mainstream ASNLH (founded in 1915), continued its long-running efforts to develop a strong African American historical tradition in order, firstly, to promote racial pride and self-esteem and, secondly, to convince whites that having played a vital role in the development of the United States, blacks were entitled to full citizenship rights. A dues-paying membership organization with branches across the country, the association disseminated information about the African American contribution to the Civil War in a variety of ways. The organization's chief scholarly vehicles, the *Journal of Negro History* and the *Negro History Bulletin,* featured several articles germane to the centennial in the early 1960s. Prominent ASNLH members, including its president, Charles H. Wesley; John Hope Franklin of Brooklyn College; and Benjamin Quarles of Morgan State College in Baltimore, delivered numerous public lectures and wrote important books, articles, and school textbooks stressing the centrality of blacks to the Civil War experience. Franklin, for example, could be heard lecturing on "Abraham Lincoln and the Politics of War" at the Brooklyn Public Library in early 1961. Wesley contributed a short pamphlet on the role of Ohio blacks in the Civil War that appeared as a publication of the Ohio state centennial commission the following year. Quarles wrote a well-received account of the relationship between Lincoln and African Americans.[10]

Throughout their endeavors mainstream black intellectuals were fully aware that they were making a positive contribution to the modern freedom struggle. They consistently highlighted the overriding importance of slavery as a factor in Civil War causation, President Lincoln's positive contribution to the emancipation process, the active role played by blacks in their own liberation, the supportive role of white abolitionists, and—a critical theme in view of the modern South's stubborn attachment to racial segregation—the conflict's ultimate confirmation of federal power. The North's victory, wrote John Hope Franklin in the second edition of *From Slavery to Freedom,* published in 1963, the year when the Kennedy administration belatedly introduced a full-blown civil rights bill into Congress, meant victory for an indestructible Union: "all states were bound henceforth to recognize the superior sovereignty of the federal government."[11]

The ASNLH also encouraged grass-roots discussion of Civil War issues by members of its local branches and backed special centennial events such as the New York Public Library's exhibition "The Negro in the Civil War" and ambitious plans by the Chicago-based American Negro Emancipation Centennial Authority (ANECA) to promote public awareness of 1963 as the centenary of the Emancipation Proclamation. Activities like these were given greater prominence by the active support of black businessmen, newspapers, and radio stations—a fact that did something to increase awareness of the centennial in black communities across the nation. They did not, moreover, go unsupported by sympathetic whites who understood well the relationship between the black countermemory and the pursuit of civil rights in the present. Bruce Catton, author of the best-selling *Centennial History of the Civil War,* sought to educate the general public about the significance of race in the Civil War, not only in his famous trilogy but also, and perhaps more strenuously, in newspaper articles and as a leading member of the New York state centennial commission.[12] Writing in the *New York Times Magazine* in February 1961, Catton described the war as "the continental divide in American history," one that had obliged the United States "at some time to build on the broad base provided by its original assertion of independence: on the belief that a democratic society knows no grades or classes in its ranks, but makes freedom equal for everyone. That the shining goal set forth in this way has not yet been reached makes no difference; the belief itself, as something which the nation must forever try to live up to, was riveted in the Eighteen Sixties."[13]

James M. McPherson, a young Princeton historian who would eventually succeed Catton as the doyen of American Civil War scholars, made a similar contribution to the cause with his book *The Struggle for Equality,* a detailed study of the antislavery movement during the Civil War and Reconstruction published during the penultimate year of the centennial. McPherson made explicit his awareness of the close connection between the struggles of the past and the modern era by dedicating the book to "all those who are working to achieve the abolitionist goal of equal rights for all men." Liberal white historians were joined in their support of black goals by white-owned businesses and white politicians who had a vested interest in being seen to advance African American goals. In Chicago, for example, the A&P grocery chain contributed to the fund-raising drive launched by the local centennial authority to commemorate the issuing of the Emancipation Proclamation. Founded by a local public relations expert, ANECA enjoyed support not only from local black ministers and civic leaders including the Reverend Joseph H. Jackson, the influential head of the National Baptist Convention, but also of no less a figure than Chicago's Democratic boss, Richard J. Daley, a man heavily reliant on black client politicians and black votes.[14]

In truth, however, while African Americans and their white allies recognized the centennial's importance from the very outset, their early efforts to foster interest in seminal historical events such as emancipation were easily eclipsed by southern white enthusiasm for Civil War observances. Although a few commentators below the Mason-Dixon Line were strongly critical of the war's importance to the regional psyche (Robert Penn Warren called it "the Great Alibi," which prevented a sophisticated understanding of the region's poverty and racial problems), large numbers of southern whites regarded the centennial as the perfect opportunity to revel in their heritage at a time when segregation was under attack from domestic and external forces. What better way to thumb one's nose at civil rights agitators and hypocritical northern liberals than by celebrating the foundation of the Confederacy and the humbling of Union forces on the battlefield? Southern white efforts to rerun the Civil War to their own advantage were aided by the CWCC determination to delegate large amounts of responsibility to the individual state commissions and to stress the bland theme of national unity above the more divisive one of racial justice. The fact that the commission was headed by Maj. Gen. Ulysses S. Grant III was certainly not a sign that the South was about be bulldozed into submission for a second time. Even though he had fond memories of his illustrious grandfather at Long Branch in 1884, Grant was a seventy-seven-year-old conservative with little or no empathy for blacks. In 1949 he had actually been attacked by radical columnist I. F. Stone for helping local real-estate interests perpetuate segregation ordinances in Washington, D.C.[15]

By the spring of 1961 a number of high-profile events revealed that the white South would commemorate the centennial in its own way, with few concessions to the official theme of unity and none at all to black sensibilities. The centennial began in earnest on January 8 with two somber ceremonies. Having laid a wreath at the tomb of his grandfather in New York City, Major General Grant attempted to set a suitably patriotic tone for the next four years by declaiming that the fundamental importance of the Civil War lay in the fact "that the country was able to reunite itself after four years of civil strife."[16] In Lexington, Virginia, another prominent member of the CWCC, William Tuck, reminded an audience at the tomb of Robert E. Lee that in the twilight of his life the great Confederate hero had urged southerners to bury the bitterness of the past and work to strengthen the Union.[17] Like the other members of the commission, Tuck, a prominent segregationist politician from southern Virginia, had no understanding of, let alone sympathy for, the black memory of the Civil War, but as a committed anticommunist he was aware that the centennial offered white southerners rather more than just an opportunity to revel in nostalgia.

Unfortunately for those who adhered to the official consensus line on the Civil War, many southern whites were unwilling to treat the centennial with the solemnity that it merited. Certainly the word from the Deep South was unambiguous. After a week-long commemoration of the founding of the Confederate government in Montgomery and a star-studded centennial ball held in Atlanta, large crowds gathered along the waterfront in Charleston, South Carolina, on April 12 to watch a full-dress pageant and a spectacular rocket display to celebrate the anniversary of the Confederate bombardment of Fort Sumter. Thousands of spectators, many of them perched on ancient guns emplaced in South Battery Park, cheered enthusiastically as geysers of flame shot up from the ruined fort in the harbor. This event, however, was overshadowed by news that a black northern delegate had been excluded from the Charleston hotel selected to host the CWCC's annual meeting. The commission's reluctance to respond to black and northern white criticism of this affront spoke volumes for the insensitivity, if not outright racism and downright incompetence, of its all-white membership. So too did its failure to intervene in plans to mark the one hundredth anniversary of the Confederate victory at First Bull Run with a well-publicized and heavily commercialized battle reenactment that was at best in dubious taste. An estimated crowd of thirty-five thousand spectators gathered on the field at Manassas to witness a recreation of the Union army's near catastrophic defeat. A watching reporter described the event as "almost ninety minutes of feigned violence in scorching heat" and remarked how "[t]he viewers came to their feet and cheered as the shouting Confederates chased the Union troops back into the woods in a panic."[18]

The sheer extent of the white South's initial domination of the centennial appears to have taken most African Americans by surprise. It was not as if they had not been warned. As early as June 1959 the Reverend John Morris of Atlanta, an active opponent of racial discrimination by dint of his involvement in the Episcopal Society for Cultural and Racial Unity, wrote to the *New York Times* claiming that segregationists were planning to use the centennial for "sounding off on present-day issues more than for commemorating a bygone event. The passions that brought forth the war between Americans are not dead and will only be exploited by many who are still grieving that the South failed to win." Yet it was not until the widely reported centennial observances of early 1961 that black leaders began to sense the danger. The Civil War was slated to be a prominent theme of Negro History Week in February 1961, but it was certainly not the only item on the agenda at the various local events sponsored by the ASNLH and a host of black community organizations. Present concerns, for example, were clearly uppermost in the minds of the association's New York City branch, which scheduled a contemporary civil rights documentary as the centerpiece of its meeting February 12 at the Uptown YMCA. Yet Negro History Week was the occasion for a number of black commentators to draw attention to the white South's capture of the centennial and the widespread ignorance among blacks and whites concerning the African American role in the Civil War. In a widely reported radio broadcast, Dorothy Sterling, the author of several black history books for teenagers, observed that no mention had been made of the black troops who had served at Fort Wagner and other military sites. "When I was in elementary school," said Sterling, "we were on the side of the North because we thought the North was right. It is no longer fashionable to take sides."[19]

Specifically, though, it was not until the segregation crisis at Charleston in April 1961 that black leaders and their liberal allies finally realized that the white South was in the process of co-opting the centennial for its own purposes. Reports that Georgia-born Madeline Williams, a black Democrat belonging to the New Jersey Centennial Commission, would not be accommodated in the downtown Charleston hotel hosting the CWCC's fourth annual meeting prompted the New Jerseyans to demand a boycott of the gathering. Support for the action was immediately forthcoming. Bruce Catton said that the New York commission had not received an invitation to Charleston but, "We would have been awfully hesitant to send a delegation to a place where one member was not invited. We have firm convictions about what came out of the war." Strong support for the boycott also came from the NAACP, whose director of public relations, Henry Lee Moon, had already written an internal memorandum suggesting that the nation's oldest civil rights organization should prepare for an independent and large-scale celebration of the Emancipation Proclamation in 1963 and formally ask the Centennial Commission "for adequate and integrated presentation of the Negro" throughout the four-year heritage bonanza. Stung into action by events in Charleston, the national NAACP issued a telegram to all its branches requesting them to pressure their state centennial commissions into joining the proposed boycott. A segregated gathering, it was alleged, would be "a betrayal of everything the Civil War was fought for."[20]

Although Karl Betts responded to the barrage of criticism by claiming that his agency had no jurisdiction over what went on in South Carolina, the adverse publicity and political pressure was sufficiently intense to secure the intervention of John F. Kennedy. On March 17 the newly inaugurated president wrote to Major General Grant expressing his view that, as a federal body, the CWCC had an obligation to ensure that everyone invited to its national assembly should receive equal treatment. Kennedy's action elicited an approving editorial from the *New York Times,* but the Centennial Commission showed few signs of altering its policy to conform with the expressed wishes of the president. A statement released on March 21 insisted that it had "no authority or jurisdiction" that would allow it to dictate to hotel owners in Charleston. This contention, of course, went to the heart of the ongoing national debate over segregation and placed President Kennedy on the horns of a dilemma, dependent as he was on the support of African Americans, northern liberals, and white southern Democrats. Continuing black pressure helped force his hand. On March 22 Roy Wilkins, the head of the NAACP, sent a scorching telegram to Karl Betts. "The national commission," he wrote, "may or may not have jurisdiction over the hotels in Charleston, but it certainly has jurisdiction over its own meeting places and the policies governing such meetings." The next day Kennedy told a news conference that the CWCC was a government body using federal funds and that, as a consequence, it had an obligation to hold its meetings at places free from racial discrimination. Confronted with public opposition from the White House and news that the boycott had begun to attract support from a number of northern state delegations, the commission finally gave in and agreed to hold its troubled meeting at the desegregated U.S. naval station outside Charleston. This represented the optimum solution for Kennedy, for it left southern segregation untouched while offering a symbolic triumph to civil rights advocates. It was, said a jubilant Madeline Williams, "a victory for the democratic process in America."[21]

In the same way that massive resistance to school desegregation in the 1950s had helped galvanize the civil rights movement, the events of early 1961 ensured that African Americans and progressive whites would contest the Civil War Centennial as vigorously as any southern white devotee of the Lost Cause. Historians were in the vanguard of attempts to counter southern white domination of the centennial. Writing in *The Nation,* the New Left scholar Jesse L. Lemisch attacked the centennial as "a surrender to the South" and urged his compatriots to "condemn theatrics which conceal the real issues of the Civil War." And a fortnight before CORE freedom riders began their historic bus journeys into the Deep South in May 1961, Lawrence D. Reddick issued his own wake-up call to the federal government. A confidant of Martin Luther King Jr. and a prominent black historian, Reddick had been dismissed from his post at Alabama State College in Montgomery because of his vocal support for civil rights. In a characteristically forthright speech to a gathering of teachers in New York City, he contended that the Civil War festivities were perpetuating historical myths about the white South, myths that were "part of the psychological and political resistance" to the administration's efforts to promote social progress. Confederate symbols then being displayed throughout the South as part of the centennial observances, he said, should be gathered up and burned, for it was time Americans exposed "the Confederate myth for the unhistorical romance much of it is." To aid the process Reddick suggested that President Kennedy himself should issue "a positive statement on the centennial celebration on what it means to the nation, requesting our mass media of communication to so portray it, and calling upon our people to so examine and honor it throughout the land." No such statement was forthcoming, but few could doubt that the segregationists' fondness for the Confederate flag reflected the close interconnection between myth, symbol, and contemporary power relations in the defiant South.[22]

The realization that the nation's plastic past was being manipulated to serve the interests of segregation brought forth a stream of criticism of the centennial from liberals of every hue. Howard Meyer, a former special assistant in the U.S. Attorney General's Office, penned a magazine article entitled "Rally around which Flag." In it Meyer criticized the centennial planners for trying to suppress all references to the moral and political issues at stake in the Civil War in order to promote national unity. An official brochure containing facts about the conflict, noted Meyer, failed to mention blacks at all, let alone the fact that they had constituted 12 percent of the Union armies and 18 percent of the North's total casualties. Observing that the Fort Sumter pageant had omitted to make clear that the original assault on the fort had been a seditious act, Meyer insisted that the war should be commemorated in such a way as not to deprive it of all meaning. "It does not serve America well, in the world of 1961," he wrote, "to ignore the evil and iniquity of slavery in marking the Centennial of the conflict." The article was given wide publicity by the National Council of Churches, a staunch supporter of the civil rights movement, and warmly welcomed by the veteran black trade unionist A. Philip Randolph. "There is no doubt," commented Randolph (unconsciously echoing the complaints of Frederick Douglass at the end of the previous century), "that this whole Civil War Centennial commemoration is a stupendous brain-washing enterprise to make the Civil War leaders of the South heroes on a par with the Civil War leaders of the North, and to strike a blow against men of color and human dignity."[23]

The sham battle at Manassas in July 1961 fueled the growing sense of outrage that many Americans felt not only at the gross commercialization of the centennial but also at the moral vacuum at the heart of the proceedings. One New Englander attacked the events at Bull Run as "a grisly pantomime" and predicted sardonically that rather more dummy corpses would be needed when it came to replicating the battle of Gettysburg. Such "frolics" were to be condemned for causing Americans "to overlook those grievous imbalances and necessities in our body politic which, one hundred years ago, made the outbreak of violence a tragic but necessary preliminary to the arduous reconstitution of our society."[24]

Incessant criticism from blacks and whites alike forced the Kennedy administration to impart greater legitimacy to the work of the CWCC. In early September the president appointed an African American, Roy Davenport, to the embattled federal agency. The same month witnessed the resignations of Grant and Betts, both men having found their authority greatly undermined by the adverse publicity generated at Charleston and Manassas. To succeed Grant as chairman of the commission, Kennedy appointed a genuine heavyweight, the California-based academic Allan Nevins. One of America's most distinguished historians (and the author of several important books on the Civil War era), Nevins shared the administration's desire for a more inclusive and dignified program of centennial events. On formally taking up office as chairman of the CWCC, he reiterated the agency's determination to emphasize the overarching theme of national unity but added, "We shall allow the just pride of no national group to be belittled or besmirched"—a clear signal that black voices were at last beginning to be heard.[25]

From mid-1961 onward, the black response to the centennial became more assertive, paralleling the growth of the civil rights movement during the early years of the decade. It took two interrelated forms. The first, essentially cultural, built on the aims and achievements of Du Bois and other black intellectuals engaged in constructing the black countermemory before the Second World War. The ASNLH redoubled its efforts to promote interest in Civil War themes among African Americans—no easy task given their preoccupation with contemporary developments above and below the Mason-Dixon Line. Insisting that "[t]he control of the presentation of history is so often the control of the future of a people," Charles H. Wesley called on blacks to forge ahead with plans to collate and disseminate information about the race's Civil War record. Community meetings, study groups, museum exhibits, essay contests, and the siting of plaques should all be used, he urged, to challenge the white South's stranglehold over the centennial. Astutely, he pointed to the fact that as time went on the very chronology of the Civil War would start to work against those who reveled in past Confederate triumphs. From the beginning of 1961, observed Wesley, there had been "a preoccupation with the glorification of the drama of the War as it opened in 1861, with Southern dominance and victories. . . . What will we see when General Grant marches through the Wilderness and General Sherman marches to the sea!"[26]

Wesley was right. As segregationists ran out of military victories to celebrate and found themselves increasingly beleaguered in the present by contemporary civil rights campaigns, they rapidly lost interest in the centennial. Civil rights organizations, moreover, were swift to seize the initiative as the opportunity came to commemorate the death throes of slavery, the enlistment of large numbers of blacks into the Union armies, and the heroic sacrifice of African American troops at sites such as Fort Wagner, Fort Pillow, and the battle of the Crater outside Petersburg, Virginia. In particular, the impending anniversary of the Emancipation Proclamation offered black activists a golden opportunity to ram home their point that the Civil War remained unfinished and that the federal government must take immediate steps to secure full and equal justice for all American citizens regardless of color. Here their efforts to utilize the centennial in the service of equality and justice were overtly and unashamedly political.

While the NAACP adopted the slogan "free by '63," Martin Luther King Jr. proceeded with his efforts to encourage, cajole, and shame the White House into providing more positive assistance for the black freedom struggle. One of his strategies was to urge President Kennedy to emulate Abraham Lincoln by issuing his own emancipation proclamation to end segregation. In the autumn of 1961 King actually spoke to Kennedy on the subject in the Lincoln Room at the White House. The president was less than enthusiastic but suggested that King might like to prepare a draft proclamation for him to peruse. King did so in May 1962, exclaiming that Kennedy, like Lincoln, "stood at a historic crossroads in the life and conscience of our nation." Political expediency outweighed any desire the president might have had of following in the footsteps of the Great Emancipator, and no blanket proclamation resulted. Undaunted, however, the leader of the Southern Christian Leadership Conference (SCLC) did not abandon his attempt to use the centennial as leverage in the battle for civil rights.[27]

In the midst of a serious desegregation crisis at the University of Mississippi in September 1962, King addressed a meeting hosted by the New York state centennial commission at the Park Sheraton Hotel in Manhattan. Before a distinguished audience, including the liberal Republican governor Nelson Rockefeller, he insisted that the defeated Confederacy retained "a veto power over the majority of the nation." The South, said King, pouring scorn on the administration's failure to confront segregation, was "an autonomous region whose posture toward the central government has elements as defiant as a hostile nation. Only the undeveloped or primitive nations of the world tolerate regions which are similar, in which feudal autocrats or military governors hold sway over the federal power. It is a condition unknown to modern industrial societies except our own." In a barbed comment directed at the White House, King added that only great presidents were deeply tortured over racial issues. "No president," he insisted, "can be great, or even fit for office, if he attempts to accommodate injustice to maintain his political balance." Dr King's efforts to ridicule federal inaction and heighten northern antagonism toward a defiantly dysfunctional South had obvious parallels with the activities of Frederick Douglass in the 1860s and showed clearly how the centennial gelled neatly with the civil rights movement's principal strategy of enlisting federal intervention in the fight against Jim Crow. The day after King's New York address, Mississippi governor Ross Barnett went on television to denounce federal attempts to secure the admission of a black student, James Meredith, to Ole Miss. "We will not surrender to the evil and illegal forces of tyranny," boasted Barnett, consciously mimicking the rhetoric of his Confederate forebears. Shortly afterward the Kennedys reluctantly dispatched U.S. troops to Oxford, Mississippi, in order to protect Meredith from a howling mob of white racists.[28]

King's attempt to elicit a powerful White House statement on segregation, however, proved to be less successful. In fact the obvious occasion for such a statement, the CWCC's obsequies in Washington to commemorate the one hundredth anniversary of the Preliminary Emancipation Proclamation, merely served to underline the movement's contention that the Civil War was not over yet. No sooner had the CWCC announced details of a suitably solemn commemorative event than Bishop Smallwood Williams of the SCLC's Washington, D.C., affiliate announced a boycott of the proceedings. Remarkably, the commission had produced an all-white list of speakers for the observances scheduled to take place on the Mall on September 22. Although the well-known black singer Mahalia Jackson had been booked to perform against the white marble backdrop of the Lincoln Memorial, a favorite venue for civil rights activists since Marian Anderson's integrated concert in 1939, the accompanying stench of tokenism had outraged Bishop Williams's group. The embarrassing controversy led to a hastily arranged meeting between CWCC members, black leaders, and Justice Department officials. The resulting agreement provided for the appointment of an African American to the speakers' roster and the seating of blacks on the platform. The name of the respected federal judge and former civil rights lawyer Thurgood Marshall was quickly added to the list of orators—a minor victory for a movement now growing in confidence and impatience.

In spite of predictions to the contrary, President Kennedy did not issue an emancipation proclamation to coincide with the official ceremonies in Washington on September 22. Declining to be present in person at the Lincoln Memorial, he prepared a taped address in which he did at least admit that much remained to be done to fulfill the glittering promises of the Declaration of Independence. Adlai Stevenson, the star attraction on the Mall, was a little bolder, suggesting that the obvious gap between American promises and American reality undermined the United States' ability to fight the Cold War effectively. But in truth nothing was said that morning to convince African Americans that the administration was serious about ending racial segregation and discrimination. As black federal judge James B. Parsons stated at a well-attended ANECA-sponsored event at Lincoln's Tomb in Springfield, Illinois, the same day, Americans seemed poorly equipped to deal with the consequences of space travel "when we can't communicate with and understand, and trust, and believe in and appreciate other people about us here on earth who may be physically or ethnically different from us." As if to emphasize the point, the Lincoln Memorial was defaced soon afterward by vandals who painted the words "nigger lover" on the rear wall of the monument.[29]

While President Kennedy did take the opportunity in November to issue a low-key order banning segregation in federal housing projects, movement campaigns and centennial observances in 1962 made it clear that the administration could not be shamed into initiating an all-out assault on Jim Crow. Only when the SCLC engineered sensational media coverage of raw segregationist violence in Birmingham in May 1963 did the Kennedys conclude that it was time to act decisively. Yet in securing the centennial high ground, blacks had contributed significantly to a genuine sense among northern whites that the South was a real threat to the health of the American polity and that the black narrative of the Civil War had rather more merit than the Lost Cause. Proof that the black countermemory had won widespread legitimacy was everywhere apparent during 1963. President Kennedy seemed to acknowledge that fact when he delivered an important civil rights address to Congress in February. "One hundred years ago," intoned Kennedy, "the Emancipation Proclamation was signed by a President who believed in the equal worth and opportunity of every human being. That Proclamation was only a first step—a step which its author unhappily did not live to follow up, a step which some of its critics dismissed as an action which 'frees the slave but ignores the Negro.' Through these long one hundred years, while slavery has vanished, progress for the Negro has been too often blocked and delayed. Equality before the law has not always meant equal treatment and opportunity."[30]

In July the centennial of the battle of Gettysburg was marked by a plethora of ceremonies in Pennsylvania. Although George Wallace, the segregationist governor of Alabama attempted to make capital from the anniversary by delivering a states' rights address at the monument to the Alabama dead, his voice was drowned out by appeals for racial justice from northern liberals. Father Theodore Hesburgh, chairman of the U.S. Civil Rights Commission, spoke at a special battlefield mass of "[t]he appalling dearth of freedom for millions of Negro Americans." Dedicating a monument to the fallen from his home state, Gov. Richard Hughes of New Jersey contended that those who had died would not sleep until their main objective had been achieved: "The Civil War was not fought to preserve the Union 'lily white' or 'Jim Crow' . . . , it was fought for liberty and justice for all." In a similar vein the Republican governor of Pennsylvania, William Scranton, used the same occasion to ask if anyone dared deny that the racial strife of the present "is justified, that it is necessary, that its purpose is fundamentally the ultimate liquidation of the cause of the Civil War?"[31]

While such statements were ahistorical (most Union troops did not fight primarily to liberate blacks let alone secure them equal rights), they underlined the centennial's usefulness to civil rights advocates in the early 1960s. Even though an expensive reenactment of Pickett's Charge on July 3 marked the end of major centennial events, the fact that 1963 had been billed by civil rights groups as the year of full emancipation continued to inform the rhetoric of black leaders like Martin Luther King Jr. In the most famous speech of his life, delivered at the Lincoln Memorial in August, King merged his voice with that of the Great Emancipator:

Fivescore years ago, a great American in whose symbolic shadow we stand today, signed the Emancipation Proclamation. This momentous decree came as a great beacon light of hope to millions of Negro slaves who had been seared in the flames of withering injustice. It came as a joyous daybreak to end the long night of their captivity. But one hundred years later, the Negro is not free; one hundred years later, the life of the Negro is still sadly crippled by the manacles of segregation and the chains of discrimination: one hundred years later, the Negro lives on a lonely island of poverty in the midst of a vast ocean of material prosperity; one hundred years later, the Negro is still languished in the corners of American society and finds himself in exile in his own land.[32]

The March on Washington was not, of course, a CWCC event, but the now dominant theme of the centennial—unfinished business—helped underpin King's eloquent calls for urgent action.

Interest in the Civil War waned considerably after 1963 as Americans abandoned expensive mock battles to mourn the death of their own martyred president and witnessed the country's steady embroilment in the Vietnam War. By the end of 1964 they already had a body count of their own without having to reflect on the carnage that finally had brought the Army of the Potomac to the outskirts of Richmond. Significantly, the civil rights movement itself began to make less use of the Civil War as a totem of full citizenship and integration. Faith in the federal government dwindled as attacks on civil rights workers in the Deep South intensified and the scourge of poverty persisted. Increasingly the commitment was to a radical reinterpretation of the black experience in the United States, not a simple restatement of the traditional black countermemory.

If the Civil War Centennial was more than background noise to the great civil rights campaigns of 1960–65, it is doubtful that the observances had a major influence on the historical consciousness of ordinary blacks and whites, most of whom may well have remained ignorant about the scale of the African American contribution to Union victory until the release of the movie *Glory* in 1989 or the subsequent appearance on PBS of Ken Burns's popular television history of the conflict. With the exception of one or two individuals such as Sam Peckinpah (whose controversial 1965 western, *Major Dundee,* did grapple with race and sectionalism in a Civil War context), moviemakers, television companies, and advertisers fought shy of controversial Civil War themes out of deference to southern white sensibilities. No monument to the African Americans who had fought for the Union was constructed during the 1960s—an indication perhaps that the war did not have a profound hold on blacks during this period. Significantly, when a monument was raised to honor the forgotten black veterans of the Union armies in 1998, it was the product less of a grass-roots surge of interest in the wartime role of African Americans than the determination of a black politician to repair the damage wrought by subway construction in inner-city Washington.[33]

But while it would probably be wrong to describe the Civil War as a fully fledged *lieu de memoire,* a value-laden memory site deeply entrenched within the consciousness of the black community in America, the determination of race leaders to contest the centennial revealed the war's enduring significance to blacks as a signifier of equal citizenship and federal power. For some it also provided important evidence that a supposedly docile and passive race possessed a vital and assertive past of immediate relevance to the mid–twentieth century. During the early days of the 1960 Greensboro student sit-ins that initiated the mass-action phase of the modern civil rights movement, members of the college football team at all-black North Carolina A&T formed a flying wedge to protect demonstrators as they entered downtown stores to protest Jim Crow facilities. Carrying small American flags they pushed confidently past jeering whites on the sidewalk. "Who the hell do you think you are?" shouted the onlookers. "We the Union Army," retorted the footballers. Small incident it may have been, but here was clear evidence that southern blacks were not about to see the Lost Cause retrieved without a struggle.[34]

4

THE CIVIL WAR IN THE MOVIES

MELVYN STOKES

Howard Strickling, studio publicity director of MGM, put out a mimeographed booklet out-
lining a promotion campaign for *The Red Badge of Courage.* "It has BIGNESS. It has GREATNESS!
First, last, and always, it is ENTERTAINMENT in the grand tradition!" the foreword stated. . . .
Civil War stories, it was asserted in another section, had long made popular movies; *Gone
with the Wind* had grossed millions of dollars and *The Birth of a Nation* had been the greatest
grosser of all time.

—LILLIAN ROSS, *Picture*

In the spring of 1950 Lillian Ross, a staff writer for the *New Yorker,* decided to
follow the making of a John Huston film, *The Red Badge of Courage,* based on Stephen Crane's classic novel of the Civil War, from its inception to final release. As a
result she wrote a series of articles, published in book form in 1952. In creating one
of the few full-length studies of the production of an individual film, Ross also shed
considerable light on how the Civil War was regarded in Hollywood. Essentially, as
the publicity release implies, the war was seen as a source of stories to entertain.
Louis B. Mayer and other MGM executives did not regard *The Red Badge of Courage*
as having much entertainment value: it did not have a conventional plot, a romance,
major female characters, or (if made as Huston wanted) stars. Huston, by contrast,
liked the simple story "of a youth who ran away from his first battle in the Civil
War, and then returned to the front and distinguished himself by performing several
heroic acts." His interest in the theme may have developed during the Second World
War, when he produced a film on the breakdown and treatment of shell-shocked
soldiers. Indeed, it was the *psychology* of heroes/cowards that primarily concerned
the director in *The Red Badge of Courage.* Having received the go-ahead to do the

film, despite Mayer's opposition, Huston insisted on avoiding as much as possible what he referred to—with great unconscious irony—as the "North vs. South" aspects of the Civil War.[1]

The promotional campaign for *The Red Badge of Courage* never happened in the way outlined in Strickling's booklet. The film went $200,000 over budget, and MGM executives were appalled at the indifferent or even hostile response of audiences at preview screenings. They insisted on cutting a number of scenes and introducing a voiceover narration linking it more closely to Stephen Crane's classic novel, all to no avail. Audiences remained considerably underwhelmed, and despite the enthusiasm of some reviewers, MGM found it impossible to find bookings for the film, eventually having to sell it internationally as the lower half of a double bill featuring an MGM musical starring Esther Williams. The second part of the publicity release was also characterized by considerable wishful thinking. While it is true that *The Birth of a Nation* (1915) and *Gone with the Wind* (1939) were enormous commercial successes, they were largely aberrations. Indeed, what strikes the historian most is not the popularity of Civil War stories used as a basis for movies but the infrequency with which such stories were used and their unpopularity with moviegoing audiences.[2]

In the days of the early silent film, it is true, there had been a genre of one- or two-reel films based on Civil War stories or settings. From about 1908 to 1917 many such films were produced. Some of these were directed by Thomas H. Ince, who came from New England but was a southern-leaning Civil War buff. Kentucky-born David W. Griffith also directed several less significant Civil War dramas before his masterpiece, *The Birth of a Nation*. After America's entry into the First World War, however, the Civil War genre largely disappeared. During the 1920s and 1930s, relatively few films with a Civil War background were produced. Among those that did appear were *Hands Up!* (1926), *The General* (1926), *The Heart of Maryland* (1927), *The Heart of General Robert E. Lee* (1928), *Morgan's Last Raid* (1929), *Only the Brave* (1930), *Secret Service* (1931), *Operator 13* (1934), *So Red the Rose* (1935), *Hearts in Bondage* (1935), and *The Littlest Rebel* (1935). Nearly all were unsuccessful at the box office. Consequently, when the notion of filming *Gone with the Wind*, Margaret Mitchell's sprawling novel of the Civil War and Reconstruction, was first raised with Louis B. Mayer of MGM, Irving Thalberg, Mayer's right-hand man, was utterly opposed. "Forget it, Louis," he is reported to have remarked, expressing the conventional Hollywood wisdom, "no Civil War picture ever made a nickel." Independent producer David O. Selznick, who would finally make the film, also probably had this tradition in mind when he, at first, hesitated over whether to buy the screen rights to Mitchell's story.[3]

The enormous popular and commercial success of *Gone with the Wind* did not open the floodgates to a series of other Civil War films. *The Man from Dakota* (1940) and *Tap Roots* (1948) were followed by a small number of films devoted to Civil War themes: *The Red Badge of Courage* (1951), *Drums in the Deep South* (1951), *Winchester Rifle* (1952), *The Raid* (1954), *Friendly Persuasion* (1956), *The Great Locomotive Chase* (1956), *Raintree County* (1957), *Band of Angels* (1957), *The Horse Soldiers* (1959), *Advance to the Rear* (1964), *Shenandoah* (1965), *Alvarez Kelly* (1966), *Journey to Shiloh* (1968), *The Beguiled* (1971), *Glory* (1989), *Gettysburg* (1993), *Pharaoh's Army* (1995), and *Ride with the Devil* (1999). With these comparatively rare exceptions, filmmakers avoided using the Civil War itself as the setting for their movies. There were practical reasons for this. Civil War pictures are costly to make (both *The Birth of a Nation* and *Gone with the Wind* were the most expensive films of their time). They need elaborate sets, many costumes, and large casts (including many extras for the hard-to-photograph battlefield shots). *The Birth of a Nation* and *Gone with the Wind,* moreover, had an intimidating effect on Hollywood producers and directors, who realized that such films would be extremely hard to match.

Taking all these things into account, however, it is still surprising that so few films have been made about the Civil War, which was almost certainly the most dramatic and defining event in American history. (Shelby Foote, in Ken Burns's television series on the war, described it as "the crossroads of our being.")[4] It cost the lives of at least 620,000 soldiers—more than were killed in all other American wars combined through Vietnam. It settled the issue of whether the United States would be one or two nations and led directly to the freeing of four million African American slaves, with all the resulting social consequences. Were there, therefore, more-complicated reasons than those outlined above for Hollywood's comparative neglect of the war? Why did audiences on the whole not like (or see) most of the films that were made? Why, conversely, did moviegoers greet two Civil War movies—*The Birth of a Nation* and *Gone with the Wind*—so enthusiastically? Finally, what kind of history of the war was recounted in the movies and how did it alter over time?

It is not only filmmakers who have largely ignored the Civil War, for novelists have tended to do the same. Indeed, C. Vann Woodward argued, the fact that the Civil War has also failed to inspire any major literary classic hints at broader, cultural reasons for the resistance of both creative artists and audiences to embrace themes from the period. Some of these, he suggested, might include an "emotional resistance" to the racial aspects of the war, a gendered response by the public, divided loyalties over the conflict itself, and soldiers' natural reluctance to discuss their experiences. The last of these was of rather more relevance to novels than to movies (although several extracts from the diary of Robert Gould Shaw, white commander of the black Fifty-fourth Massachusetts Infantry Regiment, were used in *Glory*). Questions of gender, divided loyalties, and race, however, have profoundly influenced the manner in which Hollywood approaches the subject of the Civil War.[5]

During the 1920s and 1930s, based on a substantial amount of evidence, the film industry was convinced that women formed the dominant section of the movie audience, either because they had a *numerical* majority or because they were the primary influence on what their menfolk viewed. The existence of this belief influenced the whole course of Hollywood's development. The star system itself was mainly aimed at women (one theater manager would later describe most movie houses as "Valentino traps") as was the discursive apparatus associated with it (fan magazines and stories about stars in newspapers and periodicals). Through advertising associated with "tie-ups" and licensing deals, Hollywood and its business allies also set out to appeal to women as consumers.[6] Apart from anything else, this involved making certain kinds of film: "modern" films offered better opportunities for displaying product lines such as clothes and cosmetics.[7]

In a broader sense, moreover, the movie industry set out to appeal to its dominant female audience by making the kind of films it believed they liked. A high proportion of 1920s films, therefore, were female-centered melodramas or romances. During the 1930s these gave way to a new genre, the "women's film." Conversely, filmmakers increasingly avoided the types of movies thought to have little appeal to girls and women. Prominent among these were war pictures. In a 1926 survey of ten thousand Chicago schoolchildren, Alice Miller Mitchell found that girls consistently listed war movies as the lowest of ten varieties of film. Three years earlier an even larger poll of thirty-seven thousand high school students in seventy-six cities suggested that even *The Birth of a Nation*—almost certainly the biggest-grossing film of the period—suffered from this gender bias. Less than half the number of girls than boys named it as the "Best Picture They Had Ever Seen." Even in the South girls preferred *Way down East* (1920), a tearjerker starring Lillian Gish, although boys supported Griffith's film. The perception that women disliked war movies in general may well have discouraged the making of Civil War films during this period and after, while female hostility or indifference possibly accounted for the lack of success of most of those that were made. Equally, it was no accident that *Gone with the Wind*, the most successful Civil War movie ever made, was identifiably a "women's film."[8]

Another important influence restricting the number of Civil War movies made was filmmakers' belief in what Thomas R. Cripps has dubbed "The Myth of the Southern Box Office." In the period between 1920 and 1940, it was thought inexpedient to offend the regional market of the South. Hollywood was convinced that "if it would not sell in the South, it might not sell in the North." Even if, moreover (as was the case), profits made in the South were less than those in other regions, they were still large enough to help bring a production "out of the red." Cripps uses the myth to help explain the racial stereotyping in American movies during this period, but the reluctance to offend (white) southern susceptibilities with regard to a violent and controversial period may also have helped account for the dearth of Civil War movies—and the fact that many of those that were made (including *Hands Up!*, *The General*, *The Heart of General Robert E. Lee*, *Morgan's Last Raid*, *So Red the Rose*, *The Littlest Rebel*, and *Gone with the Wind*) were based on stories told from the southern perspective.[9]

Cripps also addresses the issue of how filmmakers' approach to the Civil War has been affected by the race question. Film historians such as Douglas Gomery, Ethan Mordden, and Thomas Schatz, he maintains, have emphasized the fact that Hollywood was an economic system within which certain studio styles developed. Such styles were the result of the drive to maximize profits. Studios attempted to guarantee a "risk-free product" by varying films only a little within particular styles or genres. War movies, Cripps notes, have been especially prone to this systematization since they have appeared "so bound up in the nation's survival." Most have eventually become standardized as "a small circle of polyethnic warriors . . . seen holding fast under the stress of combat, thereby propagandizing the need for unity." On the face of it the Civil War presented a challenge to this narrative of "eventual unity," being brought about because of the existence of African American slavery. Although it led to the abolition of slavery, the freedom gained by the slaves was at best only nominal. Blacks remained as an "unassimilable Other"—a source of continuing problems and friction in American society. How, therefore, could the Civil War be presented as a "unifying epic"? The solution to this problem, Cripps contends, has by and large been for filmmakers to eliminate racial issues—and thus African Americans—from the movies they have made about the war.[10]

While there are relatively few films about the Civil War itself, the conflict is referred to in innumerable westerns. Indeed, Kim Newman writes of "the Western's obsession with the Civil War." That obsession is not, of course, with the war itself, since most fighting was east of the Mississippi, but with its consequences. Many of the main characters in westerns are depicted as war veterans. Arriving in the West, they find a way of moving beyond the conflict by concentrating on the settlement of this new region. Moreover, Confederates and Federals often purge their sin of fighting between themselves in order to unite against some other adversary or adversaries. Thus, the blue and the gray join forces against Indians in *The Outpost* (1940), *Rocky Mountain* (1950), *Winchester 73* (1950), *Run of the Arrow* (1957), *Major Dundee* (1965), and *The Undefeated* (1969). Yankees and Rebs ally together against Mexicans in *Virginia City* (1940) and *Major Dundee*. It often seems as if the drama of national reconciliation, largely impossible to apply as a formula to the Civil War because of the centrality of blacks to the conflict and its effects, as Cripps points out, is instead displaced onto the western, where African Americans are no longer regarded as a problem and the whites from both North and South can unite against more culturally permissible "others."[11]

If most of the relatively few Civil War movies made were unsuccessful at the box office, this was clearly not the case with respect to *The Birth of a Nation* and *Gone with the Wind,* both of which reached a mass audience and could be counted as the most profitable movies of their time. The success of these two films can be explained in a variety of ways. Each was based on a best-selling novel. Each was a "spectacle" within the meaning of the term for its time: *The Birth of a Nation,* in fact, by attracting a large middle-class audience to the cinema for the first time, helped in bringing about the demise of the nickelodeon. Each combined the talents of a number of highly competent actors and actresses. Each used music to extend the effect of the film itself. *Gone with the Wind* was also preceded by a long and skillful prerelease publicity campaign (the much-hyped search to identify a suitable Scarlett being one expression of this). Yet none of these reasons, either separately or in combination, seems quite sufficient to explain the remarkable success of the two films. There may well have been features of the wider American society at the time they were released that allowed Americans generally to transcend their indifference toward Civil War themes. There also may have been influences that countered the resistance of non-southerners to what was, in essence, a southern-oriented view of the Civil War and its consequences.[12]

In 1992 an eighteen-member film board added Griffith's *Birth of a Nation* to the prestigious National Registry of Film. The decision led to a protest—part of a long campaign—by the National Association for the Advancement of Colored People (NAACP). "To honor this film," argued NAACP chairman William Gibson, "is to pay tribute to America's shameful racial history." Hollywood itself has long regarded the film as an embarrassment: a landmark movie for its technical achievement and the size of its audience, but a work profoundly flawed as a consequence of its racist message. The film treats African Americans in either a patronizing or a disdainful manner. In the first part they are shown as content under the benign influence of slavery. They work hard but happily in the fields; put on a dancing show for the master's family and their northern guests, the Stonemans, during their two-hour lunch break; and if employed in the house, work loyally throughout the Civil War. The exceptions to this general rule are the mulatto housekeeper of northern politician Austin Stoneman, whose passion for his servant is hinted to be the source of his radical policy toward reconstructing the South after the war, and a unit of black Union soldiers who raid the hometown of the Cameron family in South Carolina and seem eager only to destroy. In the second part of the film, Griffith expands on his creation of what Donald Bogle calls "the brutal black buck." Carpetbaggers and aggressive blacks from the North break up the cordial relationships many early twentieth-century southern whites continued to see as characteristic of slavery, which they believed had uplifted blacks, with the consequence that African Americans regress into brutal and primitive behavior. Blacks onscreen are shown to be ignorant and untutored, to force whites off the sidewalk, to be out for revenge on former masters, and—above all—to want to marry white women. Silas Lynch, mulatto lieutenant governor of South Carolina, seeks marriage with Elsie Stoneman, the daughter of the northern Republican politician. Gus, a black soldier, wants to marry Flora, youngest daughter of the southern Camerons. When he pursues her, she throws herself off a cliff rather than surrender to his advances. This persuades the Ku Klux Klan to confront and finally overthrow what is clearly presented as the savagery and debauchery of black rule.[13]

The Birth of a Nation, in common with Gone with the Wind, is unusual in dealing with both the Civil War and its consequences during the Reconstruction period. The content of the latter part of the film was largely determined by Thomas Dixon Jr. Francis Hackett, in his contemporary review of the film, remarks that it offers what is basically Dixon's interpretation of the relations between North and South and their effects on the Negro. Dixon, from North Carolina, had studied at Johns Hopkins University under militant defenders of the Anglo-Saxon creed. Successively actor, lawyer, politician, and Baptist minister, he became a novelist in 1901 in angry response to a staging of the play based upon Harriet Beecher Stowe's Uncle Tom's Cabin, which Dixon felt dignified African Americans at the expense of southern whites. In The Leopard's Spots: A Romance of the White Man's Burden (1901) and The Clansman, an Historic Romance of the Ku Klux Klan (1905), Dixon elaborates his perception that once the institution of slavery was overthrown, African Americans "could only revert to bestiality." Part of this reversion found expression in the black male pursuit of innocent white women. Griffith, in making his film, expanded on Dixon's story in The Clansman, notably by adding an entire preliminary section on the Civil War itself but otherwise constructed The Birth of a Nation around Dixon's romance and his racial views (with which Griffith, as a southerner and the son of Col. Jake Griffith of the Confederate army, may possibly have agreed).[14]

The curious feature of Dixon's ideas on the threat from African Americans—and their later representation in The Birth of a Nation—was, on the face of it, chronology. The social crisis some had warned against during the economic depression of 1893–97 had passed. Starting in 1890 but gathering pace after the decline of Populism, African Americans had been excluded from political voting by a variety of legal stratagems. By 1905, what Joel Williamson perceives as a second wave of segregatory legislation was approaching its end in the South, separating the races in restaurants and hotels, on trains and streetcars. Blacks had been rendered both politically impotent and socially invisible. Racial violence was less common. Lynching, which reached a peak in the years after 1889, had begun to decline in the southern states, including Griffith's own Kentucky, where it had been particularly prevalent. There seemed little threat to the established racial order. Pierre Sorlin argues that there was no domestic crisis apparent when *The Birth of a Nation* was made, making the film's "alarmist tone . . . somewhat surprising," especially in view of the fact that most Americans were prepared to remain silent on the "central danger" portrayed in the film: the supposed "black problem."[15]

It has been common to see the era just before the First World War as a time of buoyant confidence in the United States. In reality, there is a good deal of evidence of social unrest and anxiety. The economic recession beginning in 1913; the continuous arrival of large numbers of immigrants, mostly from eastern and southern Europe; the processes of urbanization; a growing fear of radicalism and labor militancy; and the hysteria of the "white slave" panic make up the backdrop of the time. A number of factors conspired in these years to bring about a pervasive sense of racial threat. The forty-one volume report of the Dillingham Commission in 1911, confirming popular stereotypes of "new" versus "old" immigration; the rise of the eugenics movement and its ideas about superior breeds and unalterable racial characteristics; publicity on the "yellow peril" in California; and the feelings of ethnic disunity produced by the outbreak of the First World War all combined to promote a mood of uncertainty and unease.[16]

It is easiest to explain this phenomenon in the South. Many whites continued to believe blacks were dangerous: it was an unusual southern newspaper, as Edward Ayers points out, that did not include some stories of black wrongdoing. Segregation had failed to bring an end to the problems posed by race relations. Segregated streetcars, for example, were usually supposed to have whites at the front and "coloreds" at the back, but there was no distinct line of demarcation. To journalist Ray Stannard Baker in 1908, this seemed symbolic: the existence of a color line that neither race was able precisely to define provided a major "source of friction and bitterness." The increasing movement of African Americans to towns and cities increased the possibility of racial conflict there and provoked a further wave of segregation legislation that between 1913 and 1915 segregated facilities in factories and attempted to impose segregation in urban housing.[17]

The major change that happened before the First World War was the nationalizing of insecurities arising from race. The white South's conversion to the idea of restricting immigration, which happened in part at least because new immigrants (particularly Italians) appeared too ready to fraternize with blacks, was paralleled by growing northern white sympathy for the racial outlook of the South. One reason for this may have been the increasing black migration to the North and some of the tensions that resulted (including the race riot at Springfield, Illinois, in 1908). Enduring suspicion of Japanese immigration into California, which led the state legislature in 1913 to pass a law effectively banning Japanese land ownership there, fostered sympathy on the part of Californian whites for southern views on race. All sections by 1913 were united politically on the need to reduce the new immigration, and bills calling for a literacy test passed Congress in 1913 and 1915. This new and pervasive racial consciousness provided an ideal background for the appearance of Griffith's film, with its condemnation of racial intermixture, rampant distaste for blacks, and triumphant evocation of white superiority.

Other aspects of the time are reflected in Griffith's film. One is the crusade against alcohol. At its convention in November 1913, the Anti-Saloon League had first committed itself to pushing for nationwide prohibition. This followed a period of reverses in which, as Jack Blocker has pointed out, eight states voted to reject statewide prohibition. After 1913 this retreat ended, and prohibition resumed its forward march. Some shots in *The Birth of a Nation* can be viewed as propaganda for prohibition. It was a goal congenial to Griffith, who came from a Methodist background, and he had already made at least three films—*A Drunkard's Reformation* (1909), *What Drink Did* (1909), and *Drink's Lure* (1912)—emphasizing the dangers of alcohol. The fact that Griffith was a southerner, however, and the Civil War and Reconstruction film he was then making was about the South, led him to tie alcohol to the issue of race. Southern progressives frequently linked black crime to the effects of alcohol: reformer Alexander J. McKelway, for example, argued that "if drunkenness caused three-fourths of the crimes ascribed to it, whiskey must be taken out of the Negro's hands." What Griffith did in *The Birth of a Nation* was to provide a visual confirmation of that linkage: the renegade Gus, having driven the youngest Cameron daughter to suicide, takes refuge in Joe's gin mill. "Drunk with wine and power," the black lieutenant governor makes up his mind to marry Congressman Stoneman's daughter.[18]

Griffith's film was fortunate in the timing of its appearance. Had it been produced a decade earlier, in the same year as Dixon's novel *The Clansman* was published, it would almost certainly have attracted less attention. The main reason for this was that, in the interval, a new interracial organization had been launched to help and protect African Americans: the NAACP. Founded in the aftermath of the race riot at Springfield, Illinois, in August 1908, the NAACP was quick to recognize the threat from *The Birth of a Nation*. In putting across the "southern" view of the black race, Griffith's film damaged the cause of racial equality. The NAACP embarked upon a strategy of protest to stop the film, prompting court hearings and the lobbying of mayors and censorship boards across America. Apart from securing the reediting of a few scenes and in some locations delaying the opening of the film, these efforts invariably failed. What they did, of course, was generate priceless publicity for the movie. There was, in fact, a considerable symbiosis between *The Birth of a Nation* and the NAACP. The controversy launched by the association undoubtedly made more people want to see the film. But *The Birth of a Nation* also provided the NAACP with "an issue just when it needed one," allowing it to put its own case across with maximum publicity. In many ways it was the crusade against that movie that truly turned the NAACP into a *national* body.[19]

Gone with the Wind belongs to a different cinematic universe than *The Birth of a Nation*—one that includes sound, colors, and cinematic celebrities. Hollywood, now determined to lose no segment of its potential audience, had learned its lessons from Griffith's movie. There is no Ku Klux Klan, nor are there any more "brutal black bucks." It is not without significance, for example, that when Scarlett is attacked in Shantytown, it is the white man who assaults her, his black accomplice merely holding the horse—and she is rescued by a black (Big Sam, one of her family's ex-slaves). Both manners and morals had changed in the interim between the two movies, influencing the manner in which the Civil War years could be portrayed. The "white slave" panic was long dead, and it was possible to depict on screen the demimonde—in the form of the brothel keeper Belle Watling. Prohibition had been repealed in 1933, and alcohol could once again be depicted as part of southern (male) social life—as at the Wilkes's barbecue. With alcohol no longer a moral (or racial) issue, drunkenness can be presented in an amusing light—as when a supposedly inebriated Ashley and Dr. Meade try to outwit the Union soldiers or when a recently widowed (again) Scarlett consoles herself by drinking alone.

Two aspects of the period when *Gone with the Wind* was made may have influenced the view it presented of the Civil War era and also, perhaps, perceptions of the film on the part of female moviegoers. One scholar dates the appearance of contemporary American feminism from shortly before the First World War as radical thinkers began to challenge the idea that women were condemned by their biological natures merely to childrearing and housework. In *The Birth of a Nation* Griffith indeed may have been taking issue with such an approach by presenting an image of women as largely lacking initiative and in need of male protection. The silent films of the 1920s went beyond this view: the characteristic female image of the "flapper" portrayed women subverting social conventions in the cause of self-expression. An echo of this theme is present in *Gone with the Wind* as Scarlett shocks Atlanta society by her behavior while in mourning for her first husband, who has died (of disease) while in the service of the Confederacy.[20]

Such frivolity is swiftly abandoned, however, as Scarlett matures into a strong and independent woman. The manner in which she becomes head of the O'Hara family, the retreat to a temporary household economy at Tara after the war, the recycling of curtains as clothes (though there is no suggestion Scarlett has made them), the decision (albeit for selfish reasons) to limit the size of her family, and even the initiative to take a job (her lumber business) outside the home must have resonated with many women in the 1930s. The idea of women acting on their own seemed far less out of place in a decade in which women increasingly came to play an active role in politics and union organization. (In one sense, at least, the film also echoes male anger at the new world in which their role as breadwinner was being challenged. Sara Evans couples James Cagney's grinding a grapefruit in Mae Clark's face in *Public Enemy* with Rhett's rape of Scarlett in *Gone with the Wind* as expressions of this sentiment.)[21]

In the opinion of Marjorie Rosen, Scarlett shows "spunk and self-sufficiency." Indeed, perhaps the greatest message communicated by the film was the hope and possibility of survival. The Great Depression of the 1930s affected almost everybody. Unemployment (or the threat of unemployment) was everywhere. When *Gone with the Wind* was released in 1939, 17.2 percent of the labor force remained out of work. In the two worst years of the depression, 1932 and 1933, the number of totally unemployed never fell below twelve million, and the average unemployment rate was over 24 percent. Yet as one man told Studs Terkel years later, "In the worst hour of the Depression, if you were aggressive, if you wanted to scrounge . . . , you could survive." Scarlett embodies this spirit. To American audiences who had lived through the Great Depression, the film's message of physical survival at all costs had a tremendous appeal.[22]

The Civil War lasted just over four years. It was fought over a vast area and involved a variety of military actions. Hollywood filmmakers intent on making movies of the war period have consequently been compelled to be selective. Only a relatively small proportion of Civil War movies have actually bothered to reconstruct battles. Petersburg is featured in *The Birth of a Nation* (as is Sherman's march through Georgia). Chickamauga is depicted in *Raintree County*, Shiloh in John Ford's part of *How the West Was Won* (1963) and in *Journey to Shiloh*, Antietam and Fort Wagner in *Glory*, and Gettysburg in the film of the same name. *The Birth of a Nation*, *Gone with the Wind*, *Drums in the Deep South*, and *Raintree County* all depict in various ways the burning of Atlanta. But *Gone with the Wind*, the most successful of all Civil War movies, has no combat sequences at all. Apart from the shots of Atlanta burning, the effects of the war are conveyed through the scenes dealing with the publication of the casualty list after Gettysburg, the Atlanta hospital where Scarlett and Melanie work, the vast numbers of wounded laid out in the railroad yards, the bodies and military debris on the road to Tara, and the devastation of Twelve

Oaks. This indirect approach to representing the war was also adopted in other movies: Sherman's march through Georgia is referred to but not actually shown in *The
Beguiled* (as well as *Gone with the Wind*), and *So Red the Rose* contains a moving
scene of a mother searching for her dead son at night on the Shiloh battlefield.

As well as major battles, a number of smaller military engagements have been
used as the basis for films. These include the Andrews raid of 1862 (*The General*
and *The Great Locomotive Chase*), the Grierson raid of 1863 (*The Horse Soldiers*),
and the raid on the Vermont town of St. Albans by Confederates operating from
Canada in 1864 (*The Raid*). While the raids themselves happened, and some of the
incidents in the films are based on fact (notably the old headmaster marching his
young military-school cadets to face the Union brigade in *The Horse Soldiers*), there
are also a number of liberties taken in order to "improve" the filmed story. These
include the introduction in *The Raid* and *The Horse Soldiers* of deeply improbable
cross-sectional romances. Makers of Civil War movies often insisted on the historical
accuracy of what they were doing: Griffith at one point employed four people to
check up on details of the Civil War period, Buster Keaton insisted that the costumes and actual train used in *The General* should be as authentic as possible, and
Wilbur G. Kurz, a Georgia historian, was hired as historical adviser for *Gone with
the Wind* and *The Great Locomotive Chase*. The films themselves, however, usually
used the Civil War itself only as background to the stories they told, and—especially
once the cameras started rolling—historical accuracy was often discarded in favor of
the demands of an entertaining storyline.[23]

Civil War movies also have helped perpetuate a number of myths. One of these
is the legend of the Old South as a land of wealthy plantations, gracious ladies, and
chivalrous male cavaliers. What Rollin G. Osterweis termed a "story-book Dixie"
had its roots in the work of southern writers in the decades immediately after the
war, but Hollywood helped develop and publicize the images associated with it.
Films such as *The Birth of a Nation, Operator 13,* and *So Red the Rose* deal with
plantation life, preparing the way for what would become the culturally dominant
view of southern society after the release of *Gone with the Wind.* In Hollywood's
portrayal of that society, farmers who owned few or no slaves, the middle class, and
the poor are largely eliminated. Movies concentrate on the small minority of families
living on great plantations, depicting a world of genial masters, southern belles, loyal
black house servants, and contented field hands. In such a world, not only were
there no class tensions but also it seemed that support for the Civil War was almost
universal. There are, it is true, a number of temporary rebels in these movies—like
Duncan Bedford in *So Red the Rose* and Rhett Butler in *Gone with the Wind*—who
at first refuse to fight, but eventually they too are caught up in the struggle. This
view of solid support for the war in the South began to be questioned in *Tap Roots*

(1948), which deals with a planter family from Mississippi that opposes secession and the creation of the Confederacy. It was only with the release of *Shenandoah* in 1965, however, that Hollywood acknowledged the existence of white southern farmers who did not own slaves and opposed the war. Even so, the seductiveness of the plantation world so far as filmmakers are concerned has persisted, with this view of the South embodied in films such as *The Horse Soldiers* (1959) and *The Undefeated* (1969).[24]

A second major myth perpetuated by Civil War movies concerns slavery and its abolition. Most films show African Americans as happy and content under the slavery regime. If house servants, they are personally close to their owner's family and are linked to them by ties of affection and loyalty. If working in the fields, they are never exploited and often sing at their work. Freedom, when it comes, disrupts these benign patterns of life; house slaves often remain with their former owners, but field hands generally disappear. (The black actors and actresses who played the part of loyal servants often later reacted strongly against the roles they had portrayed. Daniel Haynes, for example, who played the butler in *So Red the Rose,* refused any further offers of work in films.) Missing from nearly all Civil War movies is any sense that blacks resisted slavery or were prepared to fight to gain their own emancipation. After *The Birth of a Nation,* the image of the black soldier with a gun in his hand disappears from films for several decades. It returned, at first, only in piecemeal fashion. Enoch, a free black worker living in the North, asks for a gun with which to fight Morgan's raiders in *Friendly Persuasion* (1956); Gabriel, a worker rather than a slave, joins Union forces in *Shenandoah* (1965). But only with *Glory* (1989) did Hollywood—covering the story of the first major black combat unit—finally deal with the subject of the 178,000 black soldiers (mainly ex-slaves) who for the most part fought courageously and well to bring an end to the institution of slavery.

Although *Glory* was the first movie to show, in a sympathetic way, black soldiers fighting together for the freedom of their race, its main focus—as Thomas Cripps points out—in the buildup to the heroic charge on Fort Wagner is not so much how African Americans experienced army life as it is the struggle between "white politicians and soldiers over the place to be taken by black soldiers in the Army." *Glory* itself does not seem to have had much influence on filmmakers. The next important Hollywood movie dealing with the Civil War was *Gettysburg* (1993), which largely set aside the issue of race and told the story of the battle from the point of view of the white officers on both sides. Also, while James McPherson expressed the hope that *Glory* would "throw a cold dash of realism over the moonlight-and-magnolia portrayal of the Confederacy," there is little sign that this has occurred. The dominant view of the Confederacy—and the Old South—in American culture continues to be that associated with *Gone with the Wind,* a movie that became a phenomenon. When it premiered on network television over two nights in 1976, NBC claimed a total audience of 162 million. Ninety percent of Americans are believed to have seen the movie at least once. The advent of the video revolution and the reissue of the film in a digitized, recolorized format as part of the celebration of its sixtieth anniversary have probably ensured its continuing appeal. Like their twentieth-century predecessors, Americans of the twenty-first century will probably derive their visual perceptions of the Civil War era predominantly from viewing the adventures of Scarlett O'Hara.[25]

II

THE LEADER
AND THE LEGACY

Politics, Patriotism, and the Civil War

5

A CONTESTED LEGACY

The Civil War and Party Politics in the North

ADAM I. P. SMITH AND PETER J. PARISH

There is an attractive clarity and simplicity about the conventional picture of the place of the Civil War in the history of the United States. According to this view, the war stands as the great divide. On one side lies the antebellum republic, animated by the ideas of republicanism, expanding boldly westward, but irreparably divided over the perpetuation of slavery in the South; on the other the increasingly recognizable shape of modern America, more self-confidently nationalist, flexing its industrial muscles, and eventually emerging as the self-described "world's only superpower" zealously exporting corporate capitalism across the globe. In American memory the Civil War serves not only as a convenient dividing line but also as the key point of transformation—what Shelby Foote has called "the crossroads of our being."[1]

To those who lived through it, the Civil War was the defining moment of their lives. It was the fiery trial through which their country was tested and affirmed, and after it, nothing, they thought, would ever be the same again. Henry James believed the war marked an era in the history of the American mind. Americans had eaten of the tree of knowledge and gained "a sense of proportion and relation, of the world being a more complicated place than it had hitherto seemed, the future more treacherous, success more difficult."[2] Strangely enough, the Civil War has loomed much larger in literary and popular memory than it often has in the accounts of those historians who have sought to trace the long-term social and economic—and political—development of the northern United States during the nineteenth century.

In contrast to contemporary reactions, recent analyses of political developments—as also of economic growth, urban and industrial expansion, and large-scale immigration—have tended to emphasize continuity rather than sudden, dramatic change, underlying structures rather than "great events." In such versions of nineteenth-century American history, the Civil War may be reduced to a digression or even a sideshow. One of the leading historians of nineteenth-century party politics, Joel Silbey, has claimed that while the war had an extraordinary influence in some areas, in others it "did not alter matters much." According to Silbey: "In the political nation, although the existing partisan system and its imperatives bent under the pressure, they did not break. Electoral coalitions shifted, and sectional tensions became a norm, but the central reality of partisanly defined and shaped political activities remained. The nation's agenda and institutions continued to reflect the dominance of two-party politics and the intense loyalties that had characterized the system since the 1830s. Neither 1861, nor 1865, nor 1877 was, then, a critical dividing line in terms of the existing values, norms, and behavior of the American political nation."[3]

The evidence in support of this view is considerable. After all, electoral politics were not suspended during the war, and the same two parties continued to fight for power. The key moment of electoral alignment, when the party system dating from the Jacksonian years collapsed, came in the 1850s, not during or after the war. Indeed, a straightforward reading of election results would appear to justify Silbey's conclusion that voter loyalties were "fixed" by 1861. Despite being caught up in the greatest war ever fought in the Western Hemisphere, the two-party system of Democrats and Republicans appears to have emerged unscathed. Undoubtedly, the institutional continuity of American political history during the last century and a half is its most striking characteristic. Furthermore, the culturally based partisan traditions represented by the Democratic party on the one hand and the Whig, Know-Nothing, and Republican parties on the other were discernible, real, and most certainly enduring. Silbey and others have emphasized the continuities of political divisions throughout the mid–nineteenth century: Democrats firmly opposed the expansion of the federal government, favoring local autonomy and cultural pluralism, whereas Whigs and Republicans were much more likely to conceive of politics and the role of government in terms of its capacity to transform society for the better, by combating social ills and through the energetic exercise of governmental power to foster economic development. Most importantly, the character of politics in a highly partisan, highly participative culture did not radically shift as a result of the war—even if wartime politics itself necessitated a rhetorical adjustment. From this viewpoint the political nation of nineteenth-century America, described so memorably by Walter Dean Burnham as a "lost Atlantis" of popular political participation, was neither created nor disrupted by the Civil War.[4]

Yet, like the opposite depiction of the war as the great watershed dividing two distinct Americas, this picture is incomplete. It achieves clarity through oversimplification and by a narrow focus on parties as institutions. Indeed, the emphasis of political historians on continuity during the Civil War period obscures some fundamental changes to the dynamics of political competition and the substance of political debate that occurred both during and after the war. It is surely possible, and potentially very fruitful, to trace more carefully the effects of the war on the way in which political life was conceived by ordinary voters and the ways in which political battles were conducted by politicians.

That influence was reflected in the language of political debate and in the symbolism or "party aura" that surrounded election campaigns. Partisan sectional alignments were reconfigured for at least two generations. Even more fundamentally, the changing issues and the political opportunities created by the war provided the soil in which the two-party system of Republicans and Democrats could take firm root—and in purely institutional terms that system endures to this day. Its durability is in marked contrast to the fragile and ephemeral character of earlier party systems. The lifespan of the second party system of Whigs and Democrats was, after all, less than two decades. It was the war—and the politicization of the legacy of the war— that allowed the inchoate anti-Democratic coalition that elected Lincoln in 1860 to emerge against all expectation as an enduring feature of the political scene and eventually to develop into the dominant force in American politics from the late nineteenth century through the early decades of the twentieth century. At the same time, the polarizing effects of the war and its aftermath provided the political tools that Democrats could use to consolidate their appeal to those sections of society alienated by the conflict's social and racial consequences and distrustful of the power of the emerging industrial corporations. In the new world of industrial America, the Democratic political tradition, which embodied the cause of the "little man" against the impersonal forces of big corporations or big government, had a new and powerful resonance, not least among the new working-class immigrants. For both parties, the bitterly contested politics of the Civil War years had implications too for the way in which party managers attempted to mobilize public support. Continuity in party structures, whether real or perceived, may mask some of the war's more elusive but equally significant political consequences.

The war thus created a contested legacy. It included a cluster of ideas and images that provided much of the substance of political language during the decades after the war, even when the immediate postwar questions—what to do with the freedmen, how to deal with the ex-Confederate South—had been resolved, compromised, or sidelined. The immediate political legacy of the war was the Republican attempt to enshrine in law and the Constitution an expansion of the guarantees of civil and political equality. But alternative lessons were learned as well, and by the 1870s these were being articulated by Democrats, by liberal reformers, and by "stalwart" Republicans. The debates over Reconstruction and the struggles for reform that replaced them can all be viewed as battles to control the public meaning of the war. Was it a lost promise or a source of continuing pride? Did veterans' organizations like the Grand Army of the Republic embody the political legacy of the war when they described it in terms of the glorious cause of nationhood? Or were the disillusioned intellectuals of the liberal reform movement closer to the mark when they bemoaned what they perceived as the debased reality: a war that had promised to create a nation purified of sin and corruption had merely expanded government, increased official venality, and robbed politics of its integrity and purpose?

The war directly affected party politics by confirming the dominance of the two-party system and giving enduring credibility to the Republican party. At the same time, it forced both parties to reexamine the basis of their electoral appeal as antebellum political divisions receded into the background or faded away. Paradoxically, however, one key element in this process for the Republicans was the strong antipartisanship that the war brought to the fore and the opportunity thus provided for the Lincoln administration to identify its own political success with the Union cause. Here was the basis of a political appeal that was partisan in the presentation of particular issues or policies but that shunned some of the tropes of party and partisanship. The appeal was explicitly addressed to "men of all previous party affiliation" and appropriated Democratic heroes like Andrew Jackson to prove the point.[5]

The resurgence of antipartisanship suggests a profound ambivalence at the heart of the political legacy of the war. At the same time, the conflict both encouraged and discouraged the normally fierce competitive nature of two-party politics. On the one hand, the great issues swirling around the war stimulated bitter controversy, giving the young Republican party an opportunity to establish and assert a clear identity for itself and thus strengthen its long-term prospects. On the other hand, the alternative view was that in a time of national crisis there was no place for divisive party politics and that everyone should rally round the flag.[6] As one Ohio newspaper explained, it seemed unpatriotic, at a time when citizens were sinking their differences and joining together to defend the Republic, to "plot for partisan ends."[7] This patriotic imperative reflected not only the understandable exigencies of wartime but also the longstanding suspicion harbored by Americans with republican sensibilities about the corrupting influence of factions. It was also a reflection of the way in which the experience of war multiplied the contexts in which citizens could become engaged in public life, thus reinforcing the political meaning of, for example, attendance at a particular church or helping make bandages for the Sanitary Commission. Harnessing this nonpartisan political energy, Lincoln ran for reelection in 1864 as the candidate of the National Union party. Given the key role that memories of the war were to play in the mobilization of support for the GOP during the later nineteenth century, it is ironic that the wartime Republican party went out of its way to distance itself from its name. An alternative antiparty perspective on politics was revived during the war and remembered by Liberal Republicans and other third-party insurgents in succeeding decades.[8]

The immediate response of northern politicians to the first shots of the war in Charleston Harbor in April 1861 revealed the underlying assumptions about the dangers of partisanship in wartime. There was a widespread feeling in the North—and in the South too—commented on frequently in newspapers, that partisanship had brought the nation to this state of "Armageddon." "The party has failed us. Party organization is dead," declared the *New York Times* in July 1861.[9] Writing this kind of premature obituary was a common response to the secession crisis, which demonstrated the inability of "normal" party politics to resolve fundamental issues. Consequently, during the first three months of the war, there was an effective cessation of interparty conflict. Until the summer of 1862, there was sufficient popular opposition to conventional political contests that, in every state under Union control, the Republican party made strenuous efforts to recast itself as a Union, National, or People's party and, with varying degrees of enthusiasm, attempted to enlist the support of local Democrats. In other words, wartime antipartisanship seemed to presage a return to the process of party dissolution or fragmentation that had characterized the 1850s. Party labels were highly fluid. Voters in New York State, for example, had the choice between ten different party names in elections in 1860, 1861, and 1862.[10]

But gradually the countervailing effect of the war in polarizing politics made itself felt. The Lincoln administration was able to create a National Union organization that embraced War Democrats and those self-described conservatives who had supported John Bell's Constitutional Union candidacy in 1860. Yet a deep, underlying hostility to the administration and the "war against slavery" that it was conducting became much more evident as the conflict continued and grew in scale. War measures—conscription in particular—and the perception that emancipation had been elevated into a war aim intensified opposition to the administration, especially in communities that had never been sympathetic to the calls for national duty and sacrifice that the war evoked. Opposing the draft both in principle and for injustices in its implementation, Democratic campaigners identified it as an abolitionist, class-based measure that hit poorer citizens and immigrants with particular severity and that would not have been necessary had propertied Republicans enlisted in the fight. The often fierce resistance encountered by enrollment officers fueled Republican fears of such "secret organizations" as the Sons of Liberty and the Knights of the Golden Circle that they believed were trying to undermine the entire war effort.[11] This violence suggests the breakdown of political order in divided communities where vigilante groups carried out attacks on proadministration newspapers, destroyed property, and fought enrolment officers. Reports in newspapers, particularly in the Midwest, suggest that this may have been a widespread phenomenon in strongly Democratic rural communities, notably in areas with a substantial population of southern origin or, to take another example, in "ethnic" mining communities. During 1863, violence broke out in intensely Democratic working-class urban areas such as lower New York City and Boston's North End.[12]

Although it was not an organized ideological response to the administration, draft rioting sharply revealed the limits of the Union party's appeal and provoked fear and anxiety within the "respectable" political community. For Democrats, conscription crystallized the feeling that the Lincoln administration was a serious threat to local autonomy and popular sovereignty. It epitomized the condemnation of Republicans as the "meddling party." Democratic newspapers commonly ran headlines like "Three Hundred Dollars or Your Life!" protesting against the commutation provision under which a man could avoid the draft by paying a three-hundred-dollar fee—or by hiring a substitute.[13] There were also allegations that agents of the Federal government were playing an increasingly active part in the suppression of internal dissent. Soldiers acting without official sanction were frequently involved in attacks on Democratic newspaper offices and Democratic public meetings. In Illinois and Indiana the normal political process broke down almost completely. Faced with recalcitrant legislatures that opposed the Emancipation Proclamation and wanted an end to the war, state governors resorted to extreme measures. In Illinois Richard Yates prorogued the legislature, and in Indiana Oliver P. Morton ran the state without the legislature for two years and raised money by a variety of unconventional and extralegal means.[14] From 1863 onward in such areas, the normal political process was replaced by a sometimes violent confrontation at the local level between rival groups struggling to assert political control. T. W. Bergley, a Union party campaigner for Lincoln in 1864, was violently attacked several times during a speaking tour of southern Indiana. On a number of occasions he reported that members of the crowd were "openly shouting for Jeff Davis."[15]

The election of 1864 clearly demonstrated not only the wartime growth of party centralization and ideological polarization but also the interconnectedness of partisanship and antipartisanship. Even as they abandoned their name and embraced the Union label, Republicans had for the first time an undisputed national leader, a unifying cause, and a rhetoric that enabled them to appeal to many Democrats. Despite the calls for national unity in the face of the rebellion, the tendency of the war was to push parties to extremes. In both the Republican Union coalition and in the Democratic party, those with the strongest views about the war tended to prevail. Quasi-secret and quasi-military organizations such the Union Leagues in the one case and the Knights of the Golden Circle in the other provided sometimes legitimate, sometimes extralegal support for party candidates.[16] While Republicans pinned the disloyalty tag on their opponents, Democrats condemned Lincoln as a tyrant who flouted the constitution. The antiwar policies of many Democrats hardened in an atmosphere of repression and deep popular division.[17]

As political discourse was polarizing over the fundamental question of the legitimacy of the war, the casualty figures continued to mount to previously unimaginable levels. The wrenching cost of the war in blood and tears, and its shattering effect on northern families and communities, entrenched feelings on both sides. Away from the halls of Congress, many communities were being torn apart by the war. While those on one side called for yet greater support for the war effort, those on the other vented their feelings of war-weariness and frustration, blaming the Lincoln administration for what was happening. The responses of political leaders revealed the pervasive cultural-political divide in northern society and had great significance for the way in which the war would be used politically in the future.[18]

During the war the Democrats faced a difficult struggle to maintain the credibility of their antebellum symbols and their common identification among activists, officeholders, and voters.[19] As for the Republicans, in 1860–61 they had no established party tradition and their "core" electorate was still in the process of formation. But by adopting the immensely important symbolism of the Union label, they were able to exploit the exceptional circumstances of a civil conflict in which political combat continued but in a dramatically heightened form. The "partisan antipartyism" of Lincoln and his administration under their National Union guise served a double purpose.[20] On the one hand, it helped them reach out to erstwhile Democrats and to those who were repelled by the "radical" image that the party had acquired in the eyes of many people even before the war. On the other hand, it served as a valuable reminder to a crucial section of their own support—Yankee Protestants in New England and far beyond it—that the Republicans were no mere political party but the vehicle of a fervent, idealistic crusade on behalf of God and country. It resonated with the moral values of a community that believed the war had been, at least in part, the result of party politics.

Antipartisanship took the form of an assertion by both parties, but especially by the Republicans, that they were the embodiment of the nation and that they transcended party in their selfless devotion to the Union. This was more than simply the natural tendency of politicians in wartime to wrap themselves in the flag. The continuation of party conflict conflated the electoral struggle with the military one. In the week of the 1864 presidential election, an editorial in *Harper's Weekly* warned its readers that the contest would decide "the most important question in history"— whether the American Republic would succumb to the fate of all previous republics and allow "party spirit" to "overpower patriotism."[21]

Just as in today's politics, antipartyism had a great deal to do with a lack of faith in the political system. An election appeal in New York City spoke of politics as having become a "synonym for all that is mean and low." It was therefore the duty of all to "labor for greater purity and higher patriotism," which meant voting for Lincoln, of course. Unionists referred to themselves as "stout-hearted, inflexible men" who transcended "mere politics." Their candidates, they said, had been chosen on the basis of "personal integrity, without regard to party," or because they were, in a rather graphic phrase, "fresh from the loins of the people." There is clearly a fine line between the exaggerated language of election campaigns and the denial of the legitimacy of the opposition. But during the Civil War partisanship and party often became dirty words; one's loyalty to a party was patriotism, one's opponent's was mere partisanship. The reelection of Lincoln, celebrated as evidence of the commitment of the northern people to the war, and the military victory when it came in April 1865 were seen as triumphs of the Union party.[22]

At the point of national reunification, wartime politics in the North seemed in retrospect more consensual and less fraught with alternative possibilities than in fact had been the case. This was a real achievement for the Republican/Union party; although the war was a partisan conflict that deeply divided northern society, its claim to be the embodiment of the entire nation created a powerful myth of national purpose and social cohesion. Lincoln's reelection followed by the final defeat of the Confederacy ensured that the war would be defined and remembered as Lincoln wanted it to be: a new birth of freedom for the Republic. The enduring power of his rhetoric is a tribute not only to Lincoln's persuasive powers but also to the effectiveness of patriotism as a political weapon.[23]

In these ways the war gave the Republican party the vital legitimacy that it needed to establish itself in the postwar years. In a context in which party identities were in a state of flux, Republicans needed to establish a long-term electoral base. Attaching their party to the successful prosecution of the war for the Union proved to be an effective way of achieving this goal. In the aftermath of the defeat of General McClellan in 1864, the Democratic party appeared demoralized and robbed of a purpose. Thinly disguised as the National Union party, the Republicans emerged from the conflict so apparently dominant that *Harper's Weekly* could confidently declare that "we are at the end of parties."[24]

Not only did the war create the conditions in which the antiparty or no-party campaign of the Republican/Union coalition would flourish, but it also irrevocably altered the terms of debate of American politics. The perceived dominance of the Unionists in 1865 was enormously enhanced by the final abolition of slavery through the Thirteenth Amendment to the Constitution. The wartime process of piecemeal emancipation by presidential proclamation had left a large number of loose ends. Furthermore, Lincoln's justification of his proclamations as an exercise of his war powers as commander in chief left doubts about the status of slaves not yet freed when the war ended. But the constitutional amendment was "a king's cure for all the evils," as Lincoln himself put it.[25] The political repercussions were also very significant. Now with the old party conflicts buried by emancipation, Secretary of State Seward could claim, overoptimistically no doubt, that "all must be friends" and that the era of parties was over. Congressman Glenni W. Schofield of Pennsylvania explained the implications for party politics of the vote on the Thirteenth Amendment: "Slavery in the end must die. . . . The only question is, shall it die now, by a constitutional amendment . . . or shall it linger in party warfare through a quarter or half a century of acrimonious debate, patchwork legislation, and conflicting adjudication?" When the two-thirds vote was finally carried in the House of Representatives, there were scenes of great jubilation, and members wept and cheered along with the public and reporters in the galleries. Reflecting on the momentousness of the vote, Indiana Republican George Julian commented, "I have felt ever since, as if I were in a new country." Not surprisingly, the months following the passage of the amendment saw feverish speculation about political realignment. The cement of the Republican party had been opposition to slavery in one form or another. With slavery dead, what issues would or could be substituted in order to give party coherence? Democrats too were left bereft of a defining issue. No wonder that the Washington correspondent of the *New York Herald* reported on February 10, 1865: "There are rumors as numerous as the frogs of Egypt of reorganization of new parties. The drift of events is in that direction."[26]

In the two months that followed, the people of the North experienced an emotional roller-coaster ride. Lee's surrender at Appomattox Court House on Palm Sunday, 1865, followed by the assassination of Lincoln on Good Friday stirred the religious passions of the North as never before. The dramatic climax of the war—a joyous emotional release followed swiftly by anguish, outrage, and calls for vengeance—fired the determination of many northerners to consolidate their victory and redeem their loss by creating a new nation purified of the sins of the past. Government was stronger than ever before, and old party disputes seemed settled. But the desire to "secure the fruits of victory," to use a ubiquitous phrase of the time, was driven by a strong antisouthern animus as much as by idealistic pursuit of national regeneration or the establishment of equal rights for the former slaves.

The wartime Union coalition that reelected Lincoln did not prove to be a stable organization once the divisive issues of Reconstruction came to the fore. Differences over interpretation of what the war's legacy should be led to ten years of confused and re-forming political identities. For some Union party leaders, notably Secretary of State William H. Seward and his allies, including the influential editor of the

New York Times Henry J. Raymond, the lesson of the war and its outcome was that the Republican party as it had been constituted in 1860 had served its purpose and was now defunct. But the Union organization, they thought, could be an enduring means of maintaining conservative principles in an antiparty coalition that might include moderate southerners and former Whigs while excluding the ideologically charged Radicals, who regarded the issues of the war as far from settled. Building on the successful wartime strategy, the National Union party of 1865 railed against the evils of division. Resolutions presented at a Union "mass meeting" at the Cooper Institute in June 1865 contained a sharp attack on parties now that the contentious issues of slavery and Union were "substantially settled and decided." Still later, in 1866, Pres. Andrew Johnson's supporters met in Philadelphia to rally support for the National Union party. Seward and Raymond were leading figures, but by then the broad coalition of support created by Lincoln had collapsed. In war the divisive issues of Reconstruction could be kept at bay with an appeal to national unity. But by 1866, with the president in conflict with Congress and the majority of the Republican party, claims to represent the entire nation sounded empty. Johnson's men did not have the authority or the influence to dominate the political agenda in the way that Lincoln's supporters could in 1864.[27]

In terms of party politics, then, the most important effect of the conflict between President Johnson and Congress was to distance the bulk of the Republican party from the Union party strategy. This was true of the "party in the electorate" as well as the politicians in Washington. It was not so much that there was a sudden reinvention of the Republican party, as William Dunning once argued in a famous article, but that Republicans had to return consciously to a party label in order to distinguish themselves from a president who was claiming to be the inheritor of the no-party Unionist strategy so effectively used by Lincoln during the war. Perhaps for the first time in the late 1860s, the Republican party as an institution became a positive reference group inducing habituated loyalty. There had scarcely been time for such loyalty to establish itself before the war. During the conflict, in their efforts to smooth the way for voters who had earlier identified with the Democracy to vote against that party, Republican leaders had broadened the antebellum coalition of anti-Democratic groups through the extensive use of Unionist rhetoric and patriotic symbols. The end of the war and the intensifying political conflict over Reconstruction made it increasingly difficult to sustain that strategy. The key moment of transition came with the midterm congressional elections of 1866, which largely turned on support for or opposition to the proposed Fourteenth Amendment. During the election campaign of that fall, Andrew Johnson's notorious stump-speaking tour in support of Democratic candidates—his "swing around the circle"—highlighted his decisive and acrimonious break with the Republicans on Capitol Hill. It was in this context that Republican party leaders began to use not only "the Democracy" as a negative reference symbol but also "Republican" as its positive and patriotic counterpart. The question for the future would be how far the Republican party, while asserting and reinforcing its positive identity, could also continue to reap some reward from its recent Unionist past as the home of all true patriots.[28]

When Henry J. Raymond commented in 1866 that the war had "wholly changed the character of our national politics," he was referring not to electoral realignment but to the transformation of the fault lines of political debate. Among the most obvious changes directly resulting from the wartime experience were the changing perceptions of blacks in the northern white mind—and the political implications of those perceptions. In the mid-1860s there was a moment when many northerners expressed great optimism about the possibility of racial progress in the South. In the eyes of some, blacks appeared as the epitome of the American worker. "Upon what grounds," asked the editor of *Harper's Weekly* in 1865, "can the ballot be refused to the loyal black citizens of the Southern States? They are the sturdy working-class." From certain sections of northern society there was even a measure of cultural acceptance that accompanied the granting of legal rights during Reconstruction. As Nina Silber has shown, even minstrel shows in the 1860s and 1870s managed to represent blacks as just another ethnic group, like the Irish or the Germans, competing within an increasingly diverse conception of American nationality. There may be doubts about how far such feelings were shared, but the Republican party as a whole did not "rejoice" at the prospect of black political equality. Antisouthern feeling, as much as any fundamental shift in popular racial attitudes in the North, provided the driving force behind new commitments to equal rights.[29]

Yet by the late 1860s the question of black voting rights had become a test of party identification, with all Democrats implacably opposed and most Republicans, with diverse motives and differing degrees of enthusiasm, accepting the idea. The mildness of Republican statements on this question was a recognition of the strong antiblack feeling among many potential party supporters. But the solid ranks of Yankee Protestants who were at the heart of the party's electoral support demanded action on the legal and voting rights of black Americans and backed this demand with their votes. Paul Kleppner explains the dilemma thus presented: "To respond to this group ran the risk of alienating other publics whose support the party needed. Failure to respond ran the risk of lost votes among a group whose mass support had been critical and whose anti-partyism had long made it resistant to mere party norms." The rhetorical solution favored by Republican politicians in the late 1860s was similar to that deployed to sell the idea of emancipation during the war: it was recast as an antisouthern issue, a means of securing the "fruits of victory."[30]

Whatever the flaws in its motivation, the enfranchisement of men who had been slaves a few years earlier was still a truly remarkable feature of the postemancipation period in the United States, as Eric Foner, among others, has emphasized. But if it was a notable achievement, it also proved to be a short-lived experiment. First through violence, intimidation, and economic pressure, then through legal disfranchisement by the turn of the century, the white South deprived black southerners of the vote. Where black Americans continued to vote, in the northern states, they remained one of the most solidly Republican groups in the electorate, still voting for the party of Abraham Lincoln, which had freed the slaves and, however fleetingly, accorded them the basic civil and political rights of American citizens. It was only the Great Depression and then the programs of the New Deal that persuaded black Americans to give precedence to desperate economic need over historic allegiances and to become overwhelmingly Democratic voters. This is one of the more dramatic examples of the complex relationship between the Civil War legacy and the more immediate concerns of the day that affected American politics for many decades after the conflict.[31]

In the early 1870s the political legacy of the war was open to diverse interpretations, and various groups and interests were busily engaged in reimagining the war and reinventing its achievements. On the one hand, Radical Republicans were still pursuing an equal-rights agenda that would require the continued exercise of federal power; on the other hand, many Democrats were hankering after a return to the values and traditions of an earlier era of laissez faire and small government, which they feared had been undermined or even destroyed by the war. In the broad area between these two positions, many mainstream Republicans settled for a vision of the war as a triumph of the national spirit—and, of course, a triumph also for their own party—in which black Americans receded further and further into the background. At the same time, liberal reformers dared to think that the war might have been a major cause of the corruption that afflicted American society in the 1870s.

Reconstruction policy took shape in an atmosphere highly charged with polarized beliefs relating to the nature and functions of government, race relations, and American citizenship. In the late 1860s, Republican party opinion had moved substantially in the direction of the Radicals' insistence on southern black suffrage and a strong federal hand in the reconstruction of the ex-Confederacy. But the appearance of policies designed to implement such a program was not adequately backed by a society that was prepared to accept all the implications of such changes. In the mind of the northern public, the Fourteenth and Fifteenth Amendments did not settle or dispose of the equal-rights issue as effectively as the Thirteenth Amendment had finally disposed of the slavery issue.

More traditional and often deeply entrenched social values—racism, localism, laissez faire—reasserted themselves in the course of what modern historians have labeled the northern "retreat from Reconstruction." This often took the form of a conscious repudiation of "wartime issues." Whatever their immediate responses had been to the outcome of the war, the end of slavery, and the constitutional amendments, most Democrats could unite in their hostility to centralized government power; in seeking to shift the focus of politics toward issues like the money question and tariffs, Democrats successfully played upon their own supporters' ambivalence about the memory of the war.[32]

It may seem surprising that, after the impressive resilience the party had shown in the difficult circumstances of the Civil War, the lowest point in the electoral fortunes of the Democrats should occur as late as 1872. But there were specific reasons why this should have happened. Low turnout in core Democratic areas was perhaps only to be expected when the party declined to run its own candidate and instead endorsed Horace Greeley, of all people—a man who for twenty years or more had been a personal symbol of most of the causes they had opposed. By 1876, in contrast, activism had revived strongly as the momentum behind the Reconstruction program in the South declined rapidly and issues associated with it became an increasing burden to the Republicans. Northern voters were increasingly influenced by a mixture of weariness with the problems in the South, prejudice against black Americans and indifference to the fate of the former slaves, and preoccupation with issues that affected them more directly. Economic distress following the Panic of 1873 also contributed to this shift in electoral priorities and reinforced the social and economic underpinning of distinct partisan traditions.[33]

The retreat from Reconstruction has often been described in terms of the "strange death of ideology." Once characterized as a moral crusade personified by the high principles of a Charles Sumner, the Republican party was now presented as being the "Grand Old Party" (still in reality only twenty years old), an organization dedicated merely to the pursuit and maintenance of power in the interests of its corporate paymasters and now personified by the rascally Roscoe Conkling. But the retreat from the immediate postwar issues relating to black civil rights is better understood simply as a shift in the focus of politics. The vast majority of northerners had never been committed to black rights in a deep or principled way. During the 1870s, as politics became more preoccupied with other matters—the questions of labor and political corruption, for example—the commitment of northern politicians to the problems of southern reconstruction was steadily eroded. The focus of concern was deflected from the distant problems of the freedmen to a real and perceived sense of crisis among congressmen's own constituents.

The corruption issue served Democrats as an extremely useful stick with which to beat their opponents. It enabled them to pull together all their disparate attacks on the Yankee meddling of the Republicans. During the war, Democrats had railed against the businessmen who, having funded Republican candidates and campaigns, proceeded to make large profits from government contracts or those who sold poor-quality "shoddy" goods to the army. By the time of Grant's presidency, Democratic warnings that corruption was undermining the fabric of republican (and Republican) government were echoed by Liberal Republicans as well. For these men, corruption served as the most glaring evidence of the nation's failure to live up to its own ideals. The focus on corruption, which became so pervasive in the 1870s, was a key factor in eroding northern support for the southern Republican governments that relied so heavily on black votes.[34]

At the same time as it hastened the retreat from government activism, the corruption issue also helped alter the meaning of the word "reform" in American politics. Whereas for Sumner's generation reform had been the great rallying cry for individual rights, it now became attenuated into a demand for more-honest government in the hands of the right people. Indeed, writers and journalists such as E. L. Godkin of *The Nation* and Charles Eliot Norton of the *North American Review* came increasingly to believe that government could do nothing effectively or honestly.[35] Was it possible, asked the liberal reformers, that the war itself had been the cause of America's moral downfall? After all, it had been the war that had bloated government functions and provided a platform for aggressive industrialists and political opportunists. To this indictment some added what they saw as the unfortunate consequences of the enfranchisement of uneducated freedmen who, together with new immigrants, debased the quality of political participation and undermined the effectiveness and the integrity of the political system. This provided the basis of yet another interpretation of the political legacy of the war. The new world of labor conflict, rampant industrialization, and corrupt politics was all so painfully different from the redeemed, virtuous Republic they had planned when the guns fell silent at Appomattox. James Russell Lowell pondered this sense of loss in his ode on the centennial in 1876:

> Is this the country that we dreamed in youth,
> Where wisdom and not numbers would have weight,
> Seed-field of simpler manners, braver truth,
> Where shame should cease to dominate
> In household, church, and state?
> Is this Atlantis?[36]

It may be argued that the political effect of the Liberal Republican presence in the 1870s was to subvert the sporadic attempts of the Grant administration to enforce Reconstruction legislation, but that was never the purpose of the elite intellectuals who supported the movement. For the most part, these liberals represented the strand of antiparty Yankee Protestantism that felt alienated by the corruption scandals that dogged the Grant administration. The impetus behind the "reform" movements of the 1870s and 1880s came from the educated eastern elite who during the war had taken a leading role in the formation of the Union Leagues, the Loyal Publication Society, and the Sanitary Commission. The taunts made in 1864 against the "ignorant" Democrats who would "unthinkingly" support their party were contrasted with the Unionists' emphasis on the ideal of responsible, respectable citizens engaging in rational-critical discourse about politics.[37] The self-described best men of the liberal elite now saw in their Civil War experience a model for their attempts to influence public opinion and to counterbalance the effect of mass organization among the working classes that made them so uneasy.[38]

In the 1870s the liberal writer Jonathan Baxter Harrison stressed the importance of popular education and envisaged an organization that would provide articles and broadsides for the press, "setting forth . . . in ever-varying forms the few great simple truths and facts which explain our present condition." Together with newspapers, "the persuasive power of public speaking, lecturing, and preaching" would serve in the cause of the "education of the people." The Loyal Publication Society of the war years provided a model for this kind of effort. The educational but participatory nature of the Union Leagues was an inspiration for Horace White and others when they founded the Free Trade League in 1866. The national Civil Service Reform League, founded in 1881, typified the liberal reformers' favored method of promoting the modernization of government through a system of local branches, public meetings, and periodicals. Led by the former head of the Sanitary Commission, it was explicitly designed to cultivate among the public a belief that government was best conducted, not through the medium of party organization, but according to "scientific" or "objective" principles.[39]

For these reformers, wartime politics had demonstrated that the respectable people of the North could respond to a higher level of politics, one that appealed to the better angels of their nature rather than the base and corrupting influence of party. Many Unionists hoped that by generating patriotic spirit and loyalty to a higher cause, the war and its legacy would bind the body politic together in face of the divisiveness of Democratic partisanship and the forces of class, ethnicity, and section.

While emphasizing equal political rights as the foundation of freedom, Republicans built an idea of an American nation that had the strength to compel loyalty and the social cohesion to prevent future disintegration. This was a very different vision from that of the Democrats, who remained wedded to the importance of locality and to a more diffuse notion of national culture. A running theme in the wartime writings of Charles Eliot Norton of the New England Loyal Publication Society was the value of "discipline." For someone like Norton, a future Liberal Republican, the strength and coherence of the political order were inevitably dependent on the moral health of society, and so war to maintain the Union was also inextricably part of a search for a more ordered society. In their thinking about the challenges of the war and its aftermath, the liberal reformers hinted at the shape of things to come. In many respects they prefigured the dilemmas of the Progressive movement of the turn of the century as they wrestled with the problems of reconciling democracy and discipline, freedom and order, and efficiency and purity in government with responsiveness to the popular will, the leadership of the "best men" with active popular participation.[40]

While reformers bemoaned the moral laxity of postwar society and Democrats sought to shift public attention to other matters, Republican election campaigns capitalized on the bonds created between the party and the electorate during the war by "waving the bloody shirt." As a supporter told Republican presidential candidate Rutherford B. Hayes in 1876, "A Bloody Shirt campaign . . . and Indiana is safe; a financial campaign [that stressed debt and currency issues] and we are beaten."[41] The Civil War remained the most potent symbol in the discourse of late-nineteenth-century politics, arousing intense feelings and reminding voters of old loyalties. Even when the rights of freedmen were ignored, the war itself remained a powerful symbol of national reunification.

After the turbulence of Reconstruction, the postwar party system settled into a new pattern with some distinctive features. One was the very close balance between the two main parties at the national level. In the four presidential elections from 1876 to 1888, the margin in the popular vote between the Republican and Democratic candidates was never more than 1 percent, and even in 1892 it was only 3 percent. Support for third parties, though often quite small, meant that neither of the major parties obtained a majority of the popular vote in the four elections from 1880 to 1892. In Congress the Democrats more often had a majority in the House of Representatives between 1876 and 1896, but the Republicans held a majority in the Senate for most of this same period. During these two decades, it was very much the exception rather than the rule for one party to control the White House and both houses of Congress. It actually happened in only six of these twenty years, and then only by the slenderest of margins. If this state of party equilibrium was a serious obstacle to major legislation or bold innovation, it also provided one more indication of the uneasy coexistence of issues and attitudes left over from the Civil War and the agenda of the emerging industrial corporate America.

Yet the national political equilibrium also concealed as much as it revealed. There were large sectional polarities buried within it, and the close alignment between sectionalism and partisanship was one of the conspicuous features of the period. The Republicans regularly led the Democrats by twenty points in New England, while the Democrats outpolled the Republicans by even larger margins in the states of the Deep South. One crucial shift in voting patterns occurred in the Midwest, where antebellum Democratic leads in most states were converted into quite steady Republican leads during the 1860s and 1870s. Strong sectional polarities—with an increasingly solid Democratic South facing a not-quite-so-solid Republican North—meant that nationally, the Republican party polled less of the national vote from 1876 to 1892 than the Whigs had achieved from 1836 to 1852. The outcome of elections often hinged on what happened in three substantial northern states, New York, Ohio, and Indiana, where the two main parties were very closely balanced. It is no coincidence that so many presidential candidates during this period came from these three states.

The contested legacy of the Civil War spread itself across many aspects of American political and public life. The appeal of antipartisanship, or "no-partyism" had been strong during the war and its immediate aftermath, and it lived on in the minds of the elite Liberal Republicans during the 1870s. But the battles of the congressional Republicans with Andrew Johnson hastened a return to pervasive two-party politics, which ushered in a period of fiercely and narrowly contested elections in the last quarter of the nineteenth century. Similarly, the reform impulse with which the Republican party had been born in the 1850s had achieved its great goal with the end of slavery by 1865, and it lost momentum during the exhausting battles over Reconstruction policy as northern voters increasingly turned their attention to other issues closer to home and to their own immediate interests. Instead of confronting great social injustices, reform dwindled into a concern for a more honest and efficient—and limited—public administration.

Above all, perhaps, the complex legacy of the Civil War derived from the interaction of historic issues dating from the war years with a whole agenda of different, though not always unrelated, issues arising from a rapidly industrializing and urbanizing United States. The relationship between these two sets of issues shaped much of American politics not only during the later decades of the nineteenth century, which have been the main focus of this discussion, but also well into the twentieth century. This interweaving of historic and contemporary political issues was often tangled and confused. Until the 1890s at least, memories of the Civil War remained very much alive, and veterans of the war were a numerous and powerful pressure group. The Grand Army of the Republic retained an influential voice in public life throughout these decades. It was no coincidence that every Republican presidential candidate from 1868 to 1900 was a Civil War veteran. Similarly, in the South the Democratic party became the political voice of the Lost Cause and the vehicle for the promotion and protection of white supremacy. One legacy of the Civil War and Reconstruction was a sectionalizing of party politics that endured well into the twentieth century.[42]

As it confronted, or failed to confront, the political agenda of a new age—tariffs and monetary policy, labor unrest and agrarian discontent, railroad monopoly and business excess—the Republican party had to fight a series of nail-bitingly close presidential contests and a series of congressional elections in which it often came off worst. In pursuit of electoral success, it regularly fell back on the strategy of "waving the bloody shirt" and reminding voters that it was the party that had saved the Union and defeated the treachery of southern secessionists. There were those too who were happy to rekindle the issues of the 1850s, the decade of the party's birth, and play upon nativist and anti-Catholic anxieties never far below the surface. Memories of the war and of earlier days could be stirred into a potent compound that reinforced underlying religious and ethnocultural party identities.

It was by means of this intertwining of historic and contemporary issues that the Republican party was able to keep going through the postwar decades and then become the normal majority party for almost forty years from the mid-1890s. It is here, perhaps, that for all its complexities, ambiguities, and ironies, the political legacy of the Civil War may be most clearly identified. Wars may be just as important for what they permit or encourage to continue as for what they destroy or what they change. In its early years the Republican party might have been destined to become just one more in the string of new parties, all of them ephemeral, that littered nineteenth-century political history—the Anti-Mason party, the Liberty party, the Free Soil party, the Know-Nothing party, the Greenback party, the Greenback-Labor party, the Prohibition party, and the People's party besides many others conceived but never actually born into the body politic. Among all these short-lived parties, the Republicans proved to be the great exception to the rule. The Civil War gave the party the opportunity, though by no means the certainty, of becoming something more enduring than all the rest. For all that, by 1865 or at the latest 1870, many in its own ranks believed that the party had fulfilled its historic mission and would fade away. The fact that it did not owed much to its ability to ride simultaneously the two unruly horses sired by "bloody shirt" historic issues from the Civil War and the economic and social concerns of the northern public in a new time. It sought to present itself as the party of prosperity as well as the party that had saved the Union. In this difficult and often uncomfortable process, the Republican party was greatly changed, but it survived. Instead of being just one more name in the roster of fragile and short-lived new parties, it became one of the two competing partners in a two-party system that has set the pattern and framework for electoral politics ever since. If the political legacy of the Civil War was hotly contested, the Republican party remained at the center of that contest.

What might be described as "the strange survival of the Republican party" gave late-nineteenth-century politics a character that was decidedly different from the world of the second party system. There are serious questions to be asked about the dominant historiographical interpretation of nineteenth-century politics, which stresses continuity and does not identify the war as a time of transition. In terms of the substance of political debate, the style of political campaigns, and attitudes to politics among both the elite and the "ordinary" voters, there was considerable change over time in the course of the "party period," and the Civil War was the forcing house of many of these changes. Viewed from outside, the structure of the house of American politics may have retained much the same appearance, but during the 1860s and 1870s, there was a good deal of renovation within and much rearrangement of the furniture.

6

ABRAHAM LINCOLN AND THE CHARACTER OF LIBERAL STATESMANSHIP

Jeffrey Leigh Sedgwick

Charles Joyner has earlier eloquently characterized how an American southerner reflects on the Civil War, using the word "tragedy," which aptly sets the stage for this examination of Abraham Lincoln. It is said that a tragedy always results from a choice, but one can carry the point a step further. Tragedies, at least in the classical sense, are characterized by the necessity to choose between alternatives, each of which has a claim to our allegiance and speaks to our most deeply held values. In short, a tragedy is not simply an error.[1]

That the Civil War was a national tragedy has less to do with the appalling casualty rates and the sheer volume of empty places at hearths and dinner tables throughout the nation than with the fact that both sides had seized upon a part of the national identity that pulled at citizens' hearts and minds. It was not just southerners who felt a sense of tragedy, nor was this tragic sensibility a product of defeat.

To identify *choice* as an intrinsic part of tragedy demands that one identifies *who* chose. That demand leads to Abraham Lincoln, for it was Lincoln who, it seems, clarified the options and asked Americans to choose, finally, between two competing interpretations of the nation's civic identity. But Lincoln's significance is more fundamental than simply clarifying the tragedy inherent in America's grasp of "the wolf by the ears" (Thomas Jefferson's peculiarly apt description of his countrymen's dalliance with chattel slavery). For as early as 1838, when he was but twenty-nine years old, Lincoln engaged in a sophisticated critique of Publius's handiwork (what we have come to know as an "extended commercial republic"), and in 1842 he issued a critique in anticipation of the coming moral "politics" (if they can be called that) of the Progressive Era.[2]

The sum of these efforts is the posing of a third way, one still unchosen, in be-

tween liberal possessive individualism (albeit modified by properly constituted political institutions and the rule of law), on the one hand, and a moralistic reformism
centered in the courts and the bureaucracy, on the other. Lincoln's alternative is
civic friendship, which entails bonds of interpersonal affection among a limited
number of persons based on shared goals or values.[3]

A study of the crisis leading to the Civil War is of value in understanding the
character of the American regime and the requirements of liberal statesmanship because the question of slavery (and how to deal with it) illuminates the problematic
relationship of principled leadership to politics in a liberal democracy. On the one
hand, the pursuit of self-interest, however enlightened, is an insufficient foundation
for free government since self-interest all too easily leads to slavery. Yet an overtly
moral politics, such as that characterizing the abolitionist movement, similarly
threatens democratic freedoms.

The peculiar character of the modern contractual or liberal regime lent a unique
character to Abraham Lincoln's attempt to preserve the Union. He had to convince
a society of self-interested beings of the utility of a point of justice while avoiding
denial of any rights guaranteed in the Constitution. This difficulty, rather than any
hypocrisy on Lincoln's part, explains the sometimes paradoxical approach Lincoln
took to the slavery issue.

Put simply, Abraham Lincoln's statesmanship was an attempt, through rhetoric,
to move a wandering nation back to a firm belief in those true principles upon which
it was founded. During the 1850s, Sen. Stephen A. Douglas's misunderstanding of
those principles had seriously endangered the future of the American regime.

What follows is an attempt to illuminate the character of the American regime,
especially its motivating principles. The Civil War provides an appropriate context
of examining this civic character for two reasons. First, the nature of a regime should
be most readily discernible in time of stress or crisis. Civil war is surely the most
severe text that a regime can experience, for each side claims to be the protector of
the government's true principles. Second, the secession crisis of the Civil War
reached its height under Lincoln's watchful eyes. Part of the reason that the crisis
produced such intellectual precision was that Lincoln himself perceived the issues so
clearly and spoke of them with such commanding insight.

To investigate Lincoln's role as a liberal statesman involves a study of three topics:
first, his understanding of the principles—the true genius—of the American government; second, his attempt to reconcile those principles with one another and thus
to preserve the Constitution; and third, his understanding of the proper way to obtain consent for the regime and its principles. A careful study of these three topics
yields an understanding of the U.S. governmental system and the place within it for
liberal statesmanship.

Lincoln's political thought emanates from his understanding of the way in which the principles of the Declaration of Independence should be understood. Certainly he understood the tension in that document between the principle of the equality of all (with regard to the rights of life, liberty, and the pursuit of happiness) and the principle of popular sovereignty (majority rule). The source of that tension is the possibility that the exercise of popular sovereignty might result in the limitation or abridgment of some citizen's or citizens' rights. Thus, a delicate balance needs to be preserved between the two principles.

In adjusting these standards and resolving the tension, Lincoln effectively engaged James Madison in a dialogue over the question posed in Federalist No. 10; that is, how can democracy be made decent? The answer to this question for Lincoln, in contrast to Madison, had less to do with proper institutional design than with the genius of the American people and the necessity to cultivate that genius through political rhetoric.

In his debates with Stephen Douglas, Lincoln explored the proper relationship between equality and popular sovereignty. He felt that in 1858 as never before, the nation was profoundly threatened. Four years previously the Kansas-Nebraska Act had been signed, allowing the matter of slavery in the territories to be decided by popular sovereignty; passage of this bill was accompanied by a professed indifference to the spread of slavery. In 1858 the author of the Kansas-Nebraska Act, Stephen Douglas, had just led antislavery forces in Congress in the anti-Lecompton battle that threw out a proslavery constitution for Kansas on the basis of its failure truly to represent public opinion in the soon-to-be-admitted state.

Consequently, it appeared that the principle of popular sovereignty alone would be sufficient to prevent the spread of slavery. So Republican leaders were seriously thinking of backing the powerful and well-known Douglas in the next presidential election. As Harry V. Jaffa has noted, "In truth, Douglas had brought the majority of the free-soil North to the point of accepting popular sovereignty and it was precisely this imminent possibility that Abraham Lincoln in the spring of 1858 regarded as the greatest disaster that could befall the American people."[4] As far as Lincoln was concerned, Douglas's professed indifference to slavery was far worse than John C. Calhoun's open endorsement of slavery. (Calhoun had referred to the Declaration of Independence's assertion of the equality of all as "a self-evident lie.") Douglas's position seemed both moderate and consonant with the Declaration, but Lincoln believed it would surely lead to the imposition of slavery everywhere.

A second event contributed to the sense of crisis in 1858, the Dred Scott decision. This Supreme Court opinion asserted that the principles of the Declaration of Independence were indeed true but that the authors of that document never meant to include Negroes as humans. As one British historian, Lord Charnwood, has observed:

This is one of the rare cases where a layman may have an opinion on a point of law, for the argument of [Chief Justice Roger B.] Taney was entirely historical and rested on the opinion as to Negroes and slavery which he ascribed to the makers of the Constitution and the authors of the Declaration of Independence. On the question of Scott's citizenship he laid down that these men had hardly counted Africans human at all, and used words such as "men," "persons," "citizens" in a sense which necessarily excluded the Negro. We have seen already that he was wrong—the Southern politician [Calhoun] who called the words of the Declaration of Independence "a self-evident lie" was a sounder historian than Taney.[5]

Lincoln also believed the ruling was wrong. Taney's assertion of this falsehood in the Declaration from a position of authority endangered the delicate balance between the principles of equality and popular sovereignty by casting into doubt the seriousness of the Founding Fathers in their assertion of the equality of all.

For Lincoln, the Illinois senatorial campaign of 1858 was to be centered solely on the issue of the proper relationship between popular sovereignty and the equality of all. The question was of crucial importance for the following reason: Lincoln was quite aware that the eyes of the world were on the United States. The Declaration of Independence had inspired revolutions throughout Europe. But it justified popular government in the United States by firmly joining it to the proposition that all persons are created equal. In a fragmentary note, Lincoln wrote: "Most governments have been based, practically, on the denial of equal rights of men, as I have in part stated them; ours began by affirming those rights. They said, some men are too ignorant and vicious, to share in government. Possibly so, said we; and by your system, you would always keep them ignorant and vicious. We propose to give all a chance; and we expected the weak to grow stronger, the ignorant, wiser; and all better and happier together."[6] Since association with the principle of equality had justified the creation of popular government, Lincoln felt that only a continued association with and respect for that same principle could maintain the cause of popular government.

The background to the Lincoln-Douglas debates of 1858 was thus set, and much has been written about the problems that Lincoln faced. For example, Richard Hofstadter observes: "It was impossible, [Lincoln] had learned, solely to disregard either the feeling that slavery is a moral wrong or the feeling—held by an even larger portion of the public—that Negroes must not be given political and social equality. He had now struck the core of the Republican problem in the Northwest; how to find a formula to reconcile the two opposing points of view held by great numbers of white people in the North."[7] But Hofstadter appears to have missed the point. If Lincoln's legacy had been simply to reconcile these two points of view, it is doubtful that history would remember him. Douglas's policy of popular sovereignty achieved the same end, and the senator was of far greater stature, especially after the Lecompton battle.

Contrary to what Hofstadter argues, it must be asked whether Lincoln's greatest feat was merely reconciling these two points of view or rather creating ex nihilo a democratically principled opposition to Douglas's apparently irresistible appeal for popular sovereignty. Lincoln, before the debates, was literally alone. Douglas had almost totally won over the Republican party to a policy that Lincoln felt would destroy not only the U.S. government but also the chance for popular government everywhere.

Lincoln argued that the old public spirit, which animated the task of the founders, was slowly dying. This was the spirit of the Revolution wherein passion and judgment were allied in opposition to the mother country, its central point was a belief in the equality of all. This belief justified the American people's endeavor to the rest of the world and established a criterion by which the success of the American experience in democracy would forever be judged. For Lincoln, the inclusion of the principle of equality in the Declaration of Independence identified the necessary condition for the establishment and maintenance of popular sovereignty. Lincoln saw Douglas's public advocacy of simple popular sovereignty as the final blow to this old public spirit.[8]

Yet it cannot be denied that Douglas also had based his advocacy of popular sovereignty on principle. In fact, much of the difficulty in the senatorial campaign debates of 1858 came as a result of the realization that both men could base their policy positions on a principle found in the Declaration of Independence. The existence of two different standards in the same document, and a misunderstanding of their natural connection, led to a debate over which one was in fact primary in the founders' minds.

Douglas held firmly to the position that the territories ought to be governed by laws reflecting the proper spirit of free political institutions. For him, the spirit of free political institutions was simply popular sovereignty, for that was the only route to political freedom. Of this argument Harry Jaffa has said: "For Douglas, the essence of free government lay in the power of decision of free men on issues of vital importance to themselves. To deprive communities of free men of their power of decision over grave questions simply because they were grave was to strike at the main ground of justification of both federalism and democracy. . . . The argument for self-government rested upon the competence of the people to decide all questions, including those of right and wrong, or there was no valid argument for self-government."[9] With this understanding, Douglas argued in the sixth debate that it was improper to discuss the morals of another state since morality was a matter that each state should decide for itself.

If the people could not choose between right and wrong, Douglas maintained, there was no justification for free government at all. Implicit in this argument was an acceptance of what the people will as being right. Rightness was not determined in free government by any external standard but rather by simple vote of the people. Sharing this same belief, one newspaper editor concluded that the colonies revolted against England not because they were ill treated by any objective standard but because they were governed without their consent. He wrote: "The mother country imposed upon the colonies local laws against their consent, and denied them the privilege of regulating their own domestic affairs—hence the revolution. The black republicans would force upon the people of the territories a law in reference to their local affairs whether they (the people of the territories) desire it or not, thus imitating the tyranny of the mother country, and denying the great principle of self-government. . . . If Mr. Lincoln denies the right of the people of the territories to so resist, then he condemns the act of the American revolution and sustains the tyranny of George the Third against our revolutionary sires."[10] Both Douglas and the editor failed to see the link between the principles of the Declaration and the legitimacy of popular government. Both failed to see that the revolution was justified by a belief in popular sovereignty derived from the equality of all. Without a belief in the equality of all, an advocacy of popular sovereignty was simply foolish. It was similarly unwise, in Lincoln's opinion, to advocate popular sovereignty while professing indifference to the spread of slavery.

The fundamental fact that Lincoln sought to emphasize was that if a majority could enslave a minority without acknowledging the injustice of its actions, then it could just as easily enslave another minority by similar reasoning. And after several minorities had been enslaved, the governing "majority" was no longer that but rather a minority of the people. Thus, popular sovereignty divorced from the principle of universal equality led directly to the downfall of popular sovereignty. In a letter to Joshua Speed, Lincoln wrote: "Our progress in degeneracy appears to me to be pretty rapid. As a nation, we began by declaring that '*all men are created equal.*' We now practically read it 'all men are created equal *except negroes.*' When the Know-Nothings get control, it will read 'all men are created equal, except negroes, *and foreigners, and catholics.*' When it comes to this I should prefer emigrating to some country where they make no pretence of loving liberty—to Russia, for instance, where despotism can be taken pure, and without the base alloy of hypocracy [*sic*]."[11] Lincoln recognized the inevitable and steady erosion of popular sovereignty where the principle of equality was ignored. Free government without a commitment to the principle of equality stated in the Declaration of Independence was not only illegitimate but also ultimately impossible.

Yet in what way did Lincoln use the word "equality" in his appeal? How are we to understand equality when Lincoln himself said: "Let it not be said I am contending for the establishment of political and social equality between whites and blacks. I have already said the contrary. I am not now combating the argument of NECESSITY, arising from the fact that the blacks are already amongst us; but I am combating what is set up as a MORAL argument for allowing them to be taken where they have never yet been—arguing against the EXTENSION of a bad thing, which where it already exists, we must of necessity, manage as best we can."[12] Clearly equality is not to be taken to mean political or social equality. Rather, Lincoln spoke of equality as it was defined, with "tolerable distinctions," in the Declaration. Men were equal in regard to life, liberty, and the pursuit of happiness.

Of the Founding Fathers, Lincoln said:

They did not mean to assert the obvious untruth, that all were then actually enjoying that equality, nor yet, that they were about to confer it immediately upon them. In fact they had no power to confer such a boon. They meant simply to declare the *right,* so that the enforcement of it might follow as fast as circumstances should permit. They meant to set up a standard maxim for free society, which should be familiar to all, and revered by all; constantly looked to, constantly labored for, and even though never perfectly attained, constantly approximated, and thereby constantly spreading and deepening its influence, and augmenting the happiness and value of life to all people of all colors everywhere.[13]

Lincoln argued that it was impossible to create political and social equality by legislative fiat. But the founders declared that right so that public opinion would eventually accomplish what the laws could not.

Lincoln conceived of this regime as precluding coercion of citizens through constitutional limitations on rule and by the existence of rights held out against the state by the individual. In such a regime the laws were said to be supreme. But in a sense the laws could not rule or coerce because they derived their power only from the attachment of the people. If the people chose to follow their unreflective desires, they might break the laws. The "good people," as Lincoln called them, would then turn to individuals of ambition for protection. Thus, the viability of republican government rested in the ability of each citizen to understand that his self-interest, rightly understood, dictated obedience to the laws. Rule in a republican regime was not by an individual, or by a group, or by the laws; rather, rule lay in the individual's sense of judgment and its ability to overcome his unreflective desires.

Once the principles of the government were understood properly, Lincoln's next task was to set about preserving the regime. In his speech to the Young Men's Lyceum of Springfield, Illinois (entitled "The Perpetuation of Our Political Institutions" and delivered in 1838), Lincoln noted that the American system was threatened, not by foreign powers, but by internal discord: "If destruction be our lot, we must ourselves be its author and finisher. As a nation of freemen, we must live through all time, or die by suicide." Lincoln said that national suicide begins with an increasing disregard for the laws, and he claimed to see evidence of such a trend. He cited the following example:

In the Mississippi case, they first commenced by hanging the regular gamblers: a set of men, certainly not following for a livelihood, a very useful, or very honest occupation; but one which, so far from being forbidden by the laws, was actually licensed by an act of the legislature, passed but a single year before. Next, negroes, suspected of conspiring to raise an insurrection, were caught up and hanged in all parts of the state: then, white men, supposed to be leagued with the negroes; and finally, strangers, from neighboring states, going thither on business, were, in many instances, subjected to the same fate. Thus went on this process of hanging, from gamblers to negroes, from negroes to white citizens, and from these to strangers; till, dead men were seen literally dangling from the boughs of trees upon every roadside; and in numbers almost sufficient to rival the native Spanish moss of the country, as a drapery of the forest.[14]

In this case the gamblers were judged to be following a dishonest and not very useful occupation. Both utilitarian calculations of self-interest and principled commitments to honesty spoke against them. And yet the law did not; indeed, the law of Mississippi sanctioned gamblers by licensing them. Lincoln's story teaches a sobering lesson about the "rule of law and not of men." When law collides with self-interest and/or moral principle, law often gives way.

But it should be carefully observed what results. First, the gamblers were not worthy of equal protection of the law, then Negroes, then white sympathizers with the Negroes, and then strangers. An action originally designed only to strike at worthless gamblers eventually was extended to a class of people, strangers (and note, visiting the state on *business*), who cannot be considered simply worthless.

Lincoln offered up a second case, that of the mulatto burned to death by a mob in St. Louis, and originally presented it in a way that ignored the question of the man's guilt. The audience was invited to feel outrage or horror at the treatment of this man regardless of his crime. Later, Lincoln revealed that the mulatto was guilty of the "outrageous murder" of a leading member of the community. Indeed, he commented that had the mob not executed the mulatto, the law surely would have condemned him to death. But lest it be concluded that the mob action was justified, Lincoln preceded the revelation of the man's guilt with the warning that the "direct consequences [of such lawlessness] are, comparatively speaking, but a small evil; and much of its danger consists, in the proneness of our minds, to regard its direct, as its only consequences. Abstractly considered, the hanging of the gamblers at Vicksburg, was of but little consequence. They constitute a portion of the population, that is worse than useless in any community; and their death, if no pernicious example be set by it, is never matter of reasonable regret with anyone."[15] The direct consequences of both cases were, abstractly considered, positive. The gamblers were worse than useless, and the mulatto was a murderer. Clearly the community was not hurt by the loss of either. But Lincoln argued that the indirect consequences were very serious, serious enough to outweigh the direct benefits.

What were these indirect consequences? They fell into two classes. First, as noted earlier, the practice of denying the rights of anyone before the law soon spreads indiscriminately to all, "the innocent, those who have ever set their faces against violations of law in every shape, alike with the guilty, fall victims to the ravages of mob law."[16]

The second class of effects concerns the spirit of attachment that the good citizens felt for their government. When the mob spirit encourages the lawless, the good become disenchanted with the existing government and seek protection elsewhere. Lincoln instructed, "Thus, then, by the operation of this mobocratic spirit, which all must admit, is now abroad in the land, the strongest bulwark of any government, and particularly of those constituted like ours, may effectually be broken down and destroyed—I mean the attachment of the people."[17] Here Lincoln pointed out that the strongest bulwark, particularly of the American experiment in free government, is the attachment of the people to the law. The very reason human beings enter into the Lockean state is in order to protect their rights to life, liberty, and property. When law is ignored, property and life itself become insecure, and citizens no longer have any reason for giving their allegiance to the state. Lincoln implied that as the attachment of the people declines, they turn increasingly to individuals "of sufficient talent and ambition." These provide protection from lawlessness but at the cost of free government.

In the latter part of the Lyceum speech, Lincoln addressed the problem of human ambition. He noted that at the founding of the American regime, ambition aided in the creation of free government. The desire for fame was linked with the success of the American experiment as defined by the Declaration. But because that experiment had succeeded, there was no longer glory to be found in free government. The founders exhausted that possibility.

Those of "the family of the lion, or the tribe of the eagle" will not be satisfied with supporting this order. Why not? Because the ambitious seek the glory of founding and of ruling. The founders were able to rule, direct, and wield power in setting up this government. But the glory of founding is greater by far than the glory that can be had in a constitutional regime. In such a system, the law divides and limits sovereignty until even rule is impossible. In addition, the power of government as a whole is radically limited by the individual's possession of rights that are held out against the government. For this reason, the ambitious, seeking to rule, will pull down the constitutional order so as to destroy the limits on his ruling power, be they laws or private rights.

Of ruling ambition Lincoln observed: "It scorns to tread in the footsteps of any predecessor, however illustrious. It thirsts and burns for distinction; and, if possible, it will have it, whether at the expense of emancipating slaves, or enslaving freemen. Is it unreasonable then to expect, that some man possessed of the loftiest genius, coupled with ambition sufficient to push it to its utmost stretch, will at some time, spring up among us? And when such a one does, it will require the people to be united with each other, attached to the government and laws, and generally intelligent, to successfully frustrate his designs."[18] The legacy of the founders was a body of law, a constitution, that limited the government's scope of action by way of assigning rights to individuals. People of ambition, however, seek to rule: one might claim to rule at the behest of justice and destroy the Constitution by emancipating the slaves in the South, or one might rule in naked self-interest and violate the Constitution by enslaving free men. But both cases are fundamentally alike in that the ambitious seek to rule and must destroy the regime to do so.

If free government is to exist, it has to prevent rule by those of ambition, whatever their justification. How can this be done? The answer is to cultivate the attachment of the people to the law. When Lincoln proposed a means of preserving this connection, he proposed that "every American, every lover of liberty, every well wisher to his posterity, swear by the blood of the Revolution, never to violate in the least particular, the laws of the country; and never to tolerate their violation by others."[19] Lincoln called upon the patriotism of each and every citizen and enlisted it in the cause of obedience to the laws. His argument of interest joined to his patriotic appeal formed a powerful argument for obedience to the laws that reached out to every person in the government, no matter how calculating the individual.

The bulwark of a free people against the danger of the ambitious had two parts. It was not only a well-calculated argument of interest but also a patriotic reverence for the laws as well. To the extent that the people revere the laws and frustrate attempts to break them, they limit the opportunities of the ambitious. But the spirit of equality is an integral part of this bulwark since it leads citizens to consider everyone equal before the laws and hence liable to them.

Lincoln's argument was that citizens in a liberal society, liberated people (that is to say citizens liberated from civil or ecclesiastical morality), love justice to such an extent that they may disdain the legal justice of the regime. Liberated people see justice in such "either-or" terms that one all-too-readily foregoes the middling sort of legal justice the government offers in favor of the pursuit of absolute justice.

This tendency results from the problematic character of law in the modern, contractual regime. Whereas the classical regime buttressed its laws with civil religion or with a "noble lie," the modern government's law is obviously a human contrivance. Thus, citizens in the modern system prefer what they feel to be a higher, natural calling to justice within themselves to obedience to an obviously conventional body of law. The result is a moral crusade that ignores the fundamental rights of individuals in favor of remaking them into more perfect beings. Lincoln was quite willing to point out that such moral intentions are capable of leading to lynching.

The solution to this problem in Lincoln's mind is to cultivate the attachment of the people to the laws rather than to justice itself. The Lyceum speech pointed out the utility of legal justice and its necessary role in a republican regime. The fact that law is based on contract and not on religion in the Lockean state makes obedience to the law tenuous. Obedience can come in one of two ways. Self-interest can stimulate a rational obedience to the law when it is realized that law secures and regulates property. Since self-interested persons manifest that interest in the acquisition of property, obedience to the law becomes a matter of fundamental interest to each individual in a Lockean state.

At the same time, civic religion or patriotism can encourage a less calculating obedience to the law. Consider the patriotic appeal of Lincoln's conclusion to the Lyceum speech. In closing he remarked of the memories of the Revolution:

They were the pillars of the temple of liberty; and now, that they have crumbled away, that temple must fall, unless we, their descendants, supply their places with other pillars, hewn from the solid quarry of sober reason. Passion has helped us; but can do so no more. It will in the future be our enemy. Reason, cold, calculating, unimpassioned reason, must furnish all the materials for our future support and defense. Let those materials be moulded into general intelligence, sound morality and, in particular, a reverence for the Constitution and laws; and, that we improved to the last; that we remained free to the last; that we revered his name to the last; that, during his long sleep, we permitted no hostile foot to pass over or desecrate his resting place; shall be that which to learn the last trump shall awaken our WASHINGTON.[20]

It should be remembered that during the Revolution, passion was allied with obedience to law. Ambitions drove individuals to make the principles of this regime and of the Declaration of Independence viable. But ambition had come to dictate something else. Lincoln therefore sought to mold reason, a calculating interest in liberty, into a political religion that would dictate obedience to the laws. And he appealed to the patriotic sentiments of his audience with his last exhortation.

The appeal to reason and to civic religion or patriotism are both found in the Lyceum speech. The middle of the oration was a precisely calculated argument directed to the self-interested, while its beginning and end were directed to the patriotic. Lincoln's fundamental goal was to point out the necessity of adhering to the law.

To summarize the Lyceum speech, it is fair to say that Lincoln hinted at the problematic character of law in the modern government as he emphasized the necessity of obedience to the laws. An integral part of this obedience was the belief in the equality of all. In essence, the great principle of the Declaration not only justified and legitimated free government but also was itself, as Hofstadter remarks, "an instrument of democracy." At the same time, Lincoln warned against persons of ambition who would tear down the Constitution and thereby destroy free government in the name of emancipating the slaves or enslaving free men. These individuals were of the same type as the Caesars and Napoleons who had come before. To control such overweening ambition, a fundamental belief in universal equality and a reverence for the laws was necessary.[21]

In his dialogue with Madison, Lincoln argued that one ambition could not always be made to counteract another within political institutions. The ambition of some is so great that it can be checked only by a "general intelligence," a civic genius of the American people.

Presumably, a statesman can be differentiated from a demagogue, not in his use of rhetoric alone, for both cultivate the talent for public speaking, but in his ability to move the people rather than simply pander to their current tastes. A republican regime is fundamentally without rule. Free government is antithetical to rule by one man, while the existence of constitutionally guaranteed rights seems to preclude human rule altogether. But as has been seen in the Lyceum speech, to speak of the rule of law is misleading. Laws can rule only through the attachment of the people.

Law, however, cannot provide for this sense of attachment. Rather, it depends on the ability of each to understand his true interests. Rule in this regime, in any meaningful sense, takes place only within the individual in the ordering of the conflict between desire and self-restraint. Lincoln had shown that a belief in the equality of all with regard to certain fundamental rights was in every man's self-interest, rightly understood. How then could this spirit of equality be asserted and cultivated in a regime characterized by the nonexistence of rule? This question could be put in another form: how could Lincoln obtain consent in a republican regime?

The answer lies in the use of rhetoric. The division of the modern regime into a public and a private sphere has been characterized by the assignment of the highest questions such as justice, morality, and religion to the private sphere, while questions of "mere life" such as the security of life and property have been assigned to the public sphere. This is a radical inversion of the classical regime, where the highest questions were of public concern and property was regulated in such a way as to facilitate the answering of the highest questions. The existence of private rights held out against the state in the modern regime prevents the state from crossing the boundary between public and private.

To the extent that Lincoln sought to change other's views of interest and morality, he had to reach into their private lives. Because he could not do this with law, Lincoln was forced to use rhetoric. Speech is the only tool of the modern statesman who seeks to enter the private sphere of modern man and elevate him to a higher plane. Thus, it is in Lincoln's speeches that one finds the statesman at work.

Lincoln's effort to prevent moral condemnation of the southern people as opposed to the institution of slavery itself is interesting in this context. In an 1854 speech at Bloomington, Illinois, protesting passage of Stephen Douglas's Kansas-Nebraska Act, which effectively repealed the 1820 Missouri Compromise limiting the spread of slavery,

He first declared that the Southern slaveholders were neither better, nor worse than we of the North, and that we of the North were no better than they. If we were situated as they are, we should act and feel as they do; and if they were situated as we are, they would act and feel as we do; and we never ought to lose sight of this fact in discussing the subject. With slavery as existing in the slave states at the time of the formation of the Union, he had nothing to do. There was a vast difference between tolerating it there, and protecting the slaveholder in the rights granted him by the Constitution, and extending slavery over a territory already free and uncontaminated with the institution.[22]

Lincoln made two important points in this speech. First, the northern people were not morally superior because of their disapproval of slavery. Second, Lincoln noted the difference between tolerating slavery and implying its utility or justness by letting it expand.

In an address to the Springfield Washington Temperance Society, Lincoln made some interesting references to the Bible. One of importance to this study was his comment, "The cause itself [temperance] seems suddenly transformed from a cold abstract theory, to a living, breathing, active and powerful chieftan, going forth 'conquering and to conquer,'" a reference to Revelations 6:2. Upon the breaking of the first seal by the Lamb, the first of the four horsemen of the Apocalypse appears. Seated on a white horse, he wears a crown and rides forth "conquering and to conquer." This biblical reference intimated that a temperance society is like a warrior, going forth to conquer and to rule. What is most interesting, though, is that the image Lincoln used is a horseman of the Apocalypse, signifying that the end is drawing near.[23]

Lincoln noted that the temperance movement was "just now" becoming successful. This was due to the fact that earlier efforts were misguided. For one thing, earlier advocates of temperance had been too distant from their subject. They had lacked "approachability" and thus were seen as being unsympathetic and disinterested. This destroyed their ability to convince or persuade their audience. Lincoln concluded the fourth paragraph of his speech by saying that only a reformed drinker had the requisite approachability to convince his audience. This is because he has seen both sides of the issue himself and is the only person in a position to know truly of what he speaks.

Lincoln then turned to a teaching on the form of a proper appeal to temperance:

When the dram-seller and drinker, were incessantly told, not in the accents of entreaty and persuasion, diffidently addressed by erring man to an erring brother; but in the thundering tones of anathema and denunciation, with which the lordly judge often groups together all the crimes of the felon's life, and thrusts them in his face just ere he passes sentence of death upon him, that they were the manufacturers and material of all the thieves and robbers and murders that infested the earth; that their houses were the workshops of the devil; and that their persons should be shunned by all the good and virtuous, as moral pestilences—I say, when they were told all this, and in this way, it is not wonderful that they were slow, *very slow,* to acknowledge the truth of such denunciations, and to join the ranks of their denouncers, in a hue and cry against themselves.[24]

Here Lincoln argued that denunciation of the sinner is counterproductive; it simply drives him away. This is human nature.

Then how might one properly make a temperance appeal? Lincoln said that to influence a man's conduct, one must gently persuade him. The first appeal must be to the man's heart. Establish a friendship; demonstrate sympathy and like interests. This appeal to the heart, to one's feelings, is crucial if reason is ever to be affected. And once the heart is captured, Lincoln concluded, "you will find but little trouble in convincing his judgment of the justice of your cause, if indeed that cause really be a just one."[25]

Lincoln's appeal to friendship, sympathy, and like interests is striking. For him, leadership based on rigid insistence on rights or strident assertions of moral judgment cannot help but fail. Nor can effective leadership or statesmanship presume to command or coerce. In seeking to lead, Lincoln said, "assume to dictate to his judgment, or to command his action, or to mark him as one to be shunned and despised," and your target will ever be beyond reach; he will never be persuaded.[26]

Notice that there are two levels to Lincoln's temperance address. On the lower level, he analyzed human nature and the proper way to influence a man's conduct. Lincoln did not say that feelings rule the man, but rather that feelings are a useful route to a man's reason. His ultimate goal surely was to affect the reason, but Lincoln was too prudent to risk his goal by using an improper form of appeal. This explains his refusal to condemn the southern people for slavery. He wished to cultivate in them a belief in the equality of all, but this would be impossible if he tried to command or condemn the South.

The higher level of the temperance address raises some disturbing questions about the effect of any effort to change human conduct and bring it more in line with moral principles. The temperance movement, regardless of its approach, was as the first horseman. It rode forth to conquer and thereby threatened to bring down the regime. A very strong parallel can be drawn between the temperance movement and the abolition movement. Both crusades had a religious impetus and nature. Both removed their central issues from the realm of politics, law, and civil justice and placed them in a religious context. At this point Lincoln realized the constitutional restraints on rule were ignored and the existence of free society threatened.

In illuminating both the character of the American regime and the requirements of statesmanship within such a government, one discovers a modern, contractual system that places definite limits on the ability of the statesman to rule in the name of principle. These limits cause the statesman to achieve his ends through the use of rhetoric, the only means by which one can cross into the private realm of each individual and influence his thinking so as to move the body politic toward a fuller realization of justice. The ability to move the citizenry toward some higher goal radically distinguishes the statesman from the demagogue, who uses rhetoric to pander to the public rather than to enlighten them.

Lincoln understood the American regime as based on a contract among self-interested individuals. These people originally entered into civil society in order to protect their lives, liberties, and private property, the latter being a visible manifestation of their self-interest. It is necessary for the statesman in such a system to present questions of justice in terms of interest, thereby appealing to self-interested, calculating individuals. At the same time, one must avoid interfering with the property of citizens, for it is the need to secure property that drives them into civil society. These two considerations explain Lincoln's presentation of the slavery question in terms of interest and his careful avoidance of an attack on southern slaveholders.

Because the modern regime is based on contract rather than on religion or moral belief, the character of law is problematic. Knowing that the law is radically conventional, modern people prefers to follow the "natural" sense of justice felt within oneself. But widespread disobedience of the law, even in the name of justice, renders property and life insecure, breaking the bonds that hold individuals together in society.

It is the statesman's task to show the fundamental interest each has in obeying the laws all of the time. But Lincoln's advocacy of a political religion indicates that, at times, something more than an appeal to interest is necessary to hold the society together. Lincoln's constant reference to the Revolution seems to serve as a patriotic appeal, encouraging citizens to feel reverence rather than to calculate interest.

Yet Lincoln also understood the limits of a moral politics, the possibility of which was to so enchant the Progressive reformers of the late nineteenth century. He understood, as did Madison, that a politics couched in moral terms promised immoderation and lawlessness. Consequently, Lincoln typically addressed moral issues in terms of interests and taught the importance of friendship and shared interests as an alternative to the politics of moral denunciation.

Lincoln's genius as a statesman can thus be attributed to his ability to understand the character of the constitutional government. He was able to stand firm on the principle of equality yet compromise on the existence of slavery in the South so as not to threaten the existence of a regime that held out the promise of eventual emancipation. He was able to call citizens to a fuller belief in the equality of all without coercing or violating the rights of others. Finally, he was able to present a point of abstract justice as a matter of interest to everyone so that even the most calculating individual was convinced of its utility.

From his unique vantage point in the mid–nineteenth century, Lincoln could gaze back upon the Founding Fathers' new science of politics and see its limitations. Yet he could also anticipate, albeit perhaps dimly, the coming Progressive Movement, with its explicit rejection of a moderate, materially oriented politics in favor of morally invigorated leadership grounded in an energetic president addressing the nation from his "bully pulpit." Lincoln's statesmanship offers a third alternative, civic friendship, well worth consideration for its depth of understanding of the problem of modern politics.

7

ABRAHAM LINCOLN AND AMERICAN NATIONHOOD

Peter J. Parish

Two great American historical anniversaries loom ahead over the next decade. First, the year 2009 will mark the bicentennial of the birth of Abraham Lincoln. Two years later, in 2011, will come the sesquicentennial of the outbreak of the Civil War. Publishers, publicists, and other lovers of anniversary celebrations will already be formulating their plans for these occasions. The close conjunction of the two may provide an opportunity for reappraisal, not only of the meaning of the war and the role of the wartime president but also, more broadly, of Lincoln's contribution to the making and shaping of American nationhood.[1]

But simply in terms of chronology, it legitimately may be asked how and where do Lincoln and the Civil War fit into this story. After all, the United States had been in existence for many decades before his election to the presidency was quickly followed by secession and civil war. Indeed, if as Lincoln himself insisted, the Declaration of Independence marked the birth of the United States, the country was over thirty years old when he was born and over eighty years old when he became president. The answer to the question, and the starting point of this whole discussion, has to be that American nationhood was in the making throughout those eighty years. Between the Revolution and the Civil War, the process of nation building went on continually, though with no guarantee of ultimate success. The American republican experiment was a very fragile one at least until 1815, and as late as the 1860s, the Union came to its greatest internal crisis when it faced the threat of permanent division and disintegration. All nations are to a greater or lesser extent artificial constructs—and this was particularly true of the United States, which embarked upon building a nation without many of the normal materials of construction: ethnic homogeneity, a language of its own, an ancient national heritage, or a nucleus of strong institutions—a monarchy, a state church, or a powerful central government. The achievement of independence from Britain was only the beginning of the nation-building process.[2]

Writing of the U.S. Constitution, Princeton historian John Murrin suggests, in a memorable turn of phrase, that "Americans had erected their constitutional roof before they put up the national walls." Other historians have pointed out that a single and enduring union consisting of all thirteen original states, with the capacity to admit others, was only one of the possible options after independence. "Americans," writes Liah Greenfeld, "held some things to be self-evident, but the Union was not among them." Kenneth Stampp has shown how the notion of a perpetual union took half a century or more to evolve. Carl Degler has described the Union as "more a means to achieve nationhood than a nation itself." He concludes that the Civil War "was not a struggle to save a failed Union, but to create a nation that until then had not come into being." This nation building went on through the early struggle for survival; the excitement and challenges of headlong territorial expansion; the development of canals, railroads, and a manufacturing industry; the influx of new population; the problems of slavery and race; and the deepening sectional division between North and South, which eventually split the Union asunder. The construction of American nationhood faced its deepest crisis in the middle decades of the nineteenth century.[3]

One of the distinguishing features of the long-running nation-building process in the United States is that much of it— indeed, most of it—was not directed or dictated by some powerful central authority. The muscles, ligaments, and nervous system of this developing national entity came from popular democracy in the form of universal suffrage, at least for adult white males, popular education and widespread literacy, improving communications, economic growth and material prosperity, and geographical and social mobility. Before the Civil War the federal government scarcely impinged on the daily life of the ordinary citizen—except through the Postal Service, which did indeed play a crucially important role in drawing the new nation together. The question would be whether a nation developing in this way could cope with the massive threat posed by internal division. Nationhood without centralization would face its severest test in the face of secession and the Civil War. Had U.S. nation building advanced far enough by the 1860s to pass that test?[4]

Examination of Lincoln's role at this crucial time must avoid any suggestion that he single-handedly saved the Union and brought about the fulfillment of American nationhood. There were other forces at work, both personal and impersonal, and Union victory in the Civil War owed much to Ulysses S. Grant, William T. Sherman, and the Union armies; the superior numbers and material resources of the

118 / PETER J. PARISH

North; the resilience and commitment to the cause of the bulk of the northern people; and the endurance and yearning for freedom of much of the slave population of the South. It is only within that broader context that one may attempt to identify the nature and the importance of Lincoln's own contribution to that outcome. The analysis that follows is conducted in four stages through the themes of salvation, definition, improvement, and legacy. These four words represent, first, the saving of the Union during the Civil War; second, the definition or redefinition of what constituted the nation and who could belong to it; third, the continuing development or improvement of the nation; and lastly, Lincoln's legacy to the nation, his place in the national memory, and his posthumous contribution to the shaping and strengthening of American nationhood.

The necessary starting point is Lincoln as the savior of the Union. There was nothing inevitable or preordained about Union victory in the Civil War, and much apparently well-informed opinion at the time believed that it would be impossible for the North to force the South back into the Union. Without the restoration of the Union, there could be no American nationhood, at least not in the form hitherto understood. In fact, Lincoln's contribution to the achievement of this goal extended back into the prewar years. Although opposition to slavery and its further extension was in the nature of things a northern sectional cause, the Republican party in its early years pulled off the remarkable feat of bringing together under one ideological umbrella its antislavery commitment and its insistence that the Union must be preserved. In her recent book, historian Susan-Mary Grant develops the point more broadly and traces the emergence of a distinctive northern version of American nationalism. Having played his part in these developments, Lincoln in 1860 became the successful presidential candidate of the Republican party. In the four-month gap between his election and his inauguration, the Union began to fall apart as seven states of the Deep South seceded even before he had assumed office. Some critics, including Allen Guelzo in his recent prize-winning study, have condemned Lincoln's silence and relative inactivity during that time. But it is not clear what the president-elect could have done, and he may have been wise to bide his time and hold his tongue. As Alexander K. McClure observes, "When he did not know what to do, he was the safest man in the world to trust to do nothing."[5]

Lincoln arrived in the White House as apparently one of the least well-qualified and least well-prepared presidents of all time. He had never held any kind of executive office and had not been elected to public office in the twelve years before he became president. In the eyes of many, he was no more than an overpromoted country lawyer and small-town fixer. Nothing in his experience, personality, or political record suggested the makings of a great war leader. And yet in the early weeks of his administration, faced with an unprecedented crisis, he displayed an implacable will and an iron determination to stand firm on what he regarded as the essentials. He flatly rejected any recognition, however indirect, of the constitutional right of a state to secede, and he had no truck at all with talk of allowing the erring sisters to depart in peace. He was indecisive in some matters and made his share of blunders and errors of judgment—for example, in allowing Secretary of State William H. Seward too much leeway to pursue his own policy and also in the confusion over the planning of the two expeditions to Fort Sumter in South Carolina and to Fort Pickens in Florida. In particular, he persisted, against the mounting weight of evidence, in his overoptimistic belief that time would allow southern unionism to reassert itself and reverse the process of secession. But for all the shortcomings in the making and execution of policy, Lincoln still ruled out any compromise that threatened the integrity of the Union or that might undermine his or his party's commitment to the prevention of any further extension of slavery. (To some modern ears there may be something quaintly old-fashioned in his protestation that he could not ditch the platform on which he had just been elected. But it is also fair to add that he never lost sight of the interests of his party and its future prospects or of the need to establish his own public authority as president).[6]

As Fort Sumter in Charleston Harbor became the major flashpoint, Lincoln dithered and wavered on the tactics to be pursued, but he remained determined that if a first shot was going to be fired, it was not going to be fired by him. As a result, when Confederate guns opened up on the U.S. fort, there was a surge of popular support in the North for a fight to save the Union against those who had fired on the Stars and Stripes. This was by no means the least of Lincoln's early services to the Union cause.[7]

In his first message to Congress in July 1861, the new president showed that, even in the midst of this great crisis, he remained aware of the deeper issues at stake. If republican government was to survive, the southern appeal to bullets rather than ballots must not be allowed to succeed. The fundamental issue at stake in the conflict, he said, "embraces more than the fate of these United States. It presents to the whole family of man, the question, whether a constitutional republic, or a democracy—a government of the people, by the same people—can, or cannot, maintain its territorial integrity, against its own domestic foes. . . . It forces us to ask: 'Is there, in all republics, this inherent and fatal weakness?' 'Must a government, of necessity, be too *strong* for the liberties of its own people, or too *weak* to maintain its own existence?'" Later in his address Lincoln developed the argument in a slightly different direction: "This is essentially a people's contest. On the side of the Union, it is a struggle for maintaining in the world that form and substance of government whose leading object is to elevate the condition of men—to lift artificial weights from all shoulders—to clear the paths of laudable pursuit for all—to afford all an unfettered start, and a fair chance, in the race of life."[8]

It may well be argued that Lincoln's firm stand was not the best recipe for avoiding war in 1861. But in addressing the question of what kind of Union was worth saving, it did much to make the nation strong enough to survive its fiery trial. Once the war had started, he showed the same iron resolution in prosecuting it. It is true that for the first year or so of the conflict, Lincoln like many others had some hopes of a limited war, of limited duration, that might end in the restoration of something not very different from the status quo antebellum. But military setbacks in 1862 convinced him that the war was becoming the "violent and remorseless revolutionary struggle" that he had dreaded, and he became implacable in waging it, urging his generals into a strategy based on relentless pressure at all points in order to exploit the North's superior numbers and resources. This kind of warfare also led him into the change of policy toward slavery that produced the Emancipation Proclamation. One of his greatest challenges during the war was to carry enough of northern public opinion with him into acceptance not only of the huge escalation of the conflict but also of the concomitant escalation of the stakes for which it was being fought. Mere restoration of the Union would no longer suffice. The casualties and sacrifices of such a war could only be justified by putting slavery on the road to extinction and by leading the way toward a cleansed and regenerated United States dedicated to the ideals enunciated in the Gettysburg Address. Thus, the war to save the Union was now a war for a better Union, or a better nation.[9]

The South's best hope of success in the war was to break the northern will to continue the fight—and Lincoln's great task was to underpin and reinforce that will. One must remember too that there were periods when the war went extremely badly for the North—for example, in the year from midsummer 1862 to July 1863, when humiliating defeats, soaring casualties, and calls for more troops with no end in sight stretched northern morale almost to the breaking point. Again in midsummer 1864, war-weariness and frustration reached a new peak as the North was unable to clinch victory over a desperate and gravely weakened enemy. Even Horace Greeley, editor of the *New York Tribune,* so often a thorn in Lincoln's side with his demands for tougher action, complained in 1864 that "our bleeding, bankrupt, almost dying country . . . longs for peace—shudders at the prospect of fresh conscriptions, of further wholesale devastations, and of new rivers of human blood." But Lincoln's will held in the face of military disasters, ever lengthening casualty lists, fierce political criticism, and popular discontent.[10]

Most remarkable of all was Lincoln's acceptance, however agonized, of a level of casualties far beyond anything in earlier American experience or imagining. Some 350,000 Union soldiers died in the war as did 250,000 Confederates—all this in a country with a population of 31,500,000 at the outbreak of the war. (The proportionate casualties for the United States in a war today would be around five million.) Lincoln's determination to carry on in face of such massive losses may be either admired or condemned, but in either case it remains a fact to be reckoned with. Alongside the gentle and humane Lincoln and the melancholy and tormented Lincoln, we have to place the tough, resolute, even ruthless Lincoln. The toll that it all took on him is graphically illustrated by the contrast between photographs of the newly elected president in 1861 and the gaunt and haunted figure of the last few weeks of his life. The point is that Lincoln's fierce commitment to the salvation and betterment of the Union drove him to maintain the escalating conflict and to accept the bloodshed and slaughter—and then to seek to understand their full meaning.[11]

The successful fight to save the Union was the essential prerequisite of all of Lincoln's other contributions to the making of American nationhood. Without that success, no great historical importance would attach to Lincoln's response to the question of the definition or redefinition of the character of this Union-becoming-a-nation, including the question of who qualified for membership in it. American nationhood was a process—Lincoln would have endorsed that view. Indeed, he gave a new and much larger meaning to that process. Along with the notion of nation-making goes nationality by choice. In the absence of many of the main props of European nationalisms—especially ethnic homogeneity—the United States substituted nationality by choice. Ideally, an American was someone who chose to be so—although, in practice, not everyone was offered the chance as the experience of Indians and black slaves amply testifies. The United States was, or was to become, a prime example of what Ernest Gellner describes as a "voluntaristic" nation. Certain consequences flow from this kind of nationality. First, citizens had a stake, an interest, in the national community. Their actual or prospective success as individuals, as families, and as communities was closely intertwined with the actual or prospective success of the nation. It is worth noting that David Potter identifies common interest as one of the mainsprings of the evolving nationalism of the pre–Civil War decades. More important still, as more and more immigrants came into the country, the collective historical memory of the moment in the not very distant past, when British colonists had chosen to become American citizens, was paralleled in the family history of many people by the moment when a decision had been made to stop being something else and to become an American. Some of the peculiar quality and strength of the voluntary principle at work in American nation-building surely derives from this convergence of the collective and the individual experience. From the mid–nineteenth century onward, each new generation reenacted the nation-making experience.[12]

The decades of Lincoln's public life, from the 1840s to the 1860s, were critical

years in the construction of American nationhood. Huge acquisitions of new territory raised questions about how geographical expansion could or could not be rec-
onciled with national unity and identity. The geographical definition of the United
States was not yet settled. The population of the territories acquired from Mexico
and then the huge wave of Irish and German immigration raised big questions about
who was or was not, could or could not be, an American. Similar questions with a
much longer history reached a new peak of concern over the black population of the
United States, almost all of whom had arrived or been born as slaves.[13]

Abraham Lincoln addressed each of these problems in a different way. On the
first, he was never a great enthusiast for further territorial expansion, particularly if
it opened up the possibility of the further expansion of slavery. His responses to the
second question—and the absolutely fundamental one of who qualified as a member
of the nation—elicited some of his most important thoughts on the definition of
American nationhood. The essential point here is that Lincoln's United States was
to be an inclusive nation, and it steadily became more so.

It has to be said that in the case of black Americans Lincoln applied his inclusive
view of nationhood only gradually, even grudgingly, often equivocally, but in the
end emphatically. On the matter of race and color, it would be idle to claim and
unreasonable to expect that Lincoln measured up to the best approved liberal standards of our time. He was the product of his early-nineteenth-century Kentucky
origins and his early life in southern Indiana and Illinois, but he did not remain the
prisoner of his upbringing. By the 1850s, if not earlier, his hatred of slavery was
clear enough, though his thoughts on what should be the place of free blacks in
American society were only slowly taking shape. His interest in colonizing freed
slaves overseas in Central America or West Africa persisted even into his presidency—but increasingly as little more than a sop to the racial views of his white
electorate. Certainly before the Civil War, he shared the prevailing view, backed by
the scientific wisdom of the day, of the inherent inferiority of the black race—and
on matters of this kind, Lincoln always remained highly sensitive to the political
need to avoid placing too much distance between white voters and himself.[14]

In his 1858 debates with Sen. Stephen A. Douglas, one constantly recurring issue
was whether the bold declaration of 1776 that "all men are created equal" applied
to black Americans. Douglas insisted that it did not, and he probably had history on
his side. After all, Thomas Jefferson and many other signatories of the Declaration of
Independence were slaveowners. In the debate at Galesburg, Illinois, Douglas stated
frankly: "in my opinion, this government was made by our fathers on the white
basis. It was made by white men for the benefit of white men and their posterity
forever." Lincoln's reply took various forms at different times and in different places.
He was ever mindful of his audience and its prejudices, and the tone of his remarks

varied between southern Illinois, where much of the population had close links with the South, and northern Illinois, with its large population of Yankee origin. While arguing that blacks were included in the terms of the Declaration, he sought to limit the implications of any such inclusion. The Declaration of Independence, he thought, did not mean that all men were created equal in all respects. But, he went on, "there is no reason in the world why the Negro is not entitled to all the rights enumerated in the Declaration of Independence—the right of life, liberty, and the pursuit of happiness. I hold that he is as much entitled to these as the white man. I agree with Judge Douglas that he is not my equal in many respects, certainly not in color—perhaps not in intellectual or moral endowments; but in the right to eat the bread without leave of anybody else which his own hand earns, he is my equal and the equal of Judge Douglas, and the equal of every other man."[15]

Perhaps the best that can be said of Lincoln's views at this stage is that he did not close the door against the inclusion of black Americans within the nation as he understood and envisaged it. Given the prevailing racial attitudes and prejudices of most white Americans of the time, this in itself was quite an advanced position for a practical and ambitious northern politician to embrace in the late 1850s. Against this background the revolution that took place during the Civil War years assumes its true dimensions. From quite early in the conflict, Lincoln was convinced that a commitment to emancipation of the slaves was both morally right and also expedient as a means of prosecuting the war against the Southern Confederacy. But he was always acutely aware of the danger of alienating the mass of northern white opinion. Lincoln pursued a tortuous and sometimes devious path toward emancipation (but there is no need to follow that in detail here). Having safely delivered the Emancipation Proclamation by the beginning of 1863, the president did not waver in his support of freedom for the slaves, and he also supported the recruitment of black soldiers to engage in their own freedom struggle. He turned sharply on those who demurred. "You say you will not fight to free Negroes," he wrote. "Some of them seem willing to fight for you; but no matter." Given the climate of the times, the decision of an American president to recruit black soldiers to fight against white Americans was one of the truly revolutionary acts of the Civil War—and, in effect, it meant that there could be no going back to earlier notions of what should happen to the former slaves after their liberation.[16]

This process culminated in the Thirteenth Amendment to the Constitution, strongly supported by Lincoln, which abolished slavery once and for all throughout the United States. It was followed, after Lincoln's death, by the Fourteenth Amendment, which among other provisions defined U.S. citizenship in a new, inclusive way. Men who had been slaves not many months earlier were soon casting their votes in elections. Despite the tragic failure to match practice with principles during the century and more that followed, it is still important to recognize the dramatic change that had taken place within the space of a decade. In his decision on the Dred Scott case in 1857, the chief justice of the Supreme Court had declared that a Negro slave could never become a citizen. Within ten years, slavery had been abolished, and the Fourteenth Amendment plainly stated that "all persons born or naturalized within the United States are citizens of the United States." It would be idle to claim that this was all Lincoln's doing, but it would be churlish to deny him a good deal of the credit. It is the most striking evidence of both the essential inclusiveness of his conception of American nationhood and of its progressive and evolutionary character.[17]

In the case of immigrants to the United States, Lincoln's inclusiveness is much clearer. By the mid-1850s, after the first really large-scale mass immigration of Europeans during the preceding decade, foreign-born residents constituted a higher proportion of the total population than at any other time in the history of the United States. Unsurprisingly, these same years witnessed a fierce nativist, anti-immigrant, and anti-Catholic backlash. The nativist Know-Nothing party made spectacular gains in elections in 1854–55 and then faded away equally rapidly once it became clear that the slavery issue, not the immigration issue, was to be the basis for a realignment of political parties. Many Whigs and former Whigs were tempted by nativism, but Lincoln, dyed-in-the-wool Whig though he had been, would have nothing to do with it. In a much quoted letter to his friend Joshua Speed, he writes: "Our progress in degeneracy appears to me to be pretty rapid. As a nation, we began by declaring that '*all men are created equal.*' We now practically read it 'all men are created equal, *except negroes.*' When the Know-Nothings get control, it will read 'all men are created equal, except negroes, *and foreigners, and catholics.*' When it comes to this I should prefer emigrating to some country where they make no pretence of loving liberty—to Russia, for instance, where despotism can be taken pure, and without the base alloy of hypocrisy."[18]

These words are in a personal letter to a friend. Even more significant are Lincoln's words in a speech in July 1858 in Chicago, where he reflects on the importance of the Fourth of July and praises the heroic achievements of those "iron men" of 1776 "whom we claim as our fathers and grandfathers"—no great surprise there. Lincoln goes on to expand on these conventional thoughts in a very striking way in a passage not always accorded the attention it merits:

We have besides these men—descended by blood from our ancestors—among us perhaps half our people who are not descendants at all of these men; they are men who have come from Europe—German, Irish, French, and Scandinavian—men that have come from Europe themselves, or whose ancestors have come hither and settled here, finding themselves our equals in all things. If they look back through this history to trace their connection with those days by blood, they find they have none, they cannot carry themselves back into that glorious epoch and make themselves feel that they are part of us. But when they look through that old Declaration of Independence they find that those old men say that "We hold these truths to be self-evident, that all men are created equal," and then they feel that that moral sentiment taught in that day evidences their relation to those men, that it is the father of all moral principle in them, and that they have a right to claim it as though they were blood of the blood, and flesh of the flesh, of the men who wrote that Declaration—and so they are. That is the electric cord in that Declaration that links the hearts of patriotic and liberty-loving men together, that will link those patriotic hearts as long as the love of freedom exists in the minds of men throughout the world.[19]

This is not one of the most elegant or eloquent examples of Lincoln's prose. If truth be told, he was not always the best of impromptu speakers, and there is a marked difference of style between a speech like this and the exquisitely crafted and carefully reworked language of his major addresses, statements, and letters. But whatever the wording, the message conveyed by this passage goes to the heart of the inclusivity of American nationhood as conceived by Lincoln. It may be added that his broad national embrace also included the white South. He always insisted that slavery was a national problem, and he was anxious—many thought too anxious—to smooth the path back into the Union for white southerners when the war ended.[20]

The passage above illustrates two key elements in Lincoln's conception of American nationhood: its basis in voluntary commitment and the inclusiveness rather than the exclusiveness of its membership. The central importance of the Declaration of Independence in that same passage introduces another element—the evolutionary character of the American national identity as understood by Lincoln. Of course, any public speaker in the mid–nineteenth century—on the Fourth of July or any other day—would invoke the Declaration of Independence at every opportunity. Yet there is a clear distinction between Lincoln's understanding and his use of the Declaration and that of most of his predecessors and many of his contemporaries. Certainly Lincoln bowed to no one in his reverence for the Declaration. In February 1861, on his way to Washington for his inauguration, he declared that he had "never had a feeling politically that did not spring from the sentiments embodied in the Declaration of Independence." (It was surely no coincidence that he was speaking in Independence Hall in Philadelphia at the time.)[21]

Many prominent figures of earlier generations—including a great champion of the Union like Daniel Webster—took an essentially preservationist view of the words of the Declaration of Independence. They saw themselves as guardians of the Ark of the Covenant and were ever on the lookout for any falling away from the ideals that the Declaration proclaimed. Theirs was an essentially backward-looking and static view of the Declaration and its continuing role in American life. There was a constant fear of derogation or degeneration from the high standards that had been set, if not indeed a pessimistic assumption of inevitable decline. Most of Webster's great set-piece orations are heavily historical and preoccupied with the search for the historical roots and the historical credentials of American nationhood. In a comparison between Webster and his New England contemporary and rival, John Quincy Adams, Major L. Wilson observes that "while Webster revered the order of the past, John Quincy Adams valued most highly the prospect of qualitative progress for the nation in the future." Ralph Waldo Emerson was scathing on the subject of Webster's reverence for the past: "Mr. Webster is a man who lives by his memory, a man of the past, not a man of faith or hope. . . . He looks at the Union as an estate, a large farm, and is excellent in the completeness of his defence of it so far. . . . What he finds already written he will defend. Lucky that so much had got well written when he came."[22]

In contrast, Lincoln and some of his Whig-Republican contemporaries took a different view, more dynamic, more progressive, and more forward looking. No one has put the point better than Daniel Walker Howe: "The Republicans' use of the Declaration of Independence looked forward in time as well as backward. In Lincoln's reinterpretation of Jefferson, 'the proposition that all men are created equal' became a positive goal for political action, not simply a prepolitical state that government should preserve by inaction."[23]

When applied to the construction of American nationhood, this understanding of the Declaration not only builds upon the idea of the nation as process but also incorporates into it concepts of betterment and improvement. In other words, Lincoln and others espoused a kind of ameliorative nationalism. The aim of improvement was directed at individuals, the nation, economic advancement, and social and moral development. Daniel Walker Howe, again, has suggested that Lincoln's personal ambitions were mirrored in his political vision for America. In 1861 Lincoln himself said, "I hold that while man exists, it is his duty to improve not only his own condition, but to assist in ameliorating mankind."[24]

In his recent book, Alan Guelzo writes of Lincoln's eagerness to break away from the poor subsistence farming background of his family, which he saw as trapping its victims in a static condition of misery. By self-education and then by adopting the law as his profession, he succeeded in making his own escape. The practice of law, mainly involved in issues of contracts, land titles, and other commercial concerns, was his avenue into the expanding world of business opportunity and the market economy. It is in this connection that Guelzo quotes Charles Sellers's description of lawyers as the "shock troops of capitalism."[25] Lincoln's mounting objection to slavery was inspired partly by the perception of it as a threat to economic improvement, both for the country as a whole and for the individual citizen and his "right to rise," to use a favorite Lincoln phrase. During the Civil War Lincoln seldom missed an opportunity, especially in his annual messages to Congress, to provide evidence of the country's continuing growth in population, resources, and output, even in face of the stresses and costs of large-scale war.[26] (Of course, Lincoln had not had the dubious benefit of reading the work of late-twentieth-century economic historians who have used their statistical magic and the benefit of hindsight to reach rather different conclusions.)[27]

Economic improvement was connected with political, social, and above all moral improvement. Here it is important to go back to how Lincoln and some of his colleagues read the message of the Declaration of Independence. In the first place, it is highly significant that Jefferson's self-evident truth that all men are created equal became a proposition in Lincoln's Gettysburg Address. A proposition is something that has to be demonstrated and proved. This resonates with the language of trial and experiment that was widely used in the political and social rhetoric of the mid–nineteenth century. Historian Rush Welter has pointed out that the notion of the United States as experiment carried a significant double meaning. On the one hand, it implied a trial, a practical test of a theory or proposition; on the other hand, it could mean a demonstration of a known principle, as with a chemistry teacher conducting an experiment before a class. The first meaning implies uncertainty, the second confidence. Some measure of accommodation between the two was offered by Lincoln in the Gettysburg Address. The president's "proposition," like his call for a new birth of freedom, is very much in line with the idea of the nation as process and as the vehicle of progress.[28]

But something more was needed if the relationship between the principles of the Declaration and the patent failure to live up to them was to be defined in some way other than as a backward-looking lament for lost virtue. In a speech at Springfield in 1857, Lincoln addressed this question. The drafters of the Declaration, he said, "did not mean to assert the obvious untruth" that everyone was already enjoying the equal rights of which they spoke or even that they were about to be granted them immediately. "They meant to set up a standard maxim for free society, which should be familiar to all, and revered by all; constantly looked to, constantly labored for, and even though never perfectly attained, constantly approximated, and thereby constantly spreading and deepening its influence, and augmenting the happiness and value of life to all people of all colors everywhere." This was a picture of a society, a nation, always looking forward to unremitting effort to come close to ideals that could never be fully achieved rather than a society trying to put the clock back to a bygone age.[29]

There are strong echoes in this interpretation of much Christian thought then and now that sees man as constantly striving to achieve an unattainable state of perfect grace but requiring frequent forgiveness for his lapses back into sin. This link is made much more explicitly in a speech by Lincoln one year later, when he invoked the scriptural admonition "as your Father in Heaven is perfect, be ye also perfect." Lincoln continued: "The Savior, I suppose, did not expect that any human creature could be perfect as the Father in Heaven; but He said: 'As your Father in Heaven is perfect, be ye also perfect.' He set that up as a standard, and he who did most towards reaching that standard, attained the highest degree of moral perfection. So I say in relation to the principle that all men are created equal, let it be as nearly reached as we can. If we cannot give freedom to every creature, let us do nothing that will impose slavery upon any other creature."[30] Guelzo describes this gap between principle and practice as "the discrepancy one had to expect between aspiration and reality." Aspiration provides a legitimate connection between present realities and ideal futures. These are telling phrases that suggest that what was earlier labeled "ameliorative nationalism" might better be described as "aspirational nationalism." Guelzo is surely not far wide of the mark when he suggests that, in this context, the Declaration of Independence assumed the role of a substitute scripture for what Lincoln himself elsewhere called a "civil religion."[31]

The constant striving for betterment, for improvement in every sense of the word, is surely at the heart of Lincoln's concept of an evolving, dynamic American nationhood. It could and often did carry religious overtones for what he himself described as "an almost chosen people." But equally, the same ideas could feed into an entirely secular sense of a nation engaged in a never-ending struggle for improvement. This was at the heart of Lincoln's vision of an American nationhood that was deeply rooted in the three principles of choice, inclusiveness, and improvement.[32]

The changes taking place in the United States during the Civil War era have often been described in terms of a transition from the Union to the nation. There is surely some connection between Lincoln's ameliorative or aspirational nationalism and this transition in thought and language, but a word of caution may be needed here. It has been pointed out more than once that, in the 272 words of the Gettysburg Address, Lincoln used the word "nation" five times and the word "Union" not at all. Some pro-Democratic and fiercely anti-Lincoln newspapers condemned him for such language; one of them described it as a "flagrant . . . perversion of history." But this emphatic preference for "nation" over "Union" may have been an exception to the rule. In his Second Inaugural Address, sixteen months after the Gettysburg Address, Lincoln referred to "Union" four times and to "nation" only three times. In the early days of his presidency, Lincoln had customarily, though not consistently, spoken of the Union. But in his first message to Congress in July 1861, he twice used the phrase "the national Union," referred several times to the 'national Constitution," and discussed "the relative matter of national power and state rights." In his message to Congress in December 1862, he did not desert the conventional term "Union," but also spoke of the "nation" and even of "the national family," warning of the dire consequences of the separation of "our common country into two nations." It has to be doubted whether every time Lincoln took up his pen he turned over in his mind whether to use the word "Union" or the word "nation." His alternating use of both, and even of the phrase "national Union" (incidentally, the label adopted by his party in the 1864 election), suggests that what is happening here is not a sudden transformation of old Union into new nation but a transition over a much longer period. But that transition was surely accelerated and its meaning clarified by four years of civil war and Lincoln's exposition of the issues at stake. A changing political vocabulary is but one more example of the American nation as process and of the role of Lincoln's ameliorative or aspirational nationalism in that process.[33]

Lincoln's own use of language was generally cool and calculated, so a measure of what was achieved during the war and under Lincoln's leadership may be more clearly obtained by turning to someone else less judicious in his own choice of words and more excitable in temperament. George Templeton Strong was a member of the New York business and social elite, a man very active and influential in public affairs during the Civil War. His diary is made wonderfully entertaining and often revealing by his volatile temperament, his uninhibited language, and his rapidly fluctuating opinions. On March 11, 1861, with Lincoln in office for barely one week and the Union apparently close to collapse, Strong wrote: "The political entity known as the United States of America is found out at last, after imposing on the community of nations for three-quarters of a century. The bird of our country is a debilitated chicken, disguised in eagle feathers. We have never been a nation; we are only an aggregate of communities, ready to fall apart at the first serious shock and without a centre of vigorous national life to keep us together." Four years later, at the end of the Civil War, Strong was in very different mood when he wrote: "The people has (I think) just been bringing forth a new American republic—an amazingly large baby—after a terribly protracted and severe labor, without chloroform."[34]

Saving the Union, defining the structure and content of the nation, injecting the notion of improvement into the nation as process—these were three key elements in Lincoln's lifetime contribution to American nationhood. But there was a fourth posthumous contribution in the shape of Lincoln's enduring legacy and his place in American memory. Some of the goals that Lincoln had not fully achieved in his life were brought closer by his death. To be killed at the hour of victory, and on Good Friday too, might be regarded by cynics as the ultimate proof of Lincoln's superb skill in political timing. In 1865, politicians, preachers, and propagandists seized eagerly on the parallel with the first Good Friday. Lincoln the martyr-president powerfully underlined the images of Lincoln the savior of the Union, the champion of American democracy, the emancipator of the slaves, and the supreme embodiment of the self-made man and the log-cabin-to-White-House myth. The emotional shock of the assassination was reinforced by the extraordinarily protracted funeral rites as Lincoln's body was conveyed on its circuitous route from Washington to its resting place in Springfield.[35]

Inevitably, the surge of emotion inspired by Lincoln's death faded with the passage of time, and it became easier to recall that the living Lincoln had been a highly controversial figure and to suggest that his reputation might be strongly contested. For many of his contemporaries, recognition that he was a great man came only after his death, if indeed it ever came at all. As president he had been belittled and reviled to a degree seldom equaled even in the annals of uninhibited nineteenth-century political invective. During the Civil War he was hated and despised by many white southerners, condemned as a tyrant by most northern Democrats, and dismissed as a buffoon or an incompetent by large sections of the press and even by some members of his own party. The waves of shock and grief set off by his death could not wash away all such feelings forever. During the last third of the nineteenth century, Lincoln was honored and memorialized in various ways, and his reputation was steadily enhanced, but there was never a shortage of dissenting voices. His name was also used or abused in support of all manner of causes. He was adopted as patron or champion of civil service reform, the protective tariff, anti-imperialism—and even white supremacy. It was only in the early twentieth century, with the help of the celebrations of the centennial of his birth in 1909, that Lincoln's status as a towering national hero was confirmed and consolidated.[36]

There are factors peculiar to Lincoln that help explain this process, but it also appears to conform to a common trend in the evolution of the reputation of national leaders. There may be a natural rhythm about the reaction of later generations to great historical figures. After the period of mourning and the tributes immediately following the death of the person concerned, there comes a reaction, perhaps a fashion for debunking, and a revival of controversies that had surrounded the person in life. After forty or fifty years, most of the dead leader's contemporaries will have passed from the scene, and if he or she survives the backlash and retains a sufficient hold on the popular memory and the popular imagination, there often comes a new high tide of interest and enthusiasm. When, in turn, that high tide recedes, either the individual will fade into the background, or if he or she retains sufficient inherent and enduring appeal, his or her reputation will settle into a less dramatic and controversial but more solid and sustained place in the public memory.

The surge in Lincoln's prestige as a truly national figure in the early twentieth century fits neatly into this pattern, though it also owed much to the specific circumstances of the time. Half a century of rapid social and economic change—the growth of large cities and giant corporations and a huge industrial workforce that included masses of recent immigrants—stimulated both a desire to enjoy the fruits of economic growth and a yearning for the values of an earlier age. The progressive movement was in part a response to these feelings, and many progressives saw Lincoln as a figure who could combine the ideals of the past with the promise of the future. According to Barry Schwartz, Lincoln was both a model for Progressivism and a model of Progressivism. Jane Addams recalled her family's devotion to Lincoln and his influence on her own political and social attitudes. For the purpose of unifying tradition and progress, Schwartz says, "Lincoln was an ideal symbol." Theodore Roosevelt identified closely with Lincoln and quoted him frequently; his secretary of state, John Hay, after all had been Lincoln's private secretary. Woodrow Wilson was another, if rather more cautious, admirer. The question "What would Lincoln do?" was a much used device in the political rhetoric of the 1912 election campaign in which the two men were rival candidates.[37]

Yet it was not only progressives who contributed at this time to the promotion of Lincoln as a great national hero. Conservatives did their best to claim a share in the new Lincoln image by using appropriate selections from his thoughts on individual self-help, property rights, and economic development. With rather more difficulty, socialists played the same game in seeking their share in the national hero. Even the hostility of some white southerners abated as they subscribed cautiously to parts of the Lincoln myth. Black Americans generally retained their affection for the Great Emancipator, though not without some ambivalence and some reservations. In different ways both Booker T. Washington and W. E. B. Du Bois expressed their admiration for him, and Washington was not unhappy to be described as the black Lincoln. It was at least equally significant that Lincoln struck a chord with many immigrants of diverse ethnic backgrounds. As they struggled to make their way in a new land, they could identify with accounts, factual or mythical, of Lincoln's struggle out of early poverty. They could find in him a personal symbol or representation of the America to which they aspired to belong. Standing for national unity and solidarity, Lincoln was, in the view of Barry Schwartz, "the perfect symbol of the inclusive dispositions of mass society."[38]

In 1909, organizers of centennial celebrations in various cities sought to incorporate this theme of inclusiveness into their Lincoln festivities. One symbolic gesture indicating Lincoln's unique status as a national figure also came in 1909 when Congress approved the use of his profile on the penny coin—"the coin of the common folk" as Carl Sandburg described it. This was the first depiction of a president on an American coin.[39]

The participation of the United States in World War I marked a further stage in the consolidation of Lincoln's position as national hero. He was the model of the president as war leader who had managed to combine firmness of purpose and an unwavering commitment to the great principles at stake with deep humanity and compassion for the victims of war. Propaganda on behalf of the war effort exploited these themes to the full; one poster distributed by the Office of Public Information quoted the final sentence of the Gettysburg Address. More than ever, the war effort of 1917–18 made the Lincoln image into a great national unifying force for almost all Americans.[40]

It was appropriate that, just before and after American participation in World War I, confirmation of Lincoln's status as national symbol and hero should be framed, so to speak, by the completion of two major memorials to him. In 1916 the Lincoln Birthplace Memorial at Hodgenville, Kentucky, was formally dedicated. It is an extraordinary monument—a classical marble temple approached by an impressive flight of fifty-six steps (one for each year of Lincoln's life) encasing a humble log cabin that looks equally fragile in its basic structure and in its claims to authenticity as Lincoln's birthplace. Six years later the Lincoln Memorial in Washington, D.C., was dedicated on Memorial Day, 1922. Inside this magnificent marble temple was Daniel Chester French's huge statue of Abraham Lincoln, unequivocally certifying his admission into the national pantheon but, by clothing him in conventional dress and showing him seated rather than standing in classic pose, retaining his essential humanity and his role as a leader close to the people. In their different ways both of these memorials sought to reconcile the two images of Lincoln: Lincoln as the common man, the folk hero, and Lincoln as the superman, the epic hero—or in the words of Barry Schwartz, "Lincoln as everyman and Lincoln as demi-god."[41]

But the key point is surely that, with the help of the centennial, the progressive temper of the times, and then the First World War, these two images of Lincoln steadily converged into one powerful symbol of American nationhood. Americans white and black, native-born and immigrant, northern and southern, radical and conservative, all had their own distinct perspective on this one truly national figure, but all had a share in him. The central themes of Lincoln's own vision of American nationhood remained as strong as ever—unity, individual commitment, inclusiveness, improvement—even if for many the prospects of converting ideals into reality remained as distant as ever. In 1909 the distinguished progressive publicist Herbert Croly commented perceptively on the nature of Lincoln's key contribution to American nationhood: "For the first time it was clearly proclaimed by a responsible politician that American nationality was a living principle rather than a legal bond." If the principle lived on, so too did the national image and reputation of the man who inspired it.[42]

For more recent generations of Americans, Lincoln has inevitably become a distant historical figure, his status no longer so hotly contested or controversial as in the years after his death, his image no longer so constantly or vividly invoked as in the early twentieth century. There are still skeptics and hostile critics ready to disparage his achievements and denigrate his character, and academic historians continue to dispute many aspects of his private and public life. But overwhelmingly, in the popular mind, his image is fixed and his place in the national memory is secure. Three historical monuments to the three great American civic gods dominate much of the center of Washington D.C., though others have been added more recently. Of the three, the Washington Monument is certainly the most conspicuous. The Jefferson Memorial is widely regarded as the most beautiful, although access to it can involve some hazard to the unwary sightseer. The Lincoln Memorial is surely the most moving of the three, and it is the one most in the public eye, serving as the focal point of great national gatherings in recent times. This may suggest that Lincoln's ameliorative or aspirational nationalism still speaks loud and clear to later generations. The gap between aspiration and achievement may sometimes seem dauntingly wide, but the concept of an American nationhood based on choice, inclusiveness, and improvement remains an attractive ideal, constantly sought, even though impossible to fully realize.

Great events provide a stage for great leaders. But for the secession crisis and the Civil War, Lincoln might have gone down in history as no more than a somewhat better than average mid-nineteenth-century president. The war came, and it propelled Lincoln into a position of vastly greater prominence and confronted him with a series of massive challenges. It follows that the legacy of the Civil War must therefore include the legacy of Abraham Lincoln. That legacy consisted not only of his significant contribution to the salvation of the Union but also of his success in giving American nationhood a stronger identity and a sense of purpose that would help sustain it through generations to come.

8

"FOR A VAST FUTURE ALSO"

Lincoln and the Millennium

JAMES M. MCPHERSON

When Abraham Lincoln breathed his last at 7:22 A.M. on April 15, 1865, Secretary of War Edwin M. Stanton intoned, "Now he belongs to the ages."

Stanton's remark was more prescient than he knew, for Lincoln's image and his legacy became the possession not only of future ages of Americans but also of people of other nations. On the centenary of Lincoln's birth in 1909, Leo Tolstoy described him as "a Christ in miniature, a saint of humanity." An Islamic leader projected a more militant image of Lincoln, declaring that America's sixteenth president "spoke with a voice of thunder . . . and his deeds were as strong as the rock." When Jacqueline Kennedy lived in the White House, she sought comfort in the Lincoln Room in times of trouble. "The kind of peace I felt in that room," she recalled, "was what you feel when going into a church. I used to feel his strength, I'd sort of be talking to him."[1]

Martin Luther King Jr. tried to persuade Jacqueline Kennedy's husband to issue a second emancipation proclamation on the hundredth anniversary of the first. John Kennedy demurred. So King went ahead on his own. When he stood on the steps of the Lincoln Memorial in August 1963 to deliver his "I Have a Dream" speech, King declared: "Fivescore years ago, a great American, in whose shadow we stand today, signed the Emancipation Proclamation. This momentous decree came as a great beacon of hope to millions of Negro slaves who had been scarred in the fame of withering injustice."[2]

Lincoln could not anticipate the reverence that millions would feel for him in future ages. But he *was* intensely aware, as he told Congress in December 1861, when America was engulfed in a tragic Civil War, that this struggle to preserve the Union "is not altogether for today—it is for a vast future also." More than any other president of the United States except perhaps Thomas Jefferson, Abraham Lincoln had a profound sense of history. He did not acquire it by formal education. Unlike Woodrow Wilson, Lincoln did not have a Ph.D. He did not study history in college or high school; indeed, he did not study it in school at all, for he had less than a year of formal schooling, which included no history courses. The only work of history Lincoln seems to have read as a boy was "Parson" Weems's famous filiopietistic biography of George Washington, with its apocryphal story of the hatchet and the cherry tree.

This book made a lasting impression on Lincoln. Forty years after he first read it, President-elect Lincoln addressed the New Jersey legislature in Trenton, near the spot where George Washington's ragged troops had won a victory the day after Christmas 1776 that saved the American Revolution from collapse. Lincoln told the legislators: "I remember all the accounts" in Weems's book "of the battle-fields and struggles for the liberty of the country, and none fixed themselves upon my imagination so deeply as the struggle here at Trenton. . . . The crossing of the river; the contest with the Hessians; the great hardships endured at that time, all fixed themselves on my memory more than any single revolutionary event. . . . I recollect thinking then, boy even though I was, that there must have been something more than common that those men struggled for."[3]

These words were not merely an exercise in nostalgia. As always, Lincoln invoked the past for a purpose. On this occasion he shifted from the Revolution to the present and future. Prospects for the United States in that present and future were dark. The country of which Lincoln would become president eleven days later was no longer the United States but the *dis*united states. Seven slave states, fearing for the future of their peculiar institution in a nation governed by the new antislavery Republican party, had seceded from the Union in response to Lincoln's election. Several more slave states were threatening to go out. Even as Lincoln spoke in Trenton, delegates from those first seven states were meeting in Montgomery, Alabama, to form the independent Confederate States of America. Civil War, or a permanent division of the country with its dire precedent for further divisions, or both loomed on the horizon. Thus, it is not surprising that when Lincoln shifted from his discussion of the Revolution to the present, he began: "I am exceedingly anxious" that what those men fought for, "that something even more than National Independence; that something that held out a great promise to all the people of the world [for] all time to come; I am exceedingly anxious that this Union, the Constitution, and the liberties of the people shall be perpetuated in accordance with the original idea for which that struggle was made."[4]

The next day, Washington's birthday, Lincoln spoke at Independence Hall in Philadelphia, where he spelled out more clearly what he believed was at stake both in the Revolution and in the crisis of 1861. "I have often inquired of myself," said Lincoln, "what great principle or idea it was that kept this [Union] so long together. It was not the mere matter of the separation of the colonies from the mother land, but that sentiment in the Declaration [of Independence] which gave liberty, not alone to the people of this country, but hope to the world for all future time." At this point in Lincoln's remarks, the newspaper text indicated "Great applause" from the audience, which included the city council and leading citizens of Philadelphia. Lincoln told them: "I have never had a feeling politically that did not spring from the sentiments embodied in the Declaration of Independence" ("Great cheering," according to the press). The ringing phrases that "all men are created equal, that they are endowed by their Creator with certain unalienable Rights, that among these are Life, Liberty, and the pursuit of Happiness," said Lincoln in 1861, "gave prom- ise," not just to Americans, but "hope to the world" that "in due time the weights should be lifted from the shoulders of all men, and that *all* should have an equal chance. (Cheers.)"[5]

The sincerity of some in the audience who cheered Lincoln's egalitarian senti- ments might be questioned. But Lincoln was quite sincere in his endorsement of them. He was, of course, painfully aware that many Americans enjoyed neither lib- erty nor equality. Four million were slaves, making the United States—the self-pro- fessed beacon of liberty to oppressed masses everywhere—the largest slaveholding country in the world. Lincoln grasped this nettle. "I hate . . . the monstrous injustice of slavery," he had said in his famous Peoria speech of 1854. "I hate it because it deprives our republican example of its just influence in the world—enables the ene- mies of free institutions, with plausibility, to taunt us as hypocrites."[6]

As for equality, said Lincoln on another occasion, the author of the Declaration of Independence and the Founding Fathers who signed it clearly "did not intend to declare all men equal *in all respects*." They did not even "mean to assert the obvious untruth" that all men in 1776 were equal in rights and opportunities. Rather, "they meant to set up a standard maxim for free society, which should be . . . constantly looked to, constantly labored for, and even though never perfectly attained, con- stantly approximated, and thereby constantly spreading and deepening its influence, and augmenting the happiness and value of life to all people of all colors every- where."[7]

Like Thomas Jefferson, Lincoln asserted a universality and timelessness for the principles of liberty, equal rights, and equal opportunity on which the nation was founded. And Lincoln acknowledged his intellectual debt to Jefferson—not Jeffer- son the slaveholder, not Jefferson the author of the Kentucky Resolutions of 1799 asserting the superiority of state over federal sovereignty, not even Jefferson the pres- ident, but Jefferson the philosopher of liberty, author of the Northwest Ordinance that kept slavery out of future states comprising 160,000 square miles at a time when most existing states of the Union still had slavery, and the Jefferson who, though he owned slaves, said of the institution that "he trembled for his country when he remembered that God was just." This was the Jefferson, said Lincoln in 1859, who "in the concrete pressure of a struggle for national independence by a single people had the coolness, forecast, and capacity to introduce into a merely revolutionary document—the Declaration of Independence—an abstract truth, applicable to all men and all times."[8]

Universal and timeless this truth may be, but in Jefferson's time it remained mostly as Lincoln described it—abstract. Fate decreed that it fell to Lincoln, not Jefferson, to give substance and meaning to what Jefferson had called a self-evident truth. Ironically, it was the slaveholders who provided Lincoln the opportunity to do so, for by taking their states out of the Union, they set in train a progression of events that destroyed the very social and political order founded on slavery that they had seceded to preserve.

Secession transformed the main issue before the country from slavery to disunion. When Lincoln became president, he confronted the question not what to do about slavery, but what to do about secession. On this question Lincoln did not hesitate. Branding secession as "the essence of anarchy," he insisted in 1861 that "the central idea pervading this struggle is the necessity that is upon us, of proving that popular government is not an absurdity. We must settle this question now, whether in a free government the minority have the right to break up the government whenever they choose. If we fail it will go far to prove the incapability of the people to govern themselves."[9]

Lincoln had come a long way in his understanding of history since his boyhood reading of Weems's biography of Washington. Like other thoughtful Americans, he was acutely conscious of the unhappy fate of most republics in the past. The United States stood almost alone in the mid–nineteenth century as a democratic republic in a world bestrode by kings, emperors, czars, petty dictators, and theories of aristocracy. Some Americans alive at midcentury had seen two French republics rise and fall. The hopes of 1848 for the triumph of popular government in Europe had been shattered by the counterrevolutions that brought a conservative reaction in the Old World. Would the American experiment in government of, by, and for the people also be swept into the dustbin of history?

Not if Lincoln could help it. "Our popular government has often been called an experiment," he told a special session of Congress that met on July 4, 1861. "Two points in it, our people have already settled—the successful *establishing,* and the successful *administering* of it. One still remains—its successful *maintenance* against a formidable internal attempt to overthrow it." If that attempt succeeded, said Lincoln, the forces of reaction in Europe would smile in smug satisfaction at this proof of their contention that the upstart republic launched in 1776 could not last.[10]

Many in the North shared Lincoln's conviction that democracy was on trial in this war. "We must fight," proclaimed an Indianapolis newspaper two weeks after Confederate guns opened fire on Fort Sumter. "We must fight because we *must*. The National Government has been assailed. The Nation has been defied. If either can be done with impunity neither Nation nor Government is worth a cent. . . . War is self preservation, if our form of Government is worth preserving. If monarchy would be better, it might be wise to quit fighting, admit that a Republic is too weak to take care of itself, and invite some deposed Duke or Prince of Europe to come over here and rule us. But otherwise, *we must fight.*"[11]

The outbreak of war brought hundreds of thousands of northern men to recruiting offices. A good many of them expressed a similar sense of democratic mission as a motive for fighting. "I do feel that the liberty of the world is placed in our hands to defend," wrote a Massachusetts soldier to his wife in 1862, "and if we are overcome then farewell to freedom." In 1863, on the second anniversary of his enlistment, an Ohio private wrote in his diary that he had not expected the war to last so long, but no matter how much longer it took it must be carried on "for the great principles of liberty and self government at stake, for should we fail, the onward march of Liberty in the Old World will be retarded at least a century, and Monarchs, Kings, and Aristocrats will be more powerful against their subjects than ever."[12]

Some foreign-born soldiers appreciated the international consequences of the war more intensely than native-born young men who took their political rights for granted. A young British immigrant in Philadelphia wrote to his father back in England explaining why he had enlisted in the Union army. "If the Unionists let the South secede," he wrote, "the West might want to separate next Presidential Election . . . , others might want to follow and this country would be as bad as the German states." Another English-born soldier, a forty-year-old corporal in an Ohio regiment, wrote to his wife in 1864 explaining why he had decided to reenlist for a second three-year hitch. "If I do get hurt I want you to remember that it will be not only for my Country and my Children but for Liberty all over the World that I risked my life, for if Liberty should be crushed here, what hope would there be for the cause of Human Progress anywhere else?" An Irish-born carpenter, a private in he Twenty-eighth Massachusetts Infantry of he famous Irish Brigade, rebuked both his wife in Boston and his father-in-law back in Ireland for questioning his judgment in risking his life for the Union. "This is the first test of a modern free government in the act of sustaining itself against internal enemys [sic]," he wrote, almost in echo of Lincoln. "If it fail then the hope of milions [sic] fall and the designs and wishes of all tyrants will succeed the old cry will be sent forth from the aristocrats of Europe that such is the common lot of all republics." It is worth noting that both this Irish-born private and the English-born Ohio corporal were killed in action in 1864.[13]

The American sense of mission invoked by Lincoln and by these soldiers—the idea that the American experiment in democracy was a beacon of liberty for oppressed people everywhere—is as old as the Mayflower Compact and as new as apparent American victory in the Cold War. In our own time this sentiment sometimes comes across as self-righteous posturing that inspires more resentment than admiration abroad. The same was true in Lincoln's time, when the resentment was expressed mainly by upper-class conservatives, especially in Britain. But many spokesmen for the middle and working classes in Europe echoed the most chauvinistic Yankees. During the debate that produced the British Reform Act of 1832, the London Working Men's Association pronounced "the Republic of America" to be a "beacon of freedom for all mankind," while a British newspaper named the *Poor Man's Guardian* pointed to American institutions as "the best precedent and guide to the oppressed and enslaved people of England in their struggle for the RIGHT OF REPRESENTATION FOR EVERY MAN."[14]

In the preface to his *Democracy in America,* written during the heady days of the 1848 democratic uprisings in Europe, Alexis de Tocqueville urges the leaders of France's newly created Second Republic to study American institutions as a guide to "the approaching irresistible and universal spread of democracy throughout the world." When instead of democracy France got the Second Empire under Napoleon III, the republican opposition to his regime looked to the United States for inspiration. "Many of the suggested reforms," wrote the historian of the French opposition, "would have remained utopic had it not been for the demonstrable existence of the United States and its republican institutions." The existence of the United States remained a thorn in the side of European reactionaries, according to a British radical newspaper, which stated in 1856, "to the oppressors of Europe, especially those of England, the [United States] is a constant terror, and an everlasting menace" because it stood as "a practical and triumphant refutation of the lying and servile sophists who maintain that without kings and aristocrats, civilized communities cannot exist."[15]

Once the war broke out, French republicans, some of them in exile, supported the North as "defenders of right and humanity." In England John Stuart Mill expressed the conviction that the American Civil War "is destined to be a turning point, for good and evil, of the course of human affairs." Confederate success, said Mills, "would be a victory for the powers of evil which would give courage to the enemies of progress and damp the spirits of its friends all over the civilized world."[16]

Some European monarchists and conservatives did indeed make no secret of their hope that the union would fall into the dustbin of history. The powerful *Times* of London considered the likely downfall of "the American colossus" a good "riddance of a nightmare. . . . Excepting a few gentlemen of republican tendencies, we all expect, we nearly all wish, success to the Confederate cause." The Earl of Shrewsbury expressed his cheerful belief "that the dissolution of the Union is inevitable, and that men before me will live to see an aristocracy established in America."[17] In Spain the royalist journal *Pensamiento Español* found it scarcely surprising that Americans were butchering each other, for the United States, it declared editorially, "was populated by the dregs of all the nations of the world. Such is the real history of the one and only state in the world which has succeeded in constituting itself according to the flaming theories of democracy. The example is too horrible to stir any desire for emulation." The minister to the United States from the Czar of all Russians echoed this opinion in 1863. "The republican form of government, so much talked about by the Europeans and so much praised by the Americans, is breaking down," he wrote. "What can be expected in a country where men of humble origin are elevated to the highest positions?" He meant Lincoln, of course. "This is democracy in practice, the democracy that European theorists rave about. If they could only see it at work they would cease their agitation and thank God for the government which they are enjoying."[18]

Clearly, opinion in Europe supported Lincoln's conviction that the very survival of democracy was at stake in the Civil War. But in the first year and a half of the war, the problem of slavery muddied the clarity of this issue. The Confederacy was a slave society, which should have strengthened the Union's image abroad as the champion of liberty and equal rights. As Lincoln put it in a private conversation in January 1862, "I cannot imagine that any European power would dare to recognize and aid the Southern Confederacy if it became clear that the Confederacy stands for slavery and the Union for freedom." The problem was at that time the Union did not yet stand for the freedom of slaves. Constitutional constraints plus Lincoln's need to keep northern Democrats and the border slave states in his was coalition inhibited efforts to make it a war against slavery. This restraint puzzled and alienated many potential European friends of the Union cause. An English observer asked in September 1861, since "the North does not proclaim abolition and never pretended to fight for anti-slavery," how "can we be fairly called upon to sympathize so warmly with the Federal cause?"[19]

Lincoln recognized the validity of this question. In September 1862 he agreed with a delegation of antislavery clergymen that "emancipation would help us in Europe, and convince them that we are incited by something more than ambition." When he said this, Lincoln had made up his mind to issue an emancipation proclamation. The balance of political forces in the North and military forces on the battlefield had shifted just enough to give this decision the impetus of public support.

Basing his action on the power of the commander in chief to seize enemy property being used to wage war against the United States—slaves were property and their labor was essential to the Confederate war economy—Lincoln issued a preliminary Emancipation Proclamation in September 1862 and the final Proclamation on January 1, 1863, justifying it as both a "military necessity" and an "act of justice."[20]

The Emancipation Proclamation not only laid the groundwork for the total abolition of slavery in the United States, which was accomplished by the Thirteenth Amendment to the Constitution in 1865, but also emancipated Lincoln from the contradiction of fighting a war for democratic liberty without fighting a war against slavery. Emancipation deepened Lincoln's sense of history. As he signed the proclamation on New Year's Day 1863, he said to colleagues who gathered to witness the historic occasion: "I never, in my life, felt more certain that I was doing right than I do in signing this paper. If my name ever goes into history it will be for this act, and my whole soul is in it."[21]

Lincoln here connected the act of emancipation with the future as he had earlier connected the war for the Union with a past that had given Lincoln's generation the legacy of a united country. Just as the sacrifices of those who had fought for independence and nationhood in 1776 inspired Lincoln and the people he led, their sacrifices in the Civil War would leave a legacy of democracy and freedom to future generations. In his first annual message to Congress—we call it today the State of the Union address—Lincoln declared that "the struggle of today is not altogether for today—it is for a vast future also." Lincoln sent his second annual message to Congress in December 1862 just before he issued the Emancipation Proclamation. On this occasion he defined the war's meaning by linking past, present, and future in a passage of unsurpassed eloquence and power. "Fellow citizens, we cannot escape history," he said. "We of this Congress and this administration, will be remembered in spite of ourselves. . . . The fiery trial through which we pass, will light us down, in honor or dishonor, to the latest generation. . . . We shall nobly save, or meanly lose, the last best, hope of earth. . . . The dogmas of the quiet past, are inadequate to the stormy present. . . . In *giving* freedom to the *slave*, we *assure* freedom to the *free*. . . . [W]e must disenthrall ourselves, and then we shall save our country."[22]

Having indicated that Lincoln's eloquence in this passage was unsurpassed, he nevertheless *did* surpass himself nearly a year later in the prose poem of 272 words that we know as the Gettysburg Address. In this elegy for Union soldiers killed during the battle of Gettysburg, Lincoln wove together past, present, and future with two other sets of three images each: continent, nation, battlefield; and birth, death, rebirth. The Gettysburg Address is so familiar that, like other things one can recite from memory, its meaning sometimes loses its import. At the risk of destroying the speech's poetic qualities, let us disaggregate these parallel images of past, present, future; continent, nation, battlefield; and birth, death, rebirth. To do this will underscore the meaning of the Civil War not only for Lincoln's time but also for generations into the future, indeed for the new millennium we have just entered.

Four score and seven years in the *past,* said Lincoln, our fathers *brought forth* on this *continent* a *nation* conceived in liberty. *Today,* our generation faces a great test whether a nation so conceived can survive. In dedicating the cemetery on this *battlefield,* the living must take inspiration to finish the task that those who lie buried here so nobly advanced by giving their last full measure of devotion. Life and *death* in this passage have a paradoxical but metaphorical relationship: men died that the nation might live, yet metaphorically the old Union also died, and with it would die the institution of slavery. After these deaths the nation must have a *"new birth* of freedom" so that government of, by, and for the people "shall not perish from the earth" but live into the vast *future,* even unto the next millennium.

Although Lincoln gave this address at the dedication of a cemetery, its rhetoric was secular. As the war went on, however, Lincoln's efforts to come to grips with the mounting toll of death, destruction, and suffering became more infused with religious inquiry. Perhaps God was punishing Americans with "this terrible war" for some great sin. By the time of his inauguration for a second term, Lincoln believed he had identified that sin. "Fondly do we hope—fervently do we pray—that this mighty scourge of war may speedily pass away," said Lincoln in his Second Inaugural Address. "Yet, if God wills that it continue, until all the wealth piled up by the bondman's two hundred and fifty years of unrequited toil shall be sunk, and until every drop of blood drawn with the lash, shall be paid by another drawn with the sword, as was said three thousand years ago, so still it must be said 'the judgments of the Lord, are true and righteous altogether.'"[23]

Fortunately, the war lasted only another few weeks after Lincoln's second inauguration. In this new millennium one may well wonder if we are still paying for the blood drawn with the lash of slavery. But the consequences abroad of Union victory were almost immediate. In Britain a disgruntled Tory member of Parliament expressed disappointment that the Union had not broken in "two or perhaps more fragments," for he considered the United States "a menace to the whole civilized world." A Tory colleague described this menace as "the beginning of an Americanizing process in England. The new Democratic ideas are gradually to find embodiment." Indeed they were. In 1865 a liberal political economist at University College London, Edward Beesly, who wanted the expansion of voting rights in Britain, pointed out the moral of Union victory across the Atlantic. "Our opponents told us that Republicanism was on trial" in the American Civil War, he said. "They insisted on our watching what they called its breakdown. They told us that it was forever discredited in England. Well, we accepted the challenge. We staked or hopes boldly upon the result. . . . Under a strain such as no aristocracy, no monarchy, no empire could have supported, Republican institutions have stood firm. It is we, now, who call upon the privileged classes to mark the result. . . . A vast impetus has been given to Republican sentiments in England."[24]

Queen Victoria's throne was safe. But a two-year debate in Parliament, in which the American example figured prominently, led to the enactment of the Reform Bill of 1867, which nearly doubled the electorate and enfranchised a large part of the British working class for the first time. With this act, the world's most powerful nation took a long stride toward democracy. What might have happened to the Reform Bill if the North had lost the Civil War, thereby confounding liberals and confirming Tory opinions of democracy, is impossible to say.

The end of slavery in the re-United States sounded the death knell of the institution in Brazil and Cuba, the only other places in the Western Hemisphere where it still existed. Commending the Brazilian government's first steps toward emancipation in 1871, an abolitionist in that country was glad, as he put it, "to see Brazil receive so quickly the moral of the Civil War in the United States."[25]

Even without northern victory in the Civil War, slavery in the United States, Brazil, and Cuba would have been unlikely to survive into the next millennium. But it might well have survived into the next century. And without the Fourteenth and Fifteenth Amendments to the Constitution, which like the Thirteenth were a direct consequence of the war and which granted equal civil and political rights to African Americans, the United States might have developed into even more of an apartheid society in the twentieth century than it did.

These amendments consummated a new interpretation of liberty in the American polity, an interpretation that may be the most important legacy of the Civil War for the new millennium. Lincoln played a crucial role in the evolution of this new concept of liberty. In April 1864 he chose the occasion of a public speech in Baltimore to define the difference between two meanings of this word so central to America's understanding of itself. "The world has never had a good definition of the word liberty," Lincoln declared in this state that still had slavery but was about to abolish it. "We all declare for liberty, but in using the same *word* we do not mean the same *thing*. With some the word liberty may mean for each man to do as he pleases with himself, and the product of his labor; while with others the same may mean for some men to do as they please with other men, and the product of other men's labors. Here are two, not only different, but incompatible things, called by the same name . . . , liberty." As he often did, Lincoln went on to illustrate his point with a parable. One of the first books he had read as a child was *Aesop's Fables,* and throughout his life Lincoln told apparently simple stories about animals to make subtle and profound points about important matters. "The shepherd drives the wolf from the sheep's throat," he said, "for which the sheep thanks the shepherd as a *liberator,* while the wolf denounces him for the same act as a destroyer of liberty, especially as the sheep is a black one. Plainly the sheep and the wolf are not agreed upon a definition of the word liberty; and precisely the same difference prevails to-day among us human creatures, even in the North, and all professing to love liberty. Hence we behold the processes by which thousands are daily passing from under the yoke of bondage, hailed by some as the advance of liberty, and bewailed by others as the destruction of all liberty."[26]

The shepherd in this fable was, of course, Lincoln himself; the black sheep was the slave, and the wolf his owner. The point of the fable was similar to a barbed comment Lincoln had made a decade earlier about southern rhetoric professing a love of liberty. "The perfect liberty they sigh for," said Lincoln on that occasion, "is the liberty of making slaves of other people."[27] More subtly, Lincoln in this parable was drawing a distinction between what the late philosopher Isaiah Berlin described as "negative liberty" and "positive liberty."[28] The concept of negative liberty is perhaps more familiar. It can be defined as the absence of restraint, a freedom from interference by outside authority with individual thought or behavior. Laws requiring automobile passengers to wear seatbelts or motorcyclists to wear helmets are a violation of their liberty to go without seatbelts or helmets. Negative liberty, therefore, is best described as freedom *from.* Positive liberty can be defined as freedom *to*—freedom to live longer and better because wearing a seatbelt or helmet has saved one from death or injury.

The example of freedom of the press perhaps provides a better illustration. This freedom is usually understood as a negative liberty—freedom from interference with what a writer writes or a reader reads. But an illiterate person suffers from a denial of positive liberty. He is unable to enjoy the freedom to read and write whatever he pleases, not because some authority prevents him from doing so, but because he cannot read or write anything. The remedy lies not in the removal of restraint but in achievement of the capacity to read and write.

Another way of defining the difference between these two concepts of liberty is to describe their relation to power. Negative liberty and power are at opposite poles; power is the enemy of liberty, especially power in the hands of a central government. Negative liberty was the preeminent concern of Americans in the eighteenth and first half of the nineteenth century. Many feared the federal government as the main threat to individual liberty; some still do today. Americans fought their Revolution against the overweening power of king and Parliament. In the Constitution they fragmented power among the three branches of the federal government, between the two houses of Congress, and between the national and state governments. But even this was not enough, in James Madison's words, to prevent the "tendency in all Governments to an augmentation of power at the expense of liberty."[29] So the founders wrote a Bill of Rights that, as the first ten amendments to the Constitution, impose limits on the power of the federal government.

Throughout early American history, political leaders remained vigilant against concentrations of power. Andrew Jackson vetoed the charter renewal of the Second Bank of the United States in 1832 because, he said, such a combination of private wealth and government power would cause "our liberties to be crushed." In 1854 the famous reformer of mental hospitals Dorothea Dix persuaded Congress to pass a bill granting public lands to the states to subsidize improved facilities for the mentally ill. Pres. Franklin Pierce vetoed the bill because, he wrote in his veto message, if Congress cold enact such a law, "it has the power to provide for the indigent who are not insane, and thus . . . the whole field of public beneficence is thrown open to the care and culture of the Federal Government." This would mean "all sovereignty vested in an absolute consolidated central power, against which the spirit of liberty has so often and in so many countries struggled in vain." Therefore, a law to improve mental health hospitals, concluded Pierce, would be "the beginning of the end . . . of our blessed inheritance of representative liberty."[30]

Owners of slaves also relied on this bulwark of negative liberty to defend their right of property in human beings. John C. Calhoun and other southern political leaders constructed an elaborate structure of state sovereignty and limitations on national power. No exercise of federal power escaped the censure of these proslavery libertarians. As Sen. Nathaniel Macon of North Carolina explained, "If Congress can make banks, roads, and canals under the Constitution, they can free slaves in the United States."[31]

The ultimate manifestation of negative liberty was secession. Southern states left the Union in 1861 because they feared that sometime in the future the growing northern antislavery majority embodied in the Republican party would exercise its power to free the slaves—a form of positive liberty that might even go so far as to empower them to read and write, to vote, and to aspire to equality with whites—a truly frightening scenario of positive liberty. Yet ironically, by seceding and provoking a war, southern whites hastened the very achievement of positive liberty they had gone to war to prevent. By 1864, when Lincoln told his parable about the shepherd protecting the black sheep from the wolf, that shepherd wielded a very big staff as commander in chief of the largest army yet known in the United States. It took every ounce of this power to accomplish the "new birth of freedom" that Lincoln invoked at Gettysburg.

Tragically, Lincoln did not live to oversee advancement toward that goal. His earlier definition of equality as a "maxim for free society . . . even though never perfectly attained . . . , constantly labored for . . . , and thereby constantly spreading and deepening its influence, and augmenting the happiness and value of life to all people of al colors" suggests the policies of positive liberty he would have pursued had he lived. But at Ford's Theater, John Wilkes Booth ended that possibility as he shouted Virginia's state motto: "*sic semper tyrannis*" (thus always to tyrants)—the slogan of negative liberty.

Lincoln's party carried on the tradition of positive liberty with its efforts to legislate and enforce equal civil rights, voting rights, and education during Reconstruction. As Republican congressman George Julian noted in 1867, the only way to achieve "justice and equality . . . for the freedmen of the South" was by "the strong arm of *power,* outstretched from the central authority here in Washington." Or as Congressman James Garfield, a future Republican president, put it also in 1867, "we must plant the heavy hand of . . . authority upon these rebel communities, and . . . plant liberty on the ruins of slavery."[32]

That is what the Thirteenth, Fourteenth, and Fifteenth Amendments to the Constitution tried to do. These amendments radically transformed the thrust of the Constitution from negative to positive liberty. Instead of the straitjacket of "thou shalt nots" imposed on the federal government by the Bill of Rights, the Civil War amendments established a precedent whereby nine of the next fourteen Constitutional amendments contained the phrase "Congress shall have the *power*" to enforce the provisions. Lincoln himself set this precedent by helping draft the Thirteenth Amendment, which was the centerpiece of the platform on which he was reelected in 1864.

Lincoln's party continued its commitment to positive liberty at least through the presidency of Theodore Roosevelt. In the twentieth century, however, the two major parties gradually reversed positions. The Democratic party, once the bastion of negative liberty, states' rights, and limited government, donned the mantle of positive liberty, while most Republicans invoked the mantra of negative liberty. How these matters will play out in the new millennium remains to be seen. But whatever happens, Lincoln's legacy of one nation, indivisible, with freedom for four million slaves and their descendants, seems likely to persist far into the millennium.

A few years ago the Huntington Library sponsored an essay contest on Lincoln for high-school students in connection with its major Lincoln exhibit. One of the finalists was a seventeen-year-old girl from Texas whose forebears had immigrated to the United States from India. She wrote that "if the United States was not in existence today, I would not have the opportunity to excel in life and education. The Union was preserved, not only for the people yesterday, but also for the lives of today."[33]

Lincoln would surely have applauded this statement. In 1861 he said that the struggle for the Union involved not only "the fate of these United States" but also "the whole family of man." It was a struggle "not altogether for today" but "for a vast future also." We are living in that vast future. Lincoln's words resonate in the twenty-first century with as much relevance as they did seven score years ago.

III

THE FRUITS OF VICTORY

*The Enduring Significance of the
American Civil War*

9

CIVIL-MILITARY RELATIONS AND THE LEGACY OF THE CIVIL WAR

Brian Holden Reid

The exact nature of the effects of war—the "impacts of war" in John Terraine's apt phrase—is one of the perennial issues confronting historians. "The impacts of war are limitless, and in many respects unfathomable," contends Terraine. The effect of the First World War on British society, for example, is a subject of considerable discussion. Did it profoundly alter society or did it merely confirm and accentuate developments that had already begun to make their influence felt before 1914? In recent years historians have gradually arrived at a consensus that emphasizes continuity with the prewar years rather than sudden and dramatic change brought about by the war itself. The First World War parallels the Civil War in this way, for if developments in civil-military relations are reviewed, it is striking how little changes in the American experience after 1865. The tenor of civil-military relations after 1865 was very largely what it was before 1861. Civil-military controversies also tended to revolve around similar issues, not least the relationship between the general in chief and the secretary of war after 1861 as well as the nature of the organizations and structures within which these and other leaders had to work. The Civil War obviously bequeathed an enormous legacy in terms of thinking about war and the nature of its future patterns; this has received considerable attention from historians, although the link between military thinking and practice is notoriously difficult to define precisely. The influence of the Civil War on American military institutions has received rather less attention.[1]

When tackling the nature of the Civil War's legacy in the area of civil-military relations, a fundamental paradox must be confronted at the outset, namely, that the Civil War represents a massive upheaval yet seems to have bequeathed little in the way of structural change or innovation. This is equally true of the civilian agencies that directed the armed forces, including the Army Department itself. Such a paradox raises a further question: does the Civil War—or any war—really promote institutional change? Prolonged warfare can certainly foster changes in the climate of ideas and attitudes that might serve as an important first step in the complex process of reform. But a desire for change is quite a different matter from actually carrying out a program and fostering a large measure of agreement and support for it. The reform of military institutions demands careful planning, deep thought, and careful consideration.

In elucidating this theme, the author enjoys the advantage of himself being personally involved in the doctrinal changes in the British army during 1987–97. The main lesson that accrues from this experience (or any other) is that it requires skilful maneuver and forethought to ensure the passage and acceptance of changes to ideas cherished by the military, which have long-established basic structures and approaches to organization. It was certainly the experience of the U.S. Army after 1865 that the challenges of peace pushed aside war-orientated reform. The army returned to its role of frontier constabulary after subduing the South. Its formations were organized around a series of frontier posts; its columns were tiny, and as a result there was no need to train sizeable formations of troops together in large numbers or conduct sizeable exercises; and consequently, there was no need to develop doctrinal publications for large-scale operations. Perhaps there was something faintly "un-American" about the practice of drawing up doctrinal pamphlets. The Leavenworth series of doctrinal publications that began appearing after 1891 were concerned with minor tactics. Clearly, the role designed for the U.S. Army after 1865, that is, the agreed policy stating what it was actually *for,* would determine any overall approach to preparing it for any future conflict. This role would also govern the attitudes of politicians toward its utility.[2]

Historians writing fairly soon after the end of the Second World War tended to argue that the Civil War had ushered in important innovations. Such an approach continued to enjoy widespread accord until the late 1960s. T. Harry Williams's superbly written, forcefully argued, and widely read book *Lincoln and His Generals* (1952) was a seminal work. He claims that the command arrangements arrived at after the appointment of Lt. Gen. Ulysses S. Grant as general in chief in March 1864 "gave the United States a modern system of command for a modern war. It was superior to anything achieved in Europe until [Field Marshal Helmuth] von Moltke forged the Prussian staff machine of 1866 and 1870." Grant's predecessor, Maj. Gen. Henry W. Halleck, was retained as chief of staff, carrying much of the administrative burden of organizing the far-flung Union armies. Maj. Gen. William T. Sherman commanded the Military Division of the Mississippi, comprising all troops deployed in the West. Competent and dynamic figures were at long last in all the key positions. The president, Abraham Lincoln, who had previously been forced to intervene in military affairs at all levels, could now allow his generals to go ahead and win the war while maintaining a close supervision of the strategy they employed. There was, in any case, close agreement between Lincoln and Grant on the need for the Union to deploy a remorseless attritional strategy against the Confederacy, exploiting the North's material and numerical superiority by mounting concentric offensives on exterior lines.[3]

Williams's argument was developed during the 1960s in several directions by his pupil Stephen E. Ambrose. In his study of Halleck, Ambrose illustrates the formal working relationship between the general in chief and the chief of staff (Grant and Halleck), on the one hand, and the close personal relations between Halleck and his friend Sherman, on the other. In the autumn of 1861 Halleck had protected Sherman from both himself and the press (which had described Sherman as "mad") when the latter suffered a nervous breakdown. Sherman was not only personally indebted to Halleck but also owed his subsequent successful military career to him. Ambrose characterizes the resulting command organization of 1864–65 as "a practical rather than a theoretical one. The command system became a loose, working arrangement that could change for an emergency." In making the system adaptable, Halleck made an important contribution. By assuming so much of the administrative work, he allowed Grant to take the field in the spring of 1864, accompanying the Army of the Potomac, commanded by Maj. Gen. George G. Meade, during its advance toward the Confederate capital, Richmond, Virginia. Further, Sherman too was able to take the field and advance on Atlanta, knowing that Halleck would oversee the administrative affairs of his military division. Ambrose lists among Halleck's activities the distribution of reinforcements, offering advice to field commanders, the supervision of supply lines, and the coordination of military and political agencies, including the president. He also made operational digests of dispatches from field commanders for Grant and served as military liaison to the president. Ambrose is more cautious in his claims for the system than Williams, but he still adheres to the basic thesis adumbrated by his mentor, namely that the Civil War witnessed the "beginnings of a modern command system."[4]

In the development of his thesis, however, Ambrose concedes several important points. First, he admits that the entire system was dependent on personalities and not structures. Second, other, more subordinate commanders found their relationships less congenial than those prevailing at the top of the command chain, and the system at those levels worked less well. Ambrose cites the example of Grant's decision to dismiss Maj. Gen. George H. Thomas in December 1864 on the eve of his great victory at the battle of Nashville. Grant had disliked him since October 1863, when Grant had assumed command at Chattanooga and received a very frosty reception from Thomas and his staff. In addition, he had received throughout the spring and summer of 1864 a series of critical reports from Sherman during the Atlanta campaign complaining about Thomas's slowness. Under such circumstances the system fell back on what Ambrose terms (but does not analyze as) "its inherent checks and balances."[5]

Ambrose fails to point out several other weaknesses of the system. Some of the duties that Halleck undertook should have been carried out by Grant's own chief of staff, John A. Rawlins. The system was overlapping and not correctly geared at the appropriate level of command. Ambrose stresses throughout his study that Halleck's main contribution to the Union victory was as an administrator. His skill in this regard represented a major step forward "from the 18th century limited war to modern, total war." Yet Ambrose fails to appreciate that under modern general-staff systems, the chief of the general staff is *not* primarily an administrator, he coordinates grand strategy. He is most certainly not subordinate to the field commanders (as Halleck was to Grant), and whatever their titles, Grant and Sherman essentially were field commanders. Finally, in Ambrose's interpretation of the 1864–65 structure, politicians (a particular *bête noire* of Halleck) were almost completely eradicated. He stresses "Lincoln's withdrawal from the picture." The president trusted his military advisers "so implicitly that he voluntarily reduced himself to exercising only an occasional veto."[6]

The argument concerning the place of administration in the direction of modern war continues to be made. For instance, John Y. Simon has claimed that Halleck's appointment as chief of staff "separated strategic command from administration, a crucial innovation in modern warfare." Modern command systems do not actually make such a distinction. The claim might have more validity if Halleck had presided over an institutionalized general staff, which he did not. In any event, the argument that the Union command system was in some important respects "modern" leads to an emphasis on its specifically military features. Williams, for instance, concedes that Halleck "was not completely a chief of staff in the modern sense. Primarily he was a channel of communication between Lincoln and Grant and between Grant and the departmental commanders." When such importance is attached to the military dimension, there is a danger that the political character of the command arrangement can be overlooked. In 1864 Grant's freedom of action was restricted by Lincoln's desire for reelection. Within the crucial Virginia theater, which Grant (coming from the West) was initially inclined to underrate, he was prepared to give important subordinate commands to generals such as Benjamin F. Butler and Franz Sigel. Even in the West he acquiesced in the unfortunate Red River campaign, directed by Maj. Gen. Nathaniel P. Banks. All three were "political generals" who would exert great sway over the electoral process, and Lincoln could not afford to alienate them by agreeing to relieve any of command. Brooks D. Simpson goes so far as to suggest that "what made the command team work was Grant's grasp of the political concerns of his civilian superior." There might be a lot of truth in this, but such a view should not, in its turn, obscure the faulty military aspects of the system that were exacerbated by political machinations.[7]

Whatever the standpoint taken on how "modern" the command system was, there can be no question that it actually worked. In the first instance, the use of the presidential war powers provided a more efficient focus for organizing strategy and the war effort than would have been possible from other likely sources of possible direction, namely Congress. Executive command embodied by one man is invariably more efficient than the deliberations of committees. Here Lincoln excelled, and his eventual choice of generals revealed shrewdness in weighing up what was required of a successful commander at the highest level. The enormous increase in presidential power and patronage (especially military) that accrued after 1861 reversed the dominance of Congress, which was so notable during the 1850s. The use of the war powers, however, could not be sanctioned after the end of the Civil War. Moreover, a major role for the army could not be justified by initiatives resulting from U.S. foreign policy such as, for example, the possibility of war with France over Mexico in 1866. Grant urged this course on a reluctant Johnson administration in 1866, but to no avail. As the president's war powers fell into disuse, the result was a major congressional counterattack that reestablished during Reconstruction the sway of the legislature over policymaking. In any case, Lincoln's successor as president, Andrew Johnson, lacked either his prestige or his tactical skill. In sum, the growth of presidential power during the Civil War did not lead to any substantial institutional change. After 1865, executive-legislative relations were very much what they were before 1861, with a series of presidents who took a limited view of the prerogatives of their office.[8]

The second reason for the success of Lincoln's system was that it represented a happy conjunction of personalities. Lincoln himself had a rare gift for not personalizing political disputes and seemed to work at his best when surrounded by men of a similar timbre. Lincoln trusted Grant. Grant and Sherman had become close friends since the spring of 1862 (indeed George Thomas, who had been Sherman's roommate at West Point, showed his jealousy of this intimacy rather too openly). Sherman and Halleck were close friends, at least until April 1865. (Sherman felt aggrieved that Halleck had taken Secretary of War Edwin Stanton's side in the controversy resulting from the discredited armistice terms Sherman had negotiated with Gen. Joseph E. Johnston at Durham Station, North Carolina; thereafter, he never spoke to Halleck again.) This general harmony was no small achievement when the atmosphere in the Union command system in 1864–65 is compared with the constant feuding to be found in the higher echelons of the U.S. command structure before 1861. Winfield Scott, general in chief, had lent the U.S. officer corps a querulous tone. He contrived to feud with every other senior general in the U.S. Army. Scott's conduct of the Mexican War (1846–48) had also been marked by a series of bitter quarrels, culminating in a final eruption after the fall of Mexico City in 1847–48 when he had Gideon Pillow, William Worth, and James Duncan arrested. Eventually, Scott himself was relieved in June 1848, and his handling of matters was examined by a court of inquiry, which exonerated his subordinates.[9]

The Confederate command system was also wracked by quarrels between generals, which were often very petty and personal. Two cases in point were the feuds between two generals, P. G. T. Beauregard and Joseph E. Johnston, and the Confederate president, Jefferson Davis. Johnston was aided and abetted by Sen. Louis T. Wigfall, the Davis administration's most persistent critic. The alliance between Johnston and Wigfall is deemed by Craig Symonds to be responsible for "the erosion of the command relationship within the Confederacy, a relationship weakened if not destroyed by Davis's political foes." It might be added that a lack of a party political mechanism resulted in a sharpening of personal spite among all the parties concerned.[10]

Personal antagonisms were not so marked, or at any rate less damaging, on the Union side. Further, since Lincoln trusted Grant, the president gave his general in chief the authority he needed to see his strategy through to a victorious conclusion. More particularly, Lincoln resolved the perennial dispute between the general in chief and the secretary of war over who enjoyed the authority to issue orders to the heads of the bureaus, coming down in Grant's favor. Such disputes had reached acrimonious (and incredibly petty) levels during the Pierce administration (1853–57), when Scott quarreled with Jefferson Davis and then took himself off in a huff to New York City. The U.S. Army appeared to function quite well without him, for he did not return to Washington until after the secession of South Carolina in December 1860. The difficulty for any general in chief was that his rank was not sanctioned by the Constitution and that his role was unclear. In 1861–62 while general in chief, George B. McClellan had made inroads against the precedent established by Davis (of issuing orders directly to the chief engineer or the quartermaster general) under the incompetent regime of Secretary of War Simon Cameron. But Cameron's irascible and dynamic replacement, Edwin M. Stanton, soon began to restore the prerogatives of his office, and this led to a series of disputes with McClellan.[11]

Stanton won this battle, and further he gained authority by securing control over the telegraph network. Progress had been made before 1861 to connect the secretary of war with all the military departments from the Potomac to the Gulf of Mexico and the Pacific Ocean. The network had been set up by Col. Anson Stager (a previous general superintendent of the Western Union Telegraph Company). Stager and his civilian operators came under the control of the Quartermaster General Department. The senior signals officer, Maj. Albert J. Myers, also enjoyed the enthusiastic support of McClellan. Cameron had shortsightedly issued an order that all telegrams should be sent to the general in chief, thus cutting the secretary of war himself out of the business of fighting the war and leaving him merely as a spectator, involved only in the preparations for any campaigns that McClellan might decide to mount. Stanton ordered the telegraph office to be transferred from McClellan's headquarters to the War Department. McClellan complained bitterly that Stanton was trying to combine the offices of secretary of war and general in chief. Indeed, Stanton had done much to break McClellan's monopoly over the making of strategy. Stanton was thus able to exert a tenacious grip over all military communications and release of information to the newspapers. He also gained an additional bonus by making this bold move. By concentrating telegraphic communication in the War Department, Stanton gained more of the president's attention than any other of his cabinet colleagues. Lincoln spent much time in the telegraph office; not only was this the first point of arrival for reports from the front but it also offered the president peace and quiet, respite from so many importunate callers. On February 26, 1862, with the endorsement of the chairman of the Joint Committee on the Conduct of the War, Sen. Benjamin F. Wade, Congress passed legislation permitting the president to take control of the entire telegraph network and allowing untrammeled use when it was required. Stager, and not McClellan's protégé Myers, was named the "supervisor [or] military superintendent of all telegraphic lines and offices in the United States."[12]

Stanton's relations with Halleck appear to have been quite amicable because the latter sought to coordinate, not direct, let alone command. In 1864 with Grant, it was quite another matter, for the general in chief intended to take the field rather than spend long hours gossiping in the Byzantine and circuitous corridors of power in Washington, D.C. The president appreciated how high the stakes were in the spring of 1864. He needed to end the war by the summer to ensure his renomination and reelection. Moreover, Lincoln recognized that Grant enjoyed a level of prestige not held by any American commander since George Washington and did not have to prove himself. Lincoln told Stanton simply to "leave him [Grant] alone to do as he pleases." No previous general in chief had enjoyed this measure of authority.[13]

Yet these structural changes in the command system were not enduring and certainly not confirmed by any kind of legislation. In September 1863 Halleck had enjoyed the services of twenty-three officers and men, and this number did not increase dramatically after March 1864. Grant had his own chief of staff and fourteen staff officers. No general staff was created to act as a buffer against civilian "interference" or to give the regular army a sense of esprit de corps and a professional edge. Of course, if such an institution had been created, there would have been no need for a general in chief, whose authority, in any case, remained vague and his position anomalous. After 1865 the problem of relations between the general in chief and the secretary of war recurred. Stanton began to reclaim authority over the bureau heads in 1866. At one point the dispute with Grant became so heated that the general decided to postpone a visit to Louisiana, Mississippi, and Texas after Grant's issue of General Orders No. 3 in January 1866 to protect soldiers, loyalists, and federal employees from southern violence. The legacy of the war years was rather confused by Grant's assumption of the portfolio of secretary of war for a short period in 1867–68 while remaining general in chief. Grant and Andrew Johnson soon quarreled over the president's desire to replace those generals who were zealously implementing congressional legislation on Reconstruction (including Philip H. Sheridan and Daniel E. Sickles). Grant took the robust view that as general in chief he was responsible for enforcing the provisions of the Third Reconstruction Act of July 1867. This was a role that the general in chief had never assumed before, but Grant's relationship with both the president and Congress was complicated at that time by his simultaneously serving as secretary of war. Grant was also perturbed to discover that the legislation did not explicitly name the general in chief as the officer entrusted to enforce the provisions of the act. Such an omission merely confirmed the longstanding ambiguity of the rank, even when its holder was also secretary of war.[14]

After Grant was elected president and during his first administration (1869–73), Stanton's success in enhancing the power of the secretary of war over the staff bureaus was completed by William W. Belknap. Sherman had succeeded Grant as general in chief in 1869, but he was pushed to the margins of military affairs by Belknap—even though Sherman too had served briefly as interim secretary of war (combining both the civil and military posts) after the death of Grant's original nominee, John A. Rawlins. Although a former soldier himself, Grant could not side politically with his old friend. Indeed, it seems to have been a high priority of Grant's administration to assert unequivocal civilian control over the military in all matters. In May 1874 Sherman moved to St Louis (as Scott had moved to New York City) and, glad to be away from the overheated political atmosphere of Washington, D.C., busied himself with inspecting frontier outposts and writing his *Memoirs* (published in two volumes in 1875). Sherman was aware of the parallel with Scott's experience, but he refused to contest Belknap's growing stranglehold over appointments and administration or seek political allies. Instead, Sherman excoriated his political masters and complained that these were his "years of frustration" by being reduced to "a nobody" who held a "mere sinecure" and thus lacked the slightest authority to influence policy and appointments. Yet the leisure that Sherman enjoyed allowed him to reflect in his *Memoirs* on the "lessons" of the Civil War. Very few Civil War commanders attempted to appraise systematically the long-term effect of their own experiences.[15]

Strong parallels are certainly evident in the tenures of Scott and Sherman as commanding generals. Yet if stress is placed on continuity in civil-military relationships, such an argument should not be pressed so forcefully that it obscures another important and parallel feature, namely that after such a momentous event as the Civil War, nothing would ever be quite the same again. The war years had led to an eclipse of the regular army as it was swamped by a huge number of volunteers. Significant commands were given to a host of important politicians, including (in addition to those mentioned above) John C. Frémont, Francis P. Blair Jr., John A. McClernand, and John A. Logan. All of these men were beholden to the administration and thus supposedly obliged to support it. However much regular officers criticized their appointment, "political generals" were an unavoidable part of the Civil War military scene. The need to reckon with the influence of politics on the making of strategy during the war represented another important legacy bequeathed by the Civil War generation. Their experience forced the leaders of the postwar regular army to refine and rationalize the American military system. It should be designed, they argued, to reduce the amount of damage that could be inflicted on the American capacity to make war by the appointment of untrained politicians to the highest echelons of command. In short, the Civil War provided the regular army with a renewed faith in its professional direction, which had not been evident before 1861. It also conferred something even more important. Commanders in the postwar period did not simply complain about the activities of politicians, as say Halleck did. Sherman and his successors as commanding general, Philip H. Sheridan and John M. Schofield, brought from their own experiences of the Civil War a strong sense of obligation to civilian society. They grasped that the regular army enjoyed an intimate relationship with its parent society. This understanding transcended their frustrations at the hands of individual politicians.

To place these important developments in their proper context, the state of the U.S. Army in the period 1865–77 must be reviewed. In 1867 the army was three times the size of what it had been in 1860; the officer corps was 258 percent larger. The numbers of regiments had been increased from nineteen to forty-five infantry and six to ten cavalry. Nonetheless, the staff departments remained untouched and operated independently. But the enlarged officer corps had witnessed important changes. Perhaps the most notable was the great increase in the number of volunteers and ex-rankers and the reduction of graduates of the U.S. Military Academy entering the service. Indeed, by 1867 the number of West Point graduates had slumped to only 23 percent of the entire officer corps, while wartime volunteers counted for 39.7 percent and ex-rankers 37.5 percent. Although West Point graduates would increase to 35.4 percent of all officers by 1877, the main feature of the overall outlook of the U.S. Army was shaped by the experience of the Civil War.

The stress on experience, especially in a conflict as challenging and destructive as the Civil War, contributed signally to the rather anti-intellectual atmosphere that prevailed after 1865. By writing his own *Memoirs,* Sherman sought to stimulate some new thought about old military issues. In the eyes of many self-made military men and veterans of the Civil War, study of war was superfluous. Veterans of the war might compare their experiences, but this was too frequently tinged by the hyperbole of reminiscence. War did not need study; to practice it effectively only required experience. One young officer wrote of his seniors that they "were tottering around in their dotage . . . [and] hadn't learned anything during the Civil War or since." Yet the Civil War had ushered in change. The military occupation of the South, for instance, was a novel test for the U.S. Army, absorbing in the years 1865–77 some 15–40 percent of its total strength.[16]

The emphasis placed by Congress on Reconstruction, which involved a large military commitment, contributed to the revival of plans for reform of the army. Sherman believed that only by strengthening the officer corps could progress be made. No precise vision of the future of the U.S. Army was possible because the threat of foreign war was remote. (For the next thirty years at least, the United States enjoyed unprecedented security from foreign attack.) The visit of Sheridan to France in 1869–70 at the time of the Franco-Prussian War and Sherman's trip to Europe in 1872 were important catalysts in shaping their views on reform. Both concluded that the U.S. Army could not absorb Prussian methods indiscriminately. Although Sherman was impressed by Helmuth von Moltke and his staff, he thought the Prussian system was "exactly adapted to their natural traditions, temperament, and moral and political organization."[17]

The whole thrust of Sherman's career hitherto brought him to the conclusion, as he hastened to inform Sheridan on his return to the United States, that "The conditions of our country, the smallness of our army the jealousy of civilians and mistrust of our authorities make our situation so different from anything abroad that I do not see that we can do any good by comparison with the military experience of others."[18] Sherman's *Memoirs* reveal that he was firmly of the opinion that the Civil War had established the pattern for future conflict. Thereafter, war would revolve around the war of entire nations; a peoples' war would be waged with mass armies and would recognize no limitation. Future wars would thus be cruel and conducted without respite until one side or the other gained a complete victory. The huge armies of the Civil War, Sherman maintained, had shown impressive qualities. He argued that in any future conflict, "a higher order of intelligence and courage on the part of the individual soldier will be an element of strength."[19]

In 1872 Sherman declared that the U.S. Army should serve as a school for the nation. West Point, an institution of which Sherman was very proud, had always served this function. In the 1870s the army as a whole would undertake the task. As Sherman wrote, "the Army should be a school that can at will infuse into the masses of volunteers and militia a spirit that shall leven [sic] the whole people into the regular army."[20] When he expanded on this theme in his *Memoirs,* the link Sherman drew between education and improvement ran to the very core of his philosophy of life. He had already established the political context for his intended reforms; in the *Memoirs* he forged the next link. The U.S. Army should always be "subject to the control of Congress," yet "for the very reason that our army is comparatively so very small, I hold that it should be the very best possible, organized and governed on true military principles, and that in time of peace we should preserve the 'habits and usages of war' so that, when war does come, we may not again be compelled to suffer the disgrace, confusion and disorder of 1861."[21]

Following the resignation of his enemy, Belknap, in 1876 after a scandal in which the secretary of war was accused of taking bribes from traders at U.S. Army posts, Sherman's public statements took on a more optimistic tone. On returning to Washington in March 1876, his relations with Belknap's successors, Alfonso Taft, and Rutherford B. Hayes's secretary of war, James D. Cameron, were more amicable and constructive. Taft agreed to accept Sherman's advice and further, that all the War Department's orders "shall be promulgated through the General of the Army"—although the staff bureaus still remained independent of that officer's authority.[22] "Our army is small and intended to be a school of instruction," Sherman would write in his Report to the Secretary of War in 1879. "The whole theory and practice of Government of the United States, has been, and continues to be, that the Regular Army must be small, as small as possible, and that for great occasions we as a people must rely on the volunteer masses of soldiery. No class of men better recognize this than the Regular Army, and as the science of war is progressive, we must keep pace with it, so as to impart to the volunteer militia, on the shortest notice, all that is known of the art and science of war up to the moment of execution. In this sense the whole Regular Army is a school."[23] To this end, Sherman wished to reintroduce fifty years later John C. Calhoun's plan, first mooted when the South Carolinian was secretary of war in 1820, for an "expansible army." In peace the U.S. Army would be prepared for the harsh challenges of war.[24]

This whole ambitious conception rested on Sherman's interpretation of the "lessons" of the Civil War and a clear understanding of the limitations of the political context in which he was forced to operate. He was realistic in assuming that, "for the near future," the U.S. Army would have to depend "on *'volunteers'* which I construe our Regular Army to be in fact." The course at West Point was revitalized and given a stronger military (as opposed to technical) thrust. In May 1881 Fort Leavenworth opened as a new school of application, which would ultimately assume the mantle of a general-staff college.[25]

Given Sherman's volatile temperament, not least his choleric temper, the manner in which he mastered his prejudices was laudable. He advanced a sensible program of reform that took into account the complex and often shifting moods of civil-military relations. He had more political sense than is often attributed to him. Sherman's experience, furthermore, illustrates the paradox that, in some ways, the Civil War had a stultifying effect on military institutions yet, in many other significant ways, the military policy of the United States was irretrievably altered. Sherman had grasped the nature of these changed circumstances and gave the U.S. Army a facelift; but it was still recognizably the same institution. Political (and financial) pressures ensured that traditional approaches were not abandoned and that the army remained dedicated to traversing well-worn roads and circling around familiar landmarks. Sherman's schemes were prudent and halting. For example, he (and his immediate successors, Sheridan and Schofield) ignored the role of staff work in modern warfare. Sheridan admired the workings of the Prussian system, although he thought American staffs were superior logistically. George B. McClellan, who visited Europe in 1874, was another admirer of Moltke's methods. But both seem to have underrated the command dimensions of the Prussian general staff system. Moltke's "demi-gods" were junior officers (often majors) who were empowered to overrule nominal army commanders when ensuring that the orders of the chief of the general staff were carried out. During the second half of the nineteenth century, there was no attempt to address the weaknesses in American staff procedures until the manuscript of Emory Upton's *Military Policy of the United States* began circulating in the 1880s. Since Sherman in 1864–65 had operated as his own chief of staff, none of his reforms touched upon such structural and operational weaknesses in the U.S. Army. As the United States enjoyed untrammeled security during this period, perhaps the low priority afforded this was not surprising.[26]

Still, the roots of prevailing misconceptions about high command and the growing importance of administration and logistics in modern warfare lay in the experience of the Civil War itself. Much of value could be learned about both during the Civil War. Yet the failure of Sherman and Sheridan especially to understand the import of the general-staff revolution brought about by Moltke in 1866 and 1870–71 resulted in (whatever the talents of individuals) the levels of command within the U.S. Army remaining rather confused. The post of general in chief and its continuing place in the structure was consistently misunderstood by politicians. Halleck had complained of this in 1863. "The responsibility and odium thrown upon it does not belong to it." Lincoln's grumpy secretary of the navy, Gideon Welles, thought Halleck "incompetent." The gibe of Sen. Benjamin F. Wade illustrates how the place of the commanding general was not appreciated. Wade thought that Halleck should conduct himself like a superior army commander; this was how in 1864 Grant eventually interpreted his position. When Halleck remained in his office to work on his papers and reports, Wade snapped that if General Halleck had forty thousand men, he could not raise six sitting geese in a farmyard. Consequently, Halleck's role as coordinator and organizer was underrated, though not by Grant, who delegated much to him while retaining the final authority in his hands.[27]

Much of this confusion over the role of military leadership has to do with the cult of Napoleon in the United States. There are innumerable photographs of Civil War generals adopting Napoleonic poses; but what is so important about the influence of Napoleonic mythology during the Civil War was that it was no less influential among civilian politicians. The trouble with this model of military action was, first, that Napoleon eventually lost (an important fact that appears to have been frequently overlooked). Second, the Emperor Napoleon was a dictator who combined in his own person the position of head of state, general in chief, and army commander. Such a triple role only served to add to American confusion over what a commander in war should actually do. It also lent a rather peculiar, if not downright hypocritical, tone to the opposition by some generals to "political" interference in military affairs. For example, McClellan, a careful student of Napoleon, was deeply enmeshed in politics himself and its underhanded maneuvers (as a Democrat) at the very same time that he denounced similar maneuvers being carried out by his political masters (and rivals in the Republican party). Nor can there be any doubting the strong antidemocratic tone adopted by the so-called Young Napoleon in some of his private correspondence, not to mention the hints that he approved of what amounted to a Federalist revival on the part of "people of quality" during the years running up to the presidential election of 1864, in which he was the Democratic nominee.[28]

The Union (Republican) victory in the 1864 presidential election and the military victory of Grant the following year appeared to vindicate the volunteer and civilian character of U.S. armies. (The imposition of West Point standards—the ethos of the regular army—on later mass armies was the achievement of John J. Pershing and his protégé George S. Patton Jr.) The war also confirmed the importance of volunteer military service as an important path to executive office. The military hero—though a hero of a particular kind—as the presidential aspirant was triumphantly reaffirmed by the experience of 1861–65. Lincoln was nervous of appointing Grant as general in chief until he had received assurances that the general would not run for the presidency in 1864. That year Maj. Gen. William S. Rosecrans had received overtures from the Radical Republicans. In later years Sherman turned down several invitations from the Democrats to run on their ticket; in 1880 Maj. Gen. Winfield Scott Hancock accepted the nomination and was beaten by his Republican opponent, Rosecrans's former chief of staff James A. Garfield. As well as Garfield, Presidents Rutherford B. Hayes, Benjamin Harrison, and William McKinley traded skillfully on their wartime records as Civil War commanders.

In an influential article, "The Macs and the Ikes," T. Harry Williams establishes two models of military presidential aspirant: first, the "Macs"—the Scott–McClellan–Douglas MacArthur type—and second, the "Ikes"—the Zachary Taylor–Grant–Eisenhower type. Williams distinguishes between them on the grounds that "the Ike generals have exemplified militarily the ideal of our industrial, democratic civilization, which took shape in the nineteenth century; the Mac generals have represented militarily the standard of an older, more aristocratic society." Williams's distinction seems largely a question of style, yet the Civil War did tend to uphold the stereotype represented by Grant and Taylor, especially in appealing to the groundswell of persistent antiparty attitudes found in a society pervaded by party politics and strident partisanship.[29]

The position of Congress also must be taken into account. The Civil War is significant in underlining the immense importance of congressional contacts and connections with the press in ensuring promotion to the higher ranks of the U.S. Army. The president might put forward the names of deserving candidates, but Congress confirms them. The appointment of Nelson A. Miles as general in chief in October 1895 illustrates the importance of congressional contacts. Miles shamelessly exploited connection to the Sherman family—he married a daughter of Sen. John Sherman and thus could rely on the patronage of both his father-in-law and the bride's uncle, Gen. William T. Sherman (although the latter was suspicious of Miles and they did quarrel). He also allied himself with ambitious western politicians who were seeking nominations for territorial governorships. He was not a West Pointer but a Civil War volunteer, and this may explain some of the antagonism he provoked among regulars. Yet they also disapproved of Miles's extraordinary appetite for publicity, self-promotion, and power, compounded by conceit and self-absorption of quite staggering proportions. His uniform as general in chief was covered with such a profusion of decorations and gold braid that wags claimed, should a run on the American gold reserves occur, it could easily be rectified by melting down General Miles's uniform. Miles certainly did not discourage those who saw in him a man of presidential timber. His career would seem to indicate that T. Harry Williams's designation of the "Macs and Ikes" is perhaps rather too neat and schematic.[30]

As for the most important congressional agency produced during the Civil War, the Joint Committee on the Conduct of the War, its legacy was not a happy one. The committee was certainly successful before 1864 in cutting into the command structure of the army and eroding the chains that bound it together; high-ranking officers were often encouraged to take its part against their seniors. The divisions (and the rancor) its success promoted tended to run along party lines. Most of the members of the committee, and particularly its chairman throughout the war, Senator Wade, and his most zealous lieutenant, Sen. Zachariah Chandler of Michigan, were convinced that the Union war effort would be revitalized if Democratic officers promoted by George B. McClellan were replaced by good Republicans. Such pressure led to some significant changes of party allegiance. Ambrose E. Burnside had been a Democrat before 1861 and a close friend of McClellan; in November 1862 he made overtures to the committee and embraced the cause of emancipation with some enthusiasm. Thereafter he was a Republican in politics, serving first as governor of Rhode Island three times (1866–68) and then as senator (1874–81). After 1862 Burnside was treated by loyal acolytes of McClellan as an apostate.[31]

Yet the committee's very success in gaining the adherence of some senior officers worked against congressional influence in later American wars. Civil War armies were large, inchoate, and essentially volunteer forces not bound together very coherently by a clear-cut regular career structure. Opposition to future congressional influence came from two directions: those who wished to impose West Point standards on any future mass army, and representatives of the executive branch, who wanted to retain the direction of any war solely in the president's hands. In 1917–18, for instance, Woodrow Wilson resisted setting up a body comparable with the Joint Committee on the Conduct of the War, arguing that it would be a "millstone around my neck." Exploiting his own knowledge of American history and relying upon a historiographical consensus that the Civil War committee's activities were both intrusive and unfortunate, Wilson explained, "It was the cause of constant and distressing harassment and rendered Mr. Lincoln's task all but impossible." The Joint Committee on the Conduct of the War, in short, showed policymakers what not to do, and members of both houses of Congress agreed with this harsh verdict.

The lesson was taken very seriously. In 1943 Sen. Harry S. Truman was appointed to chair the Special Committee to Investigate the National Defense Program. Truman consulted copies of the Joint Committee on the Conduct of the War's special report in the Library of Congress. "I became familiar with its mistakes," he recalled, "and was determined to avoid the same errors in the conduct of my special committee." He rejected all calls to use the same techniques as the joint committee and interfere directly in operational questions and in the appointment of commanders. "Thank goodness," Truman consoled himself, "I knew my history and I wouldn't do it." When some years later as president Truman's decision to move four U.S. divisions to Europe after the outbreak of the Korean War was challenged by Republican senator Kenneth Wherry, Truman claimed that as commander in chief he could deploy troops without the prior approval of Congress. Another Republican, Arthur Vandenberg, agreed with the president. "We partially tried that system in the Civil War," he admitted, "when the Committee on the Conduct of the War set a tragic precedent against any such bitter mistake."[32]

The way the higher conduct of the Civil War was treated then, over half a century later, was to greatly enhance an interpretation of the war powers that enormously favored the executive branch. Lincoln faced very special circumstances that would not be encountered by any other president—what amounted to a flagrant rebellion against the power and legitimacy of the federal government. He was forced to act immediately. While Congress was in recess, he issued a series of proclamations. He called out the state militias, announced the blockade of the seceded states, suspended the writ of habeas corpus, and underwrote expenditures with presidential authority. This dynamic employment of presidential initiative, validated by the war power, was justified by the exigencies of the unprecedented crisis that Lincoln faced. Yet as a lawyer Lincoln entertained serious doubts about the legality of his actions. He did not believe that they served as a precedent to broaden the scope of executive authority. On the contrary, he was so anxious about the possible illegality his suspension of the writ of habeas corpus that he sought confirmation of his action by congressional statute. It is possible that Lincoln realized that the Founding Fathers were keen to limit the presidential power to make war. Lincoln's caution has not been shared by post-1945 presidents, who have claimed him as a symbolic role model and have succeeded in enhancing their authority over the armed forces at the expense of Congress.[33]

There was one further legacy of the Civil War, an enduring suspicion in military circles of all politicians, whether members of the executive or legislative branches. Not only were politicians blamed for the shameful unpreparedness that had crippled the U.S. government's capacity to wage the Civil War but also, by the 1880s, army officers chose to stand aloof from the political system—or at least made it look as if they did. Soldiers might not have been so "isolated" from the mainstream of American life as was once believed, but nonetheless a view was prevalent in the officer corps that West Point graduates especially were "innocent" of politics and its nefarious activities. If soldiers showed an interest in political affairs, then they excited the suspicions of their peers. For example, in 1894, attempts were made to damage Miles's chances of becoming commanding general upon Schofield's retirement the following year by suggesting that Miles intended to run for the presidency. This notion can be linked to the strong antiparty tradition that held sway before 1861 (and during the war itself), but its continuance distorted the way that American military history was interpreted for almost three-quarters of a century by deprecating the achievements of civilian volunteers. The most brilliant exponent of what might be termed the professional point of view was Bvt. Maj. Gen. Emory Upton. In the "Uptonian" tradition, the soldiers were always right and the politicians were always wrong.[34]

Thus, according to Upton and his followers, the blunders that had been witnessed during the Civil War were less the product of operational deficiencies than of policy errors committed by those who presided over the system—the politicians. For years Upton worked on an authoritative study that he hoped would expose the faulty assumptions and miscalculations upon which policymaking was so consistently based. Although unfinished upon Upton's suicide in 1881, his work, *The Military Policy of the United States,* was a devastating diatribe against civilian interference in military affairs and repeatedly denounced the resulting foolish blunders. Upton could hardly conceal his outrage at the muddle he exposed. To him the regulars could no wrong; the volunteers were always at fault. Consequently, the dominance of volunteers over regulars had contributed to the dangerous interference of civilians in the direction of armies in the field. Upton inveighed against "that defect of our laws which, contrary to the spirit of our institutions, tempted the president to assume the character and responsibilities of a military commander." He did not (and could not) admit that it was the weaknesses of the champion of American military professionalism, McClellan, that had forced Lincoln to so reluctantly take this action. Upton's unconvincing and one-sided interpretation of this issue indicated the extent to which politicians in his account had become the universal scapegoat for every military ill.[35]

The doctrine of civilian supremacy over the military, Upton believed, was the cause of much waste of advantageous opportunities and men's lives in the indecisive campaigns of 1862. "Although constitutional Commander in Chief, he [Lincoln] did not and could not solve the military problems of the war." Upton even went so far as to suggest that the real threat to the American Constitution came, not from military action, but from the politicians. "No usurpation could have been more complete," he wrote of Lincoln's response to the secession crisis of 1861, "but what else could be done?" The lack of proper preparation for war had almost proved fatal, "the insurgents threatened the speedy overthrow of the Government, and the situation brooked no delay."[36]

The failure to put national defense on a proper footing Upton attributed to "the demagogic admonition that foreign organizations are dangerous to liberty." Upton argued in his narrow, logical way that "the principles of organization, like those of strategy, are of universal application, and that no nation has ever violated them, except at its peril." The errors of the Civil War must be avoided in the future: "The disasters which ensued [in 1862] . . . must therefore be credited to the defective laws which allowed the president to dispense with an actual general in chief and substitute in his stead a civil officer supported by military advisers disqualified by their tenure of office and occupations from giving free and enlightened opinions." Upton's reference here is to Stanton, who in March 1862 invited the sixty-four-year-old Ethan Allen Hitchcock to advise him.[37]

Upton believed that the solution to the organizational problem lay in the creation of a general staff along Prussian lines. This argument is reflective of an intense impatience with anything resembling the American system and an abandonment of Sherman's cautious attitude toward the importation of foreign institutions. On the contrary, Upton believed European methods should be used to cleanse the Augean stables. A general staff would take the running of military affairs out of the hands of civilians at all levels. Furthermore, in the conduct of operations in the field, the egregious but dangerous "political generals" would enjoy the same relationship to the staff as the Prussian princes of the blood: they would be reduced to the status of figureheads while the staff commanded.

Yet Upton, for all his military insight, failed to grasp the anomalous position of the general in chief. He wanted the commanding general to head the general staff. But this overlooked the unfortunate fact that the holders of this rank tended to interpret it in terms of field command. Moltke did not act in this manner in 1866. During the Austro-Prussian War, he had remained initially in Berlin and did not move to Bohemia until the end of June. Even when at the front, Moltke commanded by broad directives issued through the staff. He did not interfere in tactical direction as Grant did, which George G. Meade, the nominal commander of the Army of the Potomac, found so vexing but tolerated so nobly. By not acknowledging this weakness and also failing to distinguish (as modern armies do) between the chief of the general staff and the commander in chief in the field, Upton unwittingly perpetuated a structural weakness in the U.S. Army. He failed, moreover, to grasp that a close relationship between the chief executive and the head of the U.S. Army was a prerequisite for victory in American wars.[38]

The melancholy tone of Upton's book and his bitter determination to scrap our "effete organization" and start afresh by adopting a German model for American military reform is in itself a witness to the strong desire of politicians after 1865 to stand by the wisdom of the old ways. Upton brushed aside Sheridan's cautionary warning that the general-staff system gave "enormous political power to the professional soldier and the central government."[39] American political culture was deeply suspicious of any kind of centralization before 1861 and remained no less so after 1865. Upton's blind faith in the integrity and sagacity of regular officers and his enthusiasm for removing any civilian supervision of military affairs would have endangered the principle of civilian supremacy over the military. His proposals would only have contributed to the growth of professional military influence over policy, which was such an important feature of civil-military relations in all other western armies before 1916. Politicians who inveighed against the growth of professional military institutions because they threaten liberties—over the long term—were correct. John A. Logan, a politician and a successful general, warned of military cliques that might eventually "possess the power even should they never entertain the inclination, to control or, to put it more broadly, to conquer the rest of the community."[40]

Indeed, in the absence of a centralized system of military direction or a high level of preparedness for war, Americans tended to deprecate the value of both, believing they were "un-American" and a threat to liberty. In this context, the Confederacy was an important object lesson for some thirty years after the end of the Civil War. The Confederacy was the insidious creation of the "slave power." Eventually, this hostility would lessen as an interpretation of the Civil War gained ground that emphasized the idea of a shared triumph. But during the war itself and for many years afterward, people believed that the Confederacy was prepared for war. The early southern victories were explained away on the grounds of a prewar conspiracy to subvert the government and a superior organization once secession gave way to war. Lt. Roswell Lamson, U.S.N, wrote to his fiancée in the summer of 1861, "Our government will yet be forced to learn from the Rebels to employ their military knowledge and experience when it can be of service, instead of placing ignorant politicians in command."[41]

Even some of the politicians that Lamson criticized fiercely agreed in some respects with his diagnosis. Confederate successes, they believed, *were* the result of a long-prepared conspiracy. For instance, Logan's belief in the "aristocratic" habits and attitudes inculcated at West Point were shared fully by Benjamin F. Butler in his memoir, *Butler's Book* (1892). Both Logan and Butler argued that the majority of West Point graduates were hostile to American democratic egalitarianism; many betrayed its ideals during the secession crisis of 1861 by siding with their states rather than with the federal government. Logan's emphasis on the number of southern officers who graduated from the academy tended to lend weight to the spurious idea of a southern military tradition, a notion that continues to resonate.[42]

In sum, the Civil War illustrates the continuity of civil-military relations in the United States. The innovations often claimed for it in this realm—though not in others—were transient and insubstantial. Indeed, one of the bitterest, most outspoken critics of the proposed reforms of the military structure in Theodore Roosevelt's administration was Civil War veteran Nelson A. Miles. He claimed that Secretary of War Elihu Root would do much damage with his plan to set up a general staff. In 1901 Miles argued that Root's proposed reforms were more suitable to a "military aristocracy" or "monarchical Germany" than to the American Republic. Such a system, he stressed, would lead to overcentralization and would "Germanize and Russianize the small army of the United States." Furthermore, Root's bill would "accomplish no purpose except to allow the Secretary of War and the Adjutant General to promote the interests of their personal favourites." Miles's outburst was thus a restatement of the traditional fear of the general in chief that he would be pushed to the margins of decision making. On the contrary, Root's reforms would actually have provided the most senior officer in the U.S. Army with the sinew to exert control over its organization. It might perhaps be argued that the army could not be truly modernized until the last of the Civil War generation had been forced to leave the scene.[43]

10

THE ENDURING SIGNIFICANCE OF THE CIVIL WAR CONSTITUTIONAL AMENDMENTS

Patricia Lucie

Yale constitutional scholar Bruce Ackerman argues that there have been three great transformative experiences in the life of the American Constitution. Although the Philadelphia Convention is conventionally understood as the primary source of the great fundamental principles that transcend ordinary politics, he argues that both Reconstruction Republicans and New Deal Democrats engaged "in self-conscious acts of constitutional creation that rivaled the Founding Fathers' in their scope and depth." During Reconstruction the Republicans used the machinery that the Constitution provided for its own amendment. The Thirteenth Amendment abolished slavery. The Fourteenth made national citizenship primary over state, committed its "privileges or immunities" to the nation's protection, and guaranteed all persons due process and the equal protection of the laws. The Fifteenth protected voting rights against racial discrimination. Professor Ackerman concludes, "our modern disagreements about the precise meaning of these provisions should not blind us to the quantum leap the Republicans had made in nationalizing the protection of individual rights against state abridgement." Before 1865 individual rights were almost entirely state business and wholly denied to slaves. The journey from slavery to freedom transformed the Constitution.[1]

There is a relationship between transformation and endurance. The mere fact that Americans are still having "modern disagreements" about the meaning of the three amendments and that they are central to contemporary constitutional law is intriguing. Though slavery was a time-bound institution, its "badges and incidents" still stalk American life, tying the present to the past. Freedom, liberty, and equal citizenship, however, are neither time bound nor race specific. For over a century, the three constitutional amendments have carried the weight of claims for racial justice and equality through changing times and ideas about what constitutes justice and equality. But they have also become the framework within which every other contest about individual rights has been shaped for all Americans. The most modern dilemmas of gender identity and equality, access to contraceptives, and control over the technology of death come to courts across the land as cases demanding interpretation of the Civil War's legacy.

Times change. The Constitution remains the same. The Constitution was, of course, designed with that in mind. It contains a few unequivocal rules, a structure, a political philosophy, and some invitingly indeterminate language. It was, as the great chief justice John Marshall wrote, "intended to endure for ages to come, and consequently, to be adapted to the various crises of human affairs." But how and by whom was it to be adapted? Although it provided for its own amendment, this has happened infrequently. The Constitution is given life and the capacity to change by all its moving parts, its political arrangements, and by practices and institutions unknown to the text, among them the rise and importance of political parties. The final decision, however, as to whether change is compatible with the enduring fundamental meaning of the Constitution belongs to the Supreme Court.[2]

The three Civil War constitutional amendments gave Congress a potentially important role as the catalyst of further change by entrusting to it a power of enforcement. But though it was a power used to good effect immediately after the Civil War, it fell into a century's disuse when it was political death to seek votes for racial equality. The federal courts, therefore, have played the larger or more continuous role in shaping the meaning of the amendments. The amendments and early civil rights statutes put the federal courts in the frontline and greatly expanded their jurisdiction. The amendments themselves closed some choices about their meaning. Slavery was not an option. Nor was the exclusion of black Americans from citizenship. The choices that remained have sometimes seemed infinite. Through the eyes of some judges, the amendments have been part of the Constitution's "charter of negative liberties," requiring government to refrain from infringement and stay out of private lives. Others, though fewer, have shared Civil War senator Charles Sumner's vision of a Constitution "full of power, it is overrunning with power" to secure freedom, even if that meant limiting state and private choices. According to some judges, the amendments hardly altered federalism, while to others they worked a profound change. To some, freedom and citizenship rights have clear boundaries, and to others, they are, like the universe, constantly expanding. Who's right?[3]

The Supreme Court, as the Constitution's most important interpreter, fashions meanings in the context of deciding real cases. The Court would deny that it has ever made a free choice from an infinity of alternative interpretations. The meaning of freedom and citizenship is neither free floating nor in theory judge made. Judges believe themselves bound to interpret the Constitution in ways that minimize their own will. Each judgment must argue its way back from the case at hand to the text of the Constitution and to the meanings carried from its origins through history, particularly through the Court's own precedents. It is a dialogue between the present and "the deep past." Judges and their academic critics engage in endless dispute about what "interpretation" is about and what part text, history, and the exigencies of the times play in it. No case, it sometimes seems from the literature, is a model of judicial reasoning, and no theory about the process entirely satisfactory. How judges decide things has become of paramount importance to a wider public than ever before because in the twentieth century, the role of the Supreme Court changed dramatically. Americans now measure their rights largely by what the Court says they are. And more than that, they recognize that justices are political appointments whose values may have something to do with the interpretation of the Constitution.[4]

Where Congress had been the creative force of Reconstruction, the only period of comparable energy in pursuit of equal citizenship was dominated by judicial activity. In many ways, this was only able to happen because of the changes that Professor Ackerman describes as the third great transformative moment in his trilogy of moments when "we the people" made changes that went deeper than ordinary politics. The Court emerged from the New Deal having taken what in practice amounted to a self-denying vow to defer to the will of the people in matters of economic and social regulation. The Court's interventions to strike down most of the New Deal reforms had earned it opprobrium as antidemocratic. The post–New Deal Court reinvented itself as having an important role in a democracy and laid down the doctrinal foundations to justify its special vigilance in cases concerning the Bill of Rights and the rights of minorities. Twenty years later, under Chief Justice Earl Warren, the Supreme Court built a whole new jurisprudence on these foundations and began to take rights seriously. The Thirteenth, Fourteenth, and Fifteenth Amendments enjoyed what some historians described as a rediscovery, their "hour come round at last," and others described as an orgy of judicial policymaking.[5]

There are enduring core values in the Civil War amendments, and the Supreme Court in the Warren era and for some time after that engaged in what is best described as a "contemporary ratification" that transmitted something essential about those amendments to the present. But these values have always had to fight for space with some other enduring aspects of American constitutionalism. The idea that liberty is best secured in local communities predates the Civil War and has endured. So too has the idea that there are limits on the power of the federal government to reach into states and regulate the actions of private persons. The idea that the Constitution is a "charter of negative liberties" is an old one and appears to command majority support on the present Court.[6]

There is something else that survives and keeps the brakes on liberty and equality. It is the jurisprudence of the slippery slope. Judges incline toward the status quo and want to defend it against an avalanche of new claims. The Warren Court (1954–69) was a short and unusual departure from resistance to change. The longer history is one in which the Court has actively given effect to a conservative agenda. At the end of the nineteenth century, the Supreme Court retreated from the frontiers of liberty and equality in the name of preserving federalism and, in doing so, came to serve free enterprise economics and white supremacy. The Supreme Court at the end of the twentieth century is also in a conservative mode. It styles itself as self restrained, careful to keep naked judicial preferences out of constitutional interpretation and the Framers' values in it. Nonetheless, this is not a Court that is shy about making exceptions to self-restraint, either by overturning its own precedents or striking down congressional actions. The result, more often than not, is to trim back individual and minority rights. While criticizing the notion of an "imperial judiciary," it rises to the role.[7]

The Thirteenth, Fourteenth, and Fifteenth Amendments are interlinked in the one project to secure the conditions of freedom after four million slaves were emancipated during the American Civil War. All three grant Congress the power to enforce them by appropriate legislation. The very close relationship between the amendments led to some blurring of distinctions. The Reconstruction Congresses were not always explicit about which one was the source of legislative authority. Lawyers too would throw more than one into the pot of pleadings when they came to court in the hope that if one did not carry the weight of the argument, the other would. The result was that, twenty years after the Civil War ended, judges had come to develop some ideas about the meaning of the Fourteenth Amendment that affected their understandings of the other two amendments, in particular, that it allowed federal correction of state wrongs and not private ones. This expansive version of the "state action" doctrine was unhelpful to black citizens seeking redress against private discrimination and violence. The result was that some important differences in the language and structure of the amendments were obscured. The Thirteenth Amendment was a casualty of this, and its potential was untapped.[8]

The Thirteenth Amendment is uniquely radical in the U.S. Constitution. Unlike the rest of the document, it is not about "checks and balances" between units of government but a direct promise to every man, woman, and child that "neither slavery not involuntary servitude, except as a punishment for crime whereof the party shall have been duly convicted, shall exist within the United States or any place subject to its jurisdiction." As surely as it was a promise to each individual, it was also a command to each individual who would attempt to hold another in such a condition that freedom was nationalized. Power was vested in Congress "to enforce this article by appropriate legislation." It was ratified and became part of the Constitution in December 1865.

Four million slaves were free. Much of the law of property and persons in every slave state, and a good deal of criminal law too, ended the same day. Trying to find a meaning that would limit the effect of the amendment, Democrats and some conservative Republicans attempted to define freedom as the absence of slavery. Sen. Edgar Cowan put it like this: "The breaking of the bond by which the Negro slave was held to his master; that is all. It was not intended to. . . . revolutionize all the laws of the various states everywhere. It was intended, in other words, and a lawyer would have so construed it, to give the Negro the privilege of the *habeas corpus;* that is, if anyone persisted in the face of the constitutional amendment in holding him as a slave, that he should have an appropriate remedy to be delivered."[9] It was not what freedom meant to the majority of Republicans and had not been for a long time. Throughout the Civil War, Congress had plenty of opportunities in debates about confiscation, emancipation, and Reconstruction to consider what would happen to the freed slave. As early as 1862 they drafted laws that gave freedmen the protection of a writ of habeas corpus against reenslavement but, unlike Senator Cowan, did not conflate the remedy and the right.[10]

No list of ingredients of freedom could or should be compiled from speeches during these years, but undoubtedly they would disclose the pervasive Republican belief that freedom entitled a person to an equality of civil rights before the law. Once slavery was removed from state law, what was left would be the same laws that made and kept everybody else free. Thus, Sen. Lyman Trumbull stated: "With the destruction of slavery necessarily follows the destruction of the incidents of slavery . . . , those laws that prevented the colored man going from home, that did not allow him to enforce his rights; that did not allow him to be educated, were all badges of servitude made in the interests of slavery. They never would have been thought of or enacted anywhere but for slavery and when slavery falls, they fall also."[11]

It was not so simple. As Trumbull spoke in 1866, the demonstrated failure of freedom to fill the space left by slavery's demise had brought crisis. Mere reference to the "Black Codes" that southern states passed to control the lives and labor of their former "property" cannot convey their miserable inhumanity. They were grossly harassing, denying even the right of free movement, let alone free labor; made innocent behavior criminal; and created an immediate framework of reference by which Congress could begin to identify the obstacles to freedom and devise appropriate remedies.

Prof. Harold Hyman, a leading analyst of these events, identifies the great problem that confronted the Congress in 1866 as it drafted the Civil Rights Bill. "Freedom," he writes, "was a largely unstudied congeries of pragmatic customs."

Although Republicans hoped that states would regenerate these to include freedmen, it was now clear that it would not happen without making some of the responsibility for that a national one. The Republicans stumbled toward an idea that would offer a way to combine a concept of rights common to all Americans with permissible local diversity. National citizenship was the idea that pervaded all debate. Though Chief Justice Roger Taney in *Dred Scott* had denied that even free black persons were citizens, it was not a conclusion that was universally accepted and was quite positively rejected by Republicans in wartime. A free person born in the United States was a citizen who owed allegiance to the government and in return was entitled to its protection. The Civil Rights Act began with a declaration of this more inclusive version of citizenship. It proceeded to link the existence of common rights of national citizenship to the multitude of ways in which the states already made these a living sort of freedom for white citizens.[12]

The United States was on ground as new to international legal experience as space law today. No other nation attempted such a sudden change from a legal culture soaked in slavery to one guaranteeing freedom and civil rights. Federalism made that attempt an even greater adventure. There was no common experience of national citizenship enjoyed by all white Americans. Of course, there was not an American who did not believe that the Constitution secured his very substantial birthright of liberty. It was just that few understood how it was done, if indeed it was. Asked for an opinion on national citizenship in 1862, Attorney General Edward Bates spoke of a "fruitless search" in the law books. He reported that "eighty years of practical enjoyment of citizenship under the Constitution have not sufficed to teach us either the exact meaning of the word, or the constituent elements of the thing we prize so highly."[13] In fact, eighty years of enjoyment had more to do with whether or not one had the good fortune to be among the beneficiaries of state power rather than anything to do with the language of rights in the Constitution. As a matter of constitutional law, the Bill of Rights had no application to the states.[14]

In 1866, Congress made two statements about national citizenship, each of which was about common equal rights and also about equality before state law. The 1866 Civil Rights Act made the rights of white citizens its compass and entitled all citizens to the same right to "make and enforce contracts, to sue, be parties and give evidence, to inherit, purchase, lease, sell, hold and convey real and personal property, and to full and equal benefit of the laws for the security of persons and property as is enjoyed by white citizens." The act was an immediate response to overwhelming evidence of the state and private wrongs that prevented freedmen from enjoying freedom. It was not a list of all the rights the Republicans believed inherent in national citizenship. On the contrary, speakers frequently included selections from the common law and the Bill of Rights as illustrations of a commonality of rights. The phrases "such as" or "and so on" almost always accompanied the examples. This is hardly surprising in a constitutional system whose very basis was the existence of rights that could not be listed. The act only makes sense as the first use of congressional power under the Thirteenth Amendment in response to a specific set of facts.[15]

In 1866 the obstacles to freedom were the Black Codes, which were more effectively countered by the rights the Thirteenth Amendment contained than by a declaration of freedom of speech. It did not follow that the framers thought that free speech was not part of national citizenship. In the same year, Congress framed the Fourteenth Amendment in these "majestic generalities": "All persons born or naturalized in the United States and subject to the jurisdiction thereof , are citizens of the United States and of the State wherein they reside. No State shall make or enforce any law which shall abridge the privileges or immunities of citizens of the United States; nor shall any State deprive any person of life, liberty or property, without due process of law; nor deny to any person within its jurisdiction the equal protection of the laws." There is no precise answer as to what they meant by "privileges or immunities." The narrowest reading is that it was shorthand for the fundamental rights contained in the Civil Rights Act.[16] This seems to be supported by the extensive reference made in Congress to the case of *Corfield v. Coryell* in 1823. This was the leading case on the meaning of the "privileges" and "immunities" that the Constitution already guaranteed to citizens of one state when they resided in another. Judge Bushrod Washington seemed to suggest that a citizen had a portable entitlement to fundamental rights wherever he went and described them in ways that bore some resemblance to the Civil Rights Act. He did not, however, advertise these as any more than some of the relevant rights, the others being "too tedious to mention." Given the fact that Judge Washington had included the possibility of the elective franchise being among them, "as regulated and established by the laws or constitution of the state in which it is to be exercised," it seems unlikely that he intended a narrow definition of rights that a nonresident citizen would expect the Constitution to protect.[17]

The broader reading of the phrase is that it was shorthand for the entire Bill of Rights. This is supported by an impressive number of citations to congressional speeches either, as in the case of two of its prime movers, John Bingham and Jacob Howard, averring a deliberate intention to include them or, in the case of many more congressmen, references to some of its rights. Although a case against this interpretation is sometimes made out of the fact that white citizens' rights had never included an entitlement to enjoy the entire Bill of Rights in their home states, there was no evidence that the states that ratified the amendment believed it would change their laws. It seems unlikely that, even where such things as freedom of the press or religion were not specifically protected by state constitutions, that any state would put up its hand to not affording it. In practice, of course, many states had denied white citizens these rights, especially in their efforts to gag antislavery opinion. The practice of gagging bore no relationship, however, to what was in or out of the state constitution. It seems quite certain that the framers looked to the enhancement of white citizens' rights through national protection of at least the personal rights contained in the Bill of Rights as well as the *Corfield* brew of common-law rights.[18]

It was, after all, a Constitution they were writing and not a statute. They were well aware that it could have a long future in a changing world, that it would be interpreted by the Supreme Court, and that it would be the source of further congressional legislation. "Privileges and immunities" could never be mistaken for an enumeration of civil rights tied to one era, one place, or one race. It had universal application and was built to last.

The Republican design for national citizenship was one in which federal and state authorities had concurrent responsibilities to ensure an equality of civil rights. Privileges and immunities were not some special subset of law to be described once and for all, cut off from the everyday business of all other state law and entrusted to federal care. All state law had the capacity to affect them. The state end of the Republicans' design was crucial. States were to continue their traditional role in the federal system, making all the laws for the welfare and good governance of their own citizens. Indeed, they could avoid federal intervention at all by doing two things: operating a single set of laws for all, *and* ensuring that the content of these laws was protective of the civil rights of all citizens. In other words, a state that denied property rights to all of its citizens, if such a thing were imaginable, would not meet the standards of the Constitution by dint of having avoided racial discrimination. Conversely, a state whose laws recognized the right of all citizens to own property but made racially discriminatory laws for its purchase or sale would also invite federal correction. It was an idea of citizenship that brought together both an equality of real but as yet undefined, nationally held rights with an idea of intrastate equality, that is, equality before state law. The theory was that since white men were not negligent of their own privileges and immunities, states that operated a single set of laws for all citizens had nothing to fear from the Fourteenth Amendment.

There was a flaw in all this, and it was not so much in the necessary lack of precision about rights as in the lack of a coherent theory to explain the differences in citizenship, which the Republicans admitted that states could continue to make despite the universal application of the amendment to all citizens. Women were citizens, and their legal status demonstrated that the Republicans' theory of national citizenship as a fusion between universal, common civil rights and equality before state law was deficient.[19] The application of the 1866 Civil Rights Act and the Fourteenth Amendment to their situation would have accomplished a revolution in state law, particularly with respect to married women's property law. It was an irony not lost on either women or congressional Republicans. The leaders of the former protested; the latter worked hard but unconvincingly to explain why the changes in the law would not benefit women. When Sen. Charles Sumner introduced his draft proposal for what became the Thirteenth Amendment, it included the words "all persons are equal before the law." His colleague, one Senator Howard, objected to the phrase because "it might even be understood to mean that a woman would be the equal of her husband before the law!" It was not the last exchange that found Republicans scurrying to explain why states need not fear for their right to continue outright denials to married women of property and contract rights specifically covered by the 1866 Civil Rights Act. Most of these attempted explanations denied that such differences would be tolerable if applied to black citizens but fell into a morass of silly argument.[20]

At the same time, almost all Republicans admitted that some racial differences were permissible. Civil rights were distinguished from political rights, although this distinction had already begun to fade by 1867, when the majority of Republicans accepted that it was essential to citizenship. Social rights were distinguished from civil and political and frequent reassurances given to opponents who feared the collapse of the world if black and white citizens were obliged by law to mix their lives. The distinction between civil and social rights was neither clear nor immovable, however, and by 1875, Republicans passed another civil rights law, which ended racial discrimination in inns and theaters. It may be safely said that Republicans knew they lived in a world of dynamic change. It may also be said that political realities were pushing them further toward racial change than any for gender.

Suffrage is a good example of this. Although at the beginning of the Civil War there was a general acceptance among Republicans that political rights were separate from civil rights and were not conferred on anyone by being a citizen of the nation, black suffrage was nonetheless on the agenda of Reconstruction before the war ended. In 1867, Congress made it an express term for readmission of southern states to the Union. By that time it was partly a matter of political reality, a recognition that Republican political fortunes were tied to making white and black unionist votes in the South count against those of the unrepentant. It was also a matter of practical citizenship, though. Events had outpaced any theory about the divisible nature of citizenship into civil and political compartments. If freedom and civil rights were denied to the powerless, the best practical defense of them was at the polls. And if black citizens voted in South Carolina, could they be denied in Ohio? The Republican party thought not. They were well aware, however, of the extent to which this was not a universal view in the loyal states and proceeded with caution, for matters of voter qualification lay at the inner sanctum of state rights. The Fifteenth Amendment, ratified in 1870, was the survivor of a whole gamut of proposals ranging from nationally guaranteed universal suffrage and the right to hold office all the way down to a version that would have permitted states to exclude citizens on grounds of previous slavery, though not on race alone. This was the compromise: "The right of citizens of the United States to vote shall not be denied or abridged by the United States or by any State on account of race, color, or previous condition of servitude."[21]

This time there was less ambiguity, less room to argue a windfall for all citizens. Women's rights leaders argued that the right to vote was already one of their privileges or immunities as citizens under the Fourteenth Amendment. The Supreme Court decided that it was not.[22] The unanimous Court was of the opinion that if the right to vote was inherent in the Fourteenth Amendment, then the Fifteenth would not have been necessary to enfranchise black citizens. Even Virginia Minor's counsel recognized that the Fifteenth Amendment was of no use to women. Indeed, the states could exclude any citizen, provided they did so on the grounds that they were illiterate, propertyless, or for any other reason provided that the criteria was not race. The Republicans who debated the proposed Fifteenth Amendment and voted on it did so in the belief that suffrage was indeed a right of citizenship, though with the full knowledge that the language fell short of saying so. The more radical members of the party were prescient in warning that the states could easily limit black suffrage through literacy tests or property qualifications, though it turned out that the southern imagination was even more devious than anyone anticipated in finding ways to circumvent African American voting. Events would confirm this in the matter of both equality of civil rights before the law and suffrage. The strategy of relying heavily on white state lawmakers to make their own rights the measure of equality was a fragile one unless it came with a willingness to use all the ample federal powers in the amendments to remedy wrongs and to demand compliance.[23]

And this is how it was in the beginning. State noncompliance and private violence threatened to undermine the whole project of citizenship in 1870 as surely as the Black Codes had undermined freedom in 1866. Congress responded energetically with measures to protect civil rights and the right to vote. The most important feature of the statutory framework it left behind in the Enforcement Acts of 1870, the Ku Klux Klan Act of 1871, and the Civil Rights Act of 1875 is that the laws reached not only the palpable actions of states to deprive citizens of their rights but also state wrongs of omission or inaction and, crucially, private actions to violate rights. Section 6 of the Enforcement Acts provided criminal sanctions against conspiracies by "two or more persons" to deprive anyone of rights secured under the Constitution or the laws of the United States. It punished private interference with the right to vote. The Ku Klux Klan Act also reached private deprivations and imposed civil damages on offenders. The 1875 Civil Rights Act gave all persons a right to equal enjoyment of accommodation at inns, theaters, and public conveyances and punished private offenders who excluded anyone on grounds other than those established by law and applicable to citizens of every race and color, regardless of previous condition of servitude. It was powerful evidence that Republican sensitivity to states as the generators of the conditions of freedom was compatible with the seriousness that the corollary of a federal guarantee of right to each individual citizen was a remedy against any who denied it, including private persons.[24]

But were the federal courts, whose jurisdiction was greatly enlarged under all these acts, up to the challenge? The only experience they had before the Civil War of enforcing federally guaranteed rights against any and all offenders in the states was on behalf of slaveowners. Now they were called upon by statutes to wrest cases if need be from state judges, question state laws on matters that had never been federal business, and sometimes subject private citizens to fines and imprisonment for doing things that states would not punish them for. Whatever the antebellum experience of federal justice, and for African Americans it was *Dred Scott v. Sanford,* freedom and citizenship were entrusted to it. Between 1866 and 1873 all signs indicated that the Republicans' strategy was workable. In the circuit and district courts, federal judges tackled new problems in ways that suggested their understanding that the old order would have to make considerable adaptation to make freedom an everyday reality.[25]

One case is particularly instructive. On circuit in 1867, Chief Justice Salmon Chase heard a petition on behalf of a young black girl, Elizabeth Turner. She had been contracted to work for her former master under a recent Maryland apprenticeship law that differentiated between conditions for black and white apprentices in ways that Chase found analogous to involuntary servitude, prohibited by the Thirteenth Amendment and the 1866 Civil Right Act. His opinion made it clear that the law of freedom bit deep into matters of state contract and property law, interestingly, on behalf of both male and female citizens. Four years later in Alabama, a circuit court upheld the reach of the 1870 Enforcement Act to punish private conspiracies and confirmed that the right to freedom of speech and association were among the rights of citizens protected under federal law. There are other examples of vigorous opinions from freedom's frontline.[26]

Nonetheless, it would be quite misleading to suggest that until 1873 the federal courts had a clear grasp of how all the recent changes fit into the great mass of rules and doctrines of the Constitution. The law was anything but a blank slate. Judges struggled to reconcile old principles of state autonomy in criminal law with new federal interventions—for example, how murder could be a federal crime if it happened on the road to the polling station but not in a saloon fight. The law's business now was change as well as continuity, but old habits were ingrained. One of the Supreme Court's first pronouncements on the Thirteenth Amendment was to confirm that purchasers who bought slaves before the war on promise to pay later had to honor their promise irrespective of slavery's demise. Former slaveowners could thus still cash in on their former property. Continuity was something judges took seriously, and although the earliest decisions in the lower courts had begun to confront the discontinuities between slavery and freedom, the price of putting the Union back together again, to bind whites' wounds, and oil the wheels of regenerated commerce and business was to limit the influence of change. The Grant administration retreated quite deliberately from prosecuting civil rights violations by the Ku Klux Klan. The courts were not far behind, supplying the legal justifications for doing so.[27]

By 1900, if asked to explain what endured from the Civil War constitutionally, the answer would have been that the slaves were no longer property, that federalism had been preserved, and that the Fourteenth Amendment was generating a lot of business in the federal courts, though most of it about the rights of free enterprise to be free of state regulation and little about civil rights. It was a different world from the one that attempted to give freedom and citizenship real meaning for black Americans, indeed for all Americans. Courts not only reflected that changed world but also helped shape it through some important doctrines that endured into the twentieth century, piled layer upon layer on top of the original Republican design, threatening to suffocate it. The Republican framers would have recognized in these doctrines their own concerns to preserve states' rights, but not the shrinking of national rights and powers that robbed citizenship of meaning.[28]

Three of these doctrines are of special concern. Dual citizenship was not the invention of Justice Samuel F. Miller in the *Slaughterhouse Cases* in 1873, but his division of rights between nation and state was. Here was an exercise in avalanche prevention. When white butchers claimed that a state-created monopoly to a slaughterhouse abridged one of their Fourteenth Amendment privileges and immunities to follow their profession, the Court majority sensed a slippery slope, an unending stream of economic rights brought to overburdened federal courts to challenge state regulation. To avoid the prospect, Miller's opinion divided rights. National citizenship entitled the holder to the protection of the government in such things as travel on the high seas and access to post offices, that is, in aspects of life where citizen and nation met. Everything else belonged to state citizenship; thus, everything that mattered remained state business. With one stroke he killed the privileges and immunities clause. With another he restricted its influence to racial discrimination alone. The clause had no effect on the citizenship of those who already were citizens,

he said, but protected black citizens from racial discrimination. It was an interpretation at odds with the universal language of the text and its history.[29]

The state action doctrine was arguably the creation of the text of the Fourteenth
and Fifteenth Amendments rather than of the Supreme Court. The text limited the
states' abridgement or denial of rights but not ostensibly those of anyone else. Yet
clearly, Congress had passed laws punishing private violence and intimidation of
private citizens and providing civil remedies to persons deprived of civil rights.
Judges had upheld them. After *Slaughterhouse,* however, it became increasingly difficult to maintain a legal theory that acknowledged congressional power to protect
a breadth of civil rights against private action when states had been reinstated as the
fount of the rights themselves. Justice Joseph P. Bradley's opinion for the Supreme
Court in the *Civil Rights Cases* came to be read as raising high the barriers of federalism to allow federal correction only of wrongs in the laws and actions of the states.
In fact, even Justice Bradley had a broader theory that allowed for federal correction
of private acts both where the state's inaction had left citizens' rights vulnerable to
private deprivation and where legislation was based on the Thirteenth Amendment,
which was free from any state action limit. It was left to twentieth-century judges to
push these doors open, however. Citizens, for now, were not to be protected from
each other.[30]

Even protection from the laws of the state came to mean little after the Supreme
Court pronounced its opinion that a Louisiana law mandating "separate but equal"
railroad carriages for black and white passengers did not violate the equal protection
of the laws under the Fourteenth Amendment. This was the holding in *Plessy v.
Ferguson* in 1896. It was no more an inevitable outcome than the rest of the Court's
major interpretative doctrines. Like them, it took something that was undoubtedly
a part of the Republicans' intention, either in their continuing attachment to states'
rights or, as here, an ambiguity about "social rights" evident in Republican denial of
a plan to force the races to intermarry or share schoolrooms, and pushed it further,
legitimating a practice that inflicted a badge of degradation on one race, whose
members were supposedly equal before the law. Dissenting Justice John Harlan contributed something that would last longer than Jim Crow when he wrote, "Our
Constitution is colorblind, and neither knows nor tolerates classes among citizens."
It would be half a century before the colorblind phrase meant anything at all. These
judicial doctrines blew the Civil War amendments far off course. Always, the judges
cited text, precedent, and history, especially the framers' intentions, as their source
and justification.[31]

The Warren Court's approach to individual rights cannot be explained without
reference to the particular contemporary values they brought to the judicial process.
It was a Court that was greatly concerned with equality as a central principle in

American constitutionalism. The individual was entitled not just to equality before the law but to be treated as equal in dignity and moral worth. Citizenship meant belonging rather than formal inclusion. In dismantling the old judicial doctrines that had taken the life out of the three constitutional amendments, the Court, like its predecessors, created new fictions. Labeled as "activist" in playing fast and loose with text and original intent, it nonetheless came closer to transmitting the core values of the amendments to contemporary life.[32]

Though the privileges and immunities clause remained as dead as it was the day *Slaughterhouse* was decided, fundamental rights hatched in every other corner of the constitutional text, and some outside of it. Over a long period, beginning in the 1920s but gathering momentum in the 1960s, the Court made almost the entire Bill of Rights part of the liberty that states could not deny without due process. In addition, there were the "unenumerated rights," those not mentioned in the text but which were also part of "liberty."[33] The dangerous business of articulating undefined rights was not new. From the end of the nineteenth century through to the New Deal, it was a constant criticism of the Supreme Court that it had chosen to define free enterprise as a liberty under the Fourteenth Amendment and protect business interests from state regulation. Although the Court left laissez-faire economics behind in 1937, it revived the idea that there were undefined rights that state laws could not abridge. They could not, for example, ban contraceptive use because the law invaded the right to privacy protected by the amendment.[34] The list of unenumerated rights expanded later to include the controversial right to abortion.[35] Where the Court found a fundamental right at issue, it subjected the state's interests to a very high level of inquiry, or strict scrutiny, which in practice made it difficult for the state to win. This was a much more extensive nationalization of rights.

The Supreme Court began to rid constitutional law of the separate but equal doctrine as early as 1954 in the landmark case of *Brown v Board of Education*. Desegregation was a long, slow process that started with schools and extended to cover all public facilities. The Court developed a new doctrine, termed "suspect classification." Any use of race to make differences of law between the races was suspicious because it was associated with a history of discrimination and a lack of relevance to any conceivable legitimate purpose. The Constitution was indeed, as Justice Harlan had said, colorblind. Again, as with fundamental right, the Court employed strict scrutiny of laws using race as a way of classifying people. In practice it was next to impossible for the state to justify its law, though it remained just as easy as before to justify different laws based on gender.[36]

Racism was harder to prise out of private life. In housing, employment, and thousands of daily activities, black citizens faced discrimination. The state action doctrine handicapped efforts to reach private action. To some extent, the Warren

Court got around the problem by making the doctrine elastic and finding some connection—the most fragile would do—between the state and the private actor to bring the case to federal court. But it also revived interest in the Thirteenth Amendment and some century-old civil rights laws, several of which remain on the statute book.

Perhaps the vitality of the Thirteenth Amendment is the most surprising feat of endurance. In 1969 the Court decided in *Jones v. Alfred H. Mayer Co.* that the refusal of a white seller to sell his house to a black buyer was contrary to the 1866 Civil Rights Act. There followed a remarkable statement that could have opened a new era for Congress to enact new civil rights laws: "Congress has the power under the Thirteenth Amendment rationally to determine what are the badges and incidents of slavery, and the authority to translate that determination into effective action." The law journals have been more enthusiastic than the courts or Congress about how far this idea could run. With respect to race, it could reach badges and incidents of slavery that have escaped the Fourteenth Amendment. And there are aspects that are applicable to individuals regardless of race. Perhaps, some writers have suggested, there is an analogy between involuntary servitude and other conditions such as child abuse, prostitution, and some forms of labor contract that rob individuals of the power of self-determination.[37]

Although the Court was frequently criticized for its substitution of judicial will for those of the people, a feature that stands out and has never been repeated was its generous construction of congressional power as in the *Jones* case with respect to the Thirteenth Amendment. It was also true of the enforcement clause of the Fifteenth. Case by case review of discrimination against black voters had resulted in some major victories, including some long before the Warren Court, but Congress passed the Voting Rights Act in 1965 to tackle a scale of problems well beyond judicial resolution.[38] In upholding it the Court described congressional power in the broadest possible terms: "As against the reserved powers of the States, Congress may use any rational means to effectuate the constitutional prohibitions of racial discrimination in voting."[39] With respect to the Fourteenth Amendment, the Court seemed in one case to be encouraging the thought that Congress's powers were not only ones of enforcement but also perhaps of independent interpretation as a basis for further law. In other words, Congress might not be restricted to remedying only those violations the Supreme Court had identified. The case, *Katzenbach v. Morgan,* caused great controversy. What, for example, if Congress interpreted the amendment in ways that diminished rights? By what theory could Congress protect more rights than the Court but not less? The question hovered for thirty years.[40]

The current Supreme Court under Chief Justice William Rehnquist has self-consciously distanced itself from the "activism" of the Warren Court. Believing judges should exercise restraint, it will no longer pull rights out of the Constitution like rabbits out of a hat. Morally skeptical, it will not presume to know better than the elected representatives of the people what values should prevail if the Constitution does not say so. Thus, the Pandora's box that opened when abortion was held to be a fundamental right has been closed to gay sex and assisted suicide. The Court thinks it sees another slippery slope, exactly as it did a century ago: allow one claim and wait for the avalanche. Abortion itself is subject to a new standard of review that allows more state regulation. The Bill of Rights remains nationalized and is likely to continue to be. Concessions to federalism, however, are evidenced by a retreat from the most exacting standards of criminal procedure the Warren Court imposed on the states as well as a shrinking of federal habeas corpus jurisdiction to review alleged violations of these procedures. The net result is to allow more decisions about moral and criminal issues, including the death penalty, to remain stateside. In practice, this is not a liberty-expanding strategy.[41]

Far more citizens look to the equal protection clause now than was ever the case, though whether the Court has moved closer to resolving what are permissible differences between citizens is open to debate. Women are a great deal better protected than most Civil War Republicans or Warren Court liberals contemplated. The Court, beginning in 1972, edged toward something like the "suspect classification" approach to gender that it used for dismantling racial discrimination, and the latest cases show how strictly the judges review matters such as the exclusion of women from military academy.[42] Aliens and illegitimate children are among a middle tier who may be treated differently by the states on a showing of a substantial reason for doing so, but not as compelling a reason as would be needed to justify race or gender differences.[43]

Black Americans continue to be the "beneficiaries" (though a misleading term) of a colorblind Constitution. Racism, inequality, and discrimination remain. Continuing legal fictions mean that proof of actual discrimination by a particular perpetrator must be proved.[44] Thus, Georgia came away blameless in 1987 from a case in which statistics showed a death penalty system riddled with racism, but nobody could track the facts of the case down to a "smoking gun."[45] Opinion is divided on the issue, but critics have charged that colorblindness and "suspect classifications" have become a hindrance to equality. Affirmative action, that is, action that takes color into account to open up more jobs and educational opportunities to minorities without proof of purposeful discrimination, found some early support on the Court. In 1995, however, the Court made it more difficult for Congress to devise affirmative-action plans by insisting that race was a suspect classification whether it was used to help or burden its beneficiaries.[46]

"Affirmative" is not a word much heard about the Constitution. Denying that an abused four-year-old boy had any Fourteenth Amendment claim on the protection of the state against his violent father in a case where social workers had previously been involved, Chief Justice Rehnquist declared: "Nothing in the Due Process Clause itself requires the State to protect the life, liberty, and property of its citizens against invasion by private actors. The Clause is phrased as a limitation on the State's power to act, not as a guarantee of certain minimal levels of safety and security."[47]

Unlike the Warren Court, the Rehnquist Court does not invite Congress to use its powers. The question of Congress's possible independent power to interpret the Fourteenth Amendment, left hanging unanswered by the Warren Court, may have been answered in 1997, when the Court struck down the Religious Restoration Act, passed by Congress in 1993 under its Fourteenth Amendment enforcement power. Congress had legislated to undo one of the Court's own, and particularly wrong, interpretations of the free exercise clause of the First Amendment. In doing so Congress made its own interpretation of the correct meaning and earned this rebuke from the Court: "Legislation which alters the meaning," said Justice Anthony Kennedy, "cannot be said to be enforcing the Clause"; in effect, the role of Congress is limited to giving effect to the Court's interpretations. Congressmen are unlikely to be adventurous in the present judicial mood.[48]

There is, then, a certain symmetry about how the nineteenth and the twentieth centuries ended. There is no question that the three Civil War amendments have survived and that some of their core values are thriving. Lawyers and academics still write about their untapped potential and devise new and better theories of interpretation. The lesson of the last twenty years, however, is that the story does not end with the "rediscovery" of lost amendments. There is instead an ongoing dialogue about freedom and citizenship. Questions of federalism, the limits of government in private spheres, and disinclination to open a Pandora's box and sweep away society have endured as well. So too has the time-honored habit of judges of following the text, the history, and the precedents in such a way as to advise the reader to search further into such judicial prejudices.

11

"THE CHARTER OF ITS BIRTHRIGHT"

The Civil War and American Nationalism

SUSAN-MARY GRANT

This army will live, and live on, so long as soul shall answer soul, so long as that flag watches with its stars over fields of mighty memory, so long as in its red lines a regenerated people reads the charter of its birthright, and in its field of white God's covenant with man.
—JOSHUA LAWRENCE CHAMBERLAIN, *The Passing of the Armies*

[I]t is not the literal past, the "facts" of history, that shape us, but images of the past embodied in language. . . . [W]e must never cease renewing those images; because once we do, we fossilize.

—BRIAN FRIEL, *Translations,* Act III

People without a past are not a people.
—KEN BURNS

Warfare lies at the heart of the American national experience. The nation that we know as the United States is the product of two major conflicts—the Revolution of the eighteenth century and the Civil War of the nineteenth—together with two centuries' worth of violent encounters stretching from the forests of colonial New England over the Great Plains of the Wild West. In his recent study of the origins of the American Civil War, historian Brian Holden Reid highlights the importance of warfare to the United States and argues that American nationalism itself "was born in the disunity of the revolutionary struggles and nurtured in the fratricidal strife of the Civil War." This in itself does not make America unusual. As military historian Michael Howard has pointed out, "[f]rom the very beginning the principle of nationalism was almost indissolubly linked, both in theory and practice, with the idea of war." Warfare itself, the process of fighting and winning (or losing in some cases), "became a focus for national sentiment" in many nations. Americans, however, have been unwilling to concede that violence rather than voluntarism played a central role in their national development. Consequently, as far as the creation of the American nation is concerned, the subject of war is approached obliquely. The American way of war, in short, is almost always presented in quasi-mystical terms that support the national idea of freedom and equality for all.[1]

The clearest evidence of this mystical approach to warfare and its central place in the construction of U.S. nationalism can be found in the American response to the Civil War of 1861–65. The Civil War has supplanted the Revolution as the war that made the nation. It provides Americans with "a sense of identity, of resurrection through disintegration," of shared tragedy and simultaneously triumph. Writing in 1961 at the outset of the Civil War Centennial, Robert Penn Warren portrayed the Civil War as the great defining act of American nationalism. The Revolution, he argued, "did not create a nation except on paper. . . . [The United States] became a nation, only with the Civil War." Others have concurred with this view, and some have even developed it further. It has been argued, for example, that compared to the Civil War, the Revolution did little for American national construction, being "too long ago, a vague patchwork of Valley Forge and Paul Revere." The Civil War, in contrast, was the defining act: it was the nation's "holy crusade" and consequently "sacred" to Americans.[2]

Such a glib interpretation, however, serves only to obscure the complexity of the Civil War's role in American national construction and fails to explain how the war came to be seen in this way. Further, the transformation of the Civil War from a bloody internecine conflict to a glorious war of national redemption has *not* been as constructive, in terms of national unity, as it might have been and as many Americans suppose it to be. Indeed, the selective nature of American memory concerning the Civil War and its elevation to mythical status continues to operate against the successful consolidation of the United States as a nation.

The American Civil War was the conclusion of years of increasing sectional hostility and misunderstanding between the North and the South, yet its outbreak in April 1861 still came as an unwelcome shock to Americans at the time. "Civil War in our land!" Jacob Cox bemoaned, "[t]he shame, the folly, the outrage, seemed too great to be believed." Yet memories of that conflict, from the outset, were mixed. Alongside the shame, Cox recalled, "[t]he wonderful outburst of national feeling in the North in the spring of 1861 has always been a thrilling and almost supernatural thing . . . , the work of a national divinity rousing a whole people, not to terror, but to a sublime enthusiasm of self-devotion." Such sentiments reached their peak in the writings of Joshua Lawrence Chamberlain, who interpreted the war in mystical terms, recalling its battlefields "of mighty memory" with a combination of religious awe and sacrificial devotion.[3]

Chamberlain's romantic reveries jar with modern sensibilities. As Civil War historian James McPherson comments, sometimes the means of expression of nineteenth-century Americans constitutes a formidable barrier to understanding. The nineteenth century was a sentimental age, and what seems mawkish to modern readers seemed perfectly genuine to the Civil War generation. Even if it was not so, given Chamberlain's war record, he of all people should be permitted to present the war in sentimental terms. The views of those writing over a century later, though, should be more critically assessed. A twentieth-century historian's description of the Civil War as "a struggle over the nation's soul" and as proof that "a nation can abandon its birthright" should gives us pause. It is one thing to accept at face value Chamberlain's evocation of the "Angel of the Nation" approving of the North's victory in the Civil War but quite another to perpetuate his perspective in the late twentieth century.[4]

The American Civil War, however, is rarely presented in any other way. Indeed, what was a destructive and horrifying conflict has become over the years an event to rank with the myths and legends of a very distant age. Recently, one historian entitled his study of the war *An American Iliad* and justified his choice in the following terms: "The victory of the Greeks forever changed the course of Western history, and thereby of world history. More than a century ago the American people engaged in a great sectional conflict that reenacted all of the heroism and sacrifice, all of the cruelty and horror, of the Greco-Trojan war. The Union victory . . . forever changed the course of American history, and thereby of world history." Charles Roland is not the only historian to see himself as a modern-day Homer. Ken Burns, the producer of the phenomenally successful PBS series on the Civil War, has similarly drawn a comparison between the "epic verses" of Homer and his own approach to a war in which, rather than Greek killing Trojan, American killed American.[5]

The tendency to regard the Civil War in dramatic, one might say emotional, terms reveals much about the process of American national construction. It shows that a variant of Romantic nationalism played a significant role in American as in European nationalism and that this process is not yet complete. In common with Romantic nationalism in Europe, the American variant rests on the principle of voluntarism, the idea best expressed by Ernest Renan's description of the nation as a daily plebiscite. Unfortunately, this principle was seriously compromised in the American case by virtue of the fact that the United States both achieved and sustained nationhood by military rather than by voluntaristic means. The American response to this has been to elevate warfare to mystical proportions, to downplay the extent and the implications of violence within the nation, and to concentrate instead on its mythical and symbolic elements.

The focus on a mythological past is a recognized feature of European national construction. Nationalism scholar Anthony Smith, among others, has stressed the importance to a nation of myths of a glorious past, "myths of origins and descent, of liberation and migration, of the golden age and its heroes and sages, perhaps of the chosen people now to be reborn after its long sleep of decay and/or exile." Together, Smith concludes, "these myth-motifs can be formed into a composite nationalist mythology and salvation drama." Writing specifically about the Romantic nationalists, Joseph Llobera likewise emphasizes the central importance of the mythological past, which for the Romantics "embodied the loftiest and most worthy ideals." From the perspective of nationalism, he argues, "nostalgia for the past took the form of looking back to a period in the history of a nation when it achieved literary fame, political success or had flourished culturally."[6]

At first glance, much of what Smith and Llobera describe hardly seems to apply to the United States. Indeed, even a brief trawl through the voluminous and growing literature on nationalism reveals that most scholars do not believe that *any* of it applies to the United States, that it is sui generis as far as the process of national construction is concerned. America has, it is true, a shorter history in relative terms than the European nations that attract so much scholarly interest. Golden ages, and the myths associated with them, are considered to belong to the very distant past, certainly beyond the reach of actual memory. In some ways they need to be so because they are mythical in the sense that the message they convey bears a complex and sometimes vague relation to the historical truth. Yet the United States offers a unique opportunity to scholars to examine the development and refinement of the kind of myths that nations construct in order to support their national ideals. It is the very proximity to the past in the American case that offers scholars the opportunity to observe with clarity processes that are frequently obscure elsewhere.[7]

A brief consideration of the American variant of those elements that Smith has identified reveals the applicability of the European pattern to the United States. The myth of origins and descent has served America in many, frequently contradictory, ways. The myth of separate origins for North and South, for example, which developed into the stereotypes of "Cavalier" and "Yankee," constituted a significant element—albeit a contentious one—in American national construction. It provided a valuable psychological support for both North and South in the antebellum period, even though it was recognized then that the true differences between these sections were grounded more in the latter's retention of the peculiar institution rather than in any objective racial or ethnic differences. In 1855, for example, the *New York Times* noted that the "Cavaliers who emigrated to Virginia, and the Puritans who planted themselves in New-England, may be regarded as presenting the most marked dissimilarities of character of the whole bulk of those who first populated America." Yet, the paper noted, "between those two parties there were no permanent and enduring differences, such as are engraved by race and language, or even religion." It was slavery alone, the *Times* concluded, that had "deepened and confirmed their differences." The myth of separate origins, indeed, is one that continues to resonate. As late as 1980 the *Harvard Encyclopedia of American Ethnic Groups* recognized the Yankee and the southerner as ethnically distinctive. The entry for Yankees, written by Oscar Handlin, argues that the term "Yankees" applies specifically to the group whose ancestry could be traced back to the original Puritan settlers of New England and that it is a distinct "consciousness of group identity" that "held the region's people together." John Shelton Reed, who provided the entry on southerners, also identifies an awareness of group identity in the South, albeit one shaped by the sectional tensions of the nineteenth century.[8]

Myths of liberation and migration are, similarly, central to the American nation, founded as it was around the ideals of life, liberty, and the pursuit of happiness and peopled mainly by migrants from other lands. Indeed, the arrival of the Pilgrim fathers aboard the *Mayflower* and the later "Great Migration" of the Puritans in the seventeenth century were very clearly and deliberately construed as foundation myths of the American nation.[9] Similarly, the United States has no shortage of heroes and sages to inspire the population at large: the presidents George Washington, Thomas Jefferson, and Abraham Lincoln and military heroes such as Robert E. Lee. Over time the Puritan's religiously motivated "errand into the wilderness" and the republican vision of America's Founding Fathers worked together to create the idea of the United States as a nation with a clear historical mission and of Americans themselves as being a uniquely chosen people, charged with the salvation of all mankind. The Civil War, of course, threatened this vision by destroying, albeit temporarily, the republic that Abraham Lincoln described as "the last, best hope of earth." It is in the Civil War, therefore, and in the American response to it that we can detect the final component that Smith identifies, the myth of the rebirth of the chosen people, as in Lincoln's words at Gettysburg: "that this nation, under God, shall have a new birth of freedom—and that government of the people, by the people, for the people, shall not perish from the earth."[10]

Indeed, history and the myths constructed around it have always been important elements in American national development.[11] Prior to the Civil War, the focus of interest was, naturally enough, America's colonial past and its emergence to nationhood during the Revolution. Yet there was a distinct tendency even then to portray this relatively recent history in mythical terms, in particular to modify its less savory elements and to stress instead its ideals. In their focus on the frontier struggles of the colonial period and on the heroes of the Revolutionary generation, antebellum Americans revealed themselves to be very much concerned with their history, not for its own sake, but for the lessons it might teach. Via a reworking of the colonial past, a deliberate avoidance of the divisive and violent aspects of the Revolutionary War and the implications of slavery, and the elevation of the Founding Fathers to mythical status—a process providentially aided by the deaths of Thomas Jefferson and John Adams on the same day, which just happened to be Independence Day, July 4, 1826—antebellum Americans constructed "the fabled story of America."[12]

No less than Europeans, Americans in the nineteenth century sought to discover their past and reinterpret it in such a way as to give meaning to their present and direction to their future. Like the European Romantic nationalists, Americans turned to their history in order to support their national claims and support their national ambitions. Of course, Americans could not look back on the Middle Ages to any great effect, although the classical periods of Greece and Rome held a continued fascination for them. "Greek democracy and the Roman republic—emphatically not the later Rome of the Caesars—were the twin founts from which American political theory sprang."[13] American success in the Revolution offered the former colonists the opportunity to create in the New World a modern version of an ancient ideal and to move toward the establishment of what art critic Robert Hughes has termed "The Republic of Virtue." Consequently, the antebellum and Civil War generations could and did look back to the Revolution of the eighteenth century not only as the foundation of their nation but also as a time when the American national ideal was most fully expressed. For them the Revolution had not only created the American nation but also had created American nationalism by providing the symbols, history, and myths by which nationhood is constructed.[14]

The increasing sectional tension of the early and middle nineteenth century, however, undermined the efficacy of Revolutionary myths and symbols as far as national construction was concerned. Although antebellum Americans turned increasingly to the Revolution, creating through biographies, history, oratory, art, and fiction a compelling mythos around it, this was to prove insufficient for national stability. From the Revolution that they had in common, North and South during this period constructed separate, contradictory ideologies increasingly at odds with each other. In time each came to see in the other a threat to the national ideal. They accused one another of betraying the legacy of the Founding Fathers and denying the sacrifice of the Revolutionary generation. It need not have been so. Historian Michael Kammen, for example, notes that the antebellum desire to honor America's Revolutionary heroes "may have had a sectional emphasis, but it was genuinely a national gesture." Unfortunately, it was not a successful one. So far from being a unifying part of the national past, the Revolution became a bone of contention over the national future.[15]

In assessing the Civil War generation's fascination with the Revolution, Reid Mitchell describes what almost amounts to a cult of ancestor worship in the United States at this time. Americans, he argues, "thought of the nation as a community of the living and the dead. The American family extended in time. The dead remained part of the American nation; they still made claims upon the living and they could find fulfillment in the nation's destiny." Mitchell's description here fits in well with David Miller's definition of the nation as a "community of obligation," although, again, this is not an idea that is commonly applied to the United States in studies of nationalism.[16]

Historians, however, have long recognized the nineteenth century's sense of obligation to the Founding Fathers and their legacy, in particular to Jefferson and to the Declaration of Independence. This sense was perhaps best expressed by Abraham Lincoln, who in 1854 sought to alert Americans to the dangers of straying from the past and from the founders' legacy by permitting slavery to expand across the nation: "Our republican robe is soiled, and trailed in the dust. Let us repurify it. Let us turn and wash it white, in the spirit if not the blood of the Revolution. Let us turn slavery away from its claims of 'moral right.' . . . Let us return it to the position our fathers gave it; and there let it rest in peace. Let us readopt the Declaration of Independence, and with it the practices and policy which harmonize with it." Of course, by invoking the Revolutionary heritage in the way he did, Lincoln was very much placing his own interpretation on it. The position in which the Founding Fathers had left slavery was ambiguous to say the least, and the Declaration of Independence is a stirring but somewhat vague document when it comes down to it. Yet the Founding Fathers and their legacy were integral not only to Lincoln's life and ideology but also to that of his generation as a whole. Nineteenth-century Americans revered the Revolution and, in the main, "subscribed to the romantic nationalism it fostered."[17]

Specifically, for Lincoln, the Declaration of Independence offered the only valid means to nationhood for a people comprising many different ethnicities. "We are now a mighty nation," he confidently declared in 1858, but he was at the same time conscious that national ties were not necessarily obvious in a country whose people lacked a common history. Many Americans, he knew, could not trace their connections to the past "by blood" and could not "carry themselves back into that glorious epoch and make themselves feel" a part of a nation in which their ancestors had not been born. Yet they could establish American nationality through the Declaration of Independence since, Lincoln averred, they had "a right to claim it as though they were blood of the blood, and flesh of the flesh" of those who wrote it. For Lincoln, the Declaration defined "the spirit of collective American identity . . . , and it reminded succeeding generations of the obligation to preserve and extend the founding's legacy of freedom."[18]

What that legacy actually was, however, was less clear to antebellum Americans than some historians make it seem. Lincoln's was not the only available interpretation of the past, and southerners derived very different lessons from the same Revolutionary heritage. Although using the same heroic figures of the past—in particular Thomas Jefferson—as the North, the South arrived at a very different concept of the Revolution's legacy. While for Lincoln Jefferson was the author of the Declaration of Independence and an apostle of freedom, for the South he was a slaveholder, an apostle of a very different kind of liberty based on chattel slavery. Ultimately unable to square the circle of the ideals of freedom that Lincoln and many northerners invoked as the nation's heritage with the reality of slavery in their own section, southerners sought to leave a union that no longer appeared to protect their interests. Northerners may well have gone to war "to preserve the nation left them by the Revolutionary generation, meeting an obligation they felt toward that generation," but southerners felt a different obligation altogether. For the North, the Revolution had established the principle of the Union; for the South, it had established the right of secession. Justifying their respective political, economic, and social ambitions on these alternative interpretations of the past, North and South found that their common inheritance did not, in 1861, offer enough common ground to avert sectional conflict.[19]

Some years ago, one historian observed that Americans were "a martial but not a militaristic people," more impressed with the pageantry than with the reality of war. Certainly, at the outset of the Civil War, the American martial tradition comprised essentially romantic images that maintained, among other things, that "Americans only fought in defense of great moral and political principles" and that "moral fervor was more important than military experience." In many ways this sums up the respective positions of the Union and the Confederacy. For northerners, in particular, the war very soon "assumed the aura of a holy crusade" in which patriotism and religious devotion became intertwined. But southerners, equally devoted to the cause of the Confederacy, were confident that numbers alone would not decide the outcome. This belief was not entirely ill conceived. Here again the South had the example of the Revolution to sustain them, for the Continental army managed to repel the numerically superior British troops.[20]

Far from exploding the mystical concept of the American way of war, the experience of fighting in the Civil War served only to reinforce it. The Civil War generation "thought of themselves as living in an age of heroes, as performing acts of gallantry and chivalry beyond the imagination of the stay-at-home generation of their elders."[21] Neither North nor South sought to contradict this essentially romantic view of warfare and their role in it. With the example of the Revolution continuously before them, Civil War soldiers, politicians, and spokesmen saw themselves as both inheritors and defenders of the nation's glorious past. Americans who fought in the Civil War continued to keep before them their Revolutionary heritage and referred to it throughout the conflict. Indeed, the Civil War "proved curiously filled with echoes of the American Revolution." Both Union and Confederate armies observed Washington's birthday and the Fourth of July and were frequently "reminded of their Revolutionary heritage, the heroism and purity of their forefathers, and their own duty to emulate them." Yet during the war itself, each side used the Revolutionary past in different ways and toward very different ends.[22]

For southerners, the Revolutionary heritage as they interpreted it had justified the retention of slavery and ultimately propelled them toward secession from the Union. During the course of the Civil War, the South continued to refer to the Revolutionary past as a defense for the Confederacy it had created and hoped to sustain. Yet the tendency to interpret the war in mystical terms was not as pronounced during the actual conflict as it would become in the postwar cult of the Lost Cause, with its romantic invocations of the antebellum South and its glorification of Confederate heroes. The North, however, by combining the Revolutionary past with specifically religious imagery during the war itself managed both to validate the Union cause and inject it with "national" significance. In some ways it is unsurprising that the North sought to do this. It was, after all, fighting for the preservation of the Union—its interpretation of the American nation—whereas the South was fighting for the Union's destruction and for the creation of its own separate and distinct Confederate nation. Yet for an understanding of how the Civil War came to be regarded as the "salvation drama" of the American nation, it is significant to note that this process began in the North *during* and not *after* the Civil War. In this context it is worth considering historian Reid Mitchell's analysis of Julia Ward Howe's famous "Battle Hymn of the Republic." As he notes, Howe's wording—"let us *die* to make men free"—specifically links the Union soldier with Christ's suffering and death and, equally importantly, avoids any mention of what it is that soldiers actually do. He makes this last point forcibly by rephrasing the line to read "let us *kill* to make men free." The focus on death rather than on killing, Mitchell argues, "offered tautological reassurance of the legitimacy of the Union cause and the meaningfulness of Union deaths." Perhaps more importantly, such imagery reassured northern society as a whole that the Union soldier would not be brutalized by his wartime experiences but would be "ennobled" by them. Any emphasis on the actual horror of warfare, Mitchell suggests, might have resulted in troubling questions concerning the soldier's "reintegration into post-war society."[23]

A conjunction of practical and idealistic factors, therefore, prompted northerners to mythologize the Civil War even as they were involved in actually fighting it. Specifically, from a distinctly *sectional* perspective, they nevertheless interpreted the war in terms of a *national* sacrifice by which the blood of the fallen would redeem the nation. Following the Emancipation Proclamation of 1863, the North was able to add an impressive moral string to its bow. Now it was fighting not just for the preservation of the Union but also for freedom: freedom in the most immediate sense for African American slaves (at least, those in the Confederacy) as well as freedom from both the guilt and the perceived detrimental effects of the South's peculiar institution. The Thirteenth Amendment was some way off in January 1863, but many northerners, both black and white, realized that with the Emancipation Proclamation the opportunity for the nation to finally live up to the ideal of equality for all had presented itself. The subsequent compromising of such hopes in the aftermath of the conflict, which has been so ably described and analyzed in David Blight's recent study of race and reunion, lay in the future. From the perspective of the time, northern troops would "die to make men free." Nothing now could easily contradict the northern interpretation of the Civil War as a holy crusade, neither the overt and obvious racism of the North nor the bloody reality of the conflict. As one woman wrote after the battle of the Wilderness in 1864, "Oh, if this baptism of blood does not purify this country and cleanse it of greed and selfish ambitions as well as of slavery, then the nation will deserve to become extinct."[24]

In some ways, however, the old nation had already become extinct. The outbreak of Civil War "rendered the fabled age of the republic unusable," and many Americans were aware of this. "What ever happens next," declared writer Nathaniel Hawthorne, "I must say that I rejoice that the old Union is smashed. We never were one people, and never really had a country since the Constitution was formed." Frederick Douglass, the abolitionist leader, concurred, and he envisioned a radical transformation for the nation: "Men talk about saving the Union, and restoring the Union as it was. They delude themselves with the miserable idea that the old Union can be brought to life again. That old Union, whose canonized bones we so quietly inured under the shattered walls of Sumter, can never come to life again. . . . What business, then, have we to fight for the old Union? We are not fighting for it. We are fighting for something incomparably better than the old Union. We are fighting for unity; unity of object, unity of institutions, in which there shall be no North, no South, no East, no West, no black, no white, but a solidarity of the nation." For Harriet Beecher Stowe—the "little woman that made this great war," as tradition has Lincoln saying to her—the war was the "purifying chastening of a Father, rather than the avenging anger of a Destroyer," and she, like Douglass, expressed the hope that it would bring America "forth to a higher national life."[25]

For many northerners, however, what was meant by nationalism was actually northern sectional imperialism writ large. When they spoke, as Douglass did, of their desire to achieve "solidarity of the nation," they envisaged it in northern terms. As one paper put it in 1865, "There is one, and only one, sure and safe policy for the immediate future, namely: *The North must remain the absolute dictator of the Republic until the spirit of the North shall become the spirit of the whole country.*" For many northerners, the war was in some senses overdue, a long-awaited opportunity to make sectional ideals national. From this perspective the Civil War provided an opportunity to rid the North, and hopefully the nation as a whole, of the influence of slavery and the South. Writing to his brother during the war, Henry Adams expressed this viewpoint succinctly: "The nation has been dragged by this infernal cotton that had better have been burning in Hell, far away from its true course, and its worst passions and tastes have been developed by a forced and bloated growth. It will depend on the generation to which you and I belong, whether the country is to be brought back to its true course and the New England element is to carry the victory, or whether we are to be carried on from war to war and debt to debt and one military leader to another, till we lose all our landmarks and go ahead like France with a mere blind necessity to get on, without a reason or a principle."[26]

The war's eventual outcome, of course, justified Adams's confidence in the North's position. More significantly as far as American nationalism is concerned, it validated the northern interpretation of what kind of war it was, what issues were at stake, and what kind of nation had been "created." Specifically, many northerners saw in the outcome of the war the possibility for a revolutionary transformation for the United States. The Union had not only been saved but had been saved in such a way as to ensure "a new birth of freedom" for all Americans, black and white. An even greater number of northerners, of course, would not have concurred with Adams's viewpoint. For them, northern victory offered the opportunity, not for revolutionary transformation, but for a prompt return to the status quo antebellum, with all that it implied in terms of America's racial and social structure. Yet such a position was hardly defensible in the immediate aftermath of a conflict that had cost so many American lives. The impetus to transform the war from a negative conflict into a positive act of national rebirth had greater appeal. In other words, both the tendency and the need to view the Civil War as America's "salvation drama" was present from the outset.

In the immediate postwar period, Americans showed little interest in working out the revolutionary changes made possible by the North's victory. On the whole, they preferred to avoid thinking about the war altogether. This is not especially surprising. Once home from the battlefield, soldiers "became subject to an acceleration of selective memory, that strong psychological propensity to suppress the painful." Given the peculiarly internecine nature of civil wars, it is hardly surprising that noncombatants shared this desire for selective amnesia, and the assassination of Lincoln in 1865 served only to exacerbate this tendency. In the years following the Civil War, the need for national reunification overrode any desire to dwell on the memories or the lessons of the war that had divided North and South and cost so many American lives. Reunion between the sections, therefore, began tentatively and in a romantic and sentimental manner that, for the most part, ignored the war itself. Faced with the twin difficulties of coming to terms with a hostile South and drawing it back into a nation that it had clearly wished to abandon, northerners increasingly returned to antebellum ideas about that section, stressing the romance of southern life, its graciousness, its hospitality, and of course, its plantation splendor. This was, as it had been in the antebellum period, an almost wholly mythical image, but as a basis for national harmony, it was to prove effective.[27]

It was not until the 1880s and 1890s that interest in the war itself began to grow. In these decades Civil War books became popular, and between 1884 and 1887 the circulation of *Century Magazine* almost doubled when it ran its Battles and Leaders of the Civil War series. Similarly, the membership of the Union veterans society, the Grand Army of the Republic (G.A.R.), began to rise dramatically: from 30,000 in 1878, through 320,000 in 1887, and peaking at 428,000 in 1890. The G.A.R. was instrumental in the creation and promulgation of an aggressive and active patriotism that glorified the Civil War and made heroes of those who had fought it, at least those on the Union side. In the South the activities of the United Confederate Veterans, together with the emerging cult of the Lost Cause, encouraged a similar glorification of the Confederacy and its leaders that not only helped the South come to terms with defeat but also provided its means of reentry into the patriotic culture of the nation as a whole.[28]

As interest in the war escalated, however, so too did disagreements over the war's meaning and its part in American national construction. The road to reunion was paved with controversy, compromise, and an increasingly selective interpretation of what, precisely, Americans North and South had fought for. In assessing why this should have been so, historians point to the dramatic changes that late-nineteenth-century America was undergoing, particularly the rise of industrialism and the new immigration from eastern Europe. As in the antebellum period, the influx of a large number of immigrants in the 1880s and years following exacerbated the need to define and construct "100 percent Americanism" in order that a means might be found whereby these new arrivals could be successfully integrated into the national ethos. The fact that the United States had only recently been divided during the Civil War made this task potentially more difficult. The response of many patriotic societies, however, was to make the war itself the focus of the new nationalism. By elevating the Civil War to mythical status and by controlling the memory of what the war had been about, societies like the G.A.R. succeeded in creating a forceful brand of American nationalism to which all "future versions of the 'nation' would feel obliged to respond." But the fact that it was left to those who had fought the war to conclude the process of national reunification was to have a significant influence on the national perception of that war.[29]

The reconciliation process was begun shortly after Appomattox, when Joshua Lawrence Chamberlain, assigned the honor of receiving Lee's surrender, chose to acknowledge the opposing army's bravery with a salute of honor. In the years that followed, by concentrating on their battlefield experiences to the exclusion of any troubling questions over the war's causes and its legacy, Civil War soldiers managed to retrieve some middle ground on which North and South could meet. By focusing on the heroic deaths and martial bravery of the opposing side, both Union and Confederate veterans were able to approach the war less as a divisive conflict and more as a shared experience that had brought them closer together. In Chamberlain's words, the Civil War provided Americans North and South with a "rushing tide of memories which divided us, yet made us one forever." Such sentiments culminated in the dedication of the High Water Mark of the Rebellion Monument at Gettysburg in 1892. Although erected by the North, the monument paid tribute to the South, in particular to Maj. Gen. George Pickett's fateful charge on the third and final day of Gettysburg, "an unprecedented honor in an era of partisan monuments" and "a critical step in reinterpreting the battlefield as a place in which all Americans could take pride." Gettysburg, indeed, became a focus for both North and South, in turn, and finally, with the dedication of the Eternal Peace Light Memorial on July 3, 1938, for both, with its inscription "Peace Eternal in a Nation United. An enduring light to guide us in unity and friendship."[30]

It is worth bearing in mind, however, that a decade after the dedication of the Eternal Peace Light Memorial, the South's foremost author, William Faulkner, invoked Gettysburg in a very different way. It was in his novel *Intruder in the Dust* that Faulkner made his now famous observation: "For every Southern boy fourteen years old, not once but whenever he wants it, there is the instant when it's still not yet two o'clock on that July afternoon in 1863 . . . and it's all in the balance . . . and that moment doesn't need even a fourteen-year-old boy to think *This time. Maybe this time.*" The southern response to the Civil War, unsurprisingly, remained a divided one. Indeed, in some ways the Civil War and its outcome strengthened what is called the "Myth of the South" and encouraged the belief in southern distinctiveness. In the long term, however, the South could be included in the national interpretation of the Civil War as a holy crusade—at least to some degree—if the North recognized that the Confederacy had fought bravely, if not wisely, and was in this sense on an equal footing with the Union forces. By emphasizing the experience of battle at the expense of the actual issues that had divided the sections, publications like the Battles and Leaders series managed to achieve this. Its juxtaposing of articles by Union and Confederate soldiers "signaled to the South that the North recognized its achievements even if it did not applaud its motives," making it a powerful force in the reconciliation process. Over the years, in the Battles and Leaders series, in speeches, and in the oratory of commemoration ceremonies held on battlefields across the nation, North and South worked toward a new modus vivendi by portraying the Civil War as a heroic "struggle between brothers whose blood had strengthened and purified the nation."[31]

Americans, especially northerners, were encouraged in this line of thinking by the fact that, like the deaths of Jefferson and Adams on Independence Day, 1826, the day of Lincoln's death was significant for the new post–Civil War fabled story of the nation. The obvious religious overtones attendant upon his death on Good Friday, 1865, hastened the apotheosis of the savior of the Union and the liberator of the slaves, lending further support to the mystical image of the Civil War. The president himself, it seemed to many, had been sacrificed in order that the nation might endure. He became, consequently, a symbol of nationality "reborn and reinvigorated."[32] His blood was added to the blood of the fallen, and he, more so even than the Union soldier, was forever linked with Christ's suffering and death by the manner and timing of his own passing. Given the tragedy of the Civil War and the assassination of the president, many Americans were already predisposed to look for some evidence that their sacrifice and Lincoln's death had not been in vain. The portrayal of the Civil War as a holy crusade met that need. The response of Gen. William Tecumseh Sherman to the war perhaps best expresses the shift in emphasis whereby Americans sought to come to terms with the recent conflict. In 1880 he addressed a group of G.A.R. members and advised them that, so far from being glorious, war was "all hell." A decade later, addressing veterans of the Army of the Tennessee, he compared the Civil War soldier to a knight of old and declared: "Now the truth is we fought the holiest fight ever fought on God's earth."[33]

From hell to holy, the images Sherman conjured summed up the nineteenth-century American response to the Civil War. It was a cruel fight that became a sacred war, a holy crusade, America's "salvation drama." In the aftermath of the war itself, the northern interpretation of the conflict as one of a mystical blood sacrifice gradually became the national understanding. By the time of the Spanish-American War (1898), most historians agree that, in the main, northerners and southerners were once again firmly on the same side. Indeed, some argue that the process of fighting that war went a long way toward reconciliation between North and South since it offered the opportunity for the former opponents to fight a foreign foe rather than each other. Such consensus, however, was achieved at a price. The reunion of North and South was only attained via a particular and ultimately racist interpretation of the conflict, including its causes and its legacy. Groups like the G.A.R. "used a language of consensus, but beneath claims to a universal and inclusive Americanism, racial divisions deepened." In their desire both to justify their own role in the Civil War and to create new and lasting heroes and symbols for a nation so recently and comprehensively divided, these organizations returned to the millennial rhetoric of the antebellum period. They stressed preservation of past ideals rather than future possibilities of actually living up to these and deliberately avoided addressing the questions raised by the war concerning American nationality, the African American, or indeed the southern white role in it. Their patriotism was northern in origin but national in ambition and was seriously compromised by the fact that its aims were essentially contradictory. The G.A.R. wished both to promulgate a "correct" version of the war as one fought between good (Union) and bad (Confederate) forces and at the same time to create a consensus view of the Civil War and the American nation that could function in a genuinely national way.[34]

The task was an impossible one. In the end, principle gave way to practicality. The nation of "Grand Army cosmology was still the redeemer of the world, a chosen place not bound by the ordinary constraints of history . . . , a peaceable kingdom from which disorder and diversity were shut out." Theirs was not, of course, the only view of the nation to emerge in the postwar period. Other groups—including radical, immigrant, and labor associations—had their own vision of the nation's destiny, but the veterans' version of America's birthright was the strongest. Ultimately, northern and southern Civil War veterans achieved their own version of conciliation by obliterating not only troubling questions about the war's meaning but also the presence of those African American troops who had fought alongside them. The myth that the Civil War had been a white man's fight dominated postwar rhetoric. The apotheosis of Lincoln did not, in this atmosphere, prompt Americans to conclude in any satisfactory way the emancipation process that he had begun. Although slavery had been abolished, this had little immediate practical effect on the lives of the freedmen. The South remained welded to its antebellum racial outlook and policies, only now with the tacit acceptance of a North that sought stability in the face of the social upheavals of the late nineteenth century.[35]

The black leader Frederick Douglass was painfully aware of the direction that the reunion process was taking and worked hard to preserve both the memory of the African American role in the Civil War and the nation's supposed new commitment to freedom. As David Blight has argued, "Douglass hoped that Union victory, black emancipation, and the Civil War amendments would be so deeply rooted in recent American experience, so central to any conception of national regeneration, so necessary to the post-war society that they would become sacred values, ritualized in memory." He was to be disappointed. Northern ambitions for a "new birth of freedom" for the nation floundered in the face of social change in their own section coupled with the need to reach some modus vivendi with the racial ideology of the South. Despite Douglass's best efforts to "save the legacy of the Civil War for blacks," the nation as a whole showed itself to be opposed to such an inclusive legacy. The focus on military glory as the basis for postwar reconciliation worked directly against some of the ideals that the Union had supposedly fought for. Gradually, Douglass's revolutionary vision of a new "solidarity of the nation" encompassing both black and white was replaced by a conservative, preservationist impulse that defined American national identity in an exclusionary and curiously backward-looking way. From this perspective the Civil War was still regarded as America's "salvation drama," only now it had saved the nation, not from slavery and southern influence, but from disintegration. The Civil War generation succeeded in transforming a national tragedy into a triumph. They thereby achieved a persuasive form of national consensus, but it was in some ways a pyrrhic victory since the form bequeathed a divisive legacy to the nation it venerated.[36]

The importance of the Civil War for Americans cannot be denied. Robert Penn Warren even went so far as to argue that the "Civil War is, for the American imagination, the great single event of our history. Without too much wrenching, it may, in fact, be said to *be* American history. Before the Civil War we had no history in the deepest and most inward sense." This view was echoed many years later by Reid Mitchell, who argued that Civil War soldiers had "created a new American history, a potent source of myth and identity." Such statements seem distinctly at odds with one of the pervasive myths concerning the United States as a nation, namely that in such a nation the past is of less interest than the future. Americans, it has been argued, have exhibited a distinct tendency to embrace novelty at the expense of tradition. Certainly, America's relationship to the past differs from that of the European nations. Yet this lack of a long history has not presented the barrier to national construction that many scholars suppose. From the very beginnings of the settlement of North America by Europeans, its people have consistently and successfully managed to turn their very recent past into a source of myth and legend capable of inculcating nationhood. Indeed, the search for a usable past is one of the defining features of American national construction.[37]

Yet in the process of achieving a usable past, the United States, like European nations, has to be selective about its history and especially about the Civil War. The war, as one historian has argued, called into question both the ethical and the national character of America. It was the nation's "darkest hour precisely because the basest qualities in our character briefly became ascendant then." There was very little about the Civil War, he concludes, that Americans could take pride in. This, however, is the voice of the academy. It is not the voice that most Americans wish to hear, and in terms of national construction, its message is not a positive one. For those who fought in the Civil War and then did so much to reconstruct the nation in the postwar period, the impetus to derive a positive message from the conflict was strong. To do otherwise would have been to call into question their own actions and, in a very real sense, to shame the memory of their fallen comrades by implying that their deaths had been in vain. Those who fought in the war had, therefore, to be elevated to heroic status, and the war itself, by extension, became a sacred conflict. That it had held together a nation that represented "the last, best hope of earth" lent further weight to the interpretation of the Civil War as America's holy crusade. In the same way as the Revolution had to be remembered more for the ideals it represented than the manner of its achievement, so the Civil War had to be transformed into a crusade for freedom, a war for Union, and the final and decisive act of American national construction.[38]

Consequently, by the end of the nineteenth century, Americans had in place a powerful mythos surrounding the Civil War. It was seen as the conclusion of a process begun during the colonial period, honed during the Revolution, and tempered by a war that had defined, once and for all, the validity of the American experiment in self-government. Yet such an interpretation of the Civil War rested on selective assumptions about the conflict and an unquestioning acceptance of the myths surrounding it. The portrayal of the war in a semimystical way continued into the twentieth century and was not confined to Americans. In 1924 Scottish writer John Buchan advised his American audience that the Civil War "was a conflict of great men, leaders on the heroic scale," and was one fought between the South and "the larger civic organism, the Nation." Similarly, when Liah Greenfeld argues that the process of national formation in the United States was not complete until the conclusion of the Civil War, she is perpetuating the idea that the war was, in essence, a positive and constructive act. Further, her assertion that after the war "the soul of the American nation, which had been before but a resident tenant in its vast territorial body, became its owner" has a distinctly nineteenth-century ring to it. When a late-twentieth-century scholar, after rigorous analysis of the entire process of American national construction from the colonial period onward, falls back on the quasimystical interpretation of the Civil War as a battle for the "soul" of America, the continuing power of Civil War mythology becomes clear.[39]

Even those who do not regard the Civil War as a "war for nationality" per se tend to portray it in mystical terms and cite it as evidence of American exceptionalism or even superiority in the game of nation-building. Civil War historian Gabor Boritt, for example, argues that it would be wrong to regard Lincoln as a New World counterpart of "Cavour and Bismarck whose highest goal . . . was *staatsbildung*." He continues: "Without gainsaying the achievements of the Europeans, we must note that their degenerate twentieth-century descendants in the worship of the nation as an end in itself were Hitler and Mussolini. In contrast, Lincoln's dream helped lead America to the nationalism of Theodore Roosevelt, Woodrow Wilson, and Franklin Delano Roosevelt." In the context of the Civil War's legacy to the United States, it is worth recalling that one of Woodrow Wilson's first acts as president was to segregate Washington, D.C. If he was no Hitler or Mussolini, neither was Wilson a particularly inclusive nationalist, and his vision for the nation he headed in the early twentieth century was hardly different from that espoused by the G.A.R. and other Civil War veteran societies. Wilson's view of America's national purpose was in many ways "a classic expression of the self-image of a nation, born with a sense of mission." More significantly for American national development, Wilson was a national figure with a sectional agenda, one whose southern background framed his political and racial outlook. His was essentially a civic nationalism with a strong ethnic, Anglo-Saxon element that relied on a selective reading of America's past. Further, although some may argue, as Boritt does, that the worship of the nation as an end in itself has never been the American way, the fact remains that the outcome of the Civil War *did* privilege the nation at the expense of its purported ideals. The northern interpretation of the Civil War as a holy crusade, which began during the war itself and gained widespread acceptance in the postwar period, imbued the nation itself with a distinctly religious character. As Chamberlain put it, after the Civil War the American flag, in part at least, represented the charter of America's birthright, "God's covenant with man."[40]

In this sense the United States clearly represents the "first new nation" of the modern era. Joseph Llobera, for one, has highlighted the "quasi-sacred" character of the modern nation. Indeed, he concludes, "the success of nationalism in modernity has to be attributed largely to the sacred character that the nation has inherited from religion." In the American case the development of the view that the nation itself is sacred derived directly from the Civil War experience and its interpretation by Americans. It may be the case that on both Independence Day and Memorial Day, when Americans celebrate the Revolution and the Civil War respectively, they are dedicating themselves to "a nation conceived as the living fulfillment of a political doctrine that enshrines a utopian conception of men's egalitarian and fraternal relations with each other." Yet in the context of twentieth-century American nationalism, this describes the ideal rather than the reality. More plausible is the conclusion that these celebrations "have become characteristically statist or martial in form and substance, and only faintly echo the revolutionary notions of the Founders." As Liah Greenfeld notes, in "the best Romantic tradition" the American nation represented an idea, and that idea was freedom. Paradoxically, however, the process of reunification and national construction that took place after the Civil War dispersed the idea itself, leaving only the nation behind. The mythology surrounding this most crucial of all American conflicts represents both an attempt to blur this fact and at the same time to keep the idea alive.[41]

We must conclude that the idea of American exceptionalism in terms of its national construction is seriously flawed and in need of reassessment. In common with the European nations, Americans have consistently turned to their history for justification and confirmation of the present. Of necessity, that history is a highly selective one that can be more accurately described as mythical, not in the sense that it is deliberately fabricated, but rather that it interprets the past in a symbolic way with a view to establishing national identity. Much of that history too, as is the case with European nations, is concerned with warfare. As Michael Howard reminds us, for many nations, including France, Germany, and the United States, the decisive wars were ones fought by citizen armies, which linked their victories forever with the popular, national will and ensured their elevation to mythical status as the defining acts of national achievement.[42] No less than in Europe, warfare was indissolubly linked with the process of American national development.

The Civil War, specifically, is a central component in the construction of American nationalism not only because its outcome held the nation together when it might have come apart but also because the opportunity was present at that time to change the nature of the nation, to return it to the ideals of life, liberty, and the pursuit of happiness as set out in the Declaration of Independence. It was, in theory at least, the "salvation drama" of the United States. The postwar period, however, witnessed a retreat from the transformative opportunities offered by the war. This is not especially surprising. The opportunity to change the nation's racial outlook was never really present, and those who preserved the memory of the war for future generations had no desire to do so. Indeed, the requirements of the reunion process worked directly against any such revolutionary change.

The Civil War, therefore, became the central component of the new nationalist mythology of the United States, the concluding act of a drama begun two centuries before. The myths constructed around it not only reveal a specifically American response to the problem of national construction and the role of violence in this but also illuminate the motivations and impulses that lie behind the construction of a mythical past in more general terms. The Civil War's transformation from a bitter sectional conflict to a holy crusade that established and sanctified the nation was more than a product of its time and place, and it continues to resonate today. The recognition of this fact in no way diminishes the Civil War's importance to American national development but rather offers further evidence of the continued centrality of warfare and the myths constructed around it in the construction of nations. In this context as in others, it is surely time to stop regarding the United States as a nation apart.

12

FROM CIVIL WAR TO WORLD POWER

Perceptions and Realities, 1865–1914

RICHARD N. CURRENT

Between 1865 and 1914 the United States rose to recognition as one of the world's great powers. This would seem, at first glance, to be a legacy of the Civil War, one that Americans perceived and appreciated at the time. But was it really a result of that war, and did contemporary Americans perceive it as such? A review of the evidence will suggest a negative answer to both questions. The truth seems to be that people had to live down the Civil War before the country could become a great power and they could accept and applaud its new status.

To qualify as a great power, the United States needed to develop the following: (1) a party system that would tend to unite rather than to divide the country; (2) a sense of psychological as well as political reunion; (3) a strong, assertive presidency; (4) an aggressive, expansive foreign policy; (5) a large military and naval capacity; and (6) a highly industrialized and productive economy. By 1914 the United States had obtained or was on the verge of obtaining each of those half-dozen elements of national greatness. Not one of the items, however, could be traced back directly and continuously to the events of 1861–65, as even a brief look at each of them will show.

With apologies to Carl von Clausewitz, it might be said that politics is warfare carried on by other means, and American politics for many years could certainly be considered a continuation of the Civil War. The war, which followed a sectionalizing of political parties, led to an increase rather than a decrease in sectionalism. It intensified the anti-Yankee bitterness of southerners and made them less willing than before secession to acknowledge northerners as fellow citizens.

"I here declare my unmitigated hatred to Yankee rule—to all political, social and business connections with the Yankees and to the Yankee race." So wrote the Virginian Edmund Ruffin in the hour of final defeat. "Would that I could impress these sentiments, in their full force, on every living Southerner and bequeath them to every one yet to be born! May such sentiments be held universally in the outraged and down-trodden South, though in silence and stillness, until the now far-distant day shall arrive for just retribution for Yankee usurpation, oppression and atrocious outrages, and for deliverance and vengeance for the now ruined, subjugated, and enslaved Southern States!" Having written those words, Ruffin put the muzzle of a shotgun in his mouth and pushed the trigger with a forked stick.[1]

Ruffin had been a fanatical secessionist. The Georgian Howell Cobb, by contrast, had resisted extremes of sectionalism while serving as a prewar congressman, governor, and secretary of the treasury. After the war Confederate general Cobb advised Union general James H. Wilson, "The prejudices and passions which have been aroused in this contest, crimsoned in the blood of loved ones from every portion of the land, will yield only to the mellowing influence of time, and the younger participants in the struggle will scarcely live to see the last shadow pass away." The abolition of slavery, Cobb went on, was "calculated to excite the most serious apprehensions" and would be "unfortunate" for both blacks and whites. The task of statesmanship now was to find a "substitute" for slavery. "I take it for granted," Cobb concluded, "that the future relations between the negroes and their former owners . . . will be under the control and direction of the State Governments."[2]

As long as Pres. Andrew Johnson had his way, the southern states did keep control of race relations, and each of the states enacted its Black Code to limit the freedom of blacks and thus provide a substitute for slavery. To assure real freedom to the former slaves, the Republicans in 1867 launched their program of Congressional Reconstruction, which gave black men political rights. This further embittered the majority of white southerners.

A temporary dissenter from the majority was the Mississippi planter James L. Alcorn, who had been the state's largest slaveholder next to Jefferson Davis's brother Joseph but had been unenthusiastic about secession. In January 1869, shortly before Ulysses S. Grant's inauguration as president, Alcorn wrote to Grant's friend Elihu B. Washburne, an Illinois congressman: "Is there a man in Congress so stupid as to believe that there is a Democrat in the South who regards Gen. Grant with other than the most intense hatred? Who considers the American government other than a stupendous tyranny? Who would not hail with joy the overthrow of that government by France, England, or any other power, as a Christian would hail the coming of the Messiah?"[3]

Rebelliousness on the part of southern whites persisted as long as southern blacks continued to vote and hold office. The issues of the Civil War now reemerged in a somewhat altered form—states' rights instead of secession, "white supremacy" instead of slavery. The Democratic party, North as well as South, took up what had been the Confederate side. Democrats vilified the Republican state governments in the South, grossly exaggerating their extravagance and corruption and falsely characterizing them as instruments of "Negro rule." After the Democrats got control of the national House of Representatives, the federal government quit trying to enforce the political rights of southern blacks, and Reconstruction came to an end in 1877.

Republicans, with considerable justification, had been denouncing the Democratic party as the party of treason, and they continued to do so even after the Reconstruction issues were dead. Not all Democrats were traitors, Republicans said, but all the traitors were Democrats. Republicans urged ex-soldiers in the North to vote as they shot, thus appealing to the hundreds of thousands who belonged to the Union veterans' organization the Grand Army of the Republic (G.A.R.), which functioned as a virtual auxiliary of the Republican party.

Democrats accused Republicans of "waving the bloody shirt"—that is, reviving wartime hatreds for political effect—although in the South Democrats were doing likewise as they continually rearoused devotion to the Lost Cause and its heroes. In the South Confederate war service became practically a requirement for election to state or local office, and Union war service was equally essential in the North. Republican candidates were almost always former officers, almost never common soldiers. A Wisconsin member of the Grand Army of the Republic claimed in 1872 that the veteran vote had "elected 274 Generals and Colonels to the State Legislatures and not one private."[4]

In every presidential election except one between the end of the war and the end of the century, the Republicans ran a former officer of the Union army. Only Grant had been a professional soldier; all the rest of those elected—Rutherford B. Hayes, James A. Garfield, Benjamin Harrison, and William McKinley—had served as volunteers. The Democrats could not very well take advantage of the politics of patriotism in the same way. A Confederate veteran on their ticket would turn away voters in the North, and a Union veteran could not expect to attract very many in the South. Still, the Democrats tried their luck with Winfield Scott Hancock in 1880. Hancock, a West Point graduate, still held a generalship in the regular army. Against the "citizen soldier" Garfield, he had no chance.

The election of 1884 was the only one in which the Republicans risked a candidate with no war record—James G. Blaine. They tried to make up for Blaine's defect by picking John A. Logan as his running mate. Logan had been not only a general of volunteers but also a commander in chief of the G.A.R. Even so, the ticket did not attract enough of the soldier vote to carry the election. Grover Cleveland, who like Blaine had escaped war service, became the first Democrat elected president in almost thirty years.

Some observers thought that Cleveland's election marked an end to sectional politics. Once Cleveland had begun his presidency, however, Gen. William Tecumseh Sherman accused him of appointing ex-Confederates to positions as high as his cabinet. G.A.R. leaders raised the question whether the fruits of northern victory were now to be sacrificed. Republicans waved the bloody shirt with renewed vigor. Before the end of Cleveland's first term, British observer James Bryce could nevertheless declare that from 1850 to 1876, "questions, first of the extension of slavery, then of its extinction, then of the reconstruction of the Union, had divided the nation," but now the "controversies raised by the war" had been settled.[5]

During the 1890s, farmers in the South and West came together to resist the "money power" of the Northeast, and the new Populist alignment tended to offset the old sectionalism of South against North. A Populist writer quoted Abraham Lincoln (apocryphally) as having predicted that the money power would "endeavor to prolong its reign by working upon the prejudices of the people." Sure enough, "it had kept aflame the sectional bitterness engendered by the War."[6] To emphasize the spirit of reunion, the Populist party in 1892 nominated a former Union general for president and a former Confederate general for vice president.

The Spanish-American War, drawing support from both parties and both sections, contributed further to political reunion. Former Union soldiers, as represented by the G.A.R., endorsed the war. Along with them, former Confederates enlisted in it. Two ex-Confederate generals, Fitzhugh Lee and Joseph Wheeler, now served as generals in the U.S. Army. Veterans of the blue and the gray no longer refought the old war with their accustomed bitterness, and their influence for good or ill declined as they gradually died off.

Politics became still less divisive as, around the turn of the century, the southern states completed the disfranchisement of blacks by means of laws and constitutional amendments. As Bryce had said, "thoughtful observers in the South" expected that "for many years to come the negroes, naturally a good-natured and easy-going race, would be content with the position of an inferior caste, doing the hard work, and especially the field work, of the country."[7] Few northerners objected to this substitute for slavery. The war aim of reunion had finally been achieved—at the expense of the war aim of emancipation.

It took more than political reunion to bring about the psychological reunion of northerners and southerners. It also required the reeducation of northerners. They had to learn to look back on the Civil War in more or less the same way as southerners did.

In this reeducation the public schools naturally played an important part. History texts and teachers gave a great deal of attention to the war but concentrated almost exclusively on campaigns and battles, recounting them in what seemed to students like boring detail. "What a farce the teaching of American history was," an Indiana schoolboy of the 1880s later recalled; "for tomorrow take four pages, and we sat down and learned those pages over and over until we could answer how many men were shot in such and such a battle, and how many miles they marched and whether Antietam came before Gettysburg—what a waste of time."[8] Such teaching was not likely to raise a generation of Civil War enthusiasts and Yankee partisans.

Nor were the textbooks themselves likely to do so. At first, some of those used in northern schools displayed a strong Yankee bias, portraying Confederates as the veriest traitors. But the larger publishers, aiming at the southern as well as the northern market, made their books quite impartial from an early date.

Publisher A. S. Barnes and Company—with offices in New York, Chicago, and New Orleans—announced the following objective in its 1871 edition: "To write a National history by carefully avoiding all sectional or partisan views." Indeed, the book hardly expresses any views at all. It makes only a passing mention of the Emancipation Proclamation and the Thirteenth Amendment, while recounting the campaigns and battles at length. It gives equal billing to Union and Confederate heroes in the illustrations as well as the narrative. In the book Lincoln and Davis face each other in pictures of the same size on opposing pages, and Union generals appear in poses no more flattering than those of Stonewall Jackson and Robert E. Lee.[9]

Northerners seemed to accept, without complaint, that kind of bland and boring treatment of the war until the mid-1880s, when some of the Union veterans began to object to it. A Wisconsin veteran found his teenage son and daughter "lamentably ignorant" of the war's causes and the Union's aims. He discovered why when he looked at the history books that the Wisconsin schools were using. "In making textbooks for the whole country, publishers have eliminated everything that might offend the Southern people." Apparently, in Wisconsin and other northern states, young people born since the war were being brought up to feel guilty about it, while in the South they were being taught to take pride in the Lost Cause and to revere its heroes.[10]

The Grand Army of the Republic finally undertook to correct the teaching of history in the schools. At the G.A.R. national encampment in 1888, the commander in chief presented a report from the Wisconsin branch, which had appointed a committee to examine textbooks. Those used in the North, the committee found, made such concessions to the South that pupils could not tell "which was right and which was wrong." The committee concluded: "It is time that a broad, comprehensive, constitutional, Union-loving patriotism should be taught in our common schools." This the G.A.R. advocated throughout the 1890s without a great deal of success.

The G.A.R. succeeded better in its attempt during the 1890s to instill patriotism through flag worship. Local posts donated flags to schools and encouraged the schools to fly the flags. The G.A.R. instructed its own members to stand whenever "The Star-Spangled Banner" was played, and school authorities soon required students to follow the veterans' example. In 1899 the G.A.R. adopted the "Pledge of Allegiance" to the flag and began to persuade schools to adopt it.[11]

The veterans' agitation for patriotism was not a direct outgrowth of the Civil War, nor did it do much to overcome the war's legacy of sectional divisiveness. Not until twenty years after that war did the G.A.R. even start its educational program, and not until after the Spanish-American War and a new wave of patriotism did the G.A.R. make much headway with the program. The more the G.A.R. appealed to northerners, the more it alienated southerners, especially with its demand for pro-Union schoolbooks.

Unlike the G.A.R., Grant and other former officers, Confederate as well as Union, usually emphasized national harmony rather than sectional animosity when they recalled the war. Reminiscences of many of them were published in the 1880s in a series of magazine articles and then in four volumes under the title *Battles and Leaders of the Civil War*, which stressed the "skill and valor of both sides." Although Sherman had (unintentionally) stirred up southern resentment with his too-candid *Memoirs* (1875), Grant said nothing to antagonize his late foes in his *Memoirs* (1885). Southern military memoirists were too busy quarreling with one another to spend much time denouncing Federals, even if they had been inclined to do so. The ex-Confederates tried to shift the blame for losing the Lost Cause—Davis pointing the finger at various opponents; P. G. T. Beauregard and Joseph E. Johnston at Davis; John B. Hood at Johnston. Hood and Johnston were friendly enough with Sherman but could not contain their hatred for each other.[12]

Historians also contributed to the growing spirit of reunion. During the late nineteenth and the early twentieth centuries, the leading authorities—James Ford Rhodes, Frederick Jackson Turner, Edward Channing, John Bach McMaster, Woodrow Wilson—took a nationalist rather than sectionalist stance. Instead of assigning guilt for the war, they attributed it to impersonal causes. They expressed satisfaction at its consequences, the most significant of which they unanimously held was the preservation of the Union and the destruction of slavery. None of them mentioned the nation's rise to world power as one of the legacies.[13]

By 1911, a half century after its start, the war had become the subject of nearly seven thousand works of nonfiction, according to the librarian of Congress. Many of these books sold well and were widely read. Nevertheless, when Francis Trevelyan Miller was preparing his ten-volume *Photographic History of the Civil War* (1911), he noted, "military writers have informed me that they cannot understand why the American people have been so little interested in this remarkable war." (Perhaps these military writers had their own treatises in mind.) Miller came to the conclusion that the "lack of popular interest" was because the United States was "not a military nation." He dedicated his compilation "to the men in blue and gray whose valor and devotion have become the priceless heritage of a united nation."[14]

Americans were being psychologically reunited through fictional as well as historical writings. "Not only is the epoch of the war the favorite field of American fiction to-day," novelist Albion W. Tourgée noted in 1888, "but the Confederate soldier is the popular hero. Our literature has become not only Southern in type, but distinctly Confederate in sympathy." Stories by southern writers were driving "from the Northern mind the unfriendly [wartime] picture of the South," as Paul H. Buck has written. The South now appeared as a land of "noble lives . . . heroic sacrifices . . . magnolias . . . romance." In the writings of North Carolinian Thomas Dixon Jr., the South also began to appear as the bastion of white civilization against a threat of black barbarism. Dixon's 1902 book, *The Leopard's Spots: A Romance of the White Man's Burden—1805–1900,* sold more than a million copies. Two of his novels formed the basis of the racist movie *Birth of a Nation* (1915), which in turn inspired the revival of the Ku Klux Klan.[15] Columbia University historian William A. Dunning agreed with Dixon on at least one essential point—that it had been a serious error to give blacks the right to vote and hold office. Of course, suffrage had been necessary for assuring freedom to the freed and thus clinching the war aim of emancipation. By the time of World War I, most northerners were ready to abandon that aim.[16] Psychological reunion was achieved; it had been made possible by the intellectual southernization of the North.

To behave like a great power, the United States needed a strong executive, one who, at least in matters of peace and war, would be free from the constraints of the people or their representatives in Congress so as to be able to act quickly and decisively. Recent presidents have claimed this kind of authority. They, together with journalists and political scientists who cater to them, trace the authority back to the Civil War example of Abraham Lincoln.

Harry S. Truman, for one, thought the Korean War justified his seizure of steel mills in the same way that the Civil War justified Lincoln's seizure of railroad and telegraph lines between Washington and Annapolis. At a press conference Truman was asked, "Are there any limitations at all on a President's actions during an emergency?" He replied, in effect, that there were none. "Mr. Lincoln," he explained, "exercised the powers of the President to meet the emergencies with which he was faced."[17]

Actually, the Civil War was followed by a decline in the powers of the president and an increase in those of Congress. The impeachment of Andrew Johnson, though falling short of conviction, contributed to this result. Grant and his successors in the White House assumed that it was the business of Congress to make the laws and of the president to carry them out. In his book *Congressional Government* (1885), Woodrow Wilson acknowledged the dominant position of the legislative branch; he proposed a closer connection between the legislative and the executive branches, the British parliamentary system being his preferred model.[18]

But the British observer Bryce did not seem to think a reform of that kind was necessary. In *The American Commonwealth* (1889) Bryce wrote:

The domestic authority of the President is in time of peace very small. . . . In war time, however, and especially in a civil war, it expands with portentous speed. Both as commander-in-chief of the army and navy, and as charged with the "faithful execution of the laws," the President is likely to be led to assume all the powers which the emergency requires. How much he can legally do without the aid of statues is disputed, for the acts of President Lincoln during the earlier part of the War of Secession, including his proclamation suspending the writ of *Habeus Corpus,* were subsequently legalized by Congress; but it is at least clear that Congress can make him, as it did make Lincoln, almost a dictator. And how much the war power may include appears in this, that by virtue if it and without any previous legislative sanction, President Lincoln issued his emancipation proclamations of 1862 and 1863, declaring all slaves in the insurgent States to be thereafter free, although these States were deemed to be in point of law still members of the Union.[19]

As Bryce here indicated, experts in the 1880s disagreed in regard to the president's constitutional ability to act without the approval of Congress even in a time of overwhelming emergency such as the Civil War. Bryce might also have indicated—if he had known—that Lincoln himself harbored serious doubts as to the efficacy of his "war power" and the enduring constitutionality of his Emancipation Proclamation once the war should be over.

As late as 1897, Wilson believed that Lincoln's case was highly exceptional and was no model for later presidents. According to Wilson, "Lincoln made the presidency the government while the war lasted . . . , but . . . his time was a time of fearful crisis, when men studied power, not law. No one of these men [George Washington, Andrew Jackson, Lincoln] seems the normal President, or affords example of the usual course of administration."[20]

Wilson noticed a change, however, after the Spanish-American War and the diplomatic exploits of Theodore Roosevelt. "Foreign questions became leading questions," Wilson wrote in 1908, "and in them the President was of necessity leader. Our new place in the affairs of the world has . . . kept him at the front of our government, where our own thoughts and the attention of men everywhere are centered upon him." That is to say the Spanish-American War, not the Civil War, had prepared the way for the president to become the "leader" in foreign affairs.[21]

In 1913, the year Wilson took office, ex-President Roosevelt said his own principle had been the same as Jackson's and Lincoln's, namely, that the executive was "bound to serve the people affirmatively in cases where the Constitution does not explicitly forbid." But, he went on, James Buchanan and William Taft had taken the "narrowly legalistic view that the President . . . can do nothing . . . unless the Constitution explicitly commands the action." Taft was amused at Roosevelt's calling him a "Buchanan President" and himself a "Lincoln President." Later, Taft wrote that Roosevelt's notion of an "undefined residuum of power" in the executive was an "unsafe doctrine" and that Lincoln had provided no precedent for it. Lincoln had "always pointed out the [constitutional] source of the authority which in his opinion justified his acts" and "never claimed that whatever authority in government was not expressly denied to him he could exercise."[22]

In trying to maintain neutrality from 1914 to 1917, Wilson was much too cautious to suit the bellicose Roosevelt. "Whoever is too proud to fight . . . , whoever demands peace without victory . . . , is false to the teachings and lives of Washington and Lincoln," Roosevelt declaimed. "Whoever seeks office . . . on the ground that 'he kept us out of the war' . . . is treacherous to the principles of Washington and Lincoln; *they* did not 'keep us out of war.' "[23]

But Lincoln's legacy was complex and confusing. As a congressman during the war with Mexico, he had condemned James K. Polk for exceeding the constitutional powers of the president. In 1918, after the United States had entered World War I, Roosevelt denounced Wilson as a would-be wartime dictator and quoted against him Lincoln's criticism of Polk. Roosevelt said, "The President is merely the most important of a large number of public servants." This did not sound like the "Lincoln President" who could exercise any and all powers that the Constitution did not deny him in so many words.[24]

By the time of World War I, not one of Lincoln's successors had found an unequivocal precedent for the uninhibited executive in Lincoln's conduct of the Civil War.

If the Civil War had been the determining influence, the United States would not have joined the hunt for overseas possessions in the 1890s, nor would it have leaned toward Great Britain and France when the European powers formed their alliances in preparation for the war of 1914. Instead, the United States would have steered clear of imperialism, and if it had aligned itself with any of the European powers, the most likely choice (after Russia) would have been Germany.

"They [the Americans] have a well-grounded aversion, strengthened by their experience of the difficulty of ruling the South after 1865, to the incorporation or control of any community not anxious to be one with them and thoroughly in harmony with their own body." So it seemed to Bryce in 1888. "Although they would rejoice over so great an extension of their territory and resources [as Canada], they are well satisfied with the present size and progress of their own country."[25]

In *The United States as a World Power* (1908), Harvard professor Archibald Cary Coolidge agreed that after the Civil War "public opinion occupied itself but little with foreign affairs; for the nation was engaged in recovering from the effects of the struggle," and "territorial expansion did not appeal either to statesmen or to the people, the general feeling on the subject being very different from what it had been just before 1860." True, the United States acquired Alaska in 1867, "but the new territory was on the same continent," and with the anticipated annexation of Canada, "Alaska would be united to the rest of the republic." After the Alaska purchase "the feeling in America for over a generation remained hostile to further expansion."

For thirty years, expansionists made no headway in their efforts to acquire Santo Domingo, the Danish West Indies, Samoa, Hawaii, or Cuba, and they did not even think of the Philippines. If the war with Spain had occurred during the Cuban insurrection of 1868–78, the American people would not have been ready for overseas colonies or protectorates. At that time they were still preoccupied with issues growing out of the Civil War. "In 1898 the country . . . was prepared to meet the situation with a spirit quite unlike that which would have animated it twenty years earlier," as Coolidge said.[26]

Even in the 1890s, Americans retained much of their antiexpansionist feeling, and to cultivate it opponents of imperialism appealed to memories of the Civil War. "Only a very few of the public men of the time [1861–65] still delighted in 'manifest destiny' dreams," Carl Schurz reminded the people in his 1893 argument against Pres. Benjamin Harrison's proposal to annex the Hawaiian Islands. According to the well-known Presbyterian divine Henry Van Dyke, the issue in 1898 was the same as in 1860: "Could the Republic continue to exist 'half slave, half free'?" *The Arena* magazine said in 1900, "Strange things are happening in America when an Administration representing the party of Lincoln—the party that freed the blacks—stands squarely against liberty in the Philippines."

When Emilio Aguinaldo led the Filipinos in revolt against American rule, the imperialist Theodore Roosevelt also found a lesson in the Civil War. "The men in our own country who, in the name of peace, have been encouraging Aguinaldo and his people to shoot down our soldiers in the Philippines might profit not a little if they would look back to the days of the bloody draft riots . . . when the mob killed men and women in the streets and burned orphan children in the asylums as a protest against the war." The enemy at that time, the Confederacy, "was helped by the self-styled advocates of peace." So in Roosevelt's opinion, the anti-imperialists of 1899–1901 were no better than the Copperheads and draft resisters of the 1860s.

While anti-imperialists appealed to the idealism of that earlier period, expansionists made the most of racist feelings that had recently been intensified. The "little brown brother" in the Philippines, like the black brother in the southern states, seemed to need the firm hand of the master race. Alfred T. Mahan, whom Roosevelt characterized as "a Christian gentleman," confided to the imperialist senator from Massachusetts, Henry Cabot Lodge, "I try to respect, but cannot, the men who utter the shibboleth of self-government, and cloud therewith their own intelligence, by applying it to a people in the childhood stage of race development."[27]

By this time the British government was encouraging Americans, in the words of Rudyard Kipling, to "take up the white man's burden," and Mahan and Roosevelt looked upon Great Britain as a foreign-policy model for the United States. The Anglo-American rapprochement was by no means a product of the Civil War. England had been the historic enemy, the only one whose armies had ever invaded the country, and they had done it twice. By recognizing the Confederacy as a belligerent and by permitting it to obtain British-built warships, the British government antagonized the North while giving insufficient aid to satisfy the South. The Civil War led to a worsening of Anglo-American relations.

Afterward, the British deliberately cultivated American friendship. In the Treaty of Washington (1872), they agreed to a settlement of the *Alabama* claims and other U.S. grievances arising from the Civil War. They, conspicuously alone among the Europeans, were friendly during the Spanish-American War. Later, they made other concessions to win the ultimate reward of U.S. assistance in World War I.

During the Civil War the French, to an even greater degree than the British, offended northerners while failing to please southerners. The French flouted the Monroe Doctrine when they intervened in Mexico, and in the postwar decades the Monroe Doctrine became increasingly a sacred tenet of Americans, both North and South. This is one reason why most Americans favored the Prussians during the Franco-Prussian War, but there is also another reason. German immigrants vastly outnumbered French immigrants in the United States. As Coolidge said of the German Americans in 1908, "In the Civil War they played a creditable part, and they have shown themselves ready to support their adopted country on all occasions, even—if necessary—against their native one."[28] Certainly, the Civil War had nothing to do with the ultimate estrangement from Germany and reconciliation with France.

The Civil War left the United States with no strong military establishment and no tradition of militarism—even though by the war's end this country had become as mighty a military and naval power as any in the world. Congress had "provided for the assembling of a host that grew in magnitude until it surpassed in numbers the largest military force ever put in the field by a European power."[29] The navy had grown strong enough that it could have defended the American coast against any

European foe. But the navy soon dwindled to a mere skeleton of its wartime self, and only the regular army remained in 1866, after more than a million volunteers had been mustered out of the service. Congress then authorized an increase in the size of the regular army, but three years later reduced its strength to a maximum of twenty-five thousand officers and men, a limit that was to continue in effect until the Spanish-American War.

As far as the national defense was concerned, the lesson that most Americans drew from the Civil War was that a small professional army, to serve as the cadre for an expanded volunteer force, would suffice. "The two services [regular and volunteer] were rapidly and most happily combined, and demonstrated by their joint powers the strength of the country for defense, and, if need be, for offense," Blaine stated in 1884. "Without maintaining a large military establishment, which besides its expense entails multiform evils, it was shown that the Republic possesses in the strong arms and patriotic hearts of its sons an unfailing source of military power."[30]

As late as 1897, less than a year before the outbreak of the Spanish-American War, the secretary of war himself, Russell A. Alger, expressed a view similar to Blaine's. Alger, a former commander in chief of the Grand Army of the Republic, was addressing its members at a banquet. He assured his fellow veterans that the U.S. Army, "as far as it went," was "the best under God's footstool." He said that an English friend had recently asked him what the United States would do if a strong power should attack. "I answered that in thirty days we could put five millions of fighting men in the field, and back them up with a wall of fire in the person of the veteran." The G.A.R. members roared their applause.[31]

While the veteran volunteers continued to be honored, the professional soldiers of the postwar army gained little respect. They added to their unpopularity when they served as strikebreakers during the depressions of the 1870s and 1890s. In the 1870s, federal and state troops together seemed inadequate to the task. Concerned citizens then began the revitalization of the National Guard as a military reserve for war and as a strikebreaking force in times of peace.

Except in the National Guard, the army, and the military academies, there was little opportunity for military training. The Morrill Act of 1862 provided that colleges benefiting from federal land grants should teach military tactics as well as agriculture and mechanical arts, but the law did not specify whether military tactics was to be compulsory or optional. After the war the A and M colleges did little with the subject. They could seldom find qualified instructors until 1893, when Congress authorized the army to detail officers for educational duty. From time to time congressmen meanwhile introduced resolutions to discontinue the military academy at West Point.

During the Franco-Prussian War, some Americans were so well impressed by the efficiency of the Prussian army that they lauded the Prussian system of compulsory military training for all able-bodied young men. But other Americans denounced the militarism of both Prussia and France. Massachusetts senator Charles Sumner declared that Prussia was a military despotism and that compulsory service was a form of "bondage."[32] There was, at that time, no serious movement for the adoption of the Prussian system in the United States.

But there later developed a serious movement for the introduction of some kind of military training in the public schools. In the 1890s the G.A.R. advocated it, and ex-President Harrison endorsed it. The New York legislature passed a bill requiring it, despite the opposition of prominent citizens who said the measure would "encourage in America the growth of the spirit of militarism" that had "done so much to hamper the civilization and prosperity of Europe."[33] Although the governor vetoed the bill, some schools in New York and in other states soon were drilling their students.

The great majority of Americans continued to rely on untrained volunteers to fight future wars, the assumption being that the Civil War had shown they could safely do so. But some army and navy officers drew a very different lesson from that war and from subsequent events. Armies and navies of European powers were developing new technologies and techniques, and the armed forces of the United States, once so powerful, were lagging far behind.

The navy began a slight buildup in 1883, when Congress appropriated money for three small cruisers with auxiliary sails. These vessels were intended for coastal defense and commerce raiding, as ships of the Civil War had been. There was, as yet, no thought of far-flung naval engagements. As Pres. Chester A. Arthur explained in his annual message, "It is no part of our policy to create and maintain a Navy able to cope with that of the other great powers of the world."[34]

Mahan changed the concept of the navy's role with his writings on seapower, which began to appear in the 1890s. While Mahan did not neglect coastal defense, he conceived of operations a long way from American shores. To some extent he derived his ideas from the Civil War experience and study—he had written a history of the Gulf Coast blockade—but he adapted his ideas to the world scene as it had evolved since the Civil War. Mahan's doctrines had little influence on American policy until the USS *Maine* exploded and sank in Havana Harbor on February 15, 1898. Not the Civil War but the Spanish-American War gave a great impetus to the Big Navy movement.

What Mahan did for the navy, Emory Upton had tried to do for the army. Upton's *Military Policy of the United States* came out in 1904, twenty-three years after his suicide. A West Point graduate and Civil War veteran, Upton argued that the United States had never really had a military policy but had repeated the same mistake in one conflict after another and had won only with luck and with a horrific waste of time, money, and lives. "History," he wrote, "records our triumph in the Revolution, in the War of 1812, in the Florida War, in the Mexican War, and in the Great Rebellion, and as nearly all of these wars were largely begun by militia and volunteers, the conviction has been produced that with us a regular army is not a necessity." He insisted that, on the contrary, the country needed a sizable, well-trained, well-equipped professional force. "Twenty thousand regular troops at Bull Run would have routed the insurgents, settled the question of military resistance, and relieved us from the pain and suspense of four years of war."[35]

Leonard Wood took up the cause that Upton had advocated. Colonel of the Rough Riders in Cuba, commanding general in the Philippines, and then chief of staff from 1910 to 1914, Wood led the "preparedness" campaign that preceded the entry of the United States into World War I. He wanted the country to adopt a military system such as that of Germany or France, including peacetime conscription and universal military training. "Manhood suffrage," he said, "means manhood obligation for service in peace or war."[36]

Wood, like Upton, used the Civil War as a negative example to support the preparedness argument; the progress of militarism and navalism through 1914 was not a result of the war. It was, instead, a response to more-recent events and, in particular, to the military and naval developments on the part of the European powers.

"The output of American iron and steel—that measure of modern power—was, in 1870, far below the tonnage of England or France; within twenty years the United States had outstripped them and was pouring from its forges more than one-third of the world's total annual supply." So wrote Charles and Mary Beard in 1927. Moreover, "twenty-five years after the death of Lincoln, America had become, in the quantity and value of her products, the first manufacturing nation in the world." Undoubtedly, the country had industrialized at a rapid rate between the Civil War and the end of the nineteenth century. The question is how much the war had to do with the industrialization that followed it.

The Beards thought that the war, which they termed "The Second American Revolution," was a prime case of economic development. "Through financing the federal government and furnishing supplies to its armies, northern leaders in banking and industry reaped profits far greater than they had ever yet gathered during four years of peace." Thus, they "accumulated huge masses of capital" to invest in postwar enterprises. Other wartime policies, according to the Beards, also helped—tariff protection, the national banking system, grants of public land to railroad and other corporations, the provision of cheap labor through the immigration act of 1864, and the absence of hampering regulations of business.[37]

But in 1918 economic historian Victor S. Clark held that the Civil War "of itself changed no existing economic tendency in America"; "the war did not create new manufacturers" nor did it "create new forms of domestic industry." As for the tariff, it was "a post-bellum influence so far as it had permanent effect upon the growth of our manufactures." Later, in 1961, Thomas C. Cochran went even further. Undertaking to refute the Beards, Cochran raised and answered in the affirmative the question: "Did the Civil War *retard* industrialization?"[38]

Disagreeing as they do, historians since World War I have left the subject rather moot, and writers before 1914 did not even raise the issue. In 1884 Blaine boasted of the country's economic progress between 1861 and 1881, but he did not attribute it to the war, although he did say that if the Union had lost, "the progress of civilization on the American Continent" might have been "checked for generations." Wilson, in *Division and Reunion, 1829–1889,* concluded that in the "twenty-four years since the close of the War between the States . . . , these twenty-four years of steam and electricity had done more than any previous century to transform the nation." He was referring to the years 1865–89, not 1861–65, and to "steam and electricity," not to the consequences of the war. When in 1906 James Ford Rhodes completed the last of his seven volumes, he exclaimed: "What a change between 1850 and 1877! A political and social revolution had been accomplished." He did not mention an economic or industrial revolution as occurring during those years, nor did he do so when he referred to "Legacies of the War and Reconstruction" after 1877.[39]

The Civil War left a legacy that, from 1865 to 1914, discouraged more than it encouraged the rise of the United States as a world power. It left the American people with a divided psyche and divisive politics. It yielded no clear and compelling model for the "imperial presidency," despite the example of Lincoln's use of a presidential "war power." It made the nation less expansionist than before the war. It reinforced the longstanding tradition of opposing the maintenance of a large standing army, while it gave no permanence to the sizable wartime navy. And it gave no clear and certain stimulus to the industrialization of the country.

In short, the war exerted a negative rather than a positive effect on the growth of those necessary elements of a world power: political and psychological unity, presidential authority, expansionism, militarism and navalism, and industrialization. Moreover, contemporary Americans did not perceive the war as a cause of such developments.

There is, of course, one sense in which the war—resulting as it did in the defeat of the secessionists—facilitated the emergence of a world power. That power could hardly have arisen when and as it did if the continent had remained permanently divided between the United States of America and the Confederate States of America. But even the temporary division—and the struggle to overcome it—delayed the debut of the United States as a leading actor on the world's stage.

NOTES

INTRODUCTION

Susan-Mary Grant and Peter J. Parish

1. Ulysses S. Grant, *Personal Memoirs of U. S. Grant,* 2 vols. (1885; reprint, 2 vols. in 1, London: Penguin, 1999), 638–9; Abraham Lincoln, Gettysburg Address, *The Collected Works of Abraham Lincoln,* ed. Roy P. Basler et al. (1953–55; reprint, New Brunswick, N.J.: Rutgers University Press, 1988), 7:17.

2. Charles P. Roland, *An American Iliad: The Story of the Civil War* (Lexington: University Press of Kentucky, 1991), xi; David Montgomery, *The American Civil War and the Meanings of Freedom,* Harmsworth Inaugural Lecture, 1987 (Oxford, Eng.: Clarendon, 1987), 1.

3. Harold Sinclair, *The Horse Soldiers* (New York: Birlinn, 2000); Charles Frazier, *Cold Mountain* (New York: Atlantic Monthly Press, 1997); Michael Shaara, *The Killer Angels* (1974; reprint, New York: Ballantine, 1975); Jeff Shaara, *The Last Full Measure* (New York: Ballantine, 1998); Daniel Woodrell, *Woe to Live On* (1987; reprint, Harpenden, Herts., U.K.: No Exit, 1994); Tony Horwitz, *Confederates in the Attic: Dispatches from the Unfinished Civil War* (1998; reprint, New York: Vintage, 1999). For Web sites on the Civil War, which are too numerous to list, see William G. Thomas and Alice E. Carter, *The Civil War on the Web: A Guide to the Very Best Sites* (Wilmington, Del.: Scholarly Resources, 2001); and Benjamin Forgey, "A Salute to Freedom's Soldiers," *Washington Post,* July 18, 1998, E1.

4. Kenneth E. Foote, *Shadowed Ground: America's Landscapes of Violence and Tragedy* (Austin: University of Texas Press, 1997), is not devoted exclusively to the Civil War. See also Kirk Savage, *Standing Soldiers, Kneeling Slaves: Race, War, and Monument in Nineteenth-Century America* (Princeton, N.J.: Princeton University Press, 1997); Kathryn Allamong Jacob, *Testament to Union: Civil War Monuments in Washington, D.C.* (Baltimore: Johns Hopkins University Press, 1998); and Mark E. Neely Jr. and Harold Holzer, *The Union Image: Popular Prints of the Civil War North* (Chapel Hill: University of North Carolina Press, 2000).

5. See, for example, the collection of essays edited by John Bodnar, *Bonds of Affection: Americans Define Their Patriotism* (Princeton, N.J.: Princeton University Press, 1996); Stuart McConnell, *Glorious Contentment: The Grand Army of the Republic, 1865–1900* (Chapel Hill: University of North Carolina Press, 1992); Cecilia Elizabeth O'Leary, *To Die For: The Paradox of American Patriotism* (Princeton, N.J.: Princeton University Press, 1999); David Blight, " 'For Something beyond the Battlefield': Frederick Douglass and the Struggle for the Memory of the Civil War," *Journal of American History* 75 (Mar. 1989): 1156–78; Blight, *Race and Reunion: The Civil War in American Memory* (Cambridge: Harvard University Press, 2001); and Peter J. Parish, *The American Civil War,* (London: Eyre Methuen, 1975), 652.

6. David Blight, *Race and Reunion,* 387.

7. Abraham Lincoln, Address at Sanitary Fair, Baltimore, Md., Apr. 18, 1864, *Collected Works,* 7:301–2; W. E. B. Du Bois, *Black Reconstruction in America,* quoted in Montgomery, *Civil War and the Meanings of Freedom,* 1.

8. Gary Gallagher, *The Confederate War: How Popular Will, Nationalism, and Military Strategy Could Not Stave off Defeat* (Cambridge: Harvard University Press, 1999); David Madden, "Sesquicentennial News," *The United States Civil War Center,* Louisiana State University, Apr. 1, 2001 <http://www.cwc. lsu.edu/cwc/projects/sesqui.htm>, 3.

9. Brooks D. Simpson, "Quandaries of Command: Ulysses S. Grant and Black Soldiers," in, *Union and Emancipation: Essays on Politics and Race in the Civil War Era,* ed. David W. Blight and Brooks D. Simpson (Kent, Ohio: Kent State University Press, 1997), 123.

10. Abraham Lincoln, Speech at Chicago, Ill., July 10, 1858, *Collected Works,* 2:500; Alexis de Tocqueville, *Democracy in America,* 2 vols. (1855; reprint, New York: Vintage, 1945), 2:78; Robert Penn Warren, *The Legacy of the Civil War: Meditations on the Centennial* (New York: Random House, 1961), 3.

1. "FORGET, HELL!": THE CIVIL WAR IN SOUTHERN MEMORY

Charles Joyner

1. Greg Dening, "Anzac Day," in *Performances* (Melbourne, Australia: University of Melbourne Press, 1996), 225. Warren Ellem, without a single phrase of postmodern jargon, incisively deconstructs the controversial hermeneutics of one of the Civil War's last battles in his "The Fall of Fort Fisher: Contested Memories of the Civil War" (paper presented to the biennial conference of the Australian and New Zealand American Studies Association, Apr. 17, 1998). For more on this battle, see Rod Gragg, *Confederate Goliath: The Battle of Fort Fisher* (New York: HarperCollins, 1991).

2. See Shane White, " 'Down by the Riverside': An Interview with Charles Joyner," *Australasian Journal of American Studies* 13 (July 1994): 45–55.

3. Dening, "Anzac Day," 225–32.

4. Charles Joyner, "A Tale of Two Disciplines: Folklore and History" (paper presented at the Twelfth International Congress of Anthropological and Ethnological Sciences, Zagreb, Yugoslavia, July 24–31, 1988), published as "Prica o dvije discipline: folkloristika i historija," in *Folklor i povijesni proces,* ed. Dunja Rihtman-Augustin and Maja Povrzanovic (Zagreb, Yugoslavia: Zavod za istrazivanje folklora, 1989), 9–22.

5. The modern study of nationalism is much concerned with how it emerged, how its meaning has changed over time, and why it now seems to command such an aura of legitimacy. Scholars of nationalism, as the anthropologist Benedict Anderson notes, "have been perplexed, not to say irritated," by the dissonance between its objective modernity and subjective antiquity, its universality as a concept and particularity in concrete form, and its political power and philosophical poverty. See Anderson, *Imagined Communities: Reflections on the Origin and Spread of Nationalism* (1983; reprint, London: Verso, 1991), xi, 4–5. See also Aira Kemiläinen, *Nationalism: Problems Concerning the Word, the Concept, and Classification* (Jyväskylä, Finland: Jyväskylän Kasvatusopillinen Korkeakoulu, 1964), 105; Richard G. Fox, ed., *Nationalist Ideologies and the Production of National Cultures,* American Ethnological Society Monograph Series, no. 2 (Washington, D.C.: American Anthropological Society, 1990), 3; and Eric J. Hobsbawm, *Nations and Nationalism since 1780: Programme, Myth, Reality* (New York: Pantheon, 1990).

6. Arthur Link, *Wilson the Diplomatist: A Look at His Major Foreign Policies* (Baltimore: Johns Hopkins University Press, 1957), 3, 103–4, 116–7; Link, "Woodrow Wilson and Peace Moves," *The Listener* [BBC], 75 (June 16, 1966), 869–71. See also Arno J. Mayer, *Politics and Diplomacy in Peacemaking: Containment and Counterrevolution at Versailles, 1918–1919* (New York: Knopf, 1967); N. Gordon Levin

Jr., *Woodrow Wilson and World Politics: America's Response to War and Revolution* (New York: Oxford University Press, 1968); and Charles L. Mee Jr., *The End of Order* (New York: Dutton, 1980).

7. The origins of the phrase "primordial affinities and attachments" is unclear. Edward Shils used it in "Primordial, Personal, Sacred, and Civil Ties" (*British Journal of Sociology* 8 [1957]: 130–45). But Daniel Patrick Moynihan attributes the phrase (without a date) to psychiatrist Erik Erikson. See Moynihan, *Pandaemonium: Ethnicity in International Politics* (New York: Oxford University Press, 1993), 63–65. See also Harold Isaacs, "Basic Group Identity: The Idols of the Tribe?" in *Ethnicity: Theory and Experience,* ed. Nathan Glazer and Daniel Patrick Moynihan (Cambridge: Harvard University Press, 1975), 30; and James G. Kellas, *Politics of Nationalism and Ethnicity* (New York: St. Martin's, 1991), 129–31.

8. Anthony Giddens, *The Nation-State and Violence* (Cambridge: Cambridge University Press, 1985); Michael Ignatieff, *Blood and Belonging: Journeys into the New Nationalism* (New York: Hill and Wang, 1994); Anastasia N. Karakasidou, *Fields of Wheat, Hills of Blood: Passages to Nationhood in Greek Macedonia, 1870–1990* (Chicago: University of Chicago Press, 1997).

9. Abram Joseph Ryan, "The Conquered Banner" [1865], in *The Southern Poets,* ed. William Lander Weber (New York: Macmillan, 1917), 163–5.

10. John Keegan, *The Face of Battle: A Study of Agincourt, Waterloo, and the Somme* (London: Jonathan Cape, 1976), 13–77 (quotes, 64–5). There is a splendid recent translation by David Greene of Herodotus, *The History* (Chicago: University of Chicago Press, 1987). See also Thucydides, *The Peloponnesian Wars,* trans. Rex Warner(New York: Penguin, 1961); and Julius Caesar, *War Commentaries,* trans. Rex Warner (New York: Mentor, 1962). Earlier translations of Herodotus, Thucydides, and Caesar may be found in the Loeb Classical Library Series (Cambridge, Mass., 1912–).

11. C. Vann Woodward, *The Future of the Past* (New York: Oxford University Press, 1989), 187; William Faulkner, *Absalom, Absalom!* (New York: Random House, 1936), 20.

12. William Faulkner to Malcolm Cowley, *The Faulkner-Cowley File: Letters and Memories, 1944–1962,* ed. Malcolm Cowley (New York: Viking Press, 1966), 79; Robert Penn Warren, *The Legacy of the Civil War: Meditations on the Centennial* (New York: Random House, 1961).

13. Allen Tate, "The Profession of Letters in the South," *Virginia Quarterly Review* 11 (1935): 161–76.

14. The quotation is from Donald Davidson, "Lee in the Mountains," in *Lee in the Mountains and Other Poems* (New York: Charles Scribner's Sons, 1938).

15. See, for example, Faulkner, *Absalom, Absalom!;* and *The Unvanquished* (New York: Random House, 1938); Caroline Gordon, *Penhally* (New York: Charles Scribner's Sons, 1931); and *None Shall Look Back* (New York: Charles Scribner's Sons, 1937); Andrew Nelson Lytle, *The Long Night* (New York: Bobbs-Merrill, 1936); Margaret Mitchell, *Gone with the Wind* (New York: Macmillan, 1936); Allen Tate, *The Fathers* (New York: G. P. Putnam's Sons, 1938); and Stark Young, *So Red the Rose* (New York: Charles Scribner's Sons, 1934). The most comprehensive study of Civil War novels is Robert Lively, *Fiction Fights the Civil War* (Chapel Hill: University of North Carolina Press, 1957). On the Lost Cause as a civil religion, see Charles Reagan Wilson, *Baptized in Blood: The Religion of the Lost Cause, 1865–1920* (Athens: University of Georgia Press, 1980).

16. Aristotle, *Poetics,* trans. Malcolm Heath (London: Penguin, 1996), 6–18.

17. Orlando Patterson, *Slavery and Social Death* (Cambridge: Harvard University Press, 1982), vii–ix.

18. For a summary of casualties in the Civil War, see Thomas L. Livermore, *Numbers and Casualties in the Civil War* (1897; Boston: Houghton, Mifflin, 1957).

19. Among the many books of Civil War photographs are Francis Trevelyan Miller, *Photographic*

History of the Civil War, 10 vols. (1911; reprint, New York: T. Yoseloff, 1957); Richard M. Ketchum, ed., *The American Heritage Picture History of the Civil War*, 2 vols. (New York: American Heritage, 1960); and William C. Davis and Bell I. Wiley, eds., *The Image of War, 1861–1865*, 6 vols. (Garden City, N.Y.: Doubleday, 1981–84).

20. Morris tells of the Mississippi Grays in *Terrains of the Heart and Other Essays on Home* (Oxford, Miss.: Yoknapatawpha, 1981), 252. Jeremiah Gage, "A Dying Soldier's Letter to His Mother," July 3, 1863, reprinted in *The South: A Treasury of Art and Literature*, ed. Lisa Howorth (New York: Macmillan, 1993), 110.

21. The story is in Charles Kuralt, *Southerners: Portrait of a People* (Birmingham, Ala.: Oxmoor House, 1986), 137.

22. William Faulkner, quoted in Frederick L. Gwynn and Joseph L. Blotner, eds., *Faulkner in the University: Class Conferences at the University of Virginia, 1957–58* (Charlottesville: University Press of Virginia, 1959).

23. Eric J. Hobsbawm and Terence Ranger, eds., *Invented Traditions* (Cambridge: Cambridge University Press, 1983). For information on the use of this flag by the Army of Tennessee, see Robert E. Bonner, "Flag Culture and the Consolidation of Confederate Nationalism," *Journal of Southern History* 68, 2 (May 2002): 293–332 (esp. 321); and *Flags of the Confederacy* <www.ConfederateFlags.org>. It may be germane to note that Greg Dening has analyzed how a British flagpole erected on a Tahitian beach as a symbol of British possession came to symbolize something else entirely when the Union Jack was integrated by Tahitian royalty into its distinctive red-feather loincloth. "There is no evidence that they made it a sign of their deference to the English," he writes, suggesting that "they saw it as a sign of overarching sovereignty that was outside and above local politics but was imbued with all their metaphors." See Dening, *Mr. Bligh's Bad Language: Passion, Power, and Theatre on the* Bounty (Cambridge: Cambridge University Press, 1992), 279–81; and Marshall Sahlins, "The Discovery of the True Savage," in *Dangerous Liaisons: Essays in Honour of Greg Dening*, ed. Donna Merwick (Melbourne, Australia: University of Melbourne, 1994), 80. Similarly, a black-owned manufacturing business in Charleston, South Carolina, has been successfully marketing a line of sportswear featuring the Confederate flag reproduced in the colors of black nationalism.

24. Bertram Wyatt-Brown, *Southern Honor: Ethics and Behavior in the Old South* (New York: Oxford University Press, 1982), 25–62.

25. Dening, *Performances*, 231, 226. "Of all the systems that are expressions of who a people are, the sharpest and clearest is their historical consciousness," Dening maintains. "Human beings are history makers," he adds, "so when I make history, I like to make history of people making history, because that is where they reveal themselves." See Dening, "Ethnography on My Mind," in *Boundaries of the Past*, ed. Brian Attwood (Melbourne, Australia: University of Melbourne, 1990), 16–7.

26. Jefferson Davis, *The Rise and Fall of the Confederate Government*, 2 vols. (1881; reprint, New York: Da Capo, 1990), 1:77–85; Alexander M. Stephens, *A Constitutional View of the Late War between the States* (Philadelphia: National, 1868–70), 1:9; Davis, Message to the Confederate Congress, Apr. 29, 1861, in *The Rebellion Record*, ed. Frank Moore (New York: G. P. Putnam, 1861–68), 1:166–75; Stephens, Address in Savannah, Ga., Mar. 21, 1861, ibid., 1:44–9.

27. William Preston, quoted in Steven A. Channing, *Crisis of Fear: Secession in South Carolina* (New York: W. W. Norton, 1970), 222; *Declaration of the Immediate Causes which Induce and Justify the Secession of South Carolina from the Federal Union and the Ordinance of Secession* (Charleston: Evans and Coggswell, 1860).

28. Lord Charnwood, *Abraham Lincoln: A Biography* (New York: Henry Holt, 1917), chap. 6; Mary Boykin Chesnut, June 14, 15, 1861, *Mary Chesnut's Civil War*, ed. C. Vann Woodward (New Haven:

Yale University Press, 1981), 71–2. For the most complete study of southern imperialism, see Robert E. May, *The Southern Dream of a Caribbean Empire, 1854–1861* (Baton Rouge: Louisiana State University Press, 1973).

29. Francis W. Pickens, quoted in John B. Edmunds Jr., *Francis W. Pickens and the Politics of Destruction* (Chapel Hill: University of North Carolina Press, 1986), 152.

30. The pun on Victor Hugo's classic is obvious. I first used it as the title for an address at the Wilson Center in 1989. J. Tracy Power's vivid and incisive study of the last year of the war was published under that title while I was revising this essay. See Power, *Lee's Miserables: Life in the Army of Northern Virginia from the Wilderness to Appomattox* (Chapel Hill: University of North Carolina Press, 1998).

31. John Morton Blum, *Woodrow Wilson and the Politics of Morality* (Boston: Little Brown, 1956), 5–6.

32. Robert Penn Warren, *All The King's Men* (New York: Harcourt Brace, 1946).

33. Ralph Ellison, *The Territory Ahead* (New York: Random House, 1986), 86–7.

2. CONFEDERATE IDENTITY AND THE SOUTHERN MYTH SINCE THE CIVIL WAR

Bruce Collins

1. C. Vann Woodward, "The Search for Southern Identity," in *The Burden of Southern History*, rev. ed. (Baton Rouge: Louisiana State University Press, 1968), 3, 9, 16–25; John Keegan, *Warpaths: Travels of a Military Historian in North America* (London: Pimlico, 1995), 42–3. This southern sense of defeat as a result of the Confederate experiment is, of course, confined to white southerners, not all of whom were Confederate supporters. For African American southerners the sense of oppressive defeat has quite different origins.

2. I have used the list of members of the Forty-seventh Congress and the individual biographies in the *Biographical Directory of the American Congress, 1774–1961* (Washington, D.C.: Government Printing Office, 1961). I have not double counted. Thus, James L. Pugh served as a private in 1861 but spent most of the war as a member of the Confederate Congress; I have counted him under that activity. Isham G. Harris started the war as governor of Tennessee, but I have counted instead his three years as a staff officer. The historiographic consensus of the late nineteenth century involved a rejection by historians of the doctrine of secession accompanied by an acceptance of racial subordination of African Americans. Peter Novick, *That Noble Dream: The "Objectivity Question" and the American Historical Profession* (Cambridge: Cambridge University Press, 1988), 74–8.

3. Gaines M. Foster argues that the Confederate tradition became powerful in the 1890s but waned in significance two decades later. *Ghosts of the Confederacy: Defeat, the Lost Cause, and the Emergence of the New South, 1865–1913* (New York: Oxford University Press, 1987), 178–9.

4. Robert Johnson and Clarence Buel, eds., *Battles and Leaders of the Civil War*, 4 vols. (1887–88; reprint, New York: Appleton-Century, 1956), 1:ix–x, 483–4.

5. Gerald F. Linderman, *Embattled Courage: The Experience of Combat in the American Civil War* (New York: Free Press, 1987), 275, 277–9, 297. One former Confederate major general, Matthew C. Butler of South Carolina, became a major general of U.S. Volunteers in 1898.

6. Catherine Clinton, *Tara Revisited: Women, War, and the Plantation Legend* (New York: Oxford University Press, 1995), 182–3, 186; Writers' Program of the Works Projects Administration, *South Carolina: The WPA Guide to the Palmetto State* (Columbia, S.C.: University of South Carolina Press 1988),

209–10; *Cass and Birnbaum's Guide to American Colleges,* 17th ed. (New York: Harper Perennial 1996), 116, 634.

7. J. F. C. Fuller, *Grant and Lee: A Study in Personality and Generalship* (London: Eyre and Spottiswoode, 1933), 271–4; Foster, *Ghosts of the Confederacy,* 120–1; John Fraser, *America and the Patterns of Chivalry* (Cambridge: Cambridge University Press, 1982), 64–6, 215–7.

8. Woodrow Wilson, *The New Democracy: Presidential Messages, Addresses, and Other Papers,* ed. Ray Stannard Baker and William E. Dodd, vol. 1, *1913–17* (New York: Harper and Brothers, 1926), 124; Thomas L. Connelly and Barbara L. Bellows, *God and General Longstreet: The Lost Cause and the Southern Mind* (Baton Rouge: Louisiana State University Press, 1982), 26, 29–35, 109; Franklin D. Roosevelt, *The Public Papers and Addresses of Franklin D. Roosevelt,* vol. 5, *The People Approve, 1936* (New York, 1938), 215. "The classical antique virtue, at once aristocratic and republican, had become a national legend [in George Washington], and its late incarnation in Lee was to command a certain awed admiration among Northerners as well as Southerners." Edmund Wilson, *Patriotic Gore: Studies in the Literature of the American Civil War* (New York: Oxford University Press, 1962) 335.

9. John Gunther, *Inside U.S.A.* (London: Hamish Hamilton, 1947), 655, 656. Peter Novick shows how the traditional view of Reconstruction illustrated by Gunther was under attack in the 1930s. *That Noble Dream,* 77, 224–34.

10. Clinton, *Tara Revisited,* 204–6; George H. Gallup, *The Gallup Poll: Public Opinion, 1935–1971* (New York, 1972), 1:135.

11. In October 1939 some 68 percent of respondents agreed that the United States had made a mistake by entering the war of 1914–18. Gallup, *The Gallup Poll,* 1:189.

12. One such reference stresses the big improvements in African Americans' social and financial circumstances achieved during the 1930s and 1940s. Editors of *Fortune, U.SA.: The Permanent Revolution* (New York: Fortune, 1951), 154–6; William R. Taylor, *Cavalier and Yankees: The Old South and American National Character* (1957; reprint, New York: Braziller, 1961), 336, 341; Clement Eaton, *The Growth of Southern Civilization, 1790–1860* (New York: Harper, 1961), 19–24, 297, 318–24; Russell Kirk, *The Conservative Mind* (London: Faber and Faber, 1954), 212–6, 444.

13. The revisionism on slavery and subsequent modifications have spawned a vast literature. Excellent general studies include: John W. Blassingame, *The Slave Community: Plantation Life in the Antebellum South* (New York: Oxford University Press, 1972); Eugene D. Genovese, *Roll, Jordan, Roll: The World the Slaves Made* (New York: Pantheon, 1974); and Peter J. Parish, *Slavery: History and Historians* (New York: Harper, 1989).

14. Michael P. Johnson, *Toward a Patriarchal Republic: The Secession of Georgia* (Baton Rouge: Louisiana State University Press, 1977); Drew Gilpin Faust, *The Creation of Confederate Nationalism: Ideology and Identity in the Civil War South* (Baton Rouge: Louisiana State University Press, 1988), 14–6, 37–40, 52–7, 84.

15. Charles Royster, *The Destructive War: William Tecumseh Sherman, Stonewall Jackson, and the Americans* (New York: Knopf, 1993), 328–9, 331, 340, 347–8, 358; Mark Grimsley, *The Hard Hand of War: Union Military Policy toward Southern Civilians, 1861–1865* (Cambridge: Cambridge University Press, 1995), 196–205, 219–20, 223.

16. Jeffrey Rogers Hummel, *Emancipating Slaves, Enslaving Free Men* (Chicago: University of Illinois Press, 1996). I am grateful for Prof. Norman Barry's expert advice on this point.

17. William R. Brock, *Conflict and Transformation: The United States, 1844–1877* (Hammondsworth, Middlesex: Penguin, 1973), 349–51, 390–3; Confederate States of America Const, Art , Sec. 9 (4); Art IV, Sec. 2 (3); Art V, Sec. 1 (1). Reprinted in Henry Steele Commager, *Documents of American History,* vol. 1, *To 1898* (New York: Appleton-Century-Crofts, 1963), 376–84.

18. Eric Foner, *Nothing but Freedom: Emancipation and Its Legacy* (Baton Rouge: Louisiana State University Press, 1983), 6–7, 108–10.

19. Bell Irving Wiley, *The Life of Johnny Reb: The Common Soldier of the Confederacy* (Indianapolis: Bobbs Merrill, 1943); and *The Life of Billy Yank: The Common Soldier of the Union* (Indianapolis: Bobbs Merill, 1952); Linderman, *Embattled Courage,* 277–8, 287–8; Tracey Power, *Lee's Miserables: Life in the Army of Northern Virginia from the Wilderness to Appomattox* (Chapel Hill: University of North Carolina Press, 1998), xi–xii; Reid Mitchell, *Civil War Soldiers: Their Expectations and Their Experiences* (1988; reprint, New York: Viking, 1997), 209.

20. James M. McPherson, *For Cause and Comrades: Why Men Fought in the Civil War* (New York: Oxford University Press, 1997), 178; Power, *Lee's Miserables,* 321.

21. William S. McFeely, *Grant: A Biography* (New York: Norton, 1981), 121, 165–73; Connelly and Bellows, *God and General Longstreet,* 8–9. Reid Mitchell is unusual in interweaving white soldiers' reactions to African Americans into his account of African American fighting men. *Civil War Soldiers,* 184–206.

22. Woodward, "Search for Southern Identity," 18; Keegan, *Warpaths,* 356.

23. Foster, *Ghosts of the Confederacy,* 193; Connelly and Bellows, *God and General Longstreet,* 4.

24. Gunther, *Inside U.S.A.,* 660; Gallup, *The Gallup Poll,* 1:122, 183, 256, 259 (also 300–1), 261, 263 (also 275), 279–80.

25. Gallup, *The Gallup Poll,* 3:2266–7, 2316–7, 2317–8.

26. I have used the data on population, total federal government spending, and Department of Defense spending by state in Michael Barone, Grant Ujifusa, and Douglas Matthews, *The Almanac of American Politics, 1974* (New York: Facts on File, 1973), 3, 40, 187, 221, 536, 740, 903, 939, 962–3, 1033.

27. Ibid., 219, 535, 546, 742, 746, 754, 916, 1037; "Stennis, John C.," in *American National Biography,* ed. John A. Garraty and Mark C. Carnes (New York: Oxford University Press, 1999), 20:655–6.

28. Rick Atkinson, *The Long Gray Line: West Point's Class of 1966* (London: Henry Holt, Owl Books, 1990), 27, 32, 35, 236; Grimsley, *Hard Hand of War,* 219–21, 225.

29. Foster, *Ghosts of the Confederacy,* 182.

3. UNFINISHED BUSINESS: AFRICAN AMERICANS AND THE CIVIL WAR CENTENNIAL

Robert Cook

1. On the *Enola Gay,* see "History and the Public: What Can We Handle? A Round Table about History after the *Enola Gay* Controversy," *Journal of American History* 82 (Dec. 1995): 1029–1144.

2. The terms "vernacular" and "particularist" memory are drawn respectively from John Bodnar, *Remaking America: Public Memory, Commemoration, and Patriotism in the Twentieth Century* (Princeton, N.J.: Princeton University Press, 1992); and Michael Kammen, *Mystic Chords of Memory: The Transformation of Tradition in American Culture* (New York: Knopf, 1991).

3. Bayard Rustin, "From Protest to Politics: The Future of the Civil Rights Movement" [1965], in *The New Radicals,* ed. Paul Jacobs and Saul Landau (London: Penguin, 1967), 294.

4. David W. Blight, *Race and Reunion: The Civil War in American Memory* (Cambridge: Harvard University Press, 2001).

5. David W. Blight, *Frederick Douglass' Civil War: Keeping Faith in Jubilee* (Baton Rouge: Louisiana

State University Press, 1989), 235; Alistair Thomson et al., "The Memory and History Debate: Some International Perspectives," *Oral History* 22 (autumn 1994): 41.

6. Theodore Rosengarten, *All God's Dangers: The Life of Nate Shaw* (New York: Vintage, 1989), 9. Southern schools were still ignoring the role of black troops in the 1960s. One black Civil War reenactor reared in tidewater Virginia was interviewed in 1998. He recalled that "Fourth-grade history in Virginia is Virginia history. . . . And for a great portion of that you hear about the Civil War, and you hear about Lee and Jackson and Jeb Stuart, and I grew up just thinking that blacks didn't participate in the war. I just thought that all blacks were slaves during that period." *Washington City Paper,* July 17, 1998, 22.

7. David W. Blight, "W. E. B. Du Bois and the Struggle for American Historical Memory," in *History and Memory in African-American Culture,* ed. Genevieve Fabre and Robert O'Meally (New York: Oxford University Press, 1994), 46.

8. Dwight D. Eisenhower, "Statement on the Death of Last Surviving Civil War Veteran," Dec. 20, 1959, in *Public Papers of the Presidents: Dwight D. Eisenhower, 1959* (Washington, D.C.: Government Printing Office, 1960), 864.

9. Charles H. Wesley, "The Civil War and the Negro-American," *Journal of Negro History* 47 (Apr. 1962): 83–4.

10. *New York Amsterdam News,* Jan. 7, 1961, 16; Charles H. Wesley, *Ohio Negroes in the Civil War* (Columbus: Ohio State University Press, 1962); Benjamin Quarles, *Lincoln and the Negro* (New York: Oxford University Press,1962).

11. John Hope Franklin, *From Slavery to Freedom: A History of American Negroes,* 2d rev. ed. (New York: Knopf, 1963).

12. Bruce Catton, *Centennial History of the Civil War,* 3 vols. (London: Gollanz, 1961–65).

13. Bruce Catton, "Where the Great Change Took Place," *New York Times Magazine,* Feb. 5, 1961, 11.

14. James M. McPherson, *The Struggle for Equality: Abolitionists and the Negro in the Civil War and Reconstruction* (Princeton, N.J.: Princeton University Press, 1964), unnumbered dedication page. Other historians of the Middle Period writing in the early 1960s underlined the linkage between the Civil War era and the contemporary debate over race. See, for example, William Dusinberre, *Civil War Issues in Philadelphia 1856–1865* (Philadelphia: Penn State University Press, 1965), 190; William E. Gillette, *The Right to Vote: Politics and the Passage of the Fifteenth Amendment* (Baltimore: Johns Hopkins University Press, 1965), 9–11; and *Chicago Defender,* Oct. 22–28, 1960, 7; Jan. 28–Feb. 3, 1961, 6; Mar. 11–17, 1961, 2.

15. Robert P. Warren, *The Legacy of the Civil War: Meditations on the Centennial* (New York: Random House, 1961), 46; *New York Times,* Jan. 9, 1961, 23; Kammen, *Mystic Chords,* 592.

16. *New York Times,* Jan. 9, 1961, 1.

17. Ibid., 23.

18. Ibid., July 23, 1961, sec. 1, p. 1.

19. Ibid., June 7, 1959, sec. 4, p. 10; *New York Amsterdam News,* Feb. 11, 1961, 4; Mar. 4, 1961, 8.

20. *New York Times,* Mar. 10, 1961, 29; Henry Lee Moon to R. Wilkins, Jan. 26, 1960, General Office File, box A76, group 3, NAACP Papers, Library of Congress; *New York Times,* Mar. 18, 1961, 8.

21. *New York Times,* Mar. 22, 1961, 34; Mar. 23, 1961, 26; Mar. 26, 1961, sec. 1, p. 72.

22. Ibid., Mar. 27, 1961, 30; Apr. 23, 1961, sec. 1, p. 74.

23. Howard N. Meyer, "Rally around which Flag," clipping from *Interchurch News,* Bayard Rustin Papers (UPA microfilm edition, 1988), reel 2, frame 107; A. P. Randolph to H. N. Meyer, July 13, 1961, Rustin Papers, reel 2, frame 106.

24. *New York Times,* July 29, 1961, 18.

25. Ibid., Dec. 5, 1961, 31.

26. Wesley, "Civil War and the Negro-American," 78–9, 93–4.

27. Martin Luther King Jr., quoted in Merrill D. Peterson, *Lincoln in American Memory* (New York: Oxford University Press, 1994), 354.

28. Martin Luther King Jr., Address to the New York State Civil War Centennial Commission, Sept. 12, 1962, ser. 3, box 3, Martin Luther King Jr. Papers, Martin Luther King Jr. Center for Nonviolent Change, Atlanta, Ga.

29. *Public Papers of the Presidents of the United States: John F. Kennedy, 1962* (Washington, D.C.: Government Printing Office, 1963), 702–3; *New York Times,* Sept. 23, 1962, sec. 1, p. 50; Sept. 28, 1962, 30.

30. *Public Papers of the Presidents of the United States: John F. Kennedy, 1963* (Washington, D.C.: Government Printing Office, 1964), 222.

31. *New York Times,* June 30, 1963, sec. 1, p. 39; July 2, 1963, 14.

32. Martin Luther King Jr., "I Have a Dream," *A Testament of Hope: The Essential Writings and Speeches of Martin Luther King, Jr.,* ed. J. M. Washington (San Francisco: Harper Collins, 1991), 217.

33. *Washington Post,* July 18, 1998, E4.

34. William H. Chafe, *Civilities and Civil Rights: Greensboro, North Carolina, and the Black Struggle for Freedom* (New York: Oxford University Press, 1980), 119.

4. THE CIVIL WAR IN THE MOVIES

Melvyn Stokes

1. Lillian Ross, *Picture* (New York: Random House, 1952), 11, 58, 146, 158, 203.

2. Ibid., 99, 193–4, 248–9, 251–64, 278, 299–303, 306–8, 310, 314–7, 333–8, 342, 354, 362, 367, 375.

3. Jack Spears, *The Civil War on the Screen and Other Essays* (New York: A. S. Barnes, 1977), 11, 12, 21–2, 24–6, 29–30; Thalberg quoted in Leslie Halliwell, *Halliwell's Screen Greats* (London: Grafton, 1988), 155. Selznick was well aware that *So Red the Rose,* made in 1935 with Margaret Sullivan starring, had been commercially unsuccessful. David Thomson, *Showman: The Life of David O. Selznick* (London: André Deutsch, 1993), 212.

4. Jim Cullen, *The Civil War in Popular Culture: A Reusable Past* (Washington, D.C.: Smithsonian Institution Press, 1995), 2.

5. C. Vann Woodward, "The Inner Civil War," *New York Review of Books* 151:7 (Apr. 7, 1994): 36. Compare Daniel Aaron, *The Unwritten War: American Writers and the Civil War* (Madison: University of Wisconsin Press, 1987), esp. xix–xxii. The one exception to Woodward's general thesis was Stephen Crane's *The Red Badge of Courage,* published in 1895, which became a best seller. Modern fiction on Civil War themes has included Michael Shaara's Pulitzer Prize–winning *Killer Angels* (New York: McKay, 1974), whose graphic account of the battle of Gettysburg seems to have been the original inspiration for Ken Burns's documentary television series on the war, and Charles Frazier's *Cold Mountain* (New York: Atlantic Monthly Press, 1997).

6. See, for example, Charles Eckert, "The Carole Lombard in Macy's Window," *Quarterly Review of Film Studies* 3:1 (1978): 1–21.

7. Arthur Mayer, *Merely Colossal* (New York: Simon and Schuster, 1953), 178; Kathryn H. Fuller,

At the Picture Show: Small-town Audiences and the Creation of Movie Fan Culture (Washington, D.C.: Smithsonian Institution Press, 1996), esp. chap. 8.

8. Alice Miller Mitchell, *Children and Movies* (Chicago: University of Chicago Press, 1929), 104–7; Richard Koszarski, *An Evening's Entertainment: The Age of the Silent Feature Picture, 1915–1928* (Berkeley: University of California Pr ess, 1990), 28–9. The advent of audience research, beginning in 1937, confirmed the female lack of enthusiasm for war pictures. See, for example, Leo Handel, *Hollywood Looks at Its Audience* (Urbana: University of Illinois Press, 1950), 121–4. For a discussion of what women liked about *Gone with the Wind* and the meanings they continued to create from it, see Helen Taylor, *Scarlett's Women: "Gone with the Wind" and Its Female Fans* (London: Virago, 1989).

9. Thomas R. Cripps, "The Myth of the Southern Box Office: A Factor in Racial Stereotyping in American Movies, 1920–1940," in *The Black Experience in America: Selected Essays,* ed. J. C. Curtis and Lewis Gould (Austin: University of Texas Press, 1970), 121.

10. Thomas R. Cripps, "The Absent Presence in American Civil War Films," *Historical Journal of Film, Radio, and Television* 14:4 (1994): 367–9.

11. Kim Newman, *Wild West Movies: How the West Was Found, Won, Lost, Lied about, Filmed, and Forgotten* (London: Bloomsbury, 1990), 28. Cripps himself remarks that "the first reel of many westerns seemed to be about the Civil War until the action moved westward." "Absent Presence in American Civil War Films," 371–2. Exceptions to this include a number of films dealing with struggles over western gold shipments and two movies, *The Dark Command* (1940) and *Quantrill's Raiders* (1958), which covered the August 1862 burning of Lawrence, Kansas, by William C. Quantrill and his band of Confederate guerrillas.

12. For estimates of profits, see Richard Schickel, *D. W. Griffith and the Birth of Film* (London: Pavilion, 1984), 280–1, 324; and Roland Flamini, *Scarlett, Rhett, and a Cast of Thousands: The Filming of "Gone with the Wind"* (London: André Deutsch, 1976), 332–3, 336–7. On the music written by Joseph Carl Breil to be performed with *The Birth of a Nation* and Max Steiner's score for *Gone with the Wind,* see Schickel, *Griffith and the Birth of Film,* 243–4, 247; and Flamini, *Scarlett, Rhett, and a Cast of Thousands,* 300–1.

13. P. McDonald, *"Birth of a Nation* Award 'Is Racist,'" *Evening Standard* (London), Dec. 9, 1992; Donald Bogle, *Toms, Coons, Mulattoes, Mammies, and Bucks: An Interpretive History of Blacks in American Films* (New York: Continuum, 1989), 12.

14. Francis Hackett, *"The Birth of a Nation,"* in *American Film Criticism: From the Beginnings to Citizen Kane,* ed. Stanley Kauffman with Bruce Henstell (New York: Liveright, 1972), 89; David M. Chalmers, *Hooded Americanism: The History of the Ku Klux Klan* (New York: Franklin Watts, 1981), 23–5; Scott Simmon, *The Films of D. W. Griffith* (Cambridge: Cambridge University Press, 1993), 125–6.

15. J. Morgan Kousser, *The Shaping of Southern Politics: Suffrage Restriction and the Establishment of the One-Party South, 1880–1910* (New Haven: Yale University Press, 1974); Joel Williamson, *The Crucible of Race: Black-White Relations in the American South since Emancipation* (New York: Oxford University Press, 1984), 117–8, 253; George C. Wright, *Racial Violence in Kentucky, 1865–1940: Lynchings, Mob Rule, and "Legal Lynchings"* (Baton Rouge: Louisiana State University Press, 1990), 105; Pierre Sorlin, *The Film in History: Restaging the Past* (Totowa, N.J.: Barnes and Noble, 1980), 108.

16. Scott Simmon, for example, cites Walter Lippmann's later recollection of this period as "a happy time" when it was still possible to believe in "the inevitability of progress" and "the perfectability of man." *Films of D. W. Griffith,* 24.

17. Edward L. Ayers, *The Promise of the New South: Life after Reconstruction* (New York: Oxford University Press, 1992), 155; Ray Stannard Baker, *Following the Color Line: An Account of Negro Citizen-*

ship in the American Democracy (New York: Doubleday, Page, 1908), 30–1; C. Vann Woodward, *Origins of the New South, 1877–1913* (Baton Rouge: Louisiana State University Press, 1951), 354–5; Williamson, *Crucible of Race,* 253–5.

18. Jack S. Blocker, *Retreat from Reform: The Prohibition Movement in the United States 1890–1913* (Westport, Conn.: Greenwood, 1976), 214, 216, 239; McKelway quoted in Hugh C. Bailey, *Liberalism in the New South: Southern Social Reform and the Progressive Movement* (Coral Gables, Fla.: University of Miami Press, 1969), 65.

19. Schickel, *Griffith and the Birth of Film,* 300. On the background to the NAACP and its campaign against the film, see Charles Flint Kellogg, *NAACP: A History of the National Association for the Advancement of Colored People,* vol. 1, *1909–1920* (Baltimore: Johns Hopkins University Press, 1967), 9–45, 109, 142–5; and B. Joyce Ross, *J. E. Spingarn and the Rise of the NAACP, 1911–1939* (New York: Atheneum, 1972), 38–9. Also see Melvyn Stokes, "Race, Nationality, and Citizenship: The Case of *The Birth of a Nation,*" in *Federalism, Citizenship, and Collective Identities in U.S. History,* ed. Cornelis A. van Minnen and Sylvia L. Hilton (Amsterdam: VU University Press, 2000) 107–19.

20. Sara Evans, *Born for Liberty: A History of Women in America* (New York: Free Press, 1989), 167–68. On the image of the flapper, see Molly Haskell, *From Reverence to Rape: The Treatment of Women in the Movies* (Chicago: University of Chicago Press, 1987), 44, 74–82.

21. Evans, *Born for Liberty,* 204–16, 198; Susan Ware, *Holding the Line: American Women in the 1930s* (Boston: Twayne, 1982), 41–9, 90–4, 97–103, 111.

22. Marjorie Rosen, *Popcorn Venus: Women, Movies, and the American Dream* (London: Peter Owen, 1975), 169; Lester V. Chandler, *America's Greatest Depression, 1929–1941* (New York: Harper and Row, 1970), 5–6; Ray Wax quoted in Studs Terkel, *Hard Times: An Oral History of the Great Depression* (London: Allen Lane, 1970), 456.

23. Spears, *Civil War on the Screen,* 34, 55, 57.

24. Rollin G. Osterweis, *The Myth of the Lost Cause, 1865–1900* (Hamden, Conn.: Archon, 1973), 113. The divisions in northern society over the war also tended to be concealed. *Friendly Persuasion* (1956) deals with a Quaker family that opposes slavery but refuses to fight in the war. In the end, however, the eldest son of the family leaves to help the local home guard fight off Morgan's raiders.

25. Cripps, "Absent Presence," 374; James M. McPherson, "The *Glory* Story," *The New Republic,* Jan. 8, 15, 1990, 22; Thomson, *Showman,* 676; Cullen, *Civil War in Popular Culture,* 67.

5. A CONTESTED LEGACY: THE CIVIL WAR AND PARTY POLITICS IN THE NORTH

Adam I. P. Smith and Peter J. Parish

1. "Men at War: An Interview with Shelby Foote," in *The Civil War: An Illustrated History of the War between the States,* by Geoffrey C. Ward, Ken Burns, and Ric Burns (New York: Alfred A. Knopf, 1994), 264.

2. Henry James, *Hawthorne* (London, 1879), 144, quoted in George M. Fredrickson, *The Inner Civil War: Northern Intellectuals and the Crisis of the Union* (New York: Harper and Row, 1969), 1.

3. Joel Silbey, *The American Political Nation* (Stanford, Calif.: Stanford University Press, 1991), 139.

4. Walter Dean Burnham, "The Turnout Problem," in *Elections American Style,* ed. A. James Reichley (Washington, D.C.: Brookings Institution, 1997), 98.

5. A very powerful image distributed by administration supporters contrasted the "Democracy of 1832" with that of 1864. In one half of the picture a fiery President Jackson imposes his physical presence

upon a penitent John C. Calhoun and other South Carolina nullifiers. The other half of the image shows Jefferson Davis lording it over Democratic presidential nominee George B. "Little Mac" McClellan, who cravenly implores, "we should like to have Union and Peace, dear Mr. Davis, but if such is not your pleasure then please state your terms for a friendly separation." Cartoon in the Stern Collection of Lincolniana, Prints and Broadsides Collection, box 4, pt. 2, no. 30, Library of Congress, Washington, D.C.

6. The most widely distributed pamphlet on this theme was Francis Lieber, *No Party Now but All for Our Country* (New York, 1863).

7. *Cincinnati Daily Enquirer,* Oct. 11, 1861.

8. On the tradition of antipartisanship in antebellum and Civil War politics, see Michael Holt, *The Political Crisis of the 1850s* (New York: John Wiley and Sons, 1980); Ronald P. Formisano, "Political Character, Antipartyism, and the Second Party System," *American Quarterly* 21 (1969): 683–709; Mark Voss Hubbard, "The 'Third Party Tradition' Reconsidered: Third Parties and American Public Life, 1830–1900," *Journal of American History* 86 (1999): 121–50; Christopher Dell, *Lincoln and the War Democrats: The Grand Erosion of Conservative Tradition* (Cranbury, N.J.: Associated University Presses, 1975), 102–23; Adam I. P. Smith, "The Election of 1864: Political Mobilisation and Party Strategy during the American Civil War" (Ph.D. diss., Cambridge University, 1999).

9. *New York Times,* July 7, 1861.

10. As recorded in reports in the *New York Times,* the *New York Daily Tribune,* and the *New York Herald.* See Sidney D. Brummer, *Political History of New York State during the Period of the Civil War* (New York: Longmans, Green: 1911). For an overview of political developments during the early years of the war, see Philip S. Paludan, *A People's Contest: The Union and Civil War* (Lawrence: University Press of Kansas, 1988), 85–105. In the last thirty years, the only general overview of politics in the North during the Civil War is James A. Rawley, *The Politics of Union: Northern Politics during the Civil War* (Hinsdale, Ill.: Dryden, 1974); but see also Peter J. Parish, *The American Civil War* (London: Eyre Methuen, 1975), chaps. 8, 9, 16, 17. For an influential argument about the role of the party system in mobilizing support for the Union, see Eric McKitrick, "Party Politics and the Union and Confederate War Efforts," in *The American Party Systems: Stages of Political Development,* ed. William N. Chambers and Walter Dean Burnham (New York: Oxford University Press, 1967), 117–51. Paul Kleppner, *The Third Electoral System: Parties, Voters, and Political Cultures* (Chapel Hill: University of North Carolina Press, 1979), an impressive study of voting behavior in the Midwest, is extremely sensitive to the peculiar conditions of wartime. Dale E. Baum, *The Civil War Party System: The Case of Massachusetts, 1848–1876* (Chapel Hill: University of North Carolina Press, 1984), sees party loyalties as fixed by 1860 in a fervently Republican state. Joel H. Silbey, *A Respectable Minority: The Democratic Party in the Civil War Era, 1860–1869* (New York: Norton, 1979) is the only work on national Civil War politics based on a study of voting behavior. For more recent works focusing on party political strategies, see Lex Renda, *Running on the Record: Civil War Era Politics in New Hampshire* (Charlottesville: University of Virginia Press, 1997); and Michael F. Holt, "Abraham Lincoln and the Politics of Union," *Political Parties and American Political Development from the Age of Jackson to the Age of Lincoln* (Baton Rouge: Louisiana State University Press, 1992): 323–53. For an excellent discussion of the historiography of Civil War politics, see Holt, "An Elusive Synthesis: Recent Literature on Northern Politics during the Civil War," in *Writing the Civil War,* ed. James M. McPherson and William J. Cooper Jr. (Columbia: University of South Carolina Press, 1998). On the Union party strategy and the effect of the war on the character of popular political participation, see Smith, "Election of 1864," 218–50.

11. Frank L. Klement, *The Copperheads in the Middle West* (Chicago: University of Chicago Press, 1960), 190; Klement, *Dark Lanterns: Secret Political Societies, Conspiracies, and Treason Trials in the Civil War* (Baton Rouge: Louisiana State University Press, 1984).

12. On draft resistance in the Pennsylvania coalfields, see Grace Palladino, *Another Civil War: Labor, Capital, and the State in the Anthracite Regions of Pennsylvania, 1840–68* (Urbana: University of Illinois Press, 1990), 98. For descriptions of violent opposition to the war in the West, often focused on opposition to the draft, see, for example, *Chicago Tribune,* June 12, 1863; *Daily Illinois State Register,* Sept. 12, 1863; Citizens of Randolph County to Richard Yates, Aug. 23, 1864; and James Montgomery to Richard Yates, Aug. 27, 1864, Richard Yates Papers, Illinois State Historical Library, Springfield; and A. E. McNall to O. M. Hatch, Oct. 17, 1864, O. M. Hatch Papers, Illinois State Historical Library. On draft riots in eastern cities, see William Hanna, "The Boston Draft Riot," *Civil War History* 36 (1990): 260–75; Iver Bernstein, *The New York City Draft Riots: Their Significance for American Society and Politics in the Age of the Civil War* (New York: Oxford University Press, 1990); *New York Times,* July 20, 1863; and *New Hampshire Independent,* July 28, 1863.

13. James W. Geary, *We Need Men: The Union Draft in the Civil War* (De Kalb: Northern Illinois University Press, 1991), 104–8. The term "meddling party" was coined by New York governor Horatio Seymour, a Democrat. See Paludan, *People's Contest,* 91.

14. William B. Hesseltine, *Lincoln and the War Governors* (New York: A. A. Knopf, 1948); Kenneth M. Stampp, *Indiana Politics during the Civil War* (Indianapolis: Indiana Historical Bureau, 1949).

15. T. W. Bergley to Elihu B. Washburne, Oct. 3, 1864, Washburne Papers, Library of Congress.

16. For a description of the activities of several of these organizations, see *Baltimore Sun,* Sept. 2, 1864; *Chicago Tribune,* Oct. 7, 23, Nov. 4, 1864; Clement M. Silvestro, "Rally Round the Flag: The Union League in the Civil War," Clarence M. Burton Memorial Lecture 1966, Lansing, Mich., 1966; and Don H. Doyle, *The Social Order of a Frontier Community: Jacksonville, Illinois, 1825–1870* (Urbana: University of Illinois Press, 1978), 237–9. See also initiation rituals described in, for example, the *Proceedings of the National Convention, Union League of America, Held at Cleveland, May 20 and 21, 1863* (Washington, D.C., 1863).

17. There was a vocal minority within the Democratic party that openly supported peaceful separation as the only effective solution to the crisis. An example of a Democratic activist who became bitterly disillusioned by the war is S. H. Norton of Southington, Connecticut. See Nina Silber and Mary Beth Sievens, eds, *Yankee Correspondence: Civil War Letters between New England Soldiers and the Homefront* (Charlottesville: University Press of Virginia, 1996), 75–6. An example of the pamphlets produced by these genuine "southern sympathizers" is Alexander B. Johnson, *The Approaching Presidential Election* (Utica, N.Y., 1864). Johnson argues that the North was carrying on the war for purely selfish ends. "Reason cannot see why two sections of a country as large as Europe must live under one government." See also Arnold Shankman, *The Pennsylvania Antiwar Movement, 1861–1865* (Rutherford, N.J.: Fairleigh Dickinson University Press, 1980), 217–9.

18. For a discussion of wartime strikes, see David Montgomery, *Beyond Equality: Labor and the Radical Republicans, 1862–1872* (New York: A. A. Knopf, 1967), 91–101.

19. A point made by Joel Silbey. *Respectable Minority,* xii.

20. This phrase is drawn from David Waldstreicher, *In the Midst of Perpetual Fetes: The Making of American Nationalism, 1776–1820* (Chapel Hill: University of North Carolina Press, 1997), 201–10, 216–35. He writes about the practice of nationalism as "partisan antipartisanship."

21. *Harper's Weekly,* Nov. 12, 1864.

22. Manhattan Union Club, *Address to the Young Men of New York* [New York, 1864]; M. A. Croft to Simon Cameron, Aug. 31, 1864, Cameron Papers, Library of Congress; Francis Lieber, *Lincoln or McClellan?* Pamphlet 67 (New York: Loyal Publication Society, 1864); *Cincinnati Enquirer,* Oct. 12, 1864; *Chicago Tribune,* Nov. 7, 1864.

23. Smith, "Election of 1864," 273–8.

24. *Harper's Weekly,* Feb. 25, 1865.

25. Abraham Lincoln, *The Collected Works of Abraham Lincoln,* ed. Roy P. Basler et al., 8 vols. (New Brunswick, N.J.: Rutgers University Press, 1953–55), 8:254.

26. Seward and *New York Herald* quoted in John H. and Lawanda Cox, *Politics, Principle, and Prejudice, 1865–1866: Dilemma of Reconstruction America* (New York: Free Press, 1963), 39, 33; Schofield, *Congressional Globe,* 38th Cong., 2d sess. (Jan. 6, 1865), 144, quoted in Morton Keller, *Affairs of State: Public Life in Late-Nineteenth-Century America* (Cambridge: Harvard University Press, Belknap Press, 1977), 29, 30 (Julian quote).

27. *New York Times,* June 8, 1865. See Eric Foner, *Reconstruction: America's Unfinished Revolution, 1863–1877* (New York: Harper and Row, 1988), 260–6.

28. William A. Dunning, "The Second Birth of the Republican Party," *American Historical Review* 16 (1910): 56–63. On Johnson, see Eric McKitrick, *Andrew Johnson and Reconstruction* (Chicago: University of Chicago Press, 1960), and Hans L. Trefousse, *Andrew Johnson: A Biography* (New York: W. W. Norton, 1988).

29. Henry J. Raymond, "Notes for a Speech to the National Union Convention in Philadelphia in 1866," Henry J. Raymond Papers, New York Public Library; *Harpers' Weekly,* July 17, 1865; Nina Silber, *The Romance of Reunion: Northerners and the South, 1865–1900* (Chapel Hill: University of North Carolina Press, 1993), 124–31.

30. Kleppner, *Third Electoral System,* 21.

31. Foner, *Reconstruction,* 278–9.

32. On the waning of Reconstruction, see William E. Gillette, *Retreat from Reconstruction, 1869–1879* (Baton Rouge: Louisiana State University Press, 1979); Keller, *Affairs of State.*

33. See James C. Mohr, *Radical Republicans in the North: State Politics during Reconstruction* (Baltimore: Johns Hopkins University Press, 1976); and Foner, *Reconstruction,* 512–63.

34. On the corruption issue in the politics of the 1870s, see Mark W. Summers, *The Era of Good Stealings* (New York: Oxford University Press, 1993).

35. Ibid., 166–9.

36. Lowell, "Ode to the Fourth of July, 1876," quoted in Keller, *Affairs of State,* 268.

37. "Causes for National Thanksgiving: A Discourse Delivered in the First Baptist Church, Bennington, November 24th, 1864, by the Rev. Wm. S. Apsey, Pastor of the Church" (N.p., [1864]), Collection of Political Pamphlets, Election of 1864, Houghton Library, Harvard University, Cambridge, Mass.

38. On liberal reformers, see Summers, *Era of Good Stealings;* John G. Sproat, *"The Best Men": Liberal Reformers in the Gilded Age* (New York: Oxford University Press, 1968); Geoffrey Blodgett, "Reform Thought and the Genteel Tradition," in *The Gilded Age,* ed. H. Wayne Morgan (Syracuse, N.Y.: Syracuse University Press, 1970), 55–76; Blodgett, "The Mugwump Reputation, 1870 to the Present," *Journal of American History* 66 (1980): 867–87; Ari Hoogenboom, *Outlawing the Spoils: A History of the Civil Service Reform Movement, 1865–1883* (Urbana: University of Illinois Press, 1963); Michael E. McGerr, "The Meaning of Liberal Republicanism: The Case of Ohio," *Civil War History* 28 (1982): 307–23; and Fredrickson, *Inner Civil War,* 183–216.

39. Harrison quoted in Michael E. McGerr, *The Decline of Popular Politics: The American North, 1865–1928* (New York: Oxford University Press, 1986), 59. See also Summers, *Era of Good Stealings,* 221–8.

40. George Winston Smith, "Broadsides for Freedom: Civil War Propaganda in New England," *The New England Quarterly* (Sept. 1948): 291–313; McGerr, *Decline of Popular Politics,* 58–62.

41. Hayes supporter quoted in Keller, *Affairs of State,* 252.

42. On late-nineteenth-century politics and the memory of the Civil War, see Silber, *Romance of*

Reunion; and Stuart McConnell, *Glorious Contentment: The Grand Army of the Republic, 1865–1900* (Chapel Hill: University of North Carolina Press, 1992).

6. ABRAHAM LINCOLN AND THE CHARACTER OF LIBERAL STATESMANSHIP

Jeffrey Leigh Sedgwick

1. For Joyner's remarks, see chapter 1. I should confess to belonging to the portion of my discipline that believes political science is less a matter of solving problems ("who should get what, when, and why") than a matter of understanding the necessity and peculiar dignity of *tragic choices.*
2. Thomas Jefferson to John Holmes, Apr. 22, 1820, *Writings,* ed. Merrill D. Peterson (New York: Library of America, 1984), 1434.
3. Wilson Carey McWilliams, *The Idea of Fraternity in America* (Berkeley: University of California Press, 1973), 7.
4. Harry V. Jaffa, *Crisis of the House Divided* (Garden City, N.Y.: Doubleday, 1959), 276.
5. Godfrey Rathbone Benson, *Abraham Lincoln* (New York: Pocket, 1959), 124.
6. Abraham Lincoln, "Fragment on Slavery" [July 1, 1854?], *The Collected Works of Abraham Lincoln,* ed. Roy P. Basler et al., 8 vols. (New Brunswick, N.J.: Rutgers University Press, 1953–55), 2:222.
7. Richard Hofstadter, *The American Political Tradition* (New York: Alfred A. Knopf, 1948), 110.
8. Abraham Lincoln, Address before the Young Men's Lyceum of Springfield, Ill., Jan. 27, 1838, *Collected Works,* 1:114.
9. Jaffa, *Crisis of the House Divided,* 33.
10. *The (Jacksonville) Illinois Sentinal,* Sept. 12, 1856, Lincoln, *Collected Works,* 2:370.
11. Lincoln to Joshua F. Speed, Aug. 24, 1855, ibid., 2:323.
12. Abraham Lincoln, Speech at Peoria, Ill., Oct. 16, 1854, ibid., 2:266.
13. Abraham Lincoln, Speech at Springfield, Ill., June 26, 1857, ibid., 2:405.
14. Lincoln, Address before the Young Men's Lyceum, 1:109.
15. Ibid., 1:110.
16. Ibid.
17. Ibid.
18. Ibid., 1:114.
19. Ibid., 1:112.
20. Ibid., 1:115.
21. Hofstadter, *American Political Tradition,* 101.
22. Abraham Lincoln, Speech at Bloomington, Ill., Sept. 12, 1854, *Collected Works.,* 2:230.
23. Abraham Lincoln, Temperance address, Feb. 22, 1842, ibid., 1:271.
24. Ibid., 1:272.
25. Ibid., 1:273.
26. Ibid.

7. ABRAHAM LINCOLN AND AMERICAN NATIONHOOD

Peter J. Parish

1. The word "nationhood" is defined in the *New Shorter Oxford English Dictionary* (Oxford, Eng.: Clarendon Press, 1993) as "the state or fact of being a nation." This term is preferred here to other

options such as "nationality" or "nationalism" that often carry much more ideological or emotional baggage with them and that apply more properly to individual citizens or groups of citizens rather than to the nation as a whole.

2. For a brief discussion of the fragility of the early Republic and of American nationhood as a process, see Peter J. Parish, "An Exception to Most of the Rules: What Made American Nationalism Different in the Mid–Nineteenth Century?" *Prologue: Quarterly of the National Archives* 27 (1995): 218–29. For a contrary view emphasizing the fundamental strengths of American national feeling between the Revolution and the Civil War, see Donald J. Ratcliffe, "The State of the Union, 1776–1860," in *The American Civil War: Explorations and Reconsiderations,* ed. Susan-Mary Grant and Brian Holden Reid (London: Longman, 2000), 3–38.

3. John M. Murrin, "A Roof without Walls: The Dilemma of American National Identity," in *Beyond Confederation: Origins of the Constitution and American National Identity,* ed. Richard Beeman, Stephen Botein, and Edward C. Carter (Chapel Hill: University of North Carolina Press, 1987), 347; Liah Greenfeld, *Nationalism: Five Roads to Modernity* (Cambridge: Harvard University Press, 1992), 422–8 (quote, 425); Kenneth M. Stampp, "The Concept of a Perpetual Union," *The Imperiled Union: Essays on the Background of the Civil War* (New York: Oxford University Press, 1980), 3–36; Carl N. Degler, *One Among Many: The Civil War in Comparative Perspective,* Twenty-ninth Robert Fortenbaugh Lecture (Gettysburg, Pa.: Gettysburg College, 1990), 10–4.

4. Richard R. John, *Spreading the News: The American Postal System from Franklin to Morse* (Cambridge: Harvard University Press, 1995).

5. Eric Foner, *Free Soil, Free Labor, Free Men: The Ideology of the Republican Party before the Civil War* (New York: Oxford University Press, 1970), 308–10, 316; Susan-Mary Grant, *North over South: Northern Nationalism and American Identity in the Antebellum Era* (Lawrence: University Press of Kansas, 2000); Allen C. Guelzo, *Abraham Lincoln: Redeemer President* (Grand Rapids, Mich.: Eerdmans, 1999), 247–9, 252–5, 258–63; Alexander K. McClure, *Abraham Lincoln and Men of Wartimes,* 4th ed., with an introduction by James A. Rawley (Lincoln: University of Nebraska Press, 1996), 136. See also Grant's important articles and essays on American nationalism in the Civil War era, including "When Is a Nation Not a Nation? The Crisis of American Nationality in the Mid–Nineteenth Century," *Nations and Nationalism* 2 (1996): 105–29; "The Charter of Its Birthright: The Civil War and American Nationalism," *Nations and Nationalism* 4 (1998): 163–85; and "From Union to Nation: The Civil War and the Development of American Nationalism," in *The American Civil War: Explorations and Reconsiderations,* ed. Susan-Mary Grant and Brian Holden Reid (London: Longman, 2000), 333–57.

6. For two thoughtful, brief accounts of Lincoln's conduct between his election in November 1860 and his inauguration in March 1861, see Phillip Shaw Paludan, *The Presidency of Abraham Lincoln* (Lawrence: University Press of Kansas, 1994), 23–35, 49–57; and Brian Holden Reid, *The Origins of the American Civil War* (London: Longman, 1996), 239–59, 301–9.

7. There was a major historical controversy between the 1950s and the 1970s over Lincoln's handling of the Fort Sumter crisis. For a convenient summary of the main schools of thought, see James M. McPherson, *Battle Cry of Freedom: The Civil War Era* (New York: Oxford University Press, 1988), 272 n. 78. Among those historians who emphasize Lincoln's determination not to fire the first shot, see Kenneth M. Stampp, *And the War Came: The North and the Secession Crisis, 1860–61* (Chicago: University of Chicago Press, 1950), 263–93; and Richard N. Current, *Lincoln and the First Shot* (Philadelphia: Lippincott, 1963). For an excellent account of the whole crisis, see Reid, *Origins of the Civil War,* 310–59 (with a masterful conclusion on 356–8).

8. Abraham Lincoln, Message to Congress in Special Session, July 4, 1861, *The Collected Works of*

Abraham Lincoln, ed. Roy P. Basler et al., 8 vols. (New Brunswick N.J.: Rutgers University Press, 1953–55), 4:426, 438, 439.

9. Abraham Lincoln, Annual Message to Congress, Dec. 3 1861, *Collected Works,* 5:49. On Lincoln's management of the emancipation issue, see Paludan, *Presidency of Abraham Lincoln,* 142–66; and Peter J. Parish, *The American Civil War* (London: Eyre Methuen, 1975), 226–51. On Lincoln's close attention to popular support for the war, see Richard J. Carwardine, "Abraham Lincoln, the Presidency, and the Mobilization of Union Sentiment," in *The American Civil War: Explorations and Reconsiderations,* ed. Susan-Mary Grant and Brian Holden Reid (London: Longman, 2000), 68–97.

10. Greeley quoted in Guelzo, *Lincoln,* 385.

11. For examples of images best illustrating Lincoln's deterioration, see Lincoln, *Collected Works,* vol. 4, frontispiece; and vol. 8, frontispiece; and James D. Horan, *Matthew Brady: Historian with a Camera* (New York: Crown, 1955), plates 143–53.

12. See Parish, "Exception to Most of the Rules"; Ernest Gellner, *Nations and Nationalism* (Oxford: Blackwell, 1981), 7; and David M. Potter, "The Historian's Use of Nationalism and Vice Versa," in *History and American Society: Essays of David M. Potter,* ed. Don E. Fehrenbacher (New York: Oxford University Press, 1973), 80–5. See also the articles by Susan-Mary Grant cited in note 5.

13. Reginald Horsman, *Race and Manifest Destiny: The Origins of American Racial Anglo-Saxonism* (Cambridge: Harvard University Press, 1981), esp. chap. 12; Thomas R. Hietala, *Manifest Design: Anxious Aggrandizement in Late Jacksonian America* (Ithaca N.Y.: Cornell University Press, 1985), 152–72; Dale Knobel, *Paddy and the Republic: Ethnicity and Nationality in Antebellum America* (Middletown, Conn.: Wesleyan University Press, 1986), 4–18, 65–7, 95–103.

14. For two influential critical analyses of Lincoln's racial views, see Don E. Fehrenbacher, "Only His Stepchildren," *Lincoln in Text and Context: Collected Essays* (Stanford, Calif.: Stanford University Press, 1987), 95–112; and George M. Fredrickson, "A Man but Not a Brother: Abraham Lincoln and Racial Equality," *The Arrogance of Race: Historical Perspectives on Slavery, Racism, and Social Inequality* (Middletown, Conn.: Wesleyan University Press, 1988), 54–72.

15. Lincoln, *Collected Works,* 3:216–7, 212–4, 249.

16. On Lincoln's handling of the emancipation issue in 1861–63, see references in note 9 above and Lincoln to James C. Conkling, Aug. 26, 1863, Lincoln, *Collected Works,* 6:409. On black soldiers, see Dudley T. Cornish, *The Sable Arm: Black Troops in the Union Army* (New York: W. W. Norton, 1956; reprint, Lawrence: University Press of Kansas, 1987); Joseph T. Glatthaar, *Forged in Battle: The Civil War Alliance of Black Soldiers and White Officers* (New York: Free Press, 1990); and Susan-Mary Grant, "Fighting for Freedom: African American Soldiers in the Civil War," in *The American Civil War: Explorations and Reconsiderations,* ed. Susan-Mary Grant and Brian Holden Reid (London: Longman, 2000), 191–213.

17. On the Thirteenth and Fourteenth Amendments, see Harold M. Hyman and William C. Wiecek, *Equal Justice under Law: Constitutional Development, 1835–1875* (New York: Harper, 1982), 276–8, 302–3, 386–438, 463–70.

18. Tyler Anbinder, *Nativism and Slavery: The Northern Know-Nothings and the Politics of the 1850s* (New York: Oxford University Press, 1992), esp. chaps. 9–10; William E. Gienapp, *The Origins of the Republican Party, 1852–1856* (New York: Oxford University Press, 1987), esp. chaps. 3–7, 13; Michael F. Holt, *The Rise and Fall of the American Whig Party: Jacksonian Politics and the Onset of the Civil War* (New York: Oxford University Press, 1999), chaps. 23–26; Lincoln to Joshua F. Speed, Aug. 24, 1855, Lincoln, *Collected Works,* 2:323.

19. Abraham Lincoln, Speech at Chicago, July 10, 1858, *Collected Works,* 2:499–500.

20. See, for example, Guelzo, *Lincoln,* 398, 422–3.

21. Abraham Lincoln, Speech at Philadelphia, Feb. 22, 1861, *Collected Works,* 4:240.

22. Paul C. Nagel, *This Sacred Trust: American Nationality, 1798–1898* (New York: Oxford University Press, 1971), 88–90, 151–2, 158–61; Major L. Wilson, *Space, Time, and Freedom: The Quest for Nationality and the Irrepressible Conflict, 1815–1861* (Westport, Conn.: Greenwood, 1974), 102. Emerson's bitter denunciation of Webster is quoted in Irving H. Bartlett, *Daniel Webster* (New York: W. W. Norton, 1978), 268.

23. Daniel Walker Howe, *The Political Culture of the American Whigs* (Chicago: University of Chicago Press, 1979), 291.

24. Ibid., 267, 269–70; Lincoln quoted in Guelzo, *Lincoln,* 6.

25. Guelzo, *Lincoln,* 86–7. On Lincoln's determination to escape from the constraints and limited horizons of farming, see ibid., esp. 5–9, 13–15, 32–5; and Daniel Walker Howe, *Making the American Self: Jonathan Edwards to Abraham Lincoln* (Cambridge: Harvard University Press, 1997), 138–40.

26. See, for example, Abraham Lincoln, Annual Message to Congress, Dec. 3, 1861, *Collected Works,* 5:51–3; Lincoln, Annual Message to Congress, Dec. 1, 1862, ibid., 5:532–4; and Lincoln, Annual Message to Congress, Dec. 6, 1864, ibid., 8:145, 150–1.

27. During the 1960s and 1970s there was much debate among American historians on the economic effect of the Civil War. It was initiated by an article by Thomas C. Cochran, who challenged the then prevailing view by by arguing that the war set back U.S. industrial development. Cochran, "Did the Civil War Retard Industrialization?" *Mississippi Valley Historical Review* 48 (1961): 197–210. For a selection of views both for and against the Cochran thesis, see Ralph Andreano, ed., *The Economic Impact of the American Civil War* (Cambridge, Mass.: Schenkman, 1962). For a judicious recent overview of the subject, see Phillip Shaw Paludan, "What Did the Winners Win? The Social and Economic History of the North during the Civil War," in *Writing the Civil War: The Quest to Understand,* ed. James M. McPherson and William J. Cooper (Columbia: University of South Carolina Press, 1998), 175–87.

28. Rush Welter, *The Mind of America, 1820–1860* (New York: Columbia University Press, 1975), 22–5.

29. Abraham Lincoln, Speech at Springfield, Ill., June 26, 1857, *Collected Works,* 2:406.

30. Abraham Lincoln, Speech at Chicago, July 10, 1858, ibid., 2:501.

31. Guelzo, *Lincoln,* 193–8 (quotes, 196, 197).

32. Abraham Lincoln, Address to New Jersey Senate at Trenton, Feb. 21, 1861, *Collected Works,* 4:236.

33. Abraham Lincoln, Second Inaugural Address, Mar. 4, 1865, *Collected Works,* 8:442–3; Lincoln, Message to Congress, July 4, 1861, ibid., 4:421–41 (esp. 435–6); Lincoln, Annual Message to Congress, Dec. 1, 1862, ibid., 5:518–37 (esp. 527, 529). For evidence of Democratic protests at Lincoln's use of the word "nation," see Guelzo, *Lincoln,* 372.

34. Allan Nevins and Milton Halsey Thomas, eds., *The Diary of George Templeton Strong,* 4 vols. (New York: Macmillan, 1952), 3:109, 4:2.

35. Among the various recent studies of the Civil War in American memory, two books, one by a distinguished historian, the other by a sociologist, focus on Lincoln. The first, Merrill D. Peterson, *Lincoln in American Memory* (New York: Oxford University Press, 1994), is an authoritative study drawing together a mass of material. The second, Barry Schwartz, *Abraham Lincoln and the Forge of National Memory* (Chicago: University of Chicago Press, 2000), has a more ambitious theoretical framework but is less surefooted on the history; it is particularly useful on the upsurge in Lincoln's reputation in the early twentieth century. In this section of the essay, I have relied heavily on these two works. On the national mourning after Lincoln's assassination, see Schwartz, chap.1; and, more generally, Thomas Reed

Turner, *Beware the People Weeping: Public Opinion and the Assassination of Abraham Lincoln* (Baton Rouge: Louisiana State University Press, 1982).

36. In the early years of the twentieth century, Lincoln's name was exploited in the name of white supremacy by James K. Vardaman of Mississippi. Richard N. Current, *The Lincoln Nobody Knows* (New York: Hill and Wang, 1958), 231–3. Thomas Dixon, author of *The Clansman* (on which the film *The Birth of a Nation* was based), also professed admiration for Lincoln as a champion of white supremacy. Peterson, *Lincoln in American Memory,* 168–70.

37. Schwartz, *Lincoln and the Forge of National Memory,* 126–30, 161–3, 141, 136, and chap. 3; Peterson, *Lincoln in American Memory,* 164–7.

38. Peterson, *Lincoln in American Memory,* 173–4; Schwartz, *Lincoln and the Forge of National Memory,* 211–16, 195, and chap. 5.

39. Peterson, *Lincoln in American Memory,* 182.

40. Schwartz, *Lincoln and the Forge of National Memory,* 234–55.

41. Both Merrill Peterson and Barry Schwartz discuss at length the two Lincoln memorials. See Peterson, *Lincoln in American Memory,* 177–82, 206–8, 214–17; and Schwartz, *Lincoln and the Forge of National Memory,* 276–90 (quote, 268).

42. Herbert Croly, *The Promise of American Life,* ed. Arthur M. Schlesinger Jr., (Cambridge: Harvard University Press, Belknap Press, 1965), 88.

8. "FOR A VAST FUTURE ALSO": LINCOLN AND THE MILLENNIUM

James M. McPherson

1. Tolstoy and Kennedy quoted in Merrill D. Peterson, *Lincoln in American Memory* (New York: Oxford University Press, 1994) 185, 324 n.

2. Ibid., 355–6.

3. Abraham Lincoln, *The Collected Works of Abraham Lincoln,* ed. Roy P. Basler et al., 8 vols. (New Brunswick, N.J.: Rutgers University Press, 1953–55), 4235–6.

4. Ibid., 4:236.

5. Ibid., 4:240.

6. Ibid., 2:255.

7. Ibid., 2:405–6.

8. Ibid., 3:376.

9. Ibid., 4:268; Michael Burlingame and John R. Turner Ettlinger, eds., *Inside Lincoln's White House: The Complete Civil War Diary of John Hay* (Carbondale: Southern Illinois University Press, 1997), 20.

10. Lincoln, *Collected Works,* 4:439.

11. *Indianapolis Daily Journal,* Apr. 27, 1861.

12. Josiah Perry to Phebe Perry, Oct. 3, 1862, Josiah Perry Papers, Illinois State Historical Library, Springfield; Robert T. McMahan diary, Sept. 3, 1863, State Historical Society of Missouri, Columbia.

13. Titus Crenshaw to father, Nov. 10, 1861, quoted in Charlotte Erickson, *Invisible Immigrants: The Adaptation of English and Scottish Immigrants in Nineteenth Century America* (Coral Gables, Fla.: University of Miami Press, 1972), 348; George H. Cadman to Esther Cadman, Mar. 6, 1864, Cadman Papers, Southern Historical Collection, University of North Carolina, Chapel Hill; Peter Welsh to Mary Welsh, Feb. 3, 1863; and Peter Welsh to Patrick Prendergast, June 1, 1863, *Irish Green and Blue: The*

Civil War Letters of Peter Welsh, ed. Laurence Frederick Kohl and Margaret Cosee Richard (New York: Fordham University Press, 1986), 65–66, 102.

14. Quoted in George D. Lillibridge, *Beacon of Freedom: The Impact of American Democracy upon Great Britain, 1830–1870* (Philadelphia: University of Pennsylvania Press, 1955), 5, 28.

15. Alexis de Tocqueville, *Democracy in America,* 12th ed., trans. George Lawrence, ed. J. P. Mayer (New York: Harper and Row, 1966), xiii; Serge Gavronsky, *The French Liberal Opposition and the American Civil War* (New York: Humanities Press, 1968); Lillibridge, *Beacon of Freedom,* 80.

16. *Revue des Deux Mondes,* Aug. 15, 1861; and John Stuart Mill, *Autobiography,* both quoted in *Europe Looks at the Civil War,* ed. Belle Becker Sideman and Lillian Friedman (New York: Orion, 1960), 81, 117–8.

17. *Times* (London) quoted in Frank L. Owsley, *King Cotton Diplomacy: Foreign Relations of the Confederate States of America,* 2d ed., revised by Harriet C. Owsley (Chicago: University of Chicago Press, 1959), 186; Earl of Shrewsbury quoted in Ephraim D. Adams, *Great Britain and the American Civil War,* 2 vols. (New York: Russell and Russell, 1925), 2:282.

18. *Pensamiento Español,* Sept. 1862, quoted in Sideman and Friedman, *Europe Looks at the Civil War,* 173–4; Russian minister (Stoeckl) quoted in Albert A. Woldman, *Lincoln and the Russians* (Cleveland: World, 1952), 216–7.

19. Lincoln quoted in *The Reminiscences of Carl Schurz,* 3 vols. (New York: McClure, 1907–8), 2:309; *Saturday Review,* Sept. 14, 1861, quoted in Adams, *Great Britain and the American Civil War,* 1:181; *Economist,* Sept. 1861, quoted in Karl Marx and Friedrich Engels, *The Civil War in the United States,* ed. Richard Emmale (New York: International Publishers, 1937), 12.

20. Lincoln, *Collected Works,* 5:423, 6:30.

21. Frederick W. Seward, *Seward at Washington as Senator and Secretary of State* (New York: Derby and Miller, 1891), 151.

22. Lincoln, *Collected Works,* 5:53, 537.

23. Ibid., 8:333.

24. Sir Edward Bulwer-Lytton to John Bigelow, Apr. 1865, quoted in Sideman and Friedman, *Europe Looks at the Civil War,* 282; Harold M. Hyman, ed., *Heard around the World: The Impact Abroad of the Civil War* (New York: Alfred A. Knopf, 1969), xi, 73.

25. Hyman, *Heard around the World,* 323.

26. Lincoln, *Collected Works,* 7:301–2.

27. Ibid., 2:250.

28. Isaiah Berlin, *Four Essays on Liberty* (New York: Oxford University Press, 1974), 118–72.

29. Gordon S. Wood, *The Creation of the American Republic, 1776–1787* (Chapel Hill: University of North Carolina Press, 1969), 413.

30. Robert Remini, *Andrew Jackson and the Bank War* (New York: W. W. Norton, 1967), 45; James D. Richardson, comp., *Messages and Papers of the Presidents,* 20 vols. (Washington, D.C.: Government Printing Office, 1897), 12:2780–4.

31. Norman K. Risjord, *The Old Republicans: Southern Conservatism in the Age of Jefferson* (New York: Columbia University Press, 1965), 242.

32. *Congressional Globe,* 39th Cong., 2d sess. (Jan. 28, 1867), appendix, 78; *The Works of James Abram Garfield,* ed. Burke A. Hinsdale, 2 vols. (Boston: J. R. Osgood, 1882), 1:249.

33. Reena Mattew, "One Set of Footprints," essay in author's possession.

9. CIVIL-MILITARY RELATIONS AND THE LEGACY OF THE CIVIL WAR

Brian Holden Reid

1. John Terraine, *The Impacts of War, 1914 and 1918,* rev. ed. (London: Hutchinson, 1993), vi. See Jay Luvaas, *The Military Legacy of the Civil War: The European Inheritance* (1959; reprint, Lawrence: University Press of Kansas, 1988); and Brian Holden Reid, *Studies in British Military Thought: Debates with Fuller and Liddell Hart* (Lincoln: University of Nebraska Press, 1998), chap. 8.

2. Perry D. Jamieson, *Crossing the Deadly Ground: United States Army Tactics, 1865–1899* (Tuscaloosa: University of Alabama Press, 1994), 111–2, 120.

3. T. Harry Williams, *Lincoln and His Generals* (New York: Alfred A. Knopf, 1952), 302–3, 305–6.

4. Stephen E. Ambrose, *Halleck: Lincoln's Chief of Staff* (1962; reprint, Baton Rouge: Louisiana State University Press, 1990), v, 162–5.

5. See Peter Cozzens, *The Shipwreck of Their Hopes: The Battles for Chattanooga* (Urbana: University of Illinois Press, 1994), 45–6; Albert Castel, *Decision in the West: The Atlanta Campaign of 1864* (Lawrence: University of Kansas Press, 1992), 284–5; and Ambrose, *Halleck,* 193–5.

6. Ambrose, *Halleck,* 195, 208; Brian Holden Reid, "The Commander and his Chief of Staff: Ulysses S. Grant and John A. Rawlins, 1861–1865," in *Leadership and Command: The Anglo-American Experience since 1861,* ed. Gary D. Sheffield (London: Brassey's, 1997), 29.

7. John Y. Simon, "Grant, Lincoln, and Unconditional Surrender," in *Lincoln's Generals,* ed. Gabor Boritt (New York: Oxford University Press, 1994), 165; Williams, *Lincoln and His Generals,* 301; Brooks D. Simpson, "Ulysses S. Grant and the Problems of Command in 1864," in *The Art of Command in the Civil War,* ed. Steven E. Woodworth (Lincoln: University of Nebraska Press, 1998), 137–8. Simpson seems to suggest that Williams underrated Grant's understanding of the party political aspects. He did not. See T. Harry Williams, "The Military Leadership of North and South," in , *Why the North Won the Civil War,* ed. David Donald (Baton Rouge: Louisiana State University Press, 1960), 51.

8. William S. McFeely, *Grant* (New York: W. W. Norton, 1981), 221; Hans L. Trefousse, *Andrew Johnson: A Biography* (New York: W. W. Norton, 1988), 214–20; Marcus Cunliffe, *American Presidents and the Presidency,* 2d ed. (London: Fontana, 1972), 145–6, 158–9, 166–7.

9. Timothy D. Johnson, *Winfield Scott: The Quest for Military Glory* (Lawrence: University Press of Kansas, 1998), 103, 187, 192, 210–2; Marcus Cunliffe, *Soldiers and Civilians: The Martial Spirit in America, 1775–1865* (London: Eyre and Spottiswoode, 1969), 313–7.

10. Craig Symonds, "No Margin for Error: Civil War in the Confederate Government," in *The Art of Command in the Civil War,* ed. Steven E. Woodworth (Lincoln: University of Nebraska Press, 1998), 13.

11. Johnson, *Scott,* 217–9; Stephen W. Sears, *George B. McClellan: The Young Napoleon* (New York: Ticknor and Fields, 1988), 155–6, 167–8, 177–8; Cunliffe, *Soldiers and Civilians,* 325.

12. Benjamin P. Thomas and Harold M. Hyman, *Stanton: The Life and Times of Lincoln's Secretary of War* (New York: Alfred A. Knopf, 1962), 154–5; David H. Bates, *Lincoln in the Telegraph Office* (New York: Appleton, 1939), 136–7; Hans L. Trefousse, *Benjamin Franklin Wade: Radical Republican from Ohio* (New York: Twayne, 1963), 164; Paul J. Scheips, "Union Signal Communications: Innovation and Conflict," *Civil War History* 9 (Dec. 1863): 399–421.

13. Bruce Catton, *Grant Takes Command* (Boston: Little, Brown, 1968), 139.

14. Kenneth P. Williams, *Lincoln Finds a General,* 5 vols. (New York: Macmillan, 1949–58), 5:277;

Brooks D. Simpson, *Let Us Have Peace: Ulysses S. Grant and the Politics of War and Reconstruction, 1861–1868* (Chapel Hill: University of North Carolina Press, 1991), 128–9, 195–6.

15. John F. Marszalek, *Sherman: A Soldier's Passion for Order* (New York: Free Press, 1993), 385–7.

16. Mark Grandstaff, "'Preserving the Habits and Usages of War': William Tecumseh Sherman, Professional Reform in the U.S. Officer Corps, 1865–1881, Revisited," *Journal of Military History* 62 (July 1998): 525–7, 529–31.

17. Quoted in Jay Luvaas, "The Influence of the German Wars of Unification on the United States," in *On the Road to Total War: The American Civil War and the German Wars of Unification, 1861–1871,* ed. Stig Forster and Jorg Nagler (Cambridge: Cambridge University Press, 1997), 605.

18. Ibid, 605–6.

19. Russell F. Weigley, *Toward an American Army: Military Thought from Washington to Marshall* (New York: Columbia University Press, 1962), 84–5. This was not Sherman's view in 1861. After the First Battle of Manassas (Bull Run) he declared: "Our men are not good soldiers. They brag, but don't perform, complain sadly if they don't get anything they want, and a march of a few miles uses them up." Quoted in William C. Davis, *Battle at Bull Run* (New York: Doubleday, 1981), 219.

20. Grandstaff, "'Preserving the Habits and Usages of War,'" 538.

21. William T. Sherman, *Memoirs of General William T. Sherman,* 2 vols. (New York: D. Appleton, 1875), 2:406.

22. Marszalek, *Sherman,* 388–9.

23. Quoted in Weigley, *Toward an American Army,* 82, 83.

24. For a brief discussion of Calhoun's 1820 plan, see Irving H. Bartlett, *John C. Calhoun: A Biography* (New York: Norton, 1993), 91–2. The idea itself originated with Alexander Hamilton.

25. Grandstaff, "'Preserving the Habits and Usages of War,'" 539–44.

26. Luvaas, "Influence of the German Wars of the Unification," 601, 606–7; B. H. Liddell Hart, *Sherman: Soldier, Realist, American,* 2d ed. (1929; New York: Da Capo, 1993), 237.

27. Ambrose, *Halleck,* 165–8.

28. For some of George B. McClellan's hints, see *McClellan's Own Story* (New York: Charles L. Webster, 1887), 30, 59, 138–9, 141, 144, 149. See also Robert Reinders, "Militia and Public Order in Nineteenth Century America," *Journal of American Studies* 11 (Apr. 1977): 91.

29. T. Harry Williams, "The Macs and the Ikes," *American Mercury* 75 (Oct. 1952): 34, 38.

30. Robert Wooster, *Nelson A. Miles and the Twilight of the Frontier Army* (Lincoln: University Press of Nebraska, 1993), 134, 196–7.

31. William Marvel, *Burnside* (Chapel Hill: University of North Carolina Press, 1991), 419–20, 422–3.

32. Brian Holden Reid, "Historians and the Joint Committee on the Conduct of the War, 1861–1865," *Civil War History* 38 (Dec. 1992), 326–7.

33. Louis Fisher, *Presidential War Power* (Lawrence: University Press of Kansas, 1995), 38–9; David Mervin, "Presidents, Precedents, and the Use of Military Force," *Journal of American Studies* 32 (Dec. 1998): 484–5, 488, 492–4, 500.

34. John M. Gates, "The 'New' Military Professionalism," *Armed Forces and Society* 11 (spring 1985): 425–36; Peter R. DeMontravel, *A Hero to His Fighting Men: Nelson A. Miles, 1839–1925* (Kent, Ohio: Kent State University Press, 1998), 198.

35. Emory Upton, *The Military Policy of the United States from 1775* (1904; reprint, New York: Greenwood, 1968), 281; David H. Donald, *Lincoln* (London: Jonathan Cape, 1995), 319–20, 338–41.

36. Upton, *Military Policy,* 297, 229.

37. Ibid., 336, 417; Thomas and Hyman, *Stanton,* 185–6.

38. Weigley, *Toward an American Army*, 120–1; Brian Holden Reid, *The American Civil War and the Wars of the Industrial Revolution* (London: Cassell, 1999), 185; Freeman Cleaves, *Meade of Gettysburg* (Norman: University of Oklahoma Press, 1960), 234, 245–6.

39. Upton, *Military Policy*, 417; Luvaas, "Influence of the German Wars of Unification," 601.

40. John A. Logan, *The Volunteer Soldier of America* (Chicago: R. S. Peale, 1887); John Keegan, *The First World War* (London: Hutchinson, 1998), 30–4.

41. Lamson to Katie, Aug. 19, 1861, *Lamson of the* Gettysburg: *The Civil War Letters of Lieutenant Roswell H. Lamson, U.S. Navy*, edited James M. McPherson and Patricia R. McPherson (New York: Oxford University Press, 1997), 31. The "ignorant politicians" reference is to Benjamin F. Butler.

42. Logan, *Volunteer Soldier*, 455–6; Bruce Collins, "The Southern Military Tradition, 1812–61," in *Americana: Essays in Memory of Marcus Cunliffe*, ed. John White and Brian Holden Reid, 2d ed. (Hull, Eng.: University of Hull Press, 1998), 139–55; Cunliffe, *Soldiers and Civilians*, 360–1; Brian Holden Reid, *The Origins of the American Civil War* (London: Longman, 1996), 341.

43. Ronald J. Barr, "High Command in the United States: The Emergence of a Modern System," in *Leadership and Command: The Anglo-American Experience since 1861*, ed. Gary D. Sheffield (London: Brassey's, 1997), 242–3.

10. THE ENDURING SIGNIFICANCE OF THE CIVIL WAR CONSTITUTIONAL AMENDMENTS

Patricia Lucie

1. Bruce Ackerman, *We the People: Foundations* (Cambridge: Harvard University Press, Belknap Press, 1991), 44, 82.

2. *McCulloch v. Maryland*, 17 U.S. (4Wheat.) 415, 427 (1819).

3. Stanley I. Kutler, *Judicial Power and Reconstruction Politics* (Chicago: University of Chicago Press, 1968); William M. Wiecek, "The Reconstruction of Federal Judicial Power, 1863–1876," *American Journal of Legal History* 13 (1969): 333; *Congressional Globe*, 42d Cong. 2d sess. (1872), 727. For an excellent critique of the enduring power of the doctrine, see Susan Bandes, "The Negative Constitution: A Critique," *Michigan Law Review* 88 (1990): 2271–2347.

4. The literature is huge, but among the most thought provoking, see John H. Ely, *Democracy and Distrust* (Cambridge: Harvard University Press, 1980); Robert H. Bork, *The Tempting of America: The Political Seduction of the Law* (London: Sinclair-Stevenson, 1990); Erwin Cherminsky, *Interpreting the Constitution* (New York: Hill and Wang, 1987); Philip Bobbitt, *Constitutional Interpretation* (Oxford: Blackwell, 1991); and Mark Tushnet, *Red, White, and Blue: A Critical Analysis of Constitutional Law* (Cambridge: Harvard University Press, 1988).

5. Justice Stone's footnote 4 in *United States v. Carolene Products Co.* (304 U.S. 144, 152 [1938]) is credited with originating the "double standard" and mapping out a new role for the Court with respect to individual and minority rights. The justice's ideas were tentative, and the subsequent development of them was not foreseen. See Lewis F. Powell, "Carolene Products Revisited," *Columbia Law Review* 82 (1982): 1087–92. For one of the severest critics of the Warren Court's uses of history, see Raoul Berger, *Government by Judiciary: The Transformation of the Fourteenth Amendment* (Cambridge: Harvard University Press, 1977). For a different perspective, see Robert K. Kohl, "The Civil Rights Act of 1866, Its Hour Come Round at Last," *Virginia Law Review* 55 (1969): 272.

6. Justice Brennan said of the task of constitutional interpretation, "The ultimate question must be,

246 / NOTES TO PAGES 174-8

what do the words mean in our time." Justice William J. Brennan, "The Constitution of the United States: Contemporary Ratification," Symposium, Georgetown University, Oct. 12, 1985, published in *The Great Debate: Interpreting Our Written Constitution,* ed. Paul G. Cassell (N.p.: private publication, 1987).

7. The dynamics of the Court in this era are explored in Bernard Schwarz, *Super Chief: Earl Warren and His Supreme Court—A Judicial Biography* (New York and London: New York University Press, 1983); and David G. Savage, *Turning Right* (New York: John Wiley and Sons, 1992). One example of the Court reversing itself is *Adarand Constructors v. Pena* (132 L.Ed.2d 158 [1995]), overturning one of its own recent precedents, *Metro Broadcasting v. FCC* (497 U.S. 547 [1990]), which had allowed Congress more scope for affirmative action than *Adarand.* In 1995, in *U.S. v. Lopez* (514 U.S. 549 [1995]), the Court struck down the Gun-free Schools Act of 1990 on the grounds that Congress exceeded its powers under the interstate commerce clause. In 1997 it stuck down the Religious Freedom Restoration Act in *City of Boerne v. Flores* (521 U.S. 507 [1997]). Also, Justice Scalia, who would like to have seen the abortion decision of *Roe v. Wade* (410 U.S. 113 [1973]) overturned in *Planned Parenthood v. Casey* (505 U.S. 833 [1992]), spoke for himself and three colleagues when he scolded the Court for not doing so. "The Imperial Judiciary lives," he wrote, ironically setting out a decidedly imperial argument for overruling *Roe.*

8. *Civil Rights Cases,* 109 U.S. 3 (1883). For a critical analysis of the "state action" concept and its effects, see Charles L. Black, "Forward: State Action, Equal Protection, and California's Proposition 14," *Harvard Law Review* 81 (1967): 69–109. There is a huge literature on state action. One of the most interesting discussions can be found in Laurence H. Tribe, *Constitutional Choices* (Cambridge: Harvard University Press, 1985), chap.16.

9. *Congressional Globe,* 39th Cong., 1st sess. (Jan. 30, 1866), 499.

10. A proposal for a habeas guarantee of freedom was first attached to a version of the bill that became the Confiscation Act of 1862. *Congressional Globe,* 37th Cong., 2d sess. (1862), 2793. Although not adopted, the remedy was frequently discussed as a procedural remedy alongside affirmations of freedom's substantive content. See Patricia Lucie, *Freedom and Federalism, Congress and Courts, 1861–1866* (New York: Garland, 1986).

11. *Congressional Globe,* 39th Cong., 1st sess. (Jan. 19, 1866), 322.

12. Harold M. Hyman, *The Reconstruction Justice of Salmon P. Chase* (Lawrence: University Press of Kansas, 1997) 114; *Dred Scott v. Sandford,* 19 How. (60 U.S.) 393 (1857). The best general discussion is James H. Kettner, *The Development of American Citizenship, 1608–1870* (Chapel Hill: University of North Carolina Press, 1978), chap.10.

13. *Official Opinions of the Attorneys General of the United States* (Washington, D.C.: Government Printing Office, 1791–1948), 10:383.

14. This was the opinion of Chief Justice John Marshall in *Barron v. Baltimore,* 7 Pet. (32 U.S.) 243 (1833). Nonetheless, there was a growing antislavery understanding that the Bill of Rights did limit the states and empowered the nation's government to secure them. See William Wiecek, *The Source of Antislavery Constitutionalism in America* (Ithaca, N.Y.: Cornell University Press, 1977).

15. *Statutes at Large* 14 (1866): 27.

16. Berger, *Government by Judiciary.*

17. *Corfield v. Coryell,* 4 Wash.C.C. 371 (1823), interpreting Art. 4, Sec. 2 of the U.S. Constitution, guarantees reciprocity among states: "The Citizens of each State shall be entitled to all Privileges and Immunities of Citizens in the several States."

18. Justice Hugo Black's dissenting opinion in *Adamson v. California* (395 U.S. 46 [1947]), arguing that the framers intended to make the Bill of Rights applicable to the states, was the starting point for a very long academic argument. Charles Fairman made a distinguished but not definitive reply to Black.

"Does the Fourteenth Amendment Incorporate the Bill of Rights? The Original Understanding," *Stanford Law Review* 2 (1949): 5. Michael K. Curtis argues for a broad understanding of the framers intent, while Earl M. Malz takes a narrower view, as does Lambert Gingras. See Curtis, *No State Shall Abridge: The Fourteenth Amendment and the Bill of Rights* (Durham, N.C.: Duke University Press, 1986); Malz, *Civil Rights, the Constitution, and Congress, 1863–1869* (Lawrence: University Press of Kansas, 1990); and Gingras, "Congressional Misunderstandings and the Ratifiers Understanding," *The American Journal of Legal History* 40 (1996): 41–71. In practice the Supreme Court has made a selective incorporation of almost the entire Bill of Rights without accepting Black's historical argument.

19. Earl M. Malz, "The Constitution and Nonracial Discrimination: Alienage, Sex, and the Framers' Ideal of Equality," *Constitutional Commentary* 7 (1990): 251–82; Patricia Lucie, "White Rights as a Model for Black: Or—Who's Afraid of the Privileges or Immunities Clause?" *Syracuse Law Review* 38 (1987): 859–77.

20. The text and exchange of views are found in *Congressional Globe,* 38th Cong., 1st sess. (April 8, 1864), 1479–83.

21. For an edited version of the debates and the alternatives, see Bernard Schwartz, *Statutory History of the United States: Civil Rights,* vol. 1 (New York: McGraw-Hill, 1970).

22. *Minor v. Happersett,* 21 Wall. (88 U.S.) 162 (1875).

23. Aileen S. Kraditor, ed., *Up from the Pedestal* (Chicago: Quadrangle, 1970), 239. An important minority of Republicans did favor female suffrage, but the majority did not. See Ellen C. DuBois, "Outgrowing the Compact of the Fathers: Equal Rights, Woman Suffrage, and the United States Constitution, 1820–1878," *Journal of American History* 74 (1987): 836–62.

24. These statutes are reprinted in Schwartz, *Statutory History of the United States.* The surviving provisions are 18 *U.S. Code* 241 and 242 (criminal penalties derived from the 1866 and 1870 Civil Rights Acts) and civil penalties in 42 *U.S. Code* S 1981 (derived from the 1866 and 1870 acts), S 192 (from the 1866 act), S 1983 (from the 1871 act), and S 1985 (3) (from the 1871 act).

25. *Dred Scott v. Sandford,* 19 How. (60 U.S.) 393 (1857). Republican distaste for that case and wariness of the Court did not prevent their extensive use of federal courts as the only viable long-term federal presence in the states. See Kutler, *Judicial Power and Reconstruction Politics.*

26. *In re Turner,* Fed.Cas. 14,427; *United States v. Hall et al.,* discussed in Robert J. Kaczorowski, *The Politics of Judicial Interpretation: The Federal Courts, Department of Justice and Civil Rights, 1866–1876* (New York: New York University Press, 1985), 14–7. For an excellent analysis of *In re Turner,* see Hyman, *Reconstruction Justice of Salmon P. Chase.*

27. *White v. Hart,* 13 Wall. (80 U.S.) 646; *Osborn v. Nicholson,* 13 Wall. (80 U.S.) 654.

28. Michael L. Benedict, "Preserving Federalism: Reconstruction and the Waite Court," *Supreme Court Review* (1978): 39–79. Benedict emphasizes federalism concerns of framers and the Court.

29. *Slaughterhouse Cases,* 16 Wall. (83 U.S.) 36.

30. *The Civil Rights Cases,* 109 U.S. 3 (1883).

31. *Plessy v. Ferguson,* 163 U.S. 537 (1896).

32. While noting the important role of the Warren Court, Kenneth Karst is right to emphasize that a "considerable distance" is still to be traveled to achieve that sense of belonging for many Americans. *Belonging to America: Equal Citizenship and the Constitution* (New Haven: Yale University Press, 1989), 242.

33. There is an extensive literature on constitutional interpretation and the extent to which rights may be "read into" it by judicial fiat. For contrasting views, see Ronald Dworkin, *Freedom's Law: The Moral Reading of the American Constitution* (Cambridge: Harvard University Press, 1996); Richard A.

Posner, "Legal Reasoning from the Top Down and from the Bottom Up: The Question of Unenumerated Rights," *University of Chicago Law Review* 59 (1992): 433–50; and Bork, *Tempting of America*.

34. *Griswold v. Connecticut,* 381 U.S. 479 (1965). See Paul G. Kauper, "Penumbras, Peripheries, Emanations, Things Fundamental, Things Forgotten: The *Griswold* Case," *Michigan Law Review* 64 (1965): 64–197. Kauper links the new uses of substantive due process to protect individual autonomy with the old uses to protect property.

35. *Roe v. Wade.* Few cases have aroused such passion. See Laurence E. Tribe, *Abortion: The Clash of Absolutes* (New York: W. W. Norton, 1992); and Ronald Dworkin, *Life's Dominion: An Argument about Abortion, Euthanasia, and Individual Freedom* (New York: Harper Collins, 1993).

36. *Brown v. Board of Education,* 347 U.S. 483 (1954). The best case profile remains Richard Kluger, *Simple Justice: The History of Brown v. Board of Education and Black America's Struggle for Equality* (London: Deutsch, 1977). The Warren Court not only left women out of its concerns for equality but also reinforced stereotypes. In *Hoyt v. Florida* (368 U.S. 57 [1961]), the Court upheld Florida's exemption for women from jury service, unless they specifically registered, on grounds of family roles.

37. *Jones v. Alfred H. Mayer Co.,* 392 U.S. 409 (1968); Akhil R. Amar, "Remember the Thirteenth," *Constitutional Commentary* 10 (1993): 403–8; Douglas Colbert, "Liberating the Thirteenth Amendment," *Harvard Civil Rights—Civil Liberties Law Review* 30 (1995): 1–55; Lea S. Vandervelde, "The Labor Vision of the Thirteenth Amendment," *University of Pennsylvania Law Review* 138 (1989): 437–504.

38. In *Smith v. Allwright* (321 U.S. 649 [1941]) and *Terry V. Adams* (345 U.S. 461 [1953]), the Court had tackled the exclusion of black voters from primaries and preprimaries by the subterfuge of claiming that there was no state action involved in the discrimination. These were small victories in an otherwise bleak history of voter intimidation and exclusion.

39. *Katzenbach v. Morgan,* 384 U.S. 641, 650 (1966).

40. Archibald Cox argued for a broad congressional power to determine violations of equal protection itself. "The Role of Congress in Constitutional Determinations," *University of Cincinnati Law Review* 40 (1971): 199. Although there is a persuasive amount of evidence that the framers did not intend Congress to have a primary role in defining the substance of "privileges and immunities," it does not follow that Congress was restricted to remedying only violations defined by the Court.

41. *Bowers v. Hardwick* (478 U.S. 186 [1986]) decided there was no fundamental right to engage in sodomy; *Washington v. Glucksberg* (521 U.S. 702 [1997]) determined there was no right to assisted suicide; *Bowers v. Hardwick* (478 U.S. 186 [1986]) decided there was no fundamental right to engage in sodomy; *Washington v. Glucksberg* (521 U.S. 702 [1997]) decided there was no right to assisted suicide. See Yale Kamisar, Wayne R. LaFave, and Jerold H. Israel, *Modern Criminal Procedure,* 8th ed. (St. Paul, Minn.: West, 1994).

42. *United States v. Virginia,* 116 S.Ct. 2264 (1996). In this case the Court found that Virginia had not met the "exceedingly persuasive justification" that would be necessary to justify excluding women from Virginia Military Institute. With only a few exceptions (the all-male draft and a California statutory rape law), the Court has held states to a high level of justification for gender difference.

43. *Foley v. Connelie,* 435 U.S. 291 (1978); *Trimble v. Gordon,* 430 U.S. 762 (1977). The level of scrutiny in these cases, however, is unstable.

44. *Washington v. Davis,* 426 U.S. 229 (1976). This case established the requirement to prove purposeful discrimination. The Court relaxed the standards of proof in both school desegregation and affirmative action cases but has recently returned to a "perpetrator" model in which violations must be specifically attributed to a decision maker, and a recent one at that. Often, discrimination is de facto or has a general societal causation, and the plaintiff is burdened by the standard of proof.

45. *McClekey v. Kemp,* 481 U.S. 279 (1987). It was a 5–4 decision, and Justice Lewis Powell, who voted with the majority, later confessed doubts about the outcome.

46. *Adarand Constructors v. Pena,* 132 L.Ed.2d 158 (1995). The federal government's practice of using race to identify government contractors eligible for financial incentives should have been subjected to strict scrutiny and not the intermediate standard applied in previous cases involving congressional affirmative-action plans. In another recent case, *Richmond v. Croson* (488 U.S. 469 [1989]), the Court held states subject to strict scrutiny to justify the use of race to benefit minority businesses. In earlier cases the Court had shown more flexibility.

47. *DeShaney v. Winnebago Cty. Soc. Servs. Dept.,* 489 U.S.189 (1989).

48. *City of Boerne v. Flores,* 117 S.Ct. 2157 (1997); M. W. McConnell, "Institutions and Interpretation: A Critique of *Boerne v. Flores,*" *Harvard Law Review* 111 (1997).

11. "THE CHARTER OF ITS BIRTHRIGHT": THE CIVIL WAR AND AMERICAN NATIONALISM

Susan-Mary Grant

1. Brian Holden Reid, *The Origins of the American Civil War* (London: Longman, 1996), 1–3; Michael Howard, *The Lessons of History* (Oxford: Oxford University Press, 1991), 39–43.

2. Reid, *Origins,* 1; Robert Penn Warren, *The Legacy of the Civil War: Meditations on the Centennial* (New York: Random House, 1961), 3–4; Thomas P. Lowry, *The Story the Soldiers Wouldn't Tell: Sex and the American Civil War* (New York: Stackpole, 1994), 7–9.

3. Jacob D. Cox, "War Preparations in the North," in *Battles and Leaders of the Civil War,* ed. Robert Johnson and Clarence Buel, 4 vols. (1887–88; reprint, New York: T. Yoseloff, 1956), 1:84–98, 87, 84. Cox was a major general, U.S. Volunteers; a former governor of Ohio; and a former secretary of the interior. His recollection of the beginnings of the war was composed several years later.

4. James M. McPherson, *What They Fought For, 1861–1865* (Baton Rouge: Louisiana State University Press, 1994), 13; Joseph R. Fornieri, "Abraham Lincoln and the Declaration of Independence: The Meaning of Equality," in *Abraham Lincoln: Sources and Style of Leadership,* ed. Frank J. Williams et al. (Westport, Conn.: Greenwood, 1994), 45–69 (quotes, 45, 49); Joshua Lawrence Chamberlain, *The Passing of the Armies: The Last Campaign of the Armies* (1915; reprint, Gettysburg, Pa.: Stan Clark Military Books, 1994), 271. Joshua Lawrence Chamberlain was one of the Union army's most distinguished officers. He was colonel of the Twentieth Maine Infantry and in that capacity held the Union line at Little Round Top during the battle of Gettysburg, an action for which he received the Medal of Honor. Chamberlain led a brigade during the Wilderness campaign of 1864 and was promoted to divisional command following the Appomattox campaign. He also was awarded a battlefield promotion (only two were awarded during the Civil War) to brigadier general and selected to receive the surrender of Gen. Robert E. Lee's Army of Northern Virginia.

5. Charles P. Roland, *An American Iliad: The Story of the Civil War* (Lexington: University Press of Kentucky, 1991), xi; David Thelen, "The Movie Maker as Historian: Conversations with Ken Burns," *The Journal of American History* 81 (Dec. 1994): 1032; Robert Brent Toplin, ed., *Ken Burns' The American Civil War: Historians Respond* (New York: Oxford University Press, 1996), 27. The PBS series was first broadcast in September 1990, reaching an initial audience of some 13.9 million viewers. It is estimated that some 40 million Americans have seen the series in some form, and, of course, it was distributed across Europe too.

6. Anthony D. Smith, *National Identity* (London: Penguin, 1991), 66; Joseph R. Llobera, *The God of Modernity: The Development of Nationalism in Western Europe* (1994; reprint, Oxford: Berg, 1996), 172–3.

7. Ernest Gellner, *Thought and Change* (London: Weidenfeld and Nicolson, 1964), 168; Anthony D. Smith, *The Ethnic Origins of Nations* (1983; reprint, London: Blackwell, 1993), 2; Michael Kammen, *Mystic Chords of Memory: The Transformation of Tradition in American Culture* (New York: Alfred A. Knopf, 1991), 38–9; David Miller, *On Nationality* (Oxford: Clarendon, 1995), 30–6; David Archard, "Myths, Lies, and Historical Truth: A Defense of Nationalism," *Political Studies* 43 (1995): 472–81.

8. William R. Taylor, *Cavalier and Yankee: The Old South and American National Character* (1957. Reprint. Cambridge: Harvard University Press, 1979); *New York Times,* July 25, 1855; Stephen Thernstrom, ed., *The Harvard Encyclopedia of American Ethnic Groups* (Cambridge: Harvard University Press, Belknap Press, 1980), 944–8, 1028–30.

9. Kammen, *Mystic Chords,* 62–6; Virginia DeJohn Anderson, *New England's Generation: The Great Migration and the Formation of Society and Culture in the Seventeenth Century* (New York: Cambridge University Press, 1991).

10. Reinhold Niebuhr and Alan Heimert, *A Nation So Conceived: Reflections on the History of America from Its Early Visions to Its Present Power* (London: Faber and Faber, 1963), 13, 16–42; Russell Blaine Nye, *Society and Culture in America, 1830–1860* (New York: Harper and Row, 1974), 10–31; Abraham Lincoln, Annual Message to Congress, Dec. 1, 1862, *The Collected Works of Abraham Lincoln,* ed. Roy F. Basler et al., 8 vols. (1953–55; reprint, New Brunswick, N.J.: Rutgers University Press, 1988), 5:537; Lincoln, Address Delivered at the Dedication of the Cemetery at Gettysburg, Nov. 19, 1863 ibid., 7:23.

11. Fred Somkin, *Unquiet Eagle: Memory and Desire in the Idea of American Freedom, 1815–1860* (Ithaca, N.Y.: Cornell University Press, 1967), 3–4; John Hope Franklin, "The North, the South, and the American Revolution," *The Journal of American History* 62 (1975): 5–23; John V. Matthews, "Whig History: The New England Whigs and a Usable Past," *The New England Quarterly* 51 (1978): 163–82; Joyce Appleby, *Liberalism and Republicanism in the Historical Imagination* (Cambridge: Harvard University Press, 1992), 4–7.

12. Merrill D. Peterson, *The Jefferson Image in the American Mind* (New York: Oxford University Press, 1960), 5–7; John Shy, *A People Numerous and Armed: Reflections on the Military Struggle for American Independence,* rev. ed. (Ann Arbor: University of Michigan Press, 1990), 25–6; Wilbur Zelinsky, *Nation into State: The Shifting Symbolic Foundations of American Nationalism* (Chapel Hill: University of North Carolina Press, 1988), 20–46; Appleby, *Liberalism and Republicanism,* 4–5.

13. Robert Hughes, *American Visions: The Epic History of Art in America* (New York: Alfred A. Knopf, 1997), 69.

14. Reid Mitchell, *Civil War Soldiers: Their Expectations and Their Experiences* (1988; reprint, New York: Simon and Schuster, 1989), 1–2.

15. Kammen, *Mystic Chords,* 64–6; Susan-Mary Grant, "When Is a Nation Not a Nation?: The Crisis of American Nationalism in the Mid–Nineteenth Century," *Nations and Nationalism* 2 (1996): 105–29 (esp. 109–111); Susan-Mary Grant, "Making History: Myth and the Construction of American Nationhood," in *Myths and Nationhood,* ed. Geoffrey Hosking and George Sch(pflin (London: Hurst, 1997), 88–106 (esp. 95–101).

16. Reid Mitchell, *The Vacant Chair: The Northern Soldier Leaves Home* (1993; reprint, New York: Oxford University Press, 1995), 144; Miller, *On Nationality,* 23.

17. Abraham Lincoln, Speech at Peoria, Ill., Oct. 16, 1854, *Collected Works,* 2:276; Ronald D. Riet-

veld, "Lincoln's View of the Founding Fathers," in *Abraham Lincoln: Sources and Style of Leadership,* ed. Frank J. Williams et al. (Westport, Conn.: Greenwood, 1994), 17–44 (quote, 19).

18. Abraham Lincoln, Speech at Chicago, Ill., July 10, 1858, *Collected Works,* 2:400–500; Fornieri, "Lincoln and the Declaration of Independence," 46.

19. Peterson, *Jefferson Image,* 188; Randall C. Jimerson, *The Private Civil War: Popular Thought during the Sectional Conflict* (Baton Rouge: Louisiana State University Press, 1988), 33–5; Conor Cruise O'Brien, *The Long Affair: Thomas Jefferson and the French Revolution* (London: Sinclair-Stevenson, 1996), 305; Mitchell, *Vacant Chair,* 144, 154.

20. William F. Thompson, *The Image of War: The Pictorial Reporting of the American Civil War* (1959; reprint, Baton Rouge: Louisiana State University Press, 1989), 7, 28; Jimerson, *Private Civil War,* 29.

21. David Herbert Donald, "A Generation of Defeat," in *From the Old South to the New: Essays on the Transitional South,* ed. Walter J. Fraser Jr. and Winfred B. Moore Jr. (Westport, Conn.: Greenwood, 1981), 3–20 (quote, 8).

22. Mitchell, *Civil War Soldiers,* 1–2; Jimerson, *Private Civil War,* 27–8; McPherson, *What They Fought For,* 9–10.

23. Mitchell, *Vacant Chair,* 147. The passage Mitchell analyzes reads:

> In the beauty of the lilies Christ was born across the sea,
> With a glory in his bosom that transfigures you and me:
> As he died to make men holy, let us die to make men free,
> While God is marching on.

Julia Ward Howe, "The Battle-Hymn of the Republic," 1862.

24. Mitchell, *Vacant Chair,* 148–9. In general, see David Blight, *Race and Reunion: The Civil War in American Memory* (Cambridge: Harvard University Press, 2001).

25. Peterson, *Jefferson Image,* 216; Nathaniel Hawthorne to Horatio Bridge, May 26, 1861, in *"The Real War Will Never Get in the Books": Selections from Writers during the Civil War,* ed. Louis P. Masur (1993; reprint, New York: Oxford University Press, 1995), 164; Frederick Douglass, "Emancipation, Racism, and the Work before Us" (an address delivered in Philadelphia, Pennsylvania), Dec. 4, 1863, in Masur, *"The Real War,"* 118–9; Harriet Beecher Stowe, "The Chimney-Corner," *Atlantic Monthly* 15 (Jan. 1865): 109–15, ibid., 251.

26. *The Independent,* May 4, 1865; Peterson, *Jefferson Image,* 218; Jimerson, *Private Civil War,* 6; Grant, "When Is a Nation," 121; Henry Adams to Charles Francis Adams Jr., May 22, 1862, in Masur, *"The Real War,"* 8.

27. Gerald F. Linderman, *Embattled Courage: The Experience of Combat in the American Civil War* (1987; reprint, New York: Free Press, 1989), 267; Nina Silber, *The Romance of Reunion: Northerners and the South, 1865–1900* (Chapel Hill: University of North Carolina Press, 1993), 66–92.

28. Linderman, *Embattled Courage,* 271–80.

29. Paul Buck, *The Road to Reunion* (Boston: Little, Brown, 1937); Celia O'Leary, "'American All': Reforging a National Brotherhood, 1876–1917," *History Today* 44 (Oct. 1994): 19–27 (esp. 22); Stuart McConnell, *Glorious Contentment: The Grand Army of the Republic, 1865–1900* (Chapel Hill: University of North Carolina Press, 1992), xv, 220–3.

30. Chamberlain, *Passing of the Armies,* 271; Kenneth E. Foote, *Shadowed Ground: America's Landscapes of Violence and Tragedy* (Austin: University of Texas Press, 1997), 51, 127–9, 131. The High Water Mark of the Rebellion Monument takes the form of a tablet inscribed with the names of those Union

and Confederate units that took part in Pickett's Charge (a frontal assault against the Union lines on Cemetery Ridge) and in repulsing it on July 3, 1863.

31. William Faulkner, *Intruder in the Dust* (1948; reprint, London: Vintage, 1996), 194–5; Gaines M. Foster, *Ghosts of the Confederacy: Defeat, the Lost Cause, and the Emergence of the New South, 1865–1913* (1987; reprint, New York: Oxford University Press, 1988), esp. 69; Paul M. Gaston, "The New South Creed: A Study in Southern Mythmaking," in *Myth and Southern History,* ed. Patrick Gerster and Nicholas Cords, vol. 2, *The New South,* 2d ed. (Urbana: University of Illinois Press, 1989), 17–32 (esp. 31); O'Leary, "'American All,'" 26.

32. Merrill D. Peterson, *Lincoln in American Memory* (1994; reprint, New York: Oxford University Press, 1995), 29; Scott A. Sandage, "A Marble House Divided: The Lincoln Memorial, the Civil Rights Movement, and the Politics of Memory, 1939–1963," *The Journal of American History* 80 (June 1993): 135–67 (quote 141).

33. Linderman, *Embattled Courage,* 283–4.

34. O'Leary, "'American All,'" 24, 26–7.

35. McConnell, *Glorious Contentment,* 220–2; William Pencak, *For God and Country: The American Legion, 1919–1941* (Boston: Northeastern University Press, 1989), 30–1.

36. David Blight, "'For Something beyond the Battlefield': Frederick Douglass and the Struggle for the Memory of the Civil War," *The Journal of American History* 75 (Mar. 1989): 1156–78 (quote, 1158–61); Toplin, *Ken Burns's* The American Civil War, 112–3; Pencak, *For God and Country,* 29–30.

37. Warren, *Legacy,* 3; Mitchell, *Civil War Soldiers,* 209; Blight, "'For Something beyond the Battlefield,'" 1172; O'Leary, "'American All,'" 22.

38. Michael Kammen, *A Season of Youth: The American Revolution and the Historical Imagination* (New York: Alfred A. Knopf, 1978), 258–9.

39. John Buchan, *Two Ordeals of Democracy* (New York: Houghton Mifflin, 1925), 4–6; Liah Greenfeld, *Nationalism: Five Roads to Modernity* (Cambridge: Harvard University Press, 1992), 476–81.

40. Gabor S. Boritt, "Lincoln and the Economics of the American Dream," in *The Historian's Lincoln: Pseudohistory, Psychohistory, and History* (1988; reprint, Urbana: University of Illinois Press, 1996), 100; Niebuhr and Heimert, *A Nation So Conceived,* 138.

41. Seymour Martin Lipset, *The First New Nation: The United States in Historical and Comparative Perspective,* new ed. (New York: W. W. Norton, 1979), esp. 5; Llobera, *God of Modernity,* 221; Greenfeld, *Nationalism,* 481; Zelinsky, *Nation into State,* 75.

42. Howard, *Lessons of History,* 41.

12. FROM CIVIL WAR TO WORLD POWER: PERCEPTIONS AND REALITIES, 1865–1914

Richard N. Current

1. Avery Craven, *Edmund Ruffin, Southerner: A Study in Secession* (New York: D. Appleton, 1932), 259.

2. Howell Cobb to James Wilson, June 14, 1865, Andrew Johnson Papers, Library of Congress, Washington, D.C.

3. James Alcorn to Elihu B. Washburne, Jan. 1, 1869, Elihu B. Washburne Papers, Library of Congress.

4. Record of soldier from Madison, Wis.,, Apr. 30, 1872, quoted in Mary R. Dearing, *Veterans in Politics: The Story of the G.A.R.* (Baton Rouge: Louisiana State University Press, 1952), 195.

5. James Bryce, *The American Commonwealth,* 2 vols. (New York: Macmillan, 1889), 2:179–80.

6. Milford W. Howard, *The American Plutocracy* (New York, 1895), quoted in Norman Pollard, ed., *The Populist Mind* (New York: Bobbs-Merrill, 1967), 239–40.

7. Bryce, *American Commonwealth,* 2:708.

8. Mark Sullivan, *Our Times: The United States, 1900–1925,* vol. 2, *America Finding Herself* (New York: Charles Scribner's Sons, 1927), 58.

9. *A Brief History of the United States for Schools* (New York: A. S. Barnes, 1871), esp. v.

10. Richard N. Current, *Those Terrible Carpetbaggers* (New York: Oxford University Press, 1988), 404–5.

11. Dearing, *Veterans in Politics,* 402–4, 471–5.

12. Clarence C. Buel and Robert U. Johnson, eds., *Battles and Leaders of the Civil War,* 4 vols. (New York: Century, 1887–88); William T. Sherman, *Memoirs of General William T. Sherman,* 2 vols. (New York: D. Appleton, 1875); Ulysses S. Grant, *Personal Memoirs of U. S. Grant,* 2 vols. (New York: C. L. Webster, 1885–86); John A. Garraty, *The New Commonwealth, 1877–1890* (New York: Harper and Row, 1968), 287–8; John B. Hood, *Advance and Retreat,* ed. Richard N. Current (Bloomington: Indiana University Press, 1959), v.

13. Thomas J. Pressly, *Americans Interpret Their Civil War* (Princeton, N.J.: Princeton University Press, 1954), 187–90.

14. Francis Trevelyan Miller, *The Photographic History of the Civil War,* 10 vols. (New York: Review of Reviews, 1911), 9:15–6.

15. Current, *Those Terrible Carpetbaggers,* 405; Paul H. Buck, *The Road to Reunion, 1865–1900* (Boston: Little, Brown, 1937), 234–5; Raymond A. Cook, *Fire from the Flint: The Amazing Career of Thomas Dixon* (Winston-Salem, N.C.: J. F. Blair, 1968), 161–83. "Contrary to general opinion, the fiction of the Civil War is not predominantly southern," Robert A. Lively argues, but he bases his conclusion on a count of titles and does not attempt a comparison of sales. *Fiction Fights the Civil War* (Chapel Hill: University of North Carolina Press, 1957).

16. Five southerners and five northerners, including Dunning, wrote essays that were published in the *Atlantic Monthly* in 1901; republished in Richard N. Current, ed., *Reconstruction in Retrospect: Views from the Turn of the Century* (Baton Rouge: Louisiana State University Press, 1969), esp. 159. See also Buck, *Road to Reunion,* 283–97.

17. News conference, Apr. 24, 1952, in *Public Papers of the Presidents of the United States: Harry S. Truman* (Washington, D.C.: Government Printing Office, 1961–66), 8:295–6.

18. See excerpts from Woodrow Wilson, *Congressional Government,* in E. David Cronon, ed., *The Political Thought of Woodrow Wilson* (New York: Bobbs-Merrill, 1965), 61–78.

19. Bryce, *American Commonwealth,* 1:50–1.

20. Woodrow Wilson, "Mr. Cleveland as President," *Atlantic Monthly* (Mar. 1897), reprinted in Wilson, *College and State: Educational, Literary, and Political Papers (1875–1913),* ed. Ray Stannard Baker and William E. Dodd, 6 vols. (New York: Harper and Brothers, 1925), 1:286–7.

21. Woodrow Wilson, *Constitutional Government in the United States* (1908; reprinted, New York: Columbia University Press, 1917), 57–9.

22. Theodore Roosevelt, "The Presidency: Making an Old Party Progressive," *Outlook* 105 (Nov. 22, 1913): 637–8, 640, 642; William H. Taft, *Our Chief Magistrate and His Powers* (New York: Columbia University Press, 1916), 143–8.

23. Theodore Roosevelt, "Washington and Lincoln: The Great Examples," in *The Foes of Our Own Household* (New York: George H. Doran, 1917), reprinted in *The Works of Theodore Roosevelt,* 24 vols. (New York: Charles Scribner's Sons, 1923–26), 21:56.

24. Theodore Roosevelt, "Lincoln and Free Speech," *Kansas City Star,* Apr. 6, May 7, 1918.

25. Bryce, *American Commonwealth,* 2:398.

26. Archibald C. Coolidge, *The United States as a World Power* (New York: Macmillan, 1908), 37–8, 172–3.

27. Schurz, "Manifest Destiny," *Harpers' Magazine* 87 (Oct. 1893): 737–46; Van Dyke, Thanksgiving sermon, Nov. 24, 1898, in *The Independent* 50 (Dec. 1, 1898): 1579–85; Frank Parsons, "The Preservation of the Republic: The Great Issue of 1900," *The Arena* 23 (June 1900): 561–5; Theodore Roosevelt, "Expansion and Peace," *The Independent* 51 (Dec. 21, 1899): 3401–5; Mahan to Lodge, Feb. 7, 1899, manuscript in the Massachusetts Historical Society; all reprinted in Richard E. Welch, ed., *Imperialists vs. Anti-Imperialists: The Debate over Expansion in the 1890s* (Itasca, Ill.: F. E. Peacock, 1972), 45–6, 72–3, 84, 105, 116.

28. Coolidge, *United States as a World Power,* 196–7.

29. James G. Blaine, *Twenty Years of Congress: From Lincoln to Garfield,* 2 vols. (Norwich, Conn.: Henry Bill, 1884), 2:672. On the postwar demobilization, see Walter Millis, *Arms and Men: A Study in American Military History* (New York: Putnam, 1956), 132–3; and T. Harry Williams, *The History of American Wars: 1745–1918* (New York: Knopf, 1981), 303.

30. Blaine, *Twenty Years of Congress,* 2:33.

31. Graham A. Cosmas, *An Army for Empire: The United States Army in the Spanish-American War* (Columbia: University of Missouri Press, 1971), 5–6.

32. Arthur A. Ekirch Jr., *The Civilian and the Military* (New York: Oxford University Press, 1956), 120–1.

33. Dearing, *Veterans in Politics,* 479–80.

34. Millis, *Arms and Men,* 147–9.

35. Ibid., 139–40; Emory Upton, *The Military Policy of the United States from 1775* (Washington, D.C.: Government Printing Office, 1904), vii–xv (introduction dated 1880), excerpted in Walter Millis, ed., *American Military Thought* (New York: Bobbs-Merrill, 1900), 180, 192.

36. Leonard Wood, *Our Military History* (Chicago: Reilly and Britton, 1916), reprinted in Millis, *American Military Thought,* 273–4.

37. Charles A. and Mary R. Beard, *The Rise of American Civilization,* 2 vols. (New York: Macmillan, 1927), 2:106, 166, 176.

38. Victor S. Clark, "Manufacturing Development during the Civil War," in Ralph Andreano, ed., *The Economic Impact of the American Civil War* (Cambridge, Mass.: Schenkman, 1962), 41–3; Thomas C. Cochran, "Did the Civil War Retard Industrialization?" *Mississippi Valley Historical Review* 48 (Sept. 1961): 197–210.

39. Blaine, *Twenty Years of Congress,* 2: 672; Woodrow Wilson, *Division and Reunion, 1829–1889* (New York: Longmans, 1893), 298–9; James Ford Rhodes, *History of the United States from the Compromise of 1850 to the Final Restoration of Home Rule at the South in 1977,* 7 vols. (New York: Harper and Brothers, 1892–1906), 7:291.

CONTRIBUTORS

Bruce Collins is dean of the School of Humanities, University of Derby. He has formerly held the posts of dean of humanities at Ripon and York (an affiliated college of the University of Leeds), dean and deputy principal of University College, Scarborough, and professor of international history at the University of Buckingham. Educated at Cambridge, he held a Harkness Fellowship in 1972–74 and taught at Middlesex Polytechnic and the University of Glasgow. He has written *The Origins of America's Civil War* (1981) and *White Society in Antebellum America* (1985) as well as numerous articles and essays on the 1850s in, for example, *Civil War History, Georgia Historical Quarterly, Historical Journal, History Today, The Journal of American Studies, Ohio History,* and the *Pennsylvania Magazine of History and Biography.*

Robert Cook is senior lecturer in American history at the University of Sheffield. He is the author of *Baptism of Fire: The Republican Party in Iowa, 1838–1878* (1994) and *Sweet Land of Liberty?: The African American Struggle for Civil Rights in the Twentieth Century* (1998). He is currently completing a history of the United States in the Civil War era for Addison Wesley Longman and is working on a study of the Civil War centennial for Louisiana State University Press.

Richard Nelson Current has taught at the Universities of Illinois (Urbana-Champaign), Wisconsin (Madison), and North Carolina (Greensboro). He has served as Harmsworth professor at the University of Oxford and Fulbright professor at the Universities of Munich and Chile (Santiago) besides lecturing in Japan, India, Australia, and other countries. Author or coauthor of more than twenty books on U.S. history and biography, he has received the Bancroft, Bruce Catton, and Lincoln Prizes and other awards for historical writing of distinction.

Susan-Mary Grant is Reader in American History at the University of Newcastle-upon-Tyne, research fellow at the Institute of United States Studies, University of London, and cofounder of the Society of British American Nineteenth Century Historians. Her publications include *North over South: Northern Nationalism and American Identity in the Antebellum Era* (2000) and *The American Civil War: Explorations* *and Reconsiderations,* coedited with Brian Holden Reid (2000) as well as a range of articles on antebellum America and on the development of American nationalism during the Civil War era in, among others, *Nations and Nationalism* and the *Journal of American Studies.*

Charles W. Joyner is Burroughs Distinguished Professor of Southern History and Culture at Coastal Carolina University. He is the author of the prize-winning *Down by the Riverside: A South Carolina Slave Community* (1984) and *Shared Traditions: Southern History and Folk Culture* (1999). He is also the producer, writer, and host of the miniseries *Legacy of Conflict: South Carolina and the Civil War* for the South Carolina Educational Television Network.

Patricia Lucie was the director of the William J. Brennan Project, University of Glasgow, from 1973 to 1998. Her publications include *Freedom and Federalism, Congress and Courts, 1861–66* (1984); "Discrimination against Males in the U.S.A.," in *The Legal Relevance of Gender,* edited by S. McLean and N. Burrows (1988); and a range of articles in *The Judicial Review,* the *Syracuse Law Review,* and the *Denning Law Journal.*

James M. McPherson is the George Henry Davis '86 Professor of American History at Princeton University, where he has taught since 1962. He is the author of a dozen books on the era of the American Civil War and Reconstruction and the editor of numerous additional works. In 1989 he won the Pulitzer Prize in history for his book *Battle Cry of Freedom: The Civil War Era,* and in 1998 he won the Lincoln Prize for his book *For Cause and Comrades: Why Men Fought in the Civil War.* In 1982 he was the Commonwealth Fund Lecturer at University College London.

Peter Parish (1929–2002) taught American history for eighteen years at the University of Glasgow, after which he became Bonar Professor of Modern History at the University of Dundee (1976–83) and then director of the Institute of United States Studies, University of London (1983–92). He was Mellon Senior Research Fellow in American History at the University of Cambridge. Among his publications are *The American Civil War* (1975) and *Slavery: History and Historians* (1989). He edited the Everyman edition of the speeches and letters of Abraham Lincoln (1993) and the *Reader's Guide to American History* (1997). He was a former chairman of the British Association for American Studies and British American Nineteenth Century Historians.

Brian Holden Reid is professor of war studies, King's College London, and in 1987–97 was resident historian at the British Army Staff College, Camberley (of which he is a graduate). From 1984 to 1987 he was editor of the *RUSI Journal.* Since 1993 he has been a member of the Council of the Society for Army Historical Research, elected chairman in 1998. He is a fellow of the Royal Historical Society, Royal Geographical Society, and the Royal United Services Institute. His books include *J. F. C. Fuller: Military Thinker* (1987, 1990), *The Origins of the American Civil War* (1996), *Studies in British Military Thought* (1998), and *The American Civil War and the Wars of the Industrial Revolution* (1999).

Jeffrey Leigh Sedgwick is associate professor of political science at the University of Massachusetts–Amherst. He holds an A.B. from Kenyon College (1973), an M.A.P.A. from the University of Virginia (1975), and a Ph.D. in public affairs also from the University of Virginia (1978). His teaching and research interests include American national government and politics, the American presidency, and American political thought (especially of the eighteenth and nineteenth centuries). He is the author of *Law Enforcement Planning: The Limits of an Economic Approach* (1984), *Deterring Criminals: Policymaking and the American Political Tradition* (1980), and numerous book chapters and journal articles.

Adam I. P. Smith is lecturer in American history at University College London. He was, until 2001, the Kaj Arends Research Fellow in American History at Queen Mary, University of London, and is currently at Sidney Sussex, Cambridge. He is a graduate of Oxford and Sheffield Universities and in 1996–97 was a visiting fellow at Harvard University. He is currently completing his first book, *The Paradox of Partisanship: Popular Political Participation in the Civil War North.*

Melvyn Stokes teaches American history and American film history at University College London, where he has been principal organizer of the Commonwealth Fund Conference on American History since 1988. His coedited books include *Race and Class in the American South since 1890* (1994), *The Market Revolution in America* (1996), and *The United States and the European Alliance since 1945* (1999). He is coeditor (with Richard Maltby) of *American Movie Audiences: From the Turn of the Century to the Early Sound Era* (1999), *Identifying Hollywood's Audiences: Cultural Identity and the Movies* (1999), and *Hollywood Spectatorship: Changing Perceptions of Cinema Audiences* (2000). He is currently working on a book about David W. Griffith's 1915 film, *The Birth of a Nation.*

INDEX

Morris, John, 55
Morris, Willie, 23
Morton, Oliver P., 86
Movies. *See* Films
Murrin, John, 117
Myers, Albert J., 157
Mythology of Civil War, 17–78, 189–206

Napoleon, cult of, 163
National Association for the Advancement of Colored People (NAACP), 50, 56, 59, 70, 73–4
National Council of Churches, 58
National identity, 3, 8–9, 19
National Union party, 84, 88, 90
Nationalism: 11, 19–20, 188–206; aspirational/ameliorative, 10, 126, 128–9; Confederate, 6, 37; Romantic, 190–1, 193, 195–6; "separatist," 19; southern, 6; "unification," 19
Nationality by choice, 121
Nationhood: inclusive view of, 122–5, 128; Lincoln and construction of, 9–10, 116–33
Navy, 49, 217–8, 219
Neely, Mark E., 5
Negro History Bulletin, 52
Negro History Week (1961), 55
Nevins, Allan, 39, 58
New Deal, 92, 171, 173
New York Herald, 89
New York Times, 85, 191–2
Newman, Kim, 69
"No-partyism." *See* Antipartisanship
North Carolina, 45
Norton, Charles Eliot, 94, 96
Nostalgia for antebellum South, 35–6

O'Leary, Cecilia, 5
Operator 13 (film), 66, 76
Organization of American Historians, 48
Osterweis, Rollin G., 76
The Outpost (film), 69

Pacific War, 48
Parish, Peter J., 9–10, 81–99, 116–33
Parsons, James B., 61
Party politics, 8, 81–99
Patriotism, 87, 88, 110–1, 211–2

Patton, George S., Jr., 163
Peckinpah, Sam, 63
Pensamiento Español, 140
Pershing, John J., 163
Philippines, 216
Pickens, Francis W., 27
Pickett, George, 200
Pierce, Franklin, 145, 156
Pillow, Gideon, 156
Plantation life, 35–7, 40, 47, 76–7
Plessy v. Ferguson (1896), 183
Political careers, southern: 31
Political development, 9, 81–99
Political rights, 91–2, 179, 208, 209. *See also* Voting rights
Polk, James K., 215
Poor Man's Guardian, 139
Popular sovereignty, 102–6
Populist party, 210
Potter, David, 121
Power: and liberty, 144–5
Power, Tracey, 41
Presidential powers: 213–5, 221; war powers of Lincoln, 89, 155, 166, 214, 215
Progressive movement, 96, 115, 131
Prohibition, 73
Property law, 179
Public Enemy (film), 75
Puritans, 191–2

Quarles, Benjamin, 52

Racial issues, 3, 71–3, 179–81. *See also* African Americans; Civil rights; Racism/racial discrimination; Segregation; Slavery
Racism/racial discrimination, 171–2, 174, 182–3, 184–5, 186, 202–3
Radical Republicans, 90, 92
The Raid (film), 76
Raintree County (film), 75
Randolph, A. Philip, 58
Rawlins, John A., 154, 158
Raymond, Henry J., 90, 91
Reagan, Ronald, 44, 46
Reconstruction, 34, 83, 89, 90, 92, 97, 158, 160, 171, 174, 209